PUBLISHING LATINIDAD

JOSE O. FERNANDEZ

PUBLISHING LATINIDAD

Latinx Literary and Intellectual Production,
1880–1960

THE UNIVERSITY OF
ARIZONA PRESS
TUCSON

The University of Arizona Press
www.uapress.arizona.edu

We respectfully acknowledge the University of Arizona is on the land and territories of Indigenous peoples. Today, Arizona is home to twenty-two federally recognized tribes, with Tucson being home to the O'odham and the Yaqui. Committed to diversity and inclusion, the University strives to build sustainable relationships with sovereign Native Nations and Indigenous communities through education offerings, partnerships, and community service.

© 2025 by The Arizona Board of Regents
All rights reserved. Published 2025

ISBN-13: 978-0-8165-5437-9 (hardcover)
ISBN-13: 978-0-8165-5436-2 (paperback)
ISBN-13: 978-0-8165-5438-6 (ebook)

Cover design by Leigh McDonald
Cover art based on Alfio Giuffrida/AG Sinnwerke, Wandtöpfe A-exp6- 019 2019, acrylic on canvas, 110x110cm
Typeset by Leigh McDonald in Garamond Premier Pro 11/14 and Trade Gothic Next (display)

This book was made possible in part with support from the University of Iowa's Office of the Vice President for Research and the College of Liberal Arts and Sciences.

Library of Congress Cataloging-in-Publication Data
Names: Fernandez, Jose O., 1976– author.
Title: Publishing Latinidad : Latinx literary and intellectual production, 1880–1960 / Jose O. Fernandez.
Description: [Tucson] : The University of Arizona Press, 2025. | Includes bibliographical references and index.
Identifiers: LCCN 2024032654 (print) | LCCN 2024032655 (ebook) | ISBN 9780816554379 (hardcover) | ISBN 9780816554362 (paperback) | ISBN 9780816554386 (ebook)
Subjects: LCSH: American literature—Hispanic American authors—History and criticism. | Group identity in literature. | Ethnicity in literature. | Hispanic American mass media—History. | Identity (Psychology) and mass media. | Hispanic Americans—Ethnic identity. | Hispanic Americans—Intellectual life—19th century. | Hispanic Americans—Intellectual life—20th century.
Classification: LCC PS153.H56 F47 2025 (print) | LCC PS153.H56 (ebook) | DDC 810.9/8168073—dc23/eng/20241031
LC record available at https://lccn.loc.gov/2024032654
LC ebook record available at https://lccn.loc.gov/2024032655

Printed in the United States of America
♾ This paper meets the requirements of ANSI/NISO Z39.48-1992 (Permanence of Paper).

For Joy

CONTENTS

	Acknowledgments	*ix*
	Introduction: Early Latinx Authors and Alternative Print Forms and Literary Genres	3
1.	U.S. Print Culture and José Martí's *Crónicas* on U.S. Indigenous Peoples' Rights	21
2.	Arturo Schomburg's Recovery Writings and Black Print Culture	48
3.	Latinidad and Working-Class Solidarity in Jesús Colón's Sketches	73
4.	Identity and Indigeneity in José de la Luz Sáenz's World War I Diary	100
5.	Adela Sloss-Vento's Archival Practices and Mexican American Civil Rights	126
6.	Racialization and the U.S. Occupation of Japan in Américo Paredes's Writings	153
	Conclusion: Publishing Latinidad Past and Present	182
	Notes	*191*
	Bibliography	*235*
	Index	*259*

ACKNOWLEDGMENTS

SEVERAL INSTITUTIONS and individuals made possible the completion and publication of this book by their generous assistance through various stages of the writing process. The following research libraries and cultural institutions served as essential resources providing the archival materials for this project: the Schomburg Center for Research in Black Culture; the Center for Advanced Studies on Puerto Rico and the Caribbean, and the National Library and General Archive both in San Juan, Puerto Rico; the Benson Latin American Collection at the University of Texas-Austin; the M. D. Anderson Library Special Collections at the University of Houston; and the Arte Público Hispanic Historical Collection: Series 1 and 2. I would like to thank the staff of these institutions and Christian Kelleher in particular. This book would not have been possible without the resources from the University of Iowa Libraries and its dedicated staff from various units: circulation, interlibrary loans, digital collections, and media storage.

I received significant support for this project from various departments and divisions at the University of Iowa including the Office of the Vice President for Research, the Obermann Center for Advanced Studies, the College of Liberal Arts and Sciences, the Division of Interdisciplinary Programs, and the Latina/o/x Studies Program. Among these, the Obermann Center for Advanced Studies and the Office of the Vice President for Research allowed me to participate in a Book Ends Book Completion

Workshop. I would like to thank Teresa Mangum and the staff at the Obermann Center for making this event possible. I want to express my gratitude to the exceptional group of scholars who provided detailed and invaluable suggestions for the improving of an early version of this manuscript: Nicolás Kanellos, John Alba Cutler, Claire Fox, and Loren Glass. I would also like to thank the participants of the Mellon Imagining Latinidades Workshop on Latinx Scholarship and Pedagogy during summer 2022 who provided feedback on sections that would become part of this book's first chapter. Special thanks to Naomi Greyser and Aimee Carrillo Rowe for leading the workshop.

I am fortunate to have met and worked with Kristen Buckles at the University of Arizona Press. I cannot thank Kristen enough for her continued enthusiasm and support for this project. I want to thank the two external reviewers who provided incisive suggestions to improve the manuscript. Thank you also to Elizabeth Wilder, Amanda Krause, Abby Mogollón, Leigh McDonald, and other members of the staff at the University of Arizona Press who worked on this project and made this book a reality. Special thanks to Sharon Thompson and Rome Hernández Morgan for their excellent editorial assistance and Alexis Jimenez who assisted me with translations.

An earlier version of chapter 1 appeared in *Latino Studies* (2024) and is reprinted here with the permission of Palgrave Macmillan.

I am thankful to have the support of several colleagues and friends while working on this project. I would like to thank the following individuals for their assistance and friendship: María C. González, Gabriela Baeza Ventura, Carolina Villarroel, Anna M. Nogar, Vanessa Fonseca-Chávez, Sarah Quesada, Carmen Lamas, Tracy Floreani, Gary Totten, Vincent Perez, Luis Cortes, Raúl Melgoza, Evelyn Soto, Lucía Suárez, Bill Johnson González, Lois Geist, Janet Weaver, Carol Severino, Liz Mendez-Shannon, Gabriela Rivera, Maria Bruno, Carolina Kaufman, Eva Latterner, Amber Bryan, Kathleen Newman, Becky Gonzalez, Roxanna Curto, Viridiana Hernández Fernández, Julianna Pacheco, Kristine Muñoz, Stephen Warren, Deborah Whaley, Ashley Howard, María Marroquín, María Márquez Ponce, Abigail Escatel, and Thelma Trujillo.

The Latina/o/x Studies Program at the University of Iowa has provided me with everything I could have ever wished as a faculty member. I have been privileged to work with and learn from amazing students each semester. I am also grateful for working with an outstanding group of colleagues at the Latina/o/x Studies Program who have assisted at each step of my academic journey at the University of Iowa. Thanks to Rene Rocha, Claire Fox, Lina-Maria Murillo, Elizabeth Rodriguez Fielder, Eric Vázquez, Jorge Guerra, Lindsay Vella, and Tracy Meginnis. I am thankful to work at a university with administrators who have offered me their unwavering support. Thank you to Christine Getz, Roland Racevskis, Joshua Weiner, Loren Glass, Amber Bryan, Rene Rocha, Sara Sanders, Cornelia Lang, and Kristy Nabhan-Warren.

Lastly, I would like to thank friends and family members who have offered me their support and friendship over the years. I want to give special thanks to the Lockhart and Fernandez families, especially my mother-in-law Joyce Goins and my mother Martha Gallegos Fernández. This book is dedicated to the light of my life Joyce Goins-Fernandez. When I close my eyes and reflect on all the joys I have experienced, you are always the first person on my mind.

PUBLISHING LATINIDAD

INTRODUCTION

EARLY LATINX AUTHORS AND ALTERNATIVE PRINT FORMS AND LITERARY GENRES

IN THE last few decades, there has been an emphasis on recovering and studying Latinx literary and intellectual production prior to 1960, characterized by the increased scholarly attention and recovery work by Arte Público Press and the Recovering the U.S. Hispanic Literary Heritage Program both at the University of Houston and led by Nicolás Kanellos.[1] Early Latinx authors and intellectuals, while publishing, or attempting to publish, books of poetry or fiction, engaged with alternative print cultures to theorize about their distinct identities and early iterations and visions of Latinidad, and more broadly, to examine and interrogate their historical, social, and cultural position in the United States, along with those of other historically excluded groups.[2] The emergence and development of the Latinx literary and intellectual traditions have primarily been studied in conjunction with social, cultural, and political events starting in the 1960s and 1970s; moreover, scholars have continued to challenge the prevalent interpretation in American literary studies that Latinx literature represents a post-1960s social and cultural phenomenon.[3] Latinx literature and intellectual thought have a long history dating back centuries that was preserved not only in traditional books of fiction and poetry but also through an array of print cultures, nontraditional books, and literary genres. These print forms expand our appreciation of early Latinx literary and intellectual production and shed light on emerging conceptualizations of racial and ethnic identity formation within Latinx communities before the 1960s. *Publishing Latinidad* proposes that these alternative print cultures and literary genres complement and expand pre-1960 Latinx literary and intellectual history.

Due in large part to practices in mainstream U.S. book publishing, newspapers, and periodicals that, with some exceptions, systematically excluded authors of color, the writings of early Latinx authors and intellectuals were not always found in printed books of prose or poetry but rather in alternative print forms. In *Publishing Latinidad*, I argue that in addition to printed books, Latinx writers and intellectuals prior to 1960 used different print forms, including hemispheric, Black, labor, and U.S.-government-sponsored newspapers and periodicals, to enter cultural and social debates pertaining to the marginalized position of their respective groups in distinct geographical regions vis-à-vis U.S. mainstream culture and society. These writers also entered literary, cultural, and intellectual discourses through alternative forms and genres consisting of *crónicas*, translations, paratexts, bibliographies, archival practices, sketches, diaries, biographies, pamphlets, unpublished fiction, and scholarly monographs. Early Latinx writers and intellectuals debated through marginal print texts and nontraditional genres the social exclusion, disenfranchisement, racial violence, military violence, and historical erasure affecting their local communities, at times with an awareness of the historical exclusion of Black, Indigenous, and Asian American communities in the United States.

Publishing Latinidad studies the writings and ideological stance related to the racialization of non-white groups published in nontraditional print forms and genres by well-known and lesser-known authors including José Martí, Arturo Schomburg, Jesús Colón, José de la Luz Sáenz, Adela Sloss-Vento, and Américo Paredes.[4] My interpretation of these authors' writings consists of publication histories and literary analyses of some of their representative and lesser-known print texts while employing a comparative ethnic studies lens that presents instances of racial and ethnic solidarity among non-white groups dating back to the latter part of the nineteenth century. These early Latinx authors interpreted and critiqued processes of racialization and othering that affected not only their specific communities but other disenfranchised communities in the United States.

Publishing Latinidad engages with the literary and intellectual production by early Latinx authors in New York City and Texas who in their printed texts grappled with some of the most consequential moments in U.S. history, which had major repercussions for non-white groups within U.S. territories. Whether groups had a cohesive genealogy or shared group identity, communities with distinct historical, cultural, social, and political allegiances (Cubans in exile, Mexican Americans, and Puerto Ricans in New York City) developed their own notions of racial and ethnic identification vis-à-vis the larger white majority. Instead of envisioning an early pan-ethnic vision of Latinidad that united these groups, most early Latinx writers and intellectuals entered discourses related to the social, economic, historical, and cultural exclusion of their own communities marked by their histories and geography. Moreover, they theorized about their own identity and their condition as marginalized subjects in relation to the exclusion of other racialized groups in the United States.

While these authors lacked social or cultural networks with other Latinx communities in the United States, their social and intellectual trajectories were significantly altered by some of the most important historical developments in the United States, such as the aftermath of the U.S.-Mexican War, the Spanish-American War, the two world wars, and the Cold War, in which they were either active participants or their communities markedly changed as a result of these historical events. Martí wrote about the dispossession and removal of Indigenous peoples in the United States and the consequences of the Dawes Act of 1887; Schomburg interrogated the cultural erasure of Black and Black diasporic writers in the United States during Jim Crow; Colón promoted ethnic solidarity among different Latinx groups in New York City as a consequence of Puerto Rico colonial status; Sáenz advocated for the inclusion of Mexican Americans into the U.S. historical narrative as a result of his service during World War I; Sloss-Vento subverted the subordinate position of women within Mexican American communities in Texas; and Paredes grappled with the racialization of Asians and Asian Americans during the U.S. occupation of Japan after World War II. Some of their writings challenged prevailing historical narratives that either erased or minimized the history of violence against communities of color and rendering invisible their historical, social, and cultural contributions to the United States.

U.S. BOOK PUBLISHING AND EARLY LATINX LITERARY AND INTELLECTUAL PRODUCTION

Historically, the fields of American literature, American literary history, and the literary histories of minoritized groups have been dominated by critical discussions centered around the content of texts rather than how those texts were produced. The development of U.S. print culture from reproductions of British texts during the Colonial period to the emergence of early U.S. publishing houses in the nineteenth century, moving to the industrialization of printing methods to produce books, coalesced in the late nineteenth century to create the modern publishing industry, which has influenced cultural and literary production since the 1880s. More often, the history of the book in the United States has been studied by historians focusing on textual history, book history, and book studies, whose fields of inquiry more often pertain to the production, distribution, and reading of books in the United States at different historical periods.[5] Scholars of the history of the book traditionally have engaged with the printed book from an historical vantage point rather than within the field of literary studies. These dynamics are equally prevalent in literary studies pertaining to the literary production of minoritized groups within the United States.

In the context of Black literary studies, for instance, Leon Jackson has argued that "[i]f scholars of African American literature have neglected to engage with book historians, however, neither have book historians engaged too readily with African American materials."[6] As a result, Jackson argues that although there have been "fruitful encounters" between these two fields, "scholarship growing out of the history of the book and related fields has rarely spoken to, or been addressed by, scholars of African American literary and cultural history."[7] Jackson's analysis similarly applies to the field of Latinx literary studies. It is only in the last couple of decades that the fields of Black and Latinx literary studies have critically historicized and interpreted their texts in relation to the dynamics resulting from the production, editing, and reception of these books. Within the context of the history of the book in the United States, book publishing dynamics, either between minoritized writers and white publishers or within communities of color, are closely connected to the historical marginalization of non-white authors.

With a few exceptions, writers of color remained excluded by mainstream publishers, newspapers, and periodicals in the United States, with limited publishing opportunities prior to the 1960s. The exclusion of these groups in the United States from the inception of print and book publishing is associated with what Joseph Rezek describes as the "racialization of print" and the emergence and use of print technologies "to subdue, control, commodify, and dehumanize colonized and enslaved people."[8] Print cultures were used in the United States not only to exclude non-white groups but also, as the U.S. mainstream publishing industry grew and coalesced, to promote exclusionary practices that kept minoritized writers outside the industry. The expansion and proliferation of U.S. publishing houses at the turn of the twentieth century and new advances in the production and distribution of books during the first half of that century, such as the emergence of the mass-market paperback, cemented the position of the printed book as one of the prevalent forms of cultural production and cultural capital that minoritized authors were seldom able to access.

Critical discussions on the cultural function and social value of the book as markers of social distinction and cultural capital have followed Pierre Bourdieu's sociological analysis, interpreting social and class divisions in relation to a group's cultural preferences and acquired tastes.[9] Differences in economic and social status, along with access to educational opportunities, left minoritized writers at a critical disadvantage when attempting to gain the cultural capital required to gain access to publishing opportunities with mainstream publishers. As Pierre Bourdieu explains, "the structure of the distribution of economic capital is symmetrical and opposite to that of cultural capital."[10] Thus, the lack of access to book publishing opportunities for minoritized writers is not only the result of exclusionary practices by the mainstream publishing industry but also the consequence of economic inequalities that, in the case of minoritized communities in the United States, relate to their historical exclusion and disenfranchisement. Advancing Bourdieu's study of cultural capital, John Guillory argues that in the context of U.S. literature, gender, race, and class "determine[d] whether and how individuals gain[ed] access to the means of literary production..."[11] Exclusion and lack of access to social, economic, and educational opportunities for minoritized authors played a significant role in the types of Latinx books that were produced by mainstream publishing houses in the United States.

The lack of book publishing opportunities and access to mainstream publishers for minoritized writers remained a constant prior to 1960, which significantly influenced the literary traditions of different minoritized groups in the United States. A number of now-canonical Black authors, for instance, were able to publish books with mainstream publishing houses in the first half of the twentieth century; nonetheless, these Black authors represented a comparatively small number, and their relationships with white editors and publishers were characterized by an imbalance of power.[12] As George Hutchinson and John K. Young have argued, books by Black authors emerged—or failed to emerge—in a context of "cultural power inherent in literary production and distribution."[13] In other words, white publishers controlled, for the most part, the means of cultural and literary production and distribution and had the power to decide on the type and number of Black authors they published. White editors of the Harlem Renaissance, such as Alfred A. Knopf and Blanche Knopf, who published a small number of Black writers, did it from their position as "tastemakers," which in most cases meant that those authors had to adhere to European modernist aesthetics.[14] Publishing houses, moreover, were seldom unconditional in their support of previously signed Black writers. Pre-1960s authors, such as Claude McKay, Richard Wright, and Ann Petry, for instance, were able to publish some of their works with mainstream publishing houses but left a substantial number of their manuscripts unpublished since the support of white publishers fluctuated based on financial constraints and white readers' preferences.[15] Thus, it is important to consider the publication of Black literary texts prior to the 1960 as constituting what Richard Jean So cogently describes as the "history of the outlier" since most Black writers seldom had opportunities to publish their books with mainstream publishers.[16]

In the case of pre-1960 Latinx authors, the prospects of entering literary and intellectual discourses through the publication of books with U.S. mainstream publishers were as scarce as those of Black writers due in part to what Young refers to as "white publishers' control of the means of production and distribution..."[17] Young similarly discusses "the aesthetic limits for African American writers created by the economic power of mainstream publishers" and how "such a power imbalance affects almost all writers..."[18] In the case of the Latinx literary tradition, most of its representative books were published by local or regional presses, and similar to pre-1960s Black texts, they constitute "outliers" in U.S. cultural production that overwhelmingly favored texts written in English for its readers. Some of the books written either in Spanish or English representative of these trends include the novel *Jicoténcal*, published anonymously in Spanish and published in Philadelphia in 1826, María Amparo Ruiz de Burton's *Who Would Have Thought It?* (1872) and *The Squatter and the Don* (1885), Alirio Díaz Guerra's *Lucas Guevara* (1914), Conrado Espinoza's *El sol de Texas* (1926; Under the Texas Sun), Daniel Venegas's *Las Aventuras de Don Chipote* (1928; The Adventures of Don Chipote), Elena Zamora O'Shea's *El Mesquite* (1935), Américo Paredes's *Cantos de adolescencia* (1937; Songs of Youth), Josefina Niggli's *Mexican Village* (1945) and *Step Down, Elder Brother* (1947), and José Antonio Villarreal's *Pocho* (1959). As a result of these publishing dynamics in Latinx literature, especially when white publishers were involved, as in the case of Ruiz de Burton, Niggli, and Villareal, only a disproportionately small number of Latinx books were published by mainstream publishers; however, several other early Latinx writers with mainstream publishing aspirations, including Sáenz, Jovita González, and Paredes, tried unsuccessfully. As a result, the majority of early Latinx authors published their books with regional publishing houses for local or regional audiences composed of Spanish-speaking readers. The history of Latinx books in the United States is a history of exclusion in mainstream publishing; nonetheless, the story I tell in *Publishing Latinidad* is one of perseverance. While the printed book has remained a goal for most Latinx writers in a society that values the printed book of fiction and poetry as the standard of literary achievement, Latinx writers and intellectuals entered public discourses and impacted U.S. cultural production through alternative print forms and by publishing books in nontraditional genres. My study seeks to highlight the texts that have often remained on the margins of the Latinx literary and intellectual tradition.

Despite the social, economic, and cultural exclusion of Latinx communities and authors in the United States prior to 1960, Latinx literary and intellectual production developed and thrived in Spanish-language print culture in various U.S. cities, including New York City, San Antonio, Albuquerque, and Los Angeles, starting at different periods during the nineteenth century.[19] Of particular importance, *The Latino Nineteenth Century*, edited by Rodrigo Lazo and Jesse Alemán, has allowed for a reconceptualization of the field of Latinx literary history that focuses on the literary, intellectual, and artistic contributions in different print forms and particularly Spanish-language print culture. In their groundbreaking *Hispanic Periodicals in the United States: Origins to 1960*, Kanellos and Helvetia Martell argue that Spanish-language print culture served as a forum for writers and intellectuals who "often spearhead[ed] political and social movements" and was key in the development of Latinx cultural and literary production.[20] *Publishing Latinidad* builds on previous scholarship of Spanish-language print culture, and it is particularly indebted to Nicolás Kanellos and his collaborators for the digitalization of hundreds of Spanish-language newspapers and periodicals in the United States prior to 1960.[21] Spanish-language print culture in the United States was sustained in most cases by local Spanish-speaking readerships interested in local news, in addition to regional or transnational affairs; at the same time, some authors attempted to enter larger U.S. social and cultural discourses and these forms of textual production should be studied within the realm of American literary studies. As Rodrigo Lazo argues, there is a need for scholars of American literature to recognize that "Spanish-language cultures of print were in operation in the United States during much of the nineteenth century . . ." and are part of American literary history.[22] Similarly, Kirsten Silva Gruesz has argued that in the study of Spanish-language print culture, Spanish should be presented in its original as it appeared on the page in order "to push Anglophone readers into grappling seriously with Spanish as an essential literary language of the United States."[23] My study follows the lead of Lazo, Gruesz, and other scholars as I study the publishing conditions of various print texts produced in the United States, written either in English or Spanish, that contributed to the U.S. literary and intellectual heritage.

Publishing Latinidad focuses on the writings of canonical and lesser-known Latinx authors whose writings in Spanish-language, Black, and alternative publications have received less critical attention in the study of Latinx literary and intellectual history. As scholars have demonstrated, Spanish-language print culture in the United States had a hemispheric reach and formed part of a translational network of exchange of political and literary ideas and trends that originated in the United States, the Caribbean, and other Latin American countries.[24] Moreover, Spanish-language print culture developed along other print infrastructures, such as Black newspapers and periodicals that were instrumental in the development of Black intellectual, political, and cultural thought.[25] As Derrick Spires argues, the emergence of nineteenth century Black print culture worked "not simply as a response to white oppression but as a matter of course in the shaping of [Black people's] own communities and in the process meeting their own political, social, and cultural needs..."[26] Similar to Black authors, early Latinx writers developed printing infrastructures, and in the pages of Spanish-language newspapers and periodicals, they articulated strategies to claim their rightful cultural, social, and political position in the U.S. Latinx authors published their writings in Spanish-language newspapers and periodicals, Latin American newspapers, Black newspapers and periodicals, government-sponsored publications, and labor and communist newspapers and periodicals. My study focuses primarily on Martí's writings on U.S. Indigenous peoples for Latin American newspapers, Schomburg's recovery of Black authors in different Black periodicals and newspapers, Colón's sketches on Latinidad for *Pueblos Hispanos* and the *Daily Worker*, Sáenz's World War I writings in *La Prensa* of San Antonio, Sloss-Vento's writings for civil rights, also for *La Prensa*, and Paredes's reporting on the Tokyo war crimes trial for *Pacific Stars and Stripes*.

Historically, the printed book of fiction or poetry has remained the focus of literary studies and the goal for most writers but one from which minoritized writers prior to 1960s remained excluded for the most part. Scholars of book history have discussed the blurred lines between fiction and poetry printed in newspapers and periodicals in relation to the same writing printed in book format as modalities contending for equal prevalence in U.S. cultural and literary discourses during the nineteenth century;[27] however, starting in the 1880s, the industrialization of the U.S. book publishing industry shifted cultural prominence toward the printed book in United States. Literary texts became and continue to be markers of aesthetic and cultural distinction among writers, publishers, and scholars. As John Tebbel notes, publishers at the turn of the twentieth century, when literary production in the United States expanded, "were eager to publish what they called 'good literature' because they did not want to think of themselves as businessmen like the common purveyors of commodities and manipulators of money."[28] Indeed, due in part to these publishing dynamics, scholars of Latinx literature have interrogated the prevalence of the printed book as the main object of study of Latinx cultural production, particularly in relation to thriving cultural regions in the Southwest such as New Mexico during the nineteenth century.[29] These critiques concerning the prevalence of the printed book in literary studies are significant, particularly in relation to minoritized writers since white editors at mainstream publishing houses dictated the terms and aesthetic parameters during the production of books; nonetheless, books of fiction and poetry remain at the center of Latinx literary studies. Indeed, printed books of fiction and poetry had a significant place in the development of the Latinx literature as exemplified by the literary output of authors such as Martí's *Versos sencillos* (1891) or Paredes's *Cantos de adolescencia*. These authors became canonical in part because they were able to publish traditional books, albeit with local presses in the United States.

Rather than challenging the prevalence of the book of fiction and poetry in the formation of the Latinx literary tradition, *Publishing Latinidad* seeks to expand the scope of the literary tradition by studying authors and intellectuals who entered literary and intellectual discourses through the publication of nontraditional books and alternative genres. My analyses of these nontraditional print forms and genres build on critical studies of either Black and Latinx literature that have studied pamphlets, proclamations, sketches, ballads, sermons, convention minutes, letters, manuscripts, government documents, memoirs, autobiographies, biographies, and translations.[30] As Raúl Coronado suggests, "[r]ather than only search for the final form of the novel, for example, it would serve Latina/o literary and intellectual history better to historicize the development of Latina/o *writing* as a whole."[31] *Publishing Latinidad* focuses on Latinx literary and intellectual production between 1880 and 1960 and is particularly indebted to Elizabeth McHenry's excellent *To Make Negro Literature* and her study of instructional manuals, bibliographies, anthologies, "hidden" authorship, and unpublished fiction since such interpretations have allowed for a more encompassing study of the Black literary tradition of the latter part of the nineteenth century and early twentieth century.[32] As McHenry notes, these print texts and types of writings "are no less a part of literary history" even when they fall outside traditional markers of literary achievement associated with books of fiction and poetry.[33] Part of my study focuses on these alternative print forms and genres produced by some early Latinx writers that until recently have received less critical attention despite the fact that these texts were written by some of the more well-known early Latinx authors; for instance, Martí translated and published articles and novels written in English, Schomburg wrote paratexts and bibliographies included in books and anthologies, Colón used some of his previously published sketches to produce his first book, Sáenz kept a war diary that he would later publish through a book subscription method, Sloss-Vento maintained a personal archive spanning decades that she would use to write a biography, and Paredes's fiction was published decades after its original composition.

Early Latinx writers and intellectuals used alternative forms of cultural production not only to engage with Latin American and Caribbean affairs but also to enter cultural, social, and political discourses in the United States. Nineteenth-century inhabitants of Spanish and Mexican ancestry living in what would become the Southwest, and Caribbean exiles in the United States, engaged with independence movements of their respective countries and territories.[34] In the second half of the nineteenth century, writers and intellectuals in different geographies and communities in the United States (*Nuevomexicanos, Tejanos, Californios*, and Puerto Ricans in New York City) entered and influenced cultural and social debates regarding their rightful place in U.S. society. Within the pages of U.S.-based Spanish-language newspapers and periodicals, writers such as Sotero Figueroa, Clotilde Betances Jaeger, Juan Antonio Corretjer, Julia de Burgos, Eusebio Chacón, Jovita Idar, Alonso S. Perales, and Alice Dickerson Montemayor developed the Latinx intellectual tradition by theorizing about notions of nationhood and belonging within the United States.[35] These early Latinx authors and intellectuals responded to their distinct geographies, histories, and backgrounds based on their respective experiences with U.S. expansionism and colonial influence; nonetheless, their groups' experiences represent early notions of distinct racial and ethnic identities that would form part of a shared Latinidad among Latinx people in the United States. This is not to argue that these early writings reflect a direct antecedent to our present notion of Latinidad; instead, as Coronado explains, the Latinidad contained in nineteenth century texts written by "Latino" subjects in the Southwest represents "a way to conceptualize the experiences of these communities as they sedimented over time, a sedimentation that may also have had its detours and reverse-formations, but that nonetheless contributed to the formation of Latino literary and intellectual culture."[36] While most early Latinx authors did not write with an awareness of a pan-ethnic and racial group identity as Latinx subjects in the United States, they shared historical, social, cultural, and linguistic characteristics that would subsequently unite them through their Latinidad and as Latinx writers who contributed to the formation of the Latinx literary and intellectual tradition in the United States.

Some early Latinx writers and intellectuals developed local and distinct versions of Latinidad in their printed texts with an awareness not only of their marginalization vis-à-vis the larger white population but also in relation to the exclusion and racialization shared with other non-white groups in the United States. *Publishing Latinidad* takes a comparative ethnic approach and draws from the insights of scholars who have studied processes of racialization and exclusion not only of Mexican American and Afro-Caribbean populations in the United States but also other non-white groups the United States, including Black, Indigenous, and Asian Americans groups. A comparative ethnic studies lens sheds light and interprets the context of early Latinx writers' works in relation to their shared experiences of exclusion, racialization, and racial violence with other non-white groups in the United States, particularly at the height of U.S. westward territorial expansion and colonial control in the Caribbean.[37] Martí's *crónicas* for Latin American newspapers and his translations of English texts expose the forced removal and military aggression against U.S. Indigenous groups who were deemed racially inferior and unable to assimilate. Schomburg's paratexts, bibliographies, and newspaper writings reclaim a Black and Black diasporic cultural heritage and resist the historical and cultural erasure of Black writers in the United States. Colón's sketches for Spanish-language and alternative newspapers connect the social exclusion of Puerto Ricans with those of other U.S. communities of Latin American origin and other working-class communities in New York City. Sáenz's newspaper writings denounce the segregation of people of Mexican descent in Texas and in his World War I diary, he reflects on his Indigenous background in relation to the histories of Indigenous groups in the Americas. While historicizing the early Mexican American civil rights movement, Sloss-Vento inserts herself as a Latina in the movement. In Paredes' newspaper reporting and short stories written in Asia during the U.S. occupation of Japan, he writes about the racialization of Asian populations, which followed an historical pattern of exclusion of Asian Americans that continued until the Cold War. *Publishing Latinidad* seeks to connect Latinx literary and intellectual history to some of the shared histories of non-white groups as these authors theorized and sought to end their racialized and marginalized position within the United States.

OVERVIEW AND ORGANIZATION OF THE BOOK

Spanish-language print culture in the United States dates back to the early nineteenth century, but it gained prominence in the second half of the century, as it coincided with independence and revolutionary movements in Latin America, particularly in the Caribbean. A characteristic of Spanish-language print culture of this period was its hemispheric scope, as Latin American writers in exile printed newspapers in the United States primarily for transnational audiences, and similarly, Latin American writers were published and read in Spanish-language newspapers in the United States. In the case of Martí, he wrote *crónicas* in the United States for Latin American newspapers starting in 1882. Martí's contribution to Latinx intellectual history can be traced both to the influence U.S. mass-circulation newspapers and periodicals had upon Martí as well as his New York–based newspaper and periodical writings—written in Spanish for local and hemispheric audiences—pertaining to the racialization and military aggression against Indigenous communities during westward expansion. Martí's *crónicas* reflect an evolution of his thinking regarding the displacement, racialization, and military aggression against Indigenous people, a marked departure from his early views on Indigenous people from Latin America while he lived in Mexico before 1880. Martí's *crónicas* were informed by emerging sympathetic narratives toward Indigenous peoples in mass-circulation newspapers, periodicals, and books by white reformers, exemplified by Helen Hunt Jackson's *A Century of Dishonor* (1881). Martí's translation of Jackson's *Ramona* in 1887 faithfully renders some of Jackson's main arguments regarding the denial of basic rights to Indigenous people, such as restrictions to U.S. citizenship that would have protected them legally from white settlers. Around the time of the publication of Martí's translation, white reformers' efforts for Native peoples' rights resulted in the passing of the Dawes Act of 1887. Martí's subsequent *crónicas* on Indigenous peoples after the enactment of this piece of legislation moved from optimism to despair as he reflected on the disastrous consequences of the partition of Indigenous people's lands and concluded that Native peoples, and Black communities, would remain excluded and racialized under a white legislative and judicial order in the United States.

The Black press in the early decades of the twentieth century constitutes one of the most significant developments in the establishment of a Black printing infrastructure in New York City, consisting of newspapers and periodicals led by Black editors. In chapter 2, I study Schomburg's intellectual and scholarly contributions to the recovery and study of U.S. Black and Black diasporic texts that have been obscured due to his legacy as a collector of rare books and manuscripts. Schomburg's writings in Black periodicals starting in the 1910s, and particularly his contributions for the *New York Amsterdam News* during the 1930s, sought to preserve the legacy of Black authors, as he envisioned the U.S. Black literary tradition as part of a broader Black diasporic culture. Some of Schomburg's most significant scholarly contributions to the recovery and preservation of the Black literary past relate to his writings on Phillis Wheatley and his bibliographies in which he compiled the books and works of past Black writers, orators, and poets, starting with *A Bibliographical Checklist of American Negro Poetry* (1916). Schomburg's bibliographies and compilations of texts by U.S. Black and Black diasporic poets served as one of the foundations for an emerging Black academic infrastructure in the United States focusing on Black cultural production. Schomburg's "A Select List of Negro-Americana and Africana," published in Alain Locke's seminal anthology *The New Negro* (1925), contains a select compilation of representative works by Black writers that reflects Schomburg's curatorial practices in his study of Black texts in contrast to some of Locke's bibliographies, also included in *The New Negro*. Despite the encouragement by Charles S. Johnson, former editor of *Opportunity*, to publish his *Amsterdam News* essays in a book format, Schomburg's groundbreaking scholarly writing remained buried in the pages of a Black newspaper due in part to the lack of publishing opportunities for Black writers and scholars in a white-dominated newspaper and book publishing industry.

Spanish-language print culture in New York City during the first half of the twentieth century was characterized by the emergence of newspapers and periodicals that reflected the concerns of their Spanish-speaking readership in the United States. Since the early decades of the twentieth century, print publications, such as the weekly *Gráfico*, sought to create solidarity among Spanish-language readers from different Latin American backgrounds under a pan-ethnic "*Hispano*" category. Chapter 3 focuses on Colón's contribution to Latinx intellectual history as reflected in his sketches published in the New York City-based weekly *Pueblos Hispanos* during the 1940s and the *Daily Worker* in the 1950s. These sketches pertained to the social, economic, and cultural exclusion of Puerto Rican, *Hispanos*, and working-class communities in New York City. Other print cultures in New York City, such as newspapers and periodicals supported by labor and communist organizations, proved key for authors of color, as they were excluded from working or writing for mass-circulation newspapers and periodicals prior to 1960. Colón wrote sketches that were printed in the *Daily Worker*, a publication that had similarly published the newspaper writings of Richard Wright in the 1930s. In his sketches for the *Daily Worker*, Colón continues his early theorizations in *Pueblos Hispanos* regarding the need for social and labor solidarity not only among Puerto Rican New Yorkers and *Hispanos* but also with other working-class communities in New York City. In the context of Puerto Rican authors writing about the United States or residing in New York City in the 1940s and 1950s, Colón stands out as one of the few who wrote in English attempting to reach an English-speaking readership, which allows for a contextualization of his work in relation to those of Black authors such as Langston Hughes and Wright. Due in part to the exclusion of writers of color by mainstream publishing houses, Colón's collection of sketches, *A Puerto Rican in New York* (1961), in which he maps his own literary and intellectual trajectory influenced by print culture and books, was published by an alternative press in 1961 that soon went out of business, thus contributing to the book's obscurity until it was reprinted by Juan Flores in 1982.

Among the various states that developed robust Spanish-language print culture centers in the latter part of the nineteenth century and into the twentieth century, such as California, New Mexico, and Colorado, Spanish-language print culture in Texas was expanded by Mexican exiles during the Mexican Revolution. Chapter 4 moves from the East Coast to the Southwest by focusing on Sáenz's writings pertaining to the history of racialization and exclusion not only of Mexicans and Mexican Americans but also of Indigenous populations in the Southwest. Sáenz became one of the tens of thousands of Mexican nationals and Mexican Americans who participated in World War I; however, he distinguished himself by submitting letters for publication during the final years of the war to *La Prensa*, a San Antonio-based Spanish-language newspaper, that chronicled the war experiences of Mexicans and Mexican Americans on the European front. Similar to the experiences of Black soldiers, Sáenz and other Mexican American soldiers returned to the same racialized and segregated society they had left before the war despite their war contributions, which influenced the emergence of Mexican American civil rights organizations that coalesced into the League of United Latin American Citizens (LULAC) in 1929. Sáenz's social activism regarding the recognition of the contributions of Mexican American soldiers to the war effort resulted in the publication of his World War I diary *Los méxico-americanos en la gran guerra* (The Mexican Americans during the Great War) in 1933 with Artes Gráficas, a regional San Antonio press. Sáenz's participation in World War I—as depicted in his diary and contrary to his early *La Prensa* letters—allowed him to connect the shared histories of exclusion of Mexican, Mexican American, and Indigenous peoples in the Southwest. His diary complicates historical and critical interpretations regarding the racial views held by pre-1960 Mexican American civil rights activists and LULAC leaders who fought for school desegregation in Texas using the controversial legal claim to whiteness for Mexican Americans. While Sáenz actively sought connections and racial solidarity with other Indigenous soldiers, his diary lacks an engagement with the plight of other people of color, particularly Black soldiers, despite their shared racialized experiences in the army.

Before 1960, Latinas had limited social and educational opportunities, which created barriers to entering social and cultural discourses not only in mainstream publications and academic institutions but also within their respective communities. Despite these limitations, a few Latina writers entered social debates primarily through the pages of Spanish-language newspapers and periodicals in cities such as New York City, San Antonio, and Santa Fe. In chapter 5, I interpret some of Sloss-Vento's writings and social activism for civil rights in Texas, starting in 1927 and continuing almost uninterrupted to the 1970s, as an attempt to insert herself into the history of the early Mexican American rights movement in Texas. Sloss-Vento's active contributions are reflected through her archival practices, personal correspondence with key leaders of the movement, newspaper writings, and the publication of her monograph *Alonso S. Perales: His Struggle for the Rights of Mexican-Americans*, published in 1977 with Artes Gráficas. Sloss-Vento's nontraditional book serves as a *book-archive*, as she structures her text as a figurative archive of the early Mexican American civil rights movement consisting of sections containing articles from Spanish-language newspapers, books, public and private correspondence, pamphlets, lectures, and unpublished manuscripts included within the body of the text. Sloss-Vento inserts herself into her narrative by discussing her personal acquaintance and correspondence with Perales and her involvement in the movement, not as an activist on the ground, as in the case of male leaders, but through her writings published in *La Prensa* during the 1930s where she argues for the need for Mexican Americans to organize for voting rights. Rather than highlighting her role, Sloss-Vento's writings minimize her involvement due in part to the strict gender roles in Mexican American households and social organizations. While Sloss-Vento sought to create a bridge with the publication of her book between the early movement and the emerging Chicanx Movement of the late 1960s and early 1970s, her efforts were unsuccessful, as Chicanx activists rejected the social and political conservatism of pre-1960s Mexican American leaders and politicians.

Chapter 6 delves into the history of how university presses mirrored the exclusionary practices of elite and predominantly-white institutions as scholars of color, despite their academic credentials, were excluded for the most part from teaching at those institutions or publishing single-author monographs with university presses prior to 1960. Paredes's early poetry published and discussed in the pages of *La Prensa*, along with his unpublished fiction, particularly his novel *George Washington Gómez* written prior to the start of World War II, reflect his early experiences as a racialized subject and instances of racial violence against Mexican Americans in the Borderlands. Those experiences influenced Paredes's coverage of the Tokyo war crimes trial in 1946 for *Pacific Stars and Stripes*, a newspaper of the U.S. armed forces in Japan. His reporting on the Tokyo trial reflects the tensions regarding the validity and justification of the trial, as U.S. military personnel, including Paredes, believed war crimes had been committed by both sides. At the same time, Paredes's short fiction, written and set in Asia during the 1940s and early 1950s, grapples with the racialization of Asian populations by U.S. soldiers—including soldiers of color—during and after the war and the dehumanization of prisoners of war by both U.S. and Japanese soldiers. After the war, Paredes returned to the United States to continue his studies and exploration of the history of segregation and racial violence against Mexican Americans in Texas, culminating with his PhD dissertation on Gregorio Cortez. Contrary to critical interpretations regarding the attempt by the University of Texas Press to suppress sections of Paredes's scholarly monograph concerning the abuses committed by the Texas Rangers against Mexicans and Mexican Americans, the correspondence between

Paredes and his editor at the press, Frank H. Wardlaw, reflects the latter's unwavering support for the publication of *"With His Pistol in His Hand"* (1958). Before the publication of Paredes's monograph, his fiction was systematically rejected by mainstream magazines and publishing houses and remained unpublished for decades; it was only after his academic recognition that Paredes was able to publish his fiction during the 1990s with Arte Público Press.

In the conclusion, I reflect on the methodologies that contemporary scholars of Latinx literary history have formulated to study and map the Latinx literary and intellectual tradition. Before the 1960s, questions about national, ethnic, and racial identifications among distinct communities have characterized the study of early Latinx texts. The recovery, reprinting, and study of Latinx authors in traditional and alternative print forms and genres have allowed for the study of early Latinx literary and intellectual history through its primary texts and the formation and evolving views on the authors' own identities. These texts show that they were some of the earliest ethnic comparativists, as they interpreted their racialized position as one shared with other non-white groups in the United States, a position which went through periods of social, economic, and cultural turmoil due to U.S. westward expansion and colonial control in the Caribbean. The continuing efforts to map and study the Latinx literary and intellectual tradition represent an ongoing project filled with possibilities. Some Latinx writers after the 1960s were able to access publishing opportunities with mainstream publishing houses and publications; however, Latinx presses, such as Arte Público Press, also contributed to the increasing visibility of Latinx authors in the following decades. Despite some success, there is still a need for meaningful representation of Latinx authors in U.S. mainstream publishing and cultural institutions in order to righten centuries of literary and cultural marginalization.

CHAPTER 1

U.S. PRINT CULTURE AND JOSÉ MARTÍ'S *CRÓNICAS* ON U.S. INDIGENOUS PEOPLES' RIGHTS

THE LATINX literary tradition has increasingly gained depth and complexity through the incorporation of Spanish-language print culture. The late nineteenth century reflects the vibrancy of U.S.-based Spanish-language publications, as a number of literary scholars have recovered and studied the legacies and geographies of newspapers and periodicals sustained by Spanish-speaking readership in cities such as New York City, San Antonio, Los Angeles, Santa Fe, and New Orleans.[1] Spanish-speaking writers, along with other non-white writers, remained with some exceptions excluded from mainstream newspapers and periodicals, resulting in the emergence of a robust Spanish-language newspaper-publishing infrastructure in the United States. The rise of Spanish-language newspapers in these cities was connected to the establishment of an increasing number of Spanish-speaking communities where newspapers and periodicals represented the primary form for literary, intellectual, and political engagement. According to John Alba Cutler, "[i]n the absence of a robust book-publishing market in Spanish, Latinx readers in the late nineteenth and early twentieth century were much likelier to encounter literary texts in the pages of their local newspapers than bound between the covers of a book."[2] The Latinx archive is comprised of U.S.-based Spanish-language local and regional newspapers and periodicals whose readership consisted primarily of members of distinct groups (Mexican American, Puerto Rican, Cuban American, etc.).[3] Before writers and intellectuals theorized about their respective ethnic or racial identities, and what it meant to be othered in the United States, they also participated in social and political debates pertaining to their countries of origin and, more broadly, Latin America.

Spanish-language print culture and the Latinx archive are characterized by their transnational and hemispheric reach at different periods and sites in Latin America. Some Spanish-language newspapers and periodicals such as *La Verdad* and *La Patria* originated in publishing hubs such as New York City and New Orleans respectively, and their influence traveled across borders, as in the case of newspapers edited by Cuban writers in the United States during the second half of the nineteenth century. Scholars have studied early U.S.-based Cuban writers from Trans-American, transnational, and hemispheric perspectives, based in part on the geopolitical contexts of the United States and Cuba.[4] U.S. expansionism, with its sights on the Caribbean, made the United States a threat to Cubans while at the same time allowing Cuban exiles to write in U.S.-based Spanish-language newspapers with a transnational reach. Writers such as Félix Varela, Cirilo Villaverde, Miguel T. Tolón, Emilia Casanova, José Martí, Martín Morúa Delgado, and Rafael Serra were not only political exiles in the United States fighting for Cuban independence but also, as Carmen Lamas cogently argues, these writers were transnational, as their writings occupied more than one geography, and their in-between spaces created a "Latino Continuum" that simultaneously linked their "complex political and literary contexts" to Cuba and the United States.[5] These authors published some of their work in U.S.-based Spanish-language newspapers for their local readers; however, they also understood themselves as participating in the transnational and hemispheric exchange of ideas and cultural and literary trends with other audiences and writers in Latin America.[6] Some of these writers, particularly Martí, were similarly influenced by social and political discourses emerging within the United States.

In this chapter, I focus on Martí's U.S.-based newspaper writings influenced by U.S. print culture and debates that reflect his evolving views pertaining to the dispossession and racialization of U.S. Indigenous groups as reflected in his *crónicas* (chronicles) and his 1887 translation of Helen Hunt Jackson's reform novel, *Ramona* (1884). Martí's literary and political legacy is almost inseparable from Latin American letters and the fight for

Cuban independence, and as Lillian Guerra has argued, shortly after his death, his legacy was appropriated by different groups in Cuba for different purposes, and these competing interpretations have continued throughout subsequent decades;[7] however, an increasing number of literary scholars have focused on Martí in the U.S. context and have studied him as a U.S.-based writer engaging with U.S. social, cultural, historical, economic, and political topics.[8] Laura Lomas's foundational *Translating Empire* has analyzed the degree to which Martí extensively wrote, translated, and interpreted social, economic, and cultural events for U.S.-based and Latin American Spanish-speaking readers. Among the several topics covered in Martí's *crónicas*, he wrote extensively on Indigenous peoples in the United States. I argue for the centrality and increasing influence of late nineteenth century U.S. print culture, in the form of printed books, mass-circulation newspapers, and literary magazines on Martí's *crónicas* and translation of *Ramona* that reflect his gradual critical interpretation of the violence and land dispossession of Indigenous people in the United States and their lack of basic rights under U.S. jurisdiction. During his residency in Latin America, some of Martí's writings reflect his acceptance of anti-Indigenous views expressed by some of his Latin American intellectual counterparts. Technological developments in U.S. print culture that allowed for an extended news coverage in the U.S. western territories pertaining to Native groups influenced white middle-class reformers who, inspired in part by the writings of Jackson, advocated for Native peoples' rights. Once in the United States, Martí's views and newspaper writings evolved, as he became increasingly immersed in debates in U.S. mass-circulation periodicals and magazines regarding the violent removal of U.S. Indigenous people from their territories.[9] My analysis of Martí's *crónicas* on U.S. Native groups draws from Indigenous studies and Indigeneity scholarship, particularly current interpretations of the consequences of settler colonialism and notions of Indigenous sovereignty, to interpret his evolving views on U.S. Indigenous peoples.[10]

I begin by contextualizing Martí's views on U.S. Native peoples in relation to some of his previous writings on Indigenous populations in Latin America where he lived and shared anti-Indigenous views with some of his Latin American counterparts. Martí arrived in New York City at the time of technological developments in U.S. print culture that contributed to a shift in social and cultural perceptions of the conditions and histories of

U.S. Native peoples beyond Manifest Destiny historiographies prevalent in print culture before the 1880s. Martí's early *crónicas* on U.S. Indigenous people initially reflect his acceptance of received ideas on these groups published in U.S. newspapers that emphasized either their alleged violent tendencies or their successful transition to Western economic practices, such as those of the Crow and the Cheyenne respectively, while omitting or minimizing episodes of U.S. military use of force against those groups and the violent removal from their lands. In following years, influenced by U.S. newspapers and periodicals, Martí wrote in more circumspect ways regarding the role of the U.S. Army in the removal of Native groups, particularly the Nez Perce. Martí's subsequent *crónicas* focusing on U.S. Indigenous people were informed by social and legislative approaches advanced by white reformers and disseminated in print culture, particularly in Jackson's *A Century of Dishonor* (1881) and *Ramona*, which increasingly criticized the historical mistreatment of Native groups and the reservation system while advocating for legislation on their behalf, including U.S. citizenship for Native peoples.

Translations of English texts and books published in the United States represented one of the alternative print forms available for U.S.-based Spanish-speaking writers to contribute to U.S. intellectual and cultural debates while at the same time seeking to reach Spanish-speaking readers in Latin America. Martí's motivation for his translation of Jackson's *Ramona* originated in part by his support of Jackson's appeal for the protection of Native groups through legislation, including their right of representation in courts and access to U.S. citizenship, intended to avoid their land dispossession and the real prospect of complete elimination. The work of white reformers influenced the passing of the Dawes Act of 1887, which offered U.S. citizenship to Native peoples who accepted the partition of their lands; however, Martí, contrary to white reformers, came to question U.S. jurisdiction over them and their lands in part through his key realization that Indigenous and Black people in the South have shared a history of racialization, violence, and disenfranchisement in order to "mantener la raza blanca pura" (maintain white supremacy).[11] Martí's *crónicas* pertaining to U.S. Indigenous people and his translation of *Ramona* participated in discourses that questioned the territorial dispossession of non-white groups in newly conquered U.S. territories and the exclusion and racialization of non-white groups in the United States.

THE MODERN U.S. PRINT INDUSTRY AND DEPICTIONS OF U.S. INDIGENOUS PEOPLE

Prior to his arrival in New York City, Martí had already written about Indigenous people in Latin America, at times sharing prevalent negative views on Indigenous groups. These views were already widely accepted by some members of the social and intellectual elite in Latin America. In Jorge Camacho's excellent book *José Martí y la cuestión indígena* (José Martí and the Indigenous Question), he demonstrates the extent to which Martí's writings while living in Mexico in 1875 contain some of the same bias toward Indigenous peoples expressed by Mexican intellectuals, such as Francisco Pimentel and Antonio García Cubas, whom Martí admired, as he accepted the stereotype of the "lazy Indian," among other perceived negative traits.[12] As an exile in Mexico born in Cuba of Spanish parents, Martí and other members of the intellectual elite in Latin America inherited the centuries-old racial hierarchies prevalent during the Spanish control over Latin America. While notions of *mestizaje*, or racial mixing, remained the dominant racial ideology in Mexico at the time, remnants of the *casta* system prevailed in Latin America with *peninsulares* (white Spaniards) and *criollos* (creoles), such as Martí, at the top and Indigenous and Black peoples at the bottom.[13]

In an 1875 *crónica* for *La Revista Universal* of Mexico, Martí discusses the state of the Mexican economy and the shortage of agricultural workers while chastising Indigenous people in unflattering ways for their unwillingness to serve as laborers. Martí describes their participation in Mexico's economic development as something "desconocido e inútil" (unknown and useless).[14] Martí goes as far as to note that Indigenous people's intelligence is "estrecha" (narrow) just as "estrecho es todo lo que concibe y lo que hace" (everything they know and do is narrow).[15] Martí's critique of Latin American Indigenous peoples is informed in part by his emphasis on economic progress and the role of Native peoples within emerging republican ideals in Latin America. Camacho has argued that there is a tendency among critics to interpret Martí's subsequent writings on U.S. Indigenous peoples favorably while overlooking his acceptance of received ideas that contributed to the decline of Native populations in Latin America.[16] Similarly, one can wonder whether Martí's critical views on Indigenous peoples would have changed if his series of exiles would not have taken him to New York City at a time of emerging competing discourses in U.S. print culture regarding the position and histories of Indigenous peoples in the United States.

U.S. print culture went through a period of modernization in the second half of the nineteenth century as advances in technology gave rise to the mass-scale book industry and the era of mass-circulation newspapers that increased their reporting on Indigenous groups west of the Mississippi.[17] The long history of land dispossession of several Native groups and a series of catastrophes, such as the Indian removal policy, the reservation system, and the unrelenting westward movement of white settlers into Indigenous lands west of the Mississippi, grew exponentially after the passing of the Homestead Act of 1862. When it came to narratives of U.S. Native people in books, most historical and ethnographic accounts prior to the 1880s favored the U.S. government perspective and its vision of Manifest Destiny.[18] Those printed accounts contained some of the most pernicious and enduring tropes related to Native people's alleged violent tendencies and the belief that their "vanishing" was due to their own inability to assimilate into white society. Around the 1880s, sympathetic narratives about Native peoples penned by white authors—including Native peoples' struggles created by land dispossession—surfaced in print and followed in mass-circulation newspapers and magazines, along with the publication in book format of competing perspectives that challenged Manifest Destiny historiography.[19] Some of these narratives were authored by sympathizers who then turned activists and reformers for Indigenous rights; Jackson, who became one of the most well-known reformers, assisted in the dissemination of information in East Coast newspapers regarding events first reported by newspaper editor Thomas Henry Tibbles on the plight of the Poncas people by writing letters to the editor of the *New York Daily Tribune* in 1879.[20] Jackson also made use of newspaper reports and government publications during the research of her influential book *A Century of Dishonor*, a sharp denunciation on the mistreatment of Native peoples by the U.S. government. Jackson's writings in turn increased the coverage of U.S. Indigenous peoples in newspapers and periodicals, and she then continued to write articles on southern California's Indigenous populations published in *Century* magazine in 1883.[21]

Martí was able to write in New York City for almost a decade because he entered the era of mass-circulation newspapers and periodicals that changed him from a political exile into a newspaper writer engaged with U.S. print culture and its raging social, political, and economic debates.[22] Martí began to write for the English-language newspaper the *New York*

Sun and its weekly counterpart, the *Hour*, in 1880. *New York Sun*'s editor, Charles Anderson Dana, gave Martí his start as a newspaper writer based on his standing as a Latin American writer and intellectual.[23] As a light-skinned *criollo*, Martí did not experience the same degree of othering and racialization as other non-white writers in New York City or other U.S. geographies. Starting in 1881, he began to write as a New York City correspondent for Latin American newspapers such as *La Opinión Nacional* of Venezuela, *La Nación* of Argentina, and *El Partido Liberal* of Mexico, among others, primarily for their respective middle-class readerships interested in foreign affairs and European culture.[24] Martí wrote primarily for Latin American readers attracted to news and events published in the U.S. press, and he purposely attempted to write in a form that resembled articles printed in the U.S. daily newspapers.[25] Martí's writings then took the form of the *crónica*, a blend of epistolary, essayistic, and analytic writing that scholars have associated with Latin American newspaper writers, and a genre that Martí helped to popularize in the United States.[26] Martí's *crónicas* written from New York City—numbering in the hundreds spanning more than a decade—show the extent of his engagement with a myriad of U.S. historical, social, economic, and cultural topics. While Martí's varied range of U.S. subjects is difficult to quantify, his perspective and views on the United States were not static but changed over the years. As Susana Rotker rightly argues, Martí's evolving perceptions of the United States from admirer to incisive critic can be traced through his U.S.-based *crónicas*, particularly those related to political subjects.[27] While Rotker and Laura Lomas have studied Martí's trajectory from admirer to critic of the United States on various topics, I analyze Martí's evolving interpretation of U.S. Indigenous peoples that contributed to his critique of the position of non-white groups not only in the U.S. expansionist project in the Caribbean but also within the United States.

Martí wrote about the emergence of the modern print industry in the United States and high-profile national magazines such as *Harper's* and *Century* that began to compete with books for readers and whose pages included articles that contextualized some of the histories of Native peoples in the United States.[28] Laura Lomas has analyzed the extent to which some of Martí's *crónicas* on various subjects are based on his reading of U.S. magazines such as *Century*, *Harper's*, *North American Review*, and *Popular Science Monthly*.[29] In his role as editor of the Spanish-language magazine

La América printed in New York City, Martí also translated essays from some of these magazines starting in 1883.[30] During his previous stay in Spain, Martí became aware of the increased prominence of European magazines, and when he arrived in New York City, he wrote with enthusiasm on more than one occasion regarding the thriving New York City print culture that included high-profile magazines such as *Harper's* and *Century*. According to Martí, these publications rivaled some of the best magazines in France and England as "repertorio[s] de artes y letras, de todos los tiempos, de forma exquisita y amplio espíritu . . ." (depositories of arts and writings of all periods, of exquisite and broad spirit . . .).[31] Martí also praised New York City print culture for its potential for cultural and literary engagement, as he equated the production of books—the traditional form of literary dissemination—with national U.S. magazines; Martí wrote, "[l]eer una buena revista es como leer decenas de buenos libros" (reading a good magazine is as good as reading dozens of good books).[32] The emerging U.S. print culture that Martí encountered contrasted with his previous experience living in Latin America and the prevalence of high art and literary creation in the form of poetry in book format that Martí initially shared with other Latin American writers.[33] While Martí served as New York City correspondent for Latin American newspapers, he seldom roamed or left the city to acquire information and facts; instead, he primarily read, rewrote, and translated news and accounts from U.S. newspapers and magazines. A characteristic of Martí's *crónicas* then was the appropriation and synthesis of information from mass-circulation newspapers and magazines that he then combined with his writings, at times mentioning his sources, but most times omitting them.

Martí's early *crónicas* on U.S. Indigenous people reflect debates in newspapers on whether Native groups such as the Crow should fight for their rightful claim of their lands or relinquish their way of life and accept Western agricultural practices.[34] The Crow, a group of Plains Indigenous people in present-day Montana, had supported George Armstrong Custer during his military incursion in the Plains in 1876 against the Sioux and their Cheyenne allies in the so-called "Great Sioux War."[35] One of Martí's *crónicas* for *La Opinión Nacional* of April 1882 discusses newspaper reports during the early months of the same year that debated whether the U.S. government had the right to remove the Crow from their lands for economic purposes—just as the Utes had been removed from Colorado—as Crow territories became increasingly encroached upon by land speculators and railroad interests. Regarding the debate on whether the Crow should accept removal or fight back, Martí writes, "[d]e indios se habla ahora, y se teme su guerra; porque les han reconocido, cuando se les han cansado ya los brazos desnudos de pelear por el dominio de los ríos y bosques patrios que los hombres blancos violan . . ." (currently, the topic of discussion is the Indians and the fear of war; they have been recognized as their naked arms are tired of fighting for maintaining their rivers and forests that the white men have transgressed).[36] Martí's description relates to one of the main tensions in settler colonialism; that is, the belief that white settlers could impose their will over Native groups and their lands through military, economic, or cultural systems of control geared toward regulating all aspects of Indigenous peoples' lives under the "dominance of U.S. jurisdiction."[37] Martí's *crónica*, moreover, alludes to the Crow's weariness due to U.S. government officials' mismanagement of funds owed to them after signing a treaty and their willingness to fight to protect what remains of their lands; Martí writes, "[s]on los *crows* los que amenazan guerra ahora, y tienen listos sus mil guerreros y sus cuatro mil caballos de batalla" (now the Crow are threatening to wage war, and they are ready with a thousand warriors and four thousand war horses).[38] Martí's statement relates to reports in newspapers that contained similar language claiming that the Crow were ready for war and "will fight desperately before giving up their [lands]" since they are "a race of warriors."[39] Ultimately, the Crow did not engage with the U.S. Army directly and were able to remain in their vastly diminished Montana territory but under U.S. jurisdiction. Nonetheless, Martí's acknowledgement of Crow people's grievances signals a departure from his writings on Indigenous people in Latin America, as he became influenced by the coverage of these events in U.S. newspapers.

Martí presents both a critique and acceptance of the treatment of some U.S. Native groups by the U.S. government chronicled in print culture, as he participates in newspapers' depictions of them as engaging in "war" with the United States as if both sides were equals in military force. Martí initially accepts the trope of the "Indian warrior," as he describes the Cheyenne as "peleadores tremendos" (fierce warriors) only a few years back who have now taken Western agricultural practices.[40] Martí's description of the Cheyenne from warriors to western farmers, however, fails to acknowledge how the Cheyenne adapted to those conditions only after they were defeated through military force by General Nelson Miles in 1876 in the context of what Roxanne Dunbar-Ortiz describes as "genocidal campaigns against Indigenous civilians [that] took place during the administration of President [Ulysses] Grant."[41] Instead, Martí alludes to this tumultuous period of removal by the U.S. Army as a seemingly peaceful transition by the Cheyenne when he suggests they were treated "con blandura" (with kindness) by General Miles.[42] The imposition of U.S. jurisdiction over previously independent Native peoples and nations west of the Mississippi after the Civil War was made possible primarily through the unleashing of unequal military force against them.[43] Thus, the Cheyenne accepted to change their former social and economic practices only after they were defeated by the U.S. Army, or what Mark Rifkin describes as "the violence of settler colonialism."[44] The U.S. military campaign led by General Miles against the Cheyenne relates to the role that the U.S. military played in U.S. expansionism and the emergence of the United States as a nation, and as Jodi Byrd notes, "[a] democracy born out of violent occupation of lands."[45]

In the same *crónica* for *La Opinión Nacional*, Martí presents the opposing side of the debate in newspapers' coverage that portrayed the Cheyenne as an example of a Native group that successfully adopted western agricultural methods. The Cheyenne were defeated along with the Sioux in 1875 by the U.S. Army and forced to relocate to Indian Territory; they were subsequently described in newspaper accounts and U.S. government reports as a group that had successfully transitioned from their previous communal structures and sustainable agricultural practices to a U.S.-based farming model.[46] Martí's *crónica* thus contrasts the likely military defeat of the Crow in their attempt to retain their lands with the example of the Cheyenne, as he explains that the latter have gained "habilidad de agricultores ... [que han aprendido] a sembrar, y a levantar cercas" (the capacity for agriculture ... who have learned to sow and build fences).[47] While Martí accepts these conspicuous accounts circulating in newspapers, Jackson in *A Century of Dishonor* had already questioned these narratives of alleged successful economic transition by the Cheyenne as fleeting since their agricultural gains decreased in subsequent years due to weather events and led to U.S. government intervention through food rations.[48] At the core of the Cheyenne's adoption of Western agricultural practices, however, was coercion and control under a U.S. government-run system of reservations that took away agency from Indigenous groups. As Rifkin observes, control of

Native peoples' lives was enacted through "an accumulation of mundane, state-sanctioned processes,"[49] consisting of policies such as the reservation system and the imposition of settlers' modes of economic production such as farming. Initially, Martí accepted these narratives of coercive assimilation as viable alternatives for some Native groups.

Martí's subsequent writings on U.S. Native peoples contain a contextualized interpretation of these groups as in the case of the Nez Perce, whose history of violent land dispossession was featured in high-profile magazines such as *Century*. Established in 1881, *Century* was characterized by its in-depth feature articles primarily on culture, history, and the arts; among its coverage, *Century* published articles about Indigenous peoples that, while still paternalistic and hostile toward Native groups, introduced some of their past histories and customs to readers through a more nuanced lens. Martí's discussion of the plight of the Nez Perce is found in a *crónica* titled "El *Century Magazine*," published in Martí's *La América* in May 1884. This *crónica* shows the degree to which Martí's writings on Indigenous peoples were influenced by U.S. periodicals, as it is based on a May 1884 *Century* article written by C. E. S. Wood.[50] Martí writes about the use of the U.S. Army in the Great Plains and focuses on the military campaign of recent years against the Nez Perce and their leader, "Trueno que Rueda en las Montañas" (Thunder Rolling in the Mountains), also known as "Chief" Joseph.[51] This *crónica* is one of the rare instances where while discussing Native peoples, Martí mentions his source, *Century* magazine, without naming the article's author. Martí's *crónica* synthesizes and selectively takes events from Wood's article regarding the military aggression against Joseph and the Nez Perce who were relentlessly persecuted and attacked by Generals Nelson Miles and Oliver Howard in 1877, leading to the displacement of eight hundred Nez Perce from the Great Plains toward the Canadian border while sporadically engaging with the U.S. cavalry.[52] As in Wood's article, Martí's *crónica* focuses on the aftermath of the persecution that resulted in the deaths of Nez Perce's elders, women, and children.[53] Martí now challenges the accepted idea of "la barbarie de los indios" (Indian savagery) and instead describes the Nez Perce as possessing "virtudes" (virtues), "prudencia" (prudence), and "nobleza" (nobility).[54] Martí's description of the Nez Perce's social cohesion reflects a progression in his writings on Native peoples from stereotypes that present them as fearless warriors toward a more nuanced description of these groups as possessing intricate social organizations.

Martí's historical account of the Nez Perce reflects an increasingly critical interpretation regarding the role of U.S. military violence, the U.S. policy of forceful territory removal, and the legacy of broken treaties by the United States contained in emerging narratives such as Jackson's *A Century of Dishonor*. In his *crónica* on the Nez Perce, Martí emphasizes the use of U.S. military force and the tragic consequences of this violence as he notes that the Nez Perce, despite their modest fighting capabilities, were "forzados a la pelea con el [ejército] norteamericano" (forced to fight against the U.S. Army).[55] Martí now questions the use of force by the United States and the military campaign against the Nez Perce that had as its goal imprisoning and forcefully removing them to a reservation in Indian Territory. The conclusion of Martí's account alludes to the manner in which the Nez Perce were decimated as they were "engañados primero con tratados" (first cheated through treaties).[56] Jackson's *A Century of Dishonor* contains a similar poignant critique of the U.S. military aggression against the Nez Perce as she notes that the "narrative of Chief Josep[h] is profoundly touching; a very Iliad of tragedy, of dignified and hopeless sorrow; and it stands supported by the official records of the Indian Bureau."[57] In a description that seeks to capture a pathos found in Jackson's account, Martí concludes his *crónica* by describing Joseph after his surrender as "magnánimo ... y con brazo tendido, ofrec[iendo] el rifle al jefe americano" (magnanimous ... and with a stretched arm, offering his rifle to the American chief),[58] thus emphasizing the Nez Perce's defeat as the result of indiscriminate military force.

Martí's subsequent writings reflect the increasing advocacy on behalf of U.S. Native peoples that was covered in mass-circulation newspapers and periodicals as well as the degree to which this coverage influenced his views on these groups. In a *crónica* titled "Los Indios en los Estados Unidos" (Indians in the United States) published in *La Nación* in 1885, Martí presents his most sustained engagement with the condition of U.S. Indigenous people, as he focuses on their forced removal by the U.S. government, the mismanagement of the system of reservations, and the need for legislative solutions to increase their rights under U.S. jurisdiction. Martí's *crónica* is directly based on the Third Lake Mohonk Conference of 1885, an annual gathering of white sympathizers, or "friends of the Indians" seeking to improve the U.S. government's treatment of Native peoples, consisting of officials, politicians, philanthropists, academics, and religious leaders. While Martí's *crónica* reads at times as if it were written by a correspondent who attended the event, it is unclear whether he attended the conference, or if it was based in part on the conference's coverage in newspapers such as the *Sun*, the *New York Times*, or other publications.[59] Whether Martí attended the conference or not, "Indians in the United States" is significant regarding the degree to which it convincingly synthesizes field research, statistics, and arguments presented by some of the conference speakers as well as the extent to which he concurs with the platform and resolutions adopted by Mohonk Conference attendees. Martí, for instance, shares with Mohonk reformers their concerns regarding the ongoing treatment of Indigenous peoples by the U.S. government that has "burlad[o] sus derechos, engañada su fe, [y] corrompido su carácter" (cheated them of their rights, shattered their trust, and corrupted their character) and now seeks to end Native peoples' "revueltas frecuentes y justas" (frequent and justified rebellions).[60]

Based in part on the field work of Mohonk reformers, Martí's *crónica* exposes the deficiencies of the reservation system with the goal of reforming it rather than questioning its existence. Some of Martí's main critiques in "Indians in the United States" relate to the mismanagement of the system of government-run reservations based on the field work of Mohonk conference attendees, particularly ethnographer Alice Fletcher.[61] Martí notes that Native peoples have been forced to give up their lands through "tratados onerosos" (onerous treaties) and have been displaced from "la comarca en que ha[n] nacido, que es como sacar a un árbol las raíces, con lo que pierde el mayor objeto de la vida" (the region in which they have been born, which is similar to uprooting a tree from the soil; thus losing their life's purpose).[62] Treaties often contained stipulations, such as the supply of food, cattle, and tools for Native peoples, that were often mismanaged or ignored, as documented by Fletcher's field research.[63] U.S.-run reservations, Martí continues, represent "un sistema de tutela degradante que comenzó hace un siglo" (a degrading tutelage system that began a century ago), where Indigenous people were relocated, often in different territories, against their will.[64] They were at the mercy of U.S. government officials and speculators who sold them guns and alcohol "en cambio del dinero que en virtud de los tratados reparte entre las reservas el gobierno al año" (in exchange for money, which they received by virtue of treaties, divided among the reservations by the government each year).[65] Martí's critique, based on the information gathered from Mohonk Conference speakers such as Fletcher, reflects what Rifkin describes as the violent process of imposing "temporal frames generated in and by settler governance" on Native communities;⁶⁶ however, Martí and Mohonk reformers at the time stopped short of questioning the right of the U.S. government to impose a reservation system on previously sovereign groups.

"Indians in the United States" situates Martí, along with conference attendees, at the forefront of emerging U.S. political discourses disseminated in print culture that advocated for basic rights for Native peoples through legislative reform. In the same *crónica*, Martí invokes the memory of Jackson, who had passed away earlier the same year, and her influence on Mohonk reformers through her magazine articles, government reports, and books, particularly her immensely popular reform novel *Ramona*.⁶⁷ Martí recalls that one of Jackson's final gestures before she died was to write a thank-you letter to President Grover Cleveland for his determination to recognize "[el] derecho a justicia en la gente india" (the right to justice for Indian people).⁶⁸ The reason Mohonk reformers got together, according to Martí, was to attempt to "curar los males" (right the wrongs) created by the legacy of broken treaties by the U.S. government.⁶⁹ Martí states that injustices created by the reservation system, and the U.S. government's mismanagement of those reservations, rendered Native peoples at the mercy of rations, clothes, and annuities that have lasted "desde hace cien años" (for a hundred years).⁷⁰ This claim echoes Jackson's thesis in *A Century of Dishonor*, as she sought to bring attention to the history of broken treaties by the U.S. government by suggesting that the "robbery, the cruelty which were done under the cloak of this hundred years of treaty-making and treaty-breaking, are greater than can be told."⁷¹ It is well-known that Jackson sought to "appeal to the heart and the conscience of the American people" to mobilize for justice and reform;⁷² however, *A Century of Dishonor* was more influential among government officials, politicians, and religious leaders, as reflected by the Mohonk Conference attendees.

Martí's "Indians in the United States" engages with one of the key legislative measures embraced by reformers of the time, including Jackson, in proposing that an action the U.S. government can take to improve the conditions of Indigenous communities is to recognize their basic rights through U.S. citizenship. In *A Century of Dishonor*, Jackson argues that a major reason the United States was able to violently remove, displace, and relocate Native communities was due to their lack of U.S. citizenship. According to Jackson, "[a]ll judicious plans and measures for [Native peoples'] safety and salvation must embody provisions for their becoming citizens as fast as they are fit...";[73] however, a controversial aspect of this measure advocated by reformers, and Martí at the time, related to the condition that U.S. citizenship should be extended only to the Native groups who "acepten el repartimiento individual de sus tierras..." (accept the individual redistribution of their lands...).[74] Perhaps more troubling, the prospect of U.S. citizenship with the condition of ceding most of their lands relates to what Indigenous studies scholars describe as the relinquishing of Native peoples' sovereign rights. Thus, in their efforts for change, Jackson and Mohonk reformers took for granted Indigenous peoples' own sovereignty since U.S. citizenship, or as Audra Simpson calls it "Colonial citizenship,"[75] erases any claims for Native nations' sovereignty and land rights. Under this view, U.S. citizenship was envisioned as something "granted" by a foreign military power over groups who had previously considered themselves autonomous.[76] According to Simpson, the logic of settler colonialism sought to "eliminate Indigenous people; take all their land; [and] absorb them into a white, property-owning body politic."[77] Martí and reformers, nonetheless, saw U.S. citizenship as a means for Native people to gain basic rights in U.S. courts, and more importantly, the prospect of U.S. citizenship was also intended as a measure to avoid the real prospect of complete elimination as advocated by some westward expansionists in newly conquered territories that would become the states of California and Oregon.[78] Martí's evolving views on U.S. Native groups achieved a synergy with white reformers' efforts, as he further embraced Jackson's advocacy for native peoples' rights, including U.S citizenship, during his translation of Jackson's novel *Ramona*.

MARTÍ'S *RAMONA* AND INDIGENOUS PEOPLE'S RIGHTS UNDER U.S. JURISDICTION

Spanish translations of books in English published in the United States represented a prominent literary genre that in the latter part of the nineteenth century was adopted by Martí and other early Latinx writers residing in the United States, as they participated in cultural production and political debates, such as resistance to Spanish colonialism and U.S. expansionism in the Caribbean and Latin America. Lamas's outstanding book *The Latino Continuum* focuses on the role of translations of U.S. books by Latinx writers, such as Félix Varela, Miguel T. Tolón, Martí, and Martín

Morúa Delgado, who in the late nineteenth century translated U.S. texts for Spanish-speaking readers.[79] According to Lamas, these translations that form part of the Latinx archive reflect their authors' "layered and complex political and literary contexts and overlooked histories, situated as it is at the crossroads of both hemispheric and transatlantic currents of exchange that are often effaced by the logic of borders..."[80] Moreover, Lamas studies how some of these authors' translations challenged U.S. historiography and expansionism.[81] In the case of Martí, he was a respected intellectual and poet by the time he arrived in the United States and continued to write and publish poetry in Spanish for Latin American audiences; nonetheless, part of his impact in Latinx literary and intellectual history was through his writings in newspapers, periodicals, and translations. Translation represented a print form for Martí from which he was able to enter U.S. discourses pertaining to social and political events, and more specifically it allowed him to engage with the marginalized position of non-white groups in the United States. As Laura Lomas correctly argues, Spanish-language print culture in New York City served as a "medium in which he developed critical translations of [U.S.] empire."[82] While Martí indeed became increasingly critical of the treatment of U.S. Indigenous populations at the time of his translation of *Ramona*, his translation closely adheres to Jackson's reform efforts, particularly her emphasis on Indigenous people's rights.

Martí's translation of *Ramona* forms part of a group of novels that he translated over the years while living abroad and that became part of his venturing into commercial book publishing in New York City with an envisioned Latin American readership. Before arriving in the United States, Martí had already translated a French novel, Victor Hugo's *Mes Fils* (My Sons) in 1875, published in *La Revista Universal* of Mexico. Julio Ramos discusses in detail the degree to which Martí's life in New York City was not the life of a towering intellectual and author of books of poetry but rather one of a "mundane" writer seeking employment opportunities in the writing market first with U.S. newspapers and periodicals, and then through commercial enterprises in the form of magazine editor, translator, and book publisher.[83] Martí, for example, worked as a translator of Hugh Conway's bestseller *Called Back* (1883) for Appleton & Co., a U.S. book publisher, in 1886. Martí initially began to translate *Ramona* for Appleton & Co. and worked for several months on his translation; however, he began to envision his translation as part of a "pilot project of [a] transamerican publishing venture that Martí elaborated in letters to [Manuel] Mercado between 1885 and 1889."[84] He published his translation of *Ramona* independently in 1887, selling 15,000 copies mostly in Cuba and Mexico.[85] Thus, Martí's translation of Jackson's novel served the double purpose of entering both the book publishing business and a literary genre that allowed him to disseminate Jackson's social reform message among Spanish-speaking readers in the United States and Latin America.

Jackson's *A Century of Dishonor* influenced a small group of readers composed of social reformers, government officials, and legislators; however, a middle-class white readership learned about the conditions of Indigenous peoples in California through Jackson's *Ramona*. It is well-known that Jackson wanted to reach a broader readership with a novel that would equal the power of Harriet Beecher Stowe's *Uncle Tom's Cabin* (1852).[86] Jackson's novel was based on her visits to Indigenous communities in southern California that were first published in *Century* magazine in 1883 and the "Report on the Condition and Needs of the Mission Indians of California" completed by Jackson and Abbot Kinney, submitted to the Commissioner of Indians Affairs in July 1883. *Ramona* was first serialized in the *Christian Union*, a New York City weekly magazine, and published as a book by Roberts Brothers in 1884.[87] As a hybrid reform and romance novel, *Ramona*'s plot centers on Indigenous characters; Ramona Ortega, of mixed-race or "mestiza" origin, grows up with her guardian, señora Moreno, in a California hacienda. As the narrative progresses, Ramona discovers that her father was Scottish and her mother Indigenous. Alessandro Assis, a member of the Temecula Indigenous people, works at the hacienda and falls in love with Ramona. When Ramona discovers her mixed-race ancestry, both characters act on their attraction, but they would not be allowed to marry due to Alessandro's background and social position; however, after the members of Alessandro's Indigenous community are forcibly removed from their land by white settlers and his father dies, Alessandro and Ramona leave the hacienda. The narrative follows the couple through a series of resettlements, forced by white settlers' constant land encroachment; their constant relocations end when Alessandro is killed by a white settler, Jim Farrar, for allegedly attempting to steal a horse. Jackson's novel concludes with Ramona returning to the hacienda and marrying Felipe, señora Moreno's son, and the new couple moving to Mexico. While *Ramona* became a bestseller, Jackson was famously distraught at her failure to write a social reform novel, as reviewers and readers celebrated the love story while overlooking its social reform themes related to the land dispossession and injustices against Indigenous communities in California at the hands of white settlers.[88]

Martí translated and interpreted *Ramona* as a continuation of Jackson's advocacy for Native peoples' rights in the United States. Contemporary scholarship on *Ramona* has emphasized the novel's racial hierarchies, assimilationist attitudes, and white supremacist tendencies, while studies of Martí's translation of *Ramona* have focused on his aesthetic choices, revision of phrases, sentences, and omitted paragraphs and sections to demonstrate his emphasis on racial solidarity, resistance by Indigenous groups, and a critique of U.S. expansionism.[89] Laura Lomas, for instance, argues that Martí's translation "goes further than Jackson's [original] in lending much more credence to the viability and necessity of a militant revolutionary opposition within but also beyond the boundaries of the United States."[90] While Martí indeed develops a critique of the injustices and mistreatment on Native peoples in his *crónicas*, those writings reflect a desire for reform from within that does not challenge U.S. control and jurisdiction over Indigenous groups. My interpretation of Martí's translation of *Ramona* is closer to Camacho's analysis of the same work, as he shows the extent to which Martí agreed with Jackson's attempt to shed light on the removal and loss of land of Indigenous communities in California.[91] Indeed, Martí's translation of *Ramona* aligns with some of the key premises regarding the push for Native people's rights and U.S. citizenship under U.S. jurisdiction already present in Jackson's *A Century of Dishonor* and her report on the conditions of Indigenous communities in southern California. Martí's prologue to his translation, key representative scenes, and the significant shortening of the novel after Alessandro's killing show the degree to which Martí's translation centers on the dispossession of Native peoples' lands through the forced and violent displacement by white settlers sanctioned by U.S. laws. Martí's translation similarly attempted to convey Indigenous people's lack of basic rights under U.S. jurisdiction, such as the right to testify in courts, which would have protected them from the indiscriminate violence by white settlers.

Martí's prologue to his translation of *Ramona* suggests that he accepted Jackson's confluence of social reform and aesthetic elements in her novel. His prologue calls attention to Jackson's engagement with the reform novel tradition initiated by Stowe and considers *Ramona* even above *Uncle Tom's Cabin*. Martí states, "se busca la mano de la autora, que con más arte que

Harriet Beecher Stowe hizo en pro de los indios . . . lo que aquella hizo en pro de los negros con su 'Cabaña del Tío Tom'" (one seeks the hand of the author, who with more art than Harriet Beecher Stowe, did on behalf of the Indians . . . what she did on behalf of Black people with her *Uncle Tom's Cabin*).[92] Martí's prologue, however, stops short of stating what aspects of *Ramona* make it representative of the reform novel tradition; peripherally, the prologue notes that Jackson's novel "[d]ice la verdad" (tells the truth).[93] Martí could be referring to the claim that *Ramona* is based on actual historical events, just as Jackson herself wrote to editor Thomas Aldrich after its publication, "every incident in *Ramona* is true."[94] Martí's ambiguous reference to the novel's veracity, however, quickly gives way to a discussion regarding *Ramona*'s language and craft that covers the remainder of the prologue, which aligns with his own aesthetics in his fiction writings.[95] While Martí does not engage with translation theory or practice in his prologue to *Ramona*, his prologue to his translation of Conway's *Called Back* includes a statement related to following the author's intent in translation. According to Martí, a translator should work behind the scenes and should attempt to capture the qualities of the novel: "[t]raducir no es . . . mostrarse a sí propio a costa del autor, sino poner en palabra de la lengua nativa al autor entero, sin dejar ver en un solo instante la persona propia" (to translate is not . . . to reveal oneself at the expense of the original author, rather it is presenting the author through the translator's native language, avoiding even in the slightest to show oneself).[96] Based on his own aesthetics and his interpretation of translation practices as shown in his prologues, it is likely that Martí championed not only Jackson's aesthetic and stylistic choices but also her social reform goals.

Comparing Jackson's original and Martí's translation of *Ramona* shows how the translation closely renders the violence and forced displacement of Indigenous peoples from Alessandro's village in the Temecula Valley at the hands of white settlers with the backing of U.S. laws. Alessandro is from an Indigenous Temecula community, where his father and a group of Native people have settled after the dismantling of the San Luis Rey Mission, a territory formerly part of the mission system, along with its legacy of Spanish colonial rule over Indigenous peoples that continued after Mexico's independence.[97] José Aranda describes early Spanish colonial rule in California as a form of settler colonialism and as "oppressive structures that govern[ed] everyday life from political subjugation to slavery to genocide."[98] During one of his trips to his village, Alessandro discovers that his father, and all other village members, had been forcefully removed by the U.S. sheriff with the backing of an armed band, which precipitates the death of his father. Jackson, for instance, describes Alessandro's retelling these events to Ramona as follows: "I have no home; my father is dead; my people are driven out of their village. I am only a beggar now, Señorita; like those you used to feed and pity in [the] Los Angeles convent!"[99] Martí's translation remains close to the original, as it reads: "Yo no tengo casa: mi padre se ha muerto: a toda mi gente me la han echado de Temecula: ¡ya no soy más que un pordiosero, mi Señorita, un pordiosero como los que le recibían la limosna en el convento de los Angeles!"[100] Martí's translation of this key scene is consistent with Jackson's original, as both texts allude to the marginalized position of Native peoples either as servants or destitute people, which reflects the legacy of the economic system of peonage that "Christian Indians" lived under when California was part of Mexico.[101] Moreover, a major element during the forced removal of Indigenous communities in California was that they were not allowed to file land claims in California courts.[102] Both Jackson's text and Martí's translation emphasize the arbitrariness of their displacement carried out by a local authority with the backing of armed men that speaks of the use of state-sanctioned violence and the lack of any legal recourse for Native people.[103]

Martí's translation of *Ramona* faithfully renders other sections from Jackson's original text to show how California courts were used by white settlers and local officials to dispossess Indigenous people of their lands. Alessandro's community is forced to relocate on the outskirts of a canyon a few miles from Temecula, and the narrative highlights that these are state-sanctioned events since a court in San Francisco has decided that the land now belongs to a group of white settlers. When Alessandro learns that his community has been removed, Jackson's original reads, "'They are a pack of thieves and liars, every one of them!' cried Alessandro. 'They are going to steal all the land in this country; we might all just as well throw ourselves into the sea, and let them have it.'"[104] Martí's translation closely conveys Alessandro's impotence as he laments, "[¡Americanos!] ¡No hay uno que no sea ladrón, no hay uno! Toda la tierra se la van a robar: mejor fuera echarnos ya al mar ¡a que nos ahogue[mos]!"[105] The history of Indigenous land dispossession by white settlers in *Ramona* is based on Jackson's field work in southern California.[106] In the early years after California became a state, politicians in the state made deliberate choices to deny Native peoples their basic rights and legal recourses. According to Benjamin Madley, "military and civilian lawmakers, law enforcement officials, and judges stripped California Indians of legal power and rights, . . . deprived them of their land, denied them protection, [and] legalized their exploitation as both de jure and de facto unfree laborers . . ."[107] Thus, Jackson's novel and Martí's translation present how Native communities under U.S. jurisdiction lacked basic legal rights in the state; however, a major structural problem in Jackson's novel relates to what would have constituted a major moment of social denunciation—the legal erasure of Native individuals and the forced removal of the Temecula Indigenous community from their lands—instead becomes subordinated to the romance plot, as these events allow Alessandro to leave the hacienda with Ramona.

Martí could have been aware that these instances of social protest in Jackson's novel are buried under the romantic plot, and this could be the reason why he attempted to portray the killing of Alessandro at the hands of Jim Farrar in *Ramona* as the climactic scene by cutting dozens of pages from the latter part of the original. In Jackson's novel, after the killing of Alessandro, the text contains two additional chapters of approximately twenty pages each that relate to Felipe searching for Ramona, their return to the hacienda, and their eventual move to Mexico. In Martí's translation, those two concluding chapters are shortened into approximately twenty pages and combined into one final chapter.[108] Jackson and Kinney wrote in their report about white settlers attacking and killing California Indigenous people without legal repercussions; they note that their lack of legal recourses renders Indigenous lives in permanent danger since it is "a safe thing to shoot an Indian at any time when only Indian witnesses are present."[109] In the early years after California became a state, Madley explains that state "[l]egislators created a legal environment in which California Indians had almost no rights, thus granting those who attacked them virtual impunity."[110] In a latter section of Jackson's novel when Alessandro and Ramona have been forced to relocate multiple times, Alessandro takes a horse belonging to Farrar to his dwelling in a moment of physical and mental distress. Martí renders this episode as close to the original since this is the scene that would have served as the apex in the series of injustices toward California Native people. In Jackson's text, when Ramona sees the horse, her first reaction is extreme fear as the narrator states: "[o]nly too well she knew what summary punishment was dealt in that region to horse-thieves."[111] Martí's translation similarly reads: "Ella sabía con qué justicia perentoria trataban por el país a los ladrones de caballos."[112] Martí faithfully renders this significant moment since Ramona realizes that once Alessandro took the horse, he will be seen as a horse thief and could be shot indiscriminately for his act.

Consequently, Martí's translation attempts to center the killing of Alessandro as the climactic scene of the novel to accentuate the novel's critique of white settlers' legal impunity, or lack of legal consequences, when they used violence against Indigenous people. In Jackson's original narrative, Farrar traces Alessandro, shoots him twice, and rides away. Farrar's actions exemplify what Jodi Byrd describes as the underpinnings of U.S. settler colonialism and the experiences of some white settlers that "provid[e] insights into the racist, colonialist, and imperialist logics that generated the rationales for U.S. expansionism."[113] While there is a preliminary hearing on the events that led to Alessandro's killing, Jackson writes: "[Farrar would] be discharged on ground[s] of justifiable homicide, no witnesses having appeared against him."[114] Martí's translation similarly states that Farrar is acquitted "por haber sido el homicidio en defensa propia, y no aparecer testigos contra el acusado."[115] In Jackson's text, the position of Native peoples within the U.S. judicial system is described as follows: "[The judge] comforted himself by thinking—what was no doubt true—that even if the case had been brought to a jury trial, the result would have been the same; for there would never have been found a San Diego County jury that would have convicted a white man of murder for killing an Indian . . ."[116] Martí's translation offers the same legal logic: "El juez aquietó su conciencia pensando, como era la verdad, que el resultado habría sido el mismo, aun cuando hubiese él decidido que había causa de proceso: porque en todo San Diego no hubiera podido reunirse un jurado que declarase culpable a un americano por haber matado a un indio."[117] Just as with the displacement of Alessandro's community, his indiscriminate and extrajudicial killing emphasizes Jackson's claim regarding the lack of basic rights for Native peoples, which was based on an episode Jackson learned about while writing her report.[118] Similar to the theme of land dispossession in *Ramona*, the scene that should have constituted the apex of Jackson's reform novel—the indiscriminate killing of Alessandro—only lasts a few pages and is buried under the weight of the romance plot that continues for two more chapters. Martí's translation, however, shortens the novel's ending from two to one chapter perhaps with the intent of rendering the killing of Alessandro as the novel's climactic scene, thus accentuating the reform cause in Jackson's novel.

This is not to suggest that Jackson's *Ramona* contains an unprejudiced portrayal of Indigenous people since, as literary critics have shown, the novel fully participates in pseudoscientific discourses that sought to justify racial difference and hierarchies. As John M. González correctly observes, *Ramona*'s conclusion perpetuates the pernicious trope of the "vanishing Indian" prevalent in U.S. novels at the time, as Felipe and Ramona still need to leave for Mexico at the end of the novel "in order to keep the nation free from the insidious atavistic influence of mixed blood."[119] Nonetheless, Martí's translation attempts to alter the novel's narrative arch to accentuate Jackson's advocacy for basic rights and U.S. citizenship for Native peoples despite the emphasis on racial hierarchies that permeates Jackson's narrative. Jackson acknowledged that U.S. citizenship for Native people would not constitute an "instantaneous panacea" that would improve their condition;[120] however, the alternative for Jackson and other reformers was the ongoing land dispossession and attempts by state officials, such as the first Governor of California, Peter Burnett, who vowed to carry "a war of extermination" against California's Indigenous peoples and to fight "until the Indian race becomes extinct."[121] In Madley's assessment, the indiscriminate removal and killing of Native peoples in the state indeed constituted nothing more than genocide.[122] The real prospect of their elimination in California was still present at the time Jackson wrote her novel; Martí's translation of *Ramona* was in part an attempt to call attention to their lack of legal protections in territories under U.S. control.

U.S. WESTWARD EXPANSION AND THE RACIALIZATION OF INDIGENOUS PEOPLE

The work of white social reformers contributed to the passing of the Dawes Act of 1887, as it represented the legislative response for Indigenous people's rights in the form of U.S. citizenship for Native peoples who accepted allotment; that is, "the breaking up of the reservations into multiple tracts of land, owned by individuals";[123] however, the partition of land through allotment proved disastrous for Indigenous groups, as they lost most of their lands in subsequent decades. While Jackson and other reformers understood U.S. citizenship as a means to protect Indigenous communities, supporters of the

Dawes Act also attempted to avert a "war of extermination" through military means advocated by some influential westward expansionists.[124] During his reform efforts, Massachusetts Senator Henry L. Dawes, for whom the law was named after, explicitly advocated for federal legislation so that Indigenous people would not be eliminated through military force. Dawes argued, "[w]e made war on [the Indian]. We thought we would exterminate [them] if we could not civilize [them]; and we spent millions of dollars in the vain attempt to exterminate the Indian in this country."[125] As a result, the passage of the Dawes Act functioned in part as a compromise to offer U.S. citizenship to Indigenous peoples in return to their lands; however, a damaging lasting result of the legislation was the ultimate relinquishing of their sovereign rights.

Martí initially commended the passage of the Dawes Act as an appropriate legislative measure aimed to give U.S. citizenship to Native peoples without challenging the U.S. takeover of Indigenous peoples' ancestral lands. In a January 1887 *crónica* for *La Nación* titled "Sobre los Estados Unidos" (On the United States), Martí concurred with reformers welcoming the enactment of the legislation. While Martí notably does not mention the piece of legislation by name, he describes the two major provisions of the Dawes Act: the breaking of Indigenous land and U.S. citizenship for those who accept allotment; Martí writes, "[Los indios] [y]a son propietarios definidos, a tantos acres por cabeza, de las tierras que hasta ahora habían poseído en común... Y todo indio que acepte este arreglo, o entre de propia voluntad en la vida civilizada, queda por la ley investido a la ciudadanía..." (The Indians are now formally landowners, each given a number of acres of lands that until now have been owned in common... And each Indian who accepts this arrangement, or enters voluntarily into civilized life, will become a citizen by law).[126] He goes on to write how glad Jackson would have been if she had lived to see these developments sparked by her writings and reform work, concluding his *crónica* with the image of a new school for Indigenous students that has been named "Ramona."[127] Martí's optimism regarding the enactment of the Dawes Act proved to be unwarranted, as Indigenous populations were asked to cede their rights and land claims to the United States with minimal guarantees. The U.S. government's disproportionate position of power vis-à-vis Native communities that allowed for the breaking and division of Indigenous lands in the first place was not challenged by reformers; consequently, as María Josefina Saldaña-Portillo compellingly contends, "Indigenous people did not cede their lands willingly, but insofar as they were constituted as the objects of colonial and then national gazes, they became unwilling participants in historical, discursive, and geographical constructions that facilitated the conquest of their territories and continues to facilitate their ongoing dispossession."[128] This *crónica* shows that in 1887, the year his translation of Jackson's *Ramona* was published, Martí concurred with white reformers—and their legislative efforts—that would ultimately lead to the dispossession of Indigenous peoples.

After the enactment of the Dawes Act, Martí's *crónicas* on U.S. Native peoples became more sporadic and reflect a sense of disillusionment as he came to identify the racialization of those communities, and other nonwhite groups such as Black people in the South, which was at the center of the U.S. social and political order. Racialization, and the idea of a "white only" nation, had been present since the early policies of "Indian removal" and played a major role in westward expansion and how the U.S. government administrated newly conquered territories.[129] As Paul Frymer notes, "[b]ecause expansion necessitated constant confrontations with non-American populations, national lawmakers continually determined when to incorporate certain populations and when to exclude or remove those who resided on the newly acquired lands."[130] In a *crónica* for *La Nación* titled "Cartas de Martí" (Martí's Letters) of August 1887, Martí focuses on the dispossession and the racialization of Native peoples that he now equates to the position of Black people in the South. As a result, Martí formulates a crucial insight, noting that from the beginning of their contact with white settlers, Native peoples have always been excluded and have lacked basic rights similar to the way Black people have been racialized in the South despite the end of slavery. Martí realizes that for Native peoples "es vano que la ley los ampare . . ." (it is in vain that the law protects them) as legislation has failed to restrain "blancos ambiciosos" (ambitious whites) who continue to remove them from their lands, rendering them no different from "el negro perseguido en el Sur" (Black people persecuted in the South).[131] Martí argues that despite the attempts of Black people to exercise their basic rights through voting, white Southerners were willing to use violence in order to "mantener la raza blanca pura" (maintain white supremacy).[132] Thus, Martí arrives at what Byrd calls the "entanglement of colonization and racialization," and how both "have worked simultaneously to other and abject entire peoples so they can be enslaved, excluded, removed, and killed in the name of progress and capitalism."[133] Native and Black people in the South, according to Martí, share that they are "odia[dos] y abusa[dos]" (hated and abused);[134] thus he makes an explicit connection between two groups who possessed few basic rights and continued to be racialized by the white majority within the United States.

The enactment of the Dawes Act proved catastrophic for Native groups who took part in it, and Martí realized through his readings of newspapers that land reform and basic rights for Native peoples, advocated by Jackson and other reformers, had instead precipitated their further dispossession. Contemporary historians and critics have shown the degree of the dispossession created by allotment and the imposition of U.S. jurisdiction over their lands. As Rifkin notes, "[p]resented by officials and supporters as a means by which Indians could progress from a stunted and backward savagery toward civilization, allotment offered a vision of necessary development over time...";[135] however, allotment also saw "Native governance sovereignty as merely a moment within an evolutionary process of becoming [that casted] Indians as moving toward the achievement of liberal modernity rather than as struggling to retain control over their extant territories and to maintain their self-determination as peoples."[136] Contrary to Jackson, Martí lived to witness how the Dawes Act caused the opposite intended effect due to the almost insatiable desire of white settlers to acquire land in the West. This thirst for land is most evident in one of Martí's final *crónicas* on Indigenous peoples titled "Cómo se crea un pueblo nuevo en los Estados Unidos" (How a Town Is Formed in the United States), published in *La Opinión Pública* in April 1889, where he recounts the opening of newly acquired parts of the Oklahoma territory that are about to be taken by "el blanco invasor [de] la tierra" (the white invader of the land).[137] Some of the lands about to be distributed to white settlers in Oklahoma, according to Martí, were lands that the Seminoles sold to the "Padre Grande" (Great Father) in Washington, D.C., intended for other Indigenous peoples or free Black people.[138] Martí now laments the forced sale of Seminoles' land in Oklahoma in the name of economic progress.[139] As a result, Martí arrives at almost the opposite position from where he started, first describing Indigenous people in Latin America as an impediment for economic development to now identifying U.S. economic progress and territorial expansion as responsible for the racialization and reduction of U.S. Indigenous populations.

Martí's engagement with U.S. print culture, and his immersion writing on U.S. social and political discourses, including the othering and racialization of Native groups in the United States, influenced his political activism when in 1892 he shifted his focus to the fight for Cuban independence through the creation of his New York City-based newspaper *Patria*.[140] Martí's writings in *Patria* reflect a critical shift centered on the struggle for Cuban independence but with the looming danger of the U.S. expansionist project, and its racialization of non-white groups, that increasingly challenged Spain's position as the dominant colonial power in the Caribbean. Lamas has identified this connection between Martí's writings on U.S. Indigenous people and his critique of U.S. expansionism, as she correctly observes that he "placed the indigenous experience and legacy at the heart of a hemispheric resistance to U.S. expansionism and its concurrent imperialism..."[141] In addition, Martí's writings on U.S. Indigenous groups shed light on the racialization of non-white groups within the United States. Martí's "La verdad sobre los Estados Unidos" (1894; The Truth about the United States), published in *Patria* and written only a few years prior to the Spanish-American War, contains some of his most incisive statements regarding the dangerous prospect of U.S. military intervention in the Caribbean along with the emphasis on racial hierarchies in the United States attested by the treatment of Black, Indigenous, and Mexican American populations throughout each period in U.S. territorial expansion. The segregation of Black people in southern states after the end of the Civil War, and the dispossession of Indigenous peoples' lands based on laws and a judicial system predicated on racial difference, convinced Martí of the fleeting ideal of equality for non-white populations under U.S. control. Martí's *crónicas* and his translation of *Ramona* allowed him to theorize and formulate a critique of the United States that emerged from his continuous readings of U.S. newspapers and periodicals and through his reflections on the various forms of dispossession and violence against racialized subjects in the United States that in turn challenged racial hierarchies to advance alternative visions of racial equality.

CHAPTER 2

ARTURO SCHOMBURG'S RECOVERY WRITINGS AND BLACK PRINT CULTURE

STARTING IN the early nineteenth century, Black print culture functioned as the prevalent print form for literary and intellectual production where Black writers made a case for the place in U.S. society through their emphasis on previous writers who had contributed to the development of the Black literary tradition. John Ernest, in his foundational book *Chaotic Justice*, studies early nineteenth century Black authors and editors and their writings in Black newspapers and periodicals to challenge representations of their communities despite "the complex contingencies of African American literary production in a white supremacist culture . . ."[1] The Black literary tradition is composed of early texts that were produced by Black independent presses in the second half of the nineteenth century.[2] In addition, Black communities developed robust print cultures since most Black writers remained relegated to the margins of mainstream society and cultural production. Black print culture represented the primary print form used at the local and community levels by Black writers, editors, and activists not only to report on the news but also to produce knowledge and culture; in some cases, this took the form of compiling, recovering, and maintaining the legacy of past Black writers. According to Elizabeth McHenry, "central to the mission of two of the earliest African American newspapers, *Freedom's Journal* and *The Colored American*, was the development of a black readership;

they worked to illustrate the existence of a vibrant tradition of black literary arts while also encouraging black Americans to consider themselves integral to the future viability of that tradition."[3] Early Black writers and editors, including Samuel E. Cornish, John B. Russwurm, Thomas Hamilton, and Frederick Douglass, appropriated the means of literary production in the form of printing presses not only to provide a space for Black writers but also to maintain the memory and achievements of past writers such as Jupiter Hammon and Phillis Wheatley.[4]

Black print culture in the early decades of the twentieth century, particularly in New York City, served as the primary infrastructure for an extraordinary period of not only social and political engagement but also a reinvigoration of Black culture, art, and literature. Black periodicals played a crucial role in this project of social, cultural, and racial uplifting, as these publications served as venues for Black authors, artists, and intellectuals since most of them were not published in mass-circulation newspapers and mainstream magazines.[5] During this period, some New York City Black periodicals included W. E. B. Du Bois's *Crisis*; Charles S. Johnson's *Opportunity*; Chandler Owen and A. Philip Randolph's *Messenger*; *Negro World*, distributed by Marcus Garvey's Universal Negro Improvement Association; *A.M.E. Church Review*, a publication of the African Methodist Episcopal Church; and the *New York Amsterdam News*. While New York City remained the center of Black print culture, there were other Black periodicals with large readerships in other northern cities, exemplified by the *Chicago Defender*, the *Pittsburgh Courier*, and the *Philadelphia Tribune*. Most authors and intellectuals of the Harlem Renaissance wrote for these publications during different periods of their careers.[6] Black print culture allowed writers such as Katherine Tillman, William Stanley Braithwaite, Du Bois, and Arturo Schomburg to write about past Black authors and texts.[7] For instance, in his best-known essay, "The Negro Digs Up His Past," included in Alain Locke's *The New Negro* (1925), Schomburg writes about the quality of Black writing and the importance of nineteenth-century Black print culture. According to Schomburg, "[f]or a true estimate of [Black writers'] ability and scholarship, however, one must go with the antiquarian to the files of the *Anglo-African Magazine*, where page by page comparisons may be made. Their writings show Douglass, McCune Smith, Wells Brown, Delaney [sic], Wilmot Blyden and Alexander Crummell to have been as scholarly and versatile as any of the noted [white editors] with whom they were associated."[8] Beyond his often-cited essay in *The New Negro*, Schomburg wrote extensively in Black periodicals, compiled bibliographies of Black authors, and participated in the preservation of the Black literary past by writing articles for the Black press.

In this chapter, I make a case for the significance of Schomburg's recovery and mapping of the Black literary tradition during and after the Harlem Renaissance through his writings in alternative print forms and genres, including paratexts, bibliographies, and essays in Black newspapers. Schomburg sought to maintain the literary legacy of Wheatley through his scholarly preface to Charles F. Heartman's edition of *Phillis Wheatley Poems and Letters* (1915); likewise, he compiled remarkable bibliographies of Black and Black diasporic writers including *A Bibliographical Checklist of American Negro Poetry* (1916), which was revised and expanded by Dorothy Porter decades later,[9] and most prominently Schomburg's bibliography titled "A Select List of Negro-Americana and Africana," published in Locke's *The New Negro*, which offers a critical and curated compilation of "notable early books" written by Black authors. Schomburg's bibliographies reflect his knowledge of Black literature and methods of recovering the Black literary past that were comparable to the likes of Du Bois, Locke, and Braithwaite. My emphasis on Schomburg as a bibliographer is based primarily on Elizabeth McHenry's outstanding *To Make Negro Literature*, where she argues that Black literary production during the late nineteenth and early twentieth century was performed through practices and forms beyond printed works of fiction or poetry. Instead, Black literary production also included instructional manuals, anthologies, and bibliographical compilations of texts that represent alternative scholarly and intellectual endeavors in Black literary history.[10] Schomburg's essays for the *New York Amsterdam News* during the 1930s reflect his emphasis and scholarly knowledge while recovering the legacies of early Black writers and editors.

Schomburg's contributions to the Harlem Renaissance have been studied primarily through his role as a bibliophile and collector of the rare Black books and manuscripts that became the foundation for the Schomburg Center for Research in Black Culture in Harlem, rather than through his role as a writer and intellectual; for instance, Elinor Des Verney Sinnette, a biographer of Schomburg, describes him as a lender of books and materials to the leading intellectuals and scholars of the period and as the collector and "document[er]" of the movement.[11] In subsequent years, scholars of Afro-Latinx literature such as Miriam Jiménez Román and Juan Flores began to study Schomburg's writings and Black diasporic vision as containing a broader interpretation of Black history and culture beyond the U.S. context.[12] Vanessa Valdés's outstanding *Diasporic Blackness* persuasively analyzes Schomburg's contributions through the lens of *afrolatinidad* and his Afro-Latinx subjectivity.[13] Valdés rightly focuses on Schomburg's collecting endeavors and writings as reflecting his various subjectivities as Black, Afro-Latinx, and Puerto Rican.[14] Schomburg's Black diasporic thinking was recognized by the major Black editors and intellectuals during the Harlem Renaissance.[15] Nonetheless, not enough scholarly attention has been given to Schomburg's writings, particularly his participation in the recovery of Black writers that built upon the efforts of previous writers, editors, and scholars who used Black print culture to preserve the Black literary past.[16] Schomburg's interest in and writings on the Black literary past, exemplified by the figure of Wheatley, reveal the ways he envisioned the contributions of Black writers in the United States and from other geographies that included the Caribbean as representative of a broader vision of Blackness informed by his Black diasporic thinking and Afro-Latinx subjectivity.

FROM CARIBBEAN FIGHT FOR INDEPENDENCE TO SCHOLARLY RECOVERY OF WHEATLEY'S LEGACY

Schomburg arrived in New York City at the height of the fight for Cuban and Puerto Rican independence led by José Martí and other Caribbean writers who published some of their writings in New York City-based Spanish-language newspapers, such as *Patria*, starting in 1892. Schomburg was involved in the fight for independence in New York City and famously formed Las Dos Antillas (The Two Antilles), one of the various political organizations at the time.[17] During this period, Schomburg and other Afro-Latinxs involved in the movement, such as Sotero Figueroa and Rafael Serra, experienced racism and discrimination from other Cuban and Puerto Rican exiles resulting in the formation of their own organizations, such as La liga sociedad de instrucción y recreo (The Society for Instruction and Leisure).[18] When Martí led the Partido Revolucionario Cubano (Cuban Revolutionary Party), or PRC, Afro-Latinxs served in leadership roles such as Figueroa's editorship of *Patria*.[19] In the pages of *Patria*, Figueroa sought to spread his vision of an independent Cuba where people were considered equal regardless of race.[20] After Martí's death and Tomás Estrada Palma's rise to the leadership of the PRC, Afro-Latinxs were marginalized or broke away from the party. In the case of Serra, for instance, he created a new newspaper, *La Doctrina de Martí*, initially published in New York City from 1896 to 1898, in which he continued to disseminate Martí's vision of a more inclusive and equitable Cuban nation.[21] After the Spanish-American War, most of the prominent Afro-Latinx figures involved in the independence movement, such as Figueroa, Serra, and Martín Morúa Delgado, returned or moved to Cuba; Schomburg stayed in the United States and transitioned to the Black cultural and social life in New York City.

Schomburg's interest in Black history, the collecting of rare books and manuscripts, and his historical writings are connected to the influence of Figueroa and John Edward Bruce. As Nicolás Kanellos notes, "Figueroa somewhat antedates Schomburg both chronologically and in his dedication to research and the writing of history, including the history of Puerto Rico's chapter of the African diaspora."[22] Schomburg became part of a network of Black bibliophiles and collectors that included William Carl Bolivar, Henry Proctor Slaughter, and Jesse Edward Moorland, who compiled rare books, manuscripts, and artifacts not only for their private collections but also to serve as "evidence of the historical accomplishments of black people."[23] Critics have documented in detail Bruce's influence on Schomburg, particularly their shared interest in Black historical writing and historical societies.[24] A shared trait by Schomburg and Bruce was their ability to publish their historical writings in Black periodicals despite their lack of academic training.[25] It was primarily through his work as amateur historian that Schomburg was able to correspond, collaborate, and engage in intellectual exchanges with leading Black writers, editors, and scholars, or as Locke described them, the "who's who" of the Harlem Renaissance.[26] While Schomburg began as an amateur collector of rare books and manuscripts—maintaining a white-collar job as a clerk at the Bankers' Trust Company as his main source of income—he was consulted on several occasions by Du Bois, Locke, Charles S. Johnson, Carter G. Woodson, and James Weldon Johnson, who corresponded with Schomburg on matters of Black history, books, and culture.[27] Much has been written about whether some of these academically trained scholars looked down on Schomburg since he lacked an academic degree and whose writings in English were considered lacking since his first language was Spanish.[28] Nonetheless, it is significant that these writers, editors, and scholars valued Schomburg's contributions and assisted him by publishing his historical writings in leading Black publications throughout the years; equally important, they offered Schomburg an intellectual community that allowed him to write and theorize from different subjectivities, not only about Black history, but also about Black diasporic culture, and particularly literature.

Schomburg's early writings during the 1910s published in *Crisis* reflect his Black diasporic approach that characterizes several of his publications in Black periodicals.[29] Critics have discussed the significance of Schomburg's writings in *Crisis* and have concentrated on his historical writings in relation to his diasporic interpretation of Black history and culture beyond the U.S. context.[30] Lorgia García Peña, for instance, correctly explores Schomburg's work and writings through the broader lens of "Black Latinidad" that reflects his "way of knowing that is guided by the intersections of colonialism, diaspora, migration, and blackness that shape the historical processes and experiences of people who are linked—by birth, language, culture, or ancestry—to Latin America but who are also immigrants . . . in the Global North."[31] Indeed, Schomburg's writings, particularly his early essays for *Crisis*, combine multiple lenses and engage with the intersection of several geographies, political movements, and identities in the early decades of the twentieth century; for instance, one of Schomburg's early articles in *Crisis*, "General Evaristo Estenoz," published in July 1912, relates to contemporary events, as Afro-Cubans were excluded from Cuban politics after the Spanish-American War. Black Cubans on the island organized and formed the Partido Independiente de Color (Independent Party of Color) led by Estenoz. When Black political parties were banned, political clashes and increasing repression led to the infamous "Race War of 1912," in which Black political activists organized in armed resistance and were brutally suppressed, culminating with the murder of Estenoz.[32] Schomburg's disappointment with these historical developments was palpable and resulted in a gradual shift in his essays from contemporary politics toward culture, art, and literature, not only when writing in *Crisis* but also in *Opportunity*, as his interests shifted to the achievements of Black diasporic historical figures and artists such as the Spanish Black painters Sebastián Gómez and Juan de Pareja.[33]

Schomburg's essays in *Crisis* during the 1910s coincide with his scholarly contributions through different print forms and genres to maintain the legacy of past Black writers and poets, particularly the literary legacy of Wheatley. Beyond printed books and Black periodicals, Black writers during the nineteenth century engaged with other forms of knowledge production, such as compilations, instructional manuals, anthologies, critical editions, and scholarly writing in the form of introductions and prefaces. McHenry looks beyond representative Black authors and books of fiction and poetry at the turn of the twentieth century and focuses instead on other forms and genres "as a means of expanding and supplementing our knowledge of the complex literary landscape" of Black letters.[34] Since his early historical writings, Schomburg investigated and began to highlight the significance of Wheatley through different modalities and print forms; for instance, he wrote and delivered lectures at Black historical societies, such as his often-discussed "Racial Integrity: A Plea for the Establishment of a Chair of Negro History in Our Schools and Colleges," delivered in 1913, in which he invokes Wheatley when discussing the need to recover and read early Black texts.[35] Wheatley was not the first Black poet in the United States; however, as Henry L. Gates explains, Wheatley's *Poems on Various Subjects, Religious and Moral*, published in 1773, "became the first book of poetry published by a person of African descent in the English language, marking the beginning of an African-American literary tradition."[36] Schomburg's reference to Wheatley in his lecture, however, was only the beginning of a decades-long study of Wheatley and the Black literary past.

Schomburg's search to recover the poetry and writings of Wheatley relates to his collaboration with fellow book collector and writer Charles F. Heartman and their development of one of the earliest critical compilations of Wheatley's poetry.[37] Editors of Black newspapers and periodicals since the early nineteenth century sought to keep the legacy of early Black writers alive, and the remembrance of the poetry of Hammon and Wheatley were representative of those early efforts.[38] McHenry, for example, discusses how the first Black newspaper, the *Freedom's Journal*, and its editors, Cornish and Russwurm, "devoted pages of print to supplying its readers with a sense of the rich history of black literary arts" by reviewing the works of past Black writers, including Wheatley.[39] Heartman reprinted Wheatley's poems and published a critical edition in 1915 titled *Phillis Wheatley: A Critical Attempt and a Bibliography of Her Writings*. In his book, Heartman credits Schomburg as one of his advisors during the compilation of his work.[40] After receiving a copy of the book from Schomburg, Du Bois wrote a letter to Heartman describing his compilation of Wheatley's poems as "a fine piece of work."[41] Schomburg's collaboration with Heartman on Wheatley's poetry continued with Schomburg's preface on Wheatley, included in a new collection of her poems titled *Phillis Wheatley Poems and Letters*, edited and published by Heartman also in 1915. Gérard Genette describes prefaces as one of the many paratexts built within a text.[42] According to Genette, one of the functions of a preface is to "inform the reader about the origin of the work" and "the circumstances in which it was written . . ."[43] Schomburg's preface titled "An Appreciation [of Phillis Wheatley]" in Heartman's *Phillis Wheatley Poems and Letters* serves as a scholarly introduction that traces Wheatley's life and poetry and also reflects Schomburg's scholarly skills as writer and deft reader of historical and literary texts. His preface engages with eighteenth- and nineteenth-century writers and scholars from various fields who had discussed directly or indirectly Wheatley's poetry and have either praised or questioned Black people's capacity for artistic and intellectual thought.

Schomburg's "Appreciation" presents a sharp critique of slavery and the slave trade in the British colonies, particularly in Colonial Boston, that contextualizes the significance of Wheatley's early life and poetic accomplishments. Schomburg explains that "[s]lavery existed in Massachusetts as early as 1633, and continued till the Commonwealth legislated against it. The opulent colonists engaged in this traffic, for it brought wealth in return without exposing them to any of its dangers. There were slaveships, which brought their human cargo from the African coast to Boston periodically."[44] Schomburg characterizes Boston as a society that profited from the slave trade, but its reputation obscures the reality of Colonial Boston as a slave port city; instead, the city portrays itself as the "cradle of all that is refined in American manners and letters . . ."[45] Schomburg accentuates the connection between the city and its wealth generated by the profits from the slave trade and the trafficking of human beings, which aided in making possible Boston's association with cultural refinement. Schomburg is explicit regarding this connection, as he notes that the "homes of the New England aristocratic families, a good many of them built and sustained from the profit of slavery, were provided with the popular literature of the period and the standard books brought over from England . . ."[46] Paradoxically, this environment where the arts thrived—made possible in some cases by profits from the slave trade—was precisely the place where Wheatley received a literary education and became a poet.

While Schomburg's analysis of Wheatley's society sheds light on her life, his engagement with white historians challenges the white gaze and the way information about the lives of a few Black historical figures such as Wheatley was interpreted and disseminated in print books. Schomburg approaches Wheatley as a literary figure based on historical sources, as he recounts her early poems, the now-famous attestation by a group of Boston prominent citizens, and her trip to England where Wheatley was able to publish her first and only book in 1773. It is significant that Schomburg's "Appreciation" engages with the attestation in Wheatley's *Poems on Various Subjects, Religious and Moral* since this has remained a topic of scholarly discussion up to the present;[47] however, Schomburg wrote about Wheatley at the height of Jim Crow segregation and when the recovery of the Black literary tradition lacked an academic infrastructure. His description of Wheatley's travel to England is partly based on the work of popular historian Benson J. Lossing's *Eminent Americans*, first published in 1855 and updated in subsequent decades. However, Schomburg treats Wheatley's subsequent fate after her return to the United States more sympathetically than Lossing does in his piece. While writing about Wheatley's marriage to John Peters, for instance, Lossing implies that her failure to publish another book was related to her marriage, as "[m]isfortune seems to have expelled her muse."[48] In contrast, Schomburg mentions that their marriage "did not prove a happy one, and Phillis, being possessed of a susceptible mind, a delicate constitution, fell into decline."[49] Among the hundreds of American "leading statesmen, patriots, orators, and others" included in the 1890 edition of Lossing's *Eminent Americans*, Wheatley is the only Black person, which speaks not only of the erasure of Black historical figures but also of the value of Schomburg's critical intervention recovering aspects of Wheatley's biography with the sparse scholarly resources available to him during the 1910s.

Schomburg's "Appreciation" most significantly engages with past debates among some of the most well-known Enlightenment writers related to the humanity of Black people around the latter part of the eighteenth century.[50] As Gates aptly explains while discussing Wheatley's attestation by the prominent Bostonians included in *Poems on Various Subjects*, "[t]he question of whether Africans were human was less related to color than the possession of reason, a tradition inaugurated by Descartes."[51] Thus, Schomburg's "Appreciation," rather than focusing on specific aspects of Wheatley's poetic work, engages with the works of writers and scholars who had written about Black people or the worthiness of Wheatley's poetry from the start of her book publication in 1773 up until the early decades of the twentieth century during Jim Crow and the aftermath of slavery. As Saidiya Hartman observes, "[t]he abolition of slavery incited a debate on the meaning of equality.... A raging debate about the character of slavery raised questions about the meaning and scope of its abolition."[52] As a result of these ongoing debates, Schomburg emphasizes Wheatley's traits consisting of "innate intelligence," "tenderness," "gracious manner," and "kindness of heart."[53] In making some of these claims, he uses "the books of famous travelers [who] have chronicled the deeds of Negroes..."[54] Schomburg includes works from such authors as François-René de Chateaubriand, Henry Morton Stanley, and Charles Darwin. In doing this, Schomburg challenges the racialized thinking of Enlightenment writers such as David Hume by using the works of subsequent late-nineteenth-century writers. Although Schomburg does not mention specific books, he notes that "their several published works [have] given sincere and eloquent testimony to the exhibition of Samaritan and Christian endeavor shown by so-called savages."[55] The fact that Schomburg in the early twentieth century is still trying to demonstrate the qualities of Wheatley's character, based on the writings of others, speaks of the entrenched legacy of slavery still experienced by Black people under Jim Crow at the time he wrote about Wheatley.

As part of Schomburg's refutation of racialized views regarding Black people's aesthetic aptitudes, his "Appreciation" discussed at length, and in a critical manner, one of the most often-discussed aspects of the reception of Wheatley's poetry in the form of Thomas Jefferson's infamous remarks on Wheatley. The controversy derived from Jefferson's denigrating views on Wheatley contributed to the recovery and appreciation of Wheatley, as early Black writers sought to counter Jefferson's charge of lack of original thought in Wheatley's poetry; before Schomburg, early Black writers including Douglass, Martin Delany, and William Wells Brown wrote about Wheatley and the value of her poetry for Black readers.[56] Schomburg's "Appreciation" represents a continuation of these efforts, but it is also a refutation of Jefferson's views of Wheatley based on the writings of others who challenged those views during Jefferson's lifetime.[57] Schomburg's literary knowledge is significant since he has primarily been studied as a collector rather than a writer and intellectual in his own right engaging in scholarly debates. Schomburg explains that "in justice to [Wheatley's] memory[,] it is pertinent to insert the views of those who were contemporaries with Jefferson, so that [readers] may judge for [themselves]."[58] Schomburg, for example, cites Princeton President Samuel Stanhope Smith's *Essay on the Variety of Complexion and Figure in the Human Species* (1810), which directly refutes Jefferson when Smith writes: "how many of those [slave] masters could have written poems equal to those of Phillis Whately [*sic*]?"[59] Likewise, Schomburg cites another source related to Jefferson's "unwilling[ness] to acknowledge the talents of Negroes, even those of Phillis Wheatley..." from French priest and abolitionist Henri Jean-Baptiste Grégoire included in his book *De la Littérature des Nègres* (On the Literature of Negroes), published in Paris in 1808.[60] Thus, Schomburg's preface reflects the range of his scholarly knowledge in his attempt to elevate Wheatley's poetry.

Schomburg's "Appreciation," moreover, refers to writers who have written about Wheatley in the context of abolitionism and used her poetry to make a case for the end of slavery in England and the United States. Schomburg notes that Wheatley's poetry "was used by Thomas Clarkson as one of the examples to demonstrate the capabilities of Negros" in *An Essay on the Slavery and Commerce of the Human Species, Particularly the African*, published in 1785.[61] Indeed, while building his argument for the end of the slave trade, Clarkson cites three of Wheatley's poems and famously challenged his readers to consider "that if the authoress *was designed for slavery*, (as the argument must confess) the greater part of the inhabitants of Britain must lose their claim to freedom."[62] Equally compelling, Schomburg goes a step further and focuses on early abolitionists in the United States, such as Lydia Maria Child who was also critical of Jefferson's views on Wheatley in her *Appeal in Favor of That Class of Americans Called Africans* (1833). Schomburg quotes Child when she writes, "Jefferson denies that these poems have any merit; but I think he would have judged differently had he been perfectly unprejudiced."[63] Schomburg's preface succeeds at situating Wheatley's poetry not only as an important symbol for abolitionists as they made their cases for emancipation but also at developing a critical argument for the significance of Black aesthetic creation.

SCHOMBURG'S BIBLIOGRAPHIES AS ALTERNATIVE PRINT FORMS

Schomburg's bibliographies represent an alternative print form of literary and intellectual production that was instrumental in preserving Black texts and manuscripts and mapping the Black literary past. McHenry explains that bibliographies through their compilation of lists of books and authors represent "one of the most historically important features of turn-of-the-century African American literary history" and encapsulate principles on the ways Black texts were known or understood at specific historical moments.[64] Among the various purposes that bibliographies served, McHenry notes that they recorded the works of Black authors as a form of literary achievement, but rather than static, bibliographies were "simultaneously interactive, forward-thinking, and usable. They opened up the category of Black literature to inquiry and debate as they invited readers to add, subtract, redistribute, and otherwise revise them in ways that linguistically finished texts do not."[65] Schomburg's bibliographical compilations of Black poetry and early Black books fit McHenry's description of the type of intellectual, critical, and scholarly work beyond traditional print books of fiction and poetry. Moreover, alternative print forms of knowledge production were connected to Black authors' limited options while attempting to publish books with white publishers. Laura Helton succinctly captures this point when she notes that "[i]n a racially segregated information landscape, black thinkers necessarily made their arguments through files and filing structures as well as through poetry and prose."[66] Schomburg's scholarly writing indeed necessitated different print forms and genres. As Valdés correctly argues, "[a] consideration of Arturo Schomburg's collecting habits compels us as scholars and students alike to consider different modes of scholarship when we think of knowledge production."[67] Schomburg's bibliographical compilations, starting with his *A Bibliographical Checklist of American Negro Poetry*, published by Heartman in 1916, represent a form of participation in scholarly and intellectual conversations through the compilation of texts that speaks of similar efforts by past and subsequent Black bibliographers and scholars.

Schomburg was one among other practitioners of the bibliography genre who assisted in the preservation of the Black literary past with his *Bibliographical Checklist*, which is characterized by its thoroughness and length consisting of more than two hundred entries of titles of books, poetry compilations, and individual poems.[68] Schomburg's *Bibliographical Checklist* has not received enough critical attention or recognition as part of his efforts to preserve elements of the Black literary tradition at a time when the academic infrastructure for the study of Black literature was just starting to emerge. Sinnette, for example, briefly mentions Schomburg's

Bibliographical Checklist and notes that while it "was a landmark effort to record the works of black poets," he was dissatisfied with his work.[69] Bibliographies represented critical endeavors and Schomburg's bibliography is exceptional in its compilation of books and published poems by Black poets known to him from the start of the tradition up to 1916. In her influential *Early Negro Writing*, Dorothy Porter notes, "scholars of all colors and creeds eagerly [sought] out historical documentation that [would] help to restore the Negro to his rightful place in history."[70] Schomburg's bibliography does not include sections that discuss the structure, choices, or methodology behind his entries; instead, his *Bibliographical Checklist* includes entries of authors, titles of books or poems, publisher, and date of publication, but in some cases, entries contain only partial information. One of the functions of Schomburg's bibliography was to serve as a reference for experts, collectors, and librarians; however, it was also intended to showcase the various reprints and subsequent editions of books of poetry, as in the case of Paul Laurence Dunbar, in which among his twenty-one entries, there are five different editions of Dunbar's *Lyrics of Lowly Life* published between 1896 and 1908.[71] Schomburg could have conceived subsequent editions as almost distinct texts based on the readers' reception of those texts in subsequent years and in relation to the social or historical events that may have altered their meaning for readers.[72] While Schomburg's meticulous inclusion of Dunbar's work seems expected based on Dunbar's notoriety at the time, due in part to the patronage of white editors such as William Dean Howells, Schomburg similarly includes the various published works of other early poets as in the case of different editions of George Moses Horton's works, the first Black poet who published a book of poetry in the South before the Civil War.[73]

Schomburg's *Bibliographical Checklist* is distinct in its inclusion of Afro-Caribbean poets and poetry from Haiti, Cuba, and Puerto Rico, which reflects the uniqueness of Schomburg's Black diasporic vision in contrast to the work of previous and subsequent Black bibliographers. Among the several Haitian poets, some better-known and others less studied, Schomburg includes Alcibiade Fleury Battier, Barbaud Royer Boisrond, Oswald Durand, Emmanuel Édouard, Tertulien Guilbaud, Edmond Héraux, Paul Lochard, Solon Ménos, Charles Moravia, Georges Sylvain, Justin Therison, and Etzer Vilaire. The inclusion of Haitian poets is significant since the intended audience for Schomburg's *Bibliographical Checklist* seemed to be experts and collectors primarily in the United States; however, the addition of these poets' book titles in the original French seeks to insert these poets within his larger Black diasporic literary vision, one that most likely lacked a robust readership in the United States. Something similar occurs when Schomburg includes the works of Black Cuban and Puerto Rican poets who wrote in Spanish, such as Tomás Carrión Maduro, Eleuterio Derkes, José del Carmen Díaz (Narciso Blanco), Juan Francisco Manzano, Antonio Medina y Céspedes, Gabriel de la Concepción Valdés (Plácido), and Vicente Silveira. Schomburg lists most of their poetry titles in the original Spanish, as his addition of untranslated poetry titles attempts to showcase Black diasporic aesthetic production that echoes the cosmopolitan vision of some of his Harlem Renaissance counterparts, such as Du Bois, Locke, and James Weldon Johnson, who traveled abroad and spent time in Europe, and particularly in France.[74]

The importance of Schomburg's *Bibliographical Checklist* in Black literary history is reflected by Porter's use of Schomburg's bibliographical compilation as the basis for her bibliography titled *North American Negro Poets: A Bibliographical Checklist of Their Writings 1760–1944*, published in 1945.[75] Porter's bibliography is a reinterpretation of Schomburg's *Bibliographical Checklist* with important revisions and additions that acknowledge his foundational work as "the first considerable bibliography of American Negro poetry."[76] Decades later, Porter emphasized the importance of bibliographies in collecting and documenting the Black literary past, stating that the "importance of librarians, archivists, and bibliographers who are also collectors and builders of our African American library collections cannot be minimized."[77] In the same essay, Porter argued for the need of additional descriptive components in bibliographies consisting of "brief annotations or notes," explaining the goals and choices made by the bibliographers.[78] This may be the reason why one of the first sections in Porter's *North American Negro Poets* is a preface that explains the goals and methods used in her bibliography. In her preface, Porter specifically outlines her bibliography's goals, stating that "one of the principal objectives of this bibliography is to afford an index to the relative distribution of books and other published materials of Negro poetry among our libraries and thus indirectly to reflect the richness of American holdings in this sphere."[79] Schomburg's bibliography implicitly shared similar goals, as it showcased the considerable literary production of Black and Black diasporic poets but also served as a resource for libraries and scholars such as Porter. Another stated objective of Porter's bibliography is to incite a conversation in which other experts and librarians can participate in the knowledge-production process; Porter writes, "[i]t is hoped that omissions or corrections when determined by the reader will be forwarded to the compiler."[80] That is, rather than a fixed text, Porter envisions her bibliography as susceptible to revisions based on experts' input.

Indeed, Porter's *North American Negro Poets* enters in conversation with Schomburg's *Bibliographical Checklist* since Porter is precisely engaging in the type of revision that she is proposing when reimagining his bibliography. Notably, Porter refers to her bibliography as "an expansion of the Schomburg checklist";[81] however, Porter's bibliography is more than an "expansion" but rather a reinterpretation that benefited from the emerging academic infrastructure in the form of university special collections and an increasing number of resources and scholars committed to the study of Black literary texts that were unavailable to Schomburg in the 1910s. Porter, for instance, was able to network with librarians at Howard and other universities and organizations such as the New York Public Library and the Library of Congress. Thus, Porter's bibliography almost doubles the number of entries in Schomburg's *Bibliographical Checklist*. For instance, while the number of entries on Dunbar in Schomburg's bibliography is twenty-one,[82] Porter's number of Dunbar references in *North American Negro Poets* almost doubles at thirty-eight.[83] Porter also includes a list of institutions, research centers, and university libraries where every single title included in her bibliography is located; for example, Wheatley's 1804 edition of *Poems on Various Subjects, Religious and Moral* published by Oliver Steele in Hartford, Connecticut, can be located at the American Antiquarian Society and the Yale University Library.[84] While Porter recognizes "the usefulness of [Schomburg's] bibliography of Negro poetry," she argues in her preface to *North American Negro Poets* that there is a need not only for "expansion" but also for "revision";[85] this is most recognizable in Porter's decision to remove all of Schomburg's references to Black diasporic poets outside the United States in her version, a decision that speaks of his choices and goals as he imagined a more inclusive vision of Black letters.

Schomburg's subsequent scholarly participation in the bibliography genre after *Bibliographical Checklist* included his bibliography titled "A Select List of Negro-Americana and Africana," included in Locke's *The New Negro* anthology. Since the late nineteenth century, anthologies and bibliographies served as alternative forms of literary production for Black authors. From the start of the tradition, there have been attempts by Black authors and specialists to select works through anthologies for readers, educators, and specialists, which increased at the turn of the twentieth century and during the Harlem Renaissance; these efforts are exemplified by Gertrude Bustill Mossell's *The Work of the Afro-American Woman* (1894), James Weldon Johnson's *The Book of American Negro Poetry* (1922), Locke's *The New Negro* (1925), Charles S. Johnson's *Ebony and Topaz* (1927), and Countee Cullen's *Caroling Dusk: An Anthology of Verse by Negro Poets* (1927).[86] Locke's anthology famously sought to showcase the historical, artistic, and literary output of Black writers by including essays, poems, short fiction, drama, and music by almost all the major figures of the Harlem Renaissance;[87] however, a lesser studied aspect of Locke's anthology is the various bibliographies that constitute one of its three main sections and begins with a bibliography written by Schomburg followed by a series of bibliographies compiled primarily by Locke. Schomburg's bibliography in *The New Negro* contains distinct markers that reflect his knowledge of Black texts and critical choices, not merely as a collector of books, but as a researcher with specialized knowledge of Black texts and manuscripts. As the subtitle of Schomburg's bibliography establishes, his compilation focuses on "Notable Early Books by Negroes," signaling that it does not merely contain books he read or was able to locate, but it presents works he and previous readers deemed valuable for various reasons. Schomburg, for instance, knew about the works of contemporary Black authors such as Langston Hughes and Claude McKay; however, the most recent work included in his compilation is Paul Laurence Dunbar's *Majors and Minors* published in 1895.[88] Schomburg's bibliography instead stands as a curated list of past Black texts he considers worth preserving.

Schomburg's "A Select List of Negro-Americana and Africana" reflects his curatorial practices and methodology implied by the number of texts that emphasize aesthetic quality, historical significance, and the inclusion of different print forms and genres. It is difficult to ascertain precisely Schomburg's method in compiling his bibliography since almost by definition, bibliographies consist primarily of compilations of authors and books lacking sections that discuss compilers' choices or selection criteria; nonetheless, as McHenry notes, it is possible to make inferences about the compiler's intentions in bibliographies by studying the text's content and structure.[89]

As previous practitioners used bibliographies for different purposes, such as lists of books based on their literary significance, as reading guides, and for library classification, among others, Schomburg seeks to include a select number of Black texts and documents in different genres worth studying for experts and future generations. Schomburg's bibliography contains approximately eighty-four authors, and an additional number of publications by some authors as in the case of William Wells Brown, whose entry includes six books.[90] Within this relatively small compilation, however, Schomburg includes some of the most representative Black texts in various genres that closely align with contemporary mappings of the Black literary tradition. Among works of fiction and poetry, Schomburg includes, for example, Brown's *Clotel*; Douglass's *Heroic Slave*; Dunbar's *Oak and Ivy*; Frances E. W. Harper's *Poems on Miscellaneous Subjects*; Frank Webb's *The Garies and Their Friends*; and Wheatley's *Poems on Various Subjects, Religious and Moral*. Schomburg's bibliography also contains nonfiction, represented by Brown's *The Black Man: His Antecedents, His Genius and His Achievements*; William Cooper Nell's *The Colored Patriots of the American Revolution*; and William Still's *The Underground Railroad*. Schomburg also includes a relatively small but important number of slave narratives, such as Henry Bibb's *Narrative of the Life and Adventures of H.B.*; Brown's *Narrative of W. W. B., a Fugitive Slave*; and Douglass's *Narrative of the Life of Frederick Douglass*. While clearly a selective list, it is worth asking whether Schomburg considered these works more significant than others, or if these books reflect his own choices, or a consensus among experts and collectors.

Schomburg's bibliography, moreover, reflects his curatorial practices, as he includes texts in various print forms beyond the printed book and by including Black diasporic texts. Schomburg's bibliography, for example, includes sermons, addresses, and pamphlets, such as Absalom Jones and Richard Allen's *Narrative of the Proceedings of the Black People*; Benjamin Banneker's almanacs; Samuel Cornish and Theodore Wright's *The Colonization Scheme Considered*; Delany's *The Condition, Elevation, Emigration, . . .* ; Jupiter Hammon's *An Address to the Negroes in the State of New York*; Absalom Jones's *A Thanksgiving Sermon on Account of the Abolition of the African Slave Trade*; David Walker's *Appeal*; and Peter Williams Jr.'s *Oration on the Abolition of the Slave Trade*. In a similar approach that reflects Schomburg's appreciation of Black print culture as repository of Black cultural production, he includes Black periodicals and the editors that led them, such as Hamilton's the *Anglo-African Magazine*; Cornish and Russwurm's *Freedom's Journal*; and Douglass's *The North Star* and *Frederick Douglass' Paper*. In alignment with Schomburg's Black diasporic vision, he includes works such as Juan Francisco Manzano's *Poems by a Slave in the Island of Cuba*; Ignatius Sancho's *Letters of the Late I. S.*, and Gustavus Vassa's *Narrative of Olaudah Equiano*. Schomburg's compilation, however, contains gaps that speak of the difficulty of recovery efforts of Black texts that were only undertaken in a systematic manner after the 1960s through the institutionalization of Black studies in colleges and universities; these omissions include Hannah Crafts's *The Bondwoman's Narrative*; Delany's *Blake*; Pauline Hopkins's *Contending Forces*; and Harriet Wilson's *Our Nig*. Schomburg's bibliography, thus, reflects his own knowledge gained by decades of collecting, researching, and reading not only Black books but other print forms and genres.

Schomburg's "A Select List of Negro-Americana and Africana" reveals much as it is, but an analysis of his structure and implied choices can be studied further through a comparison with Locke's bibliography titled "The Negro in Literature," also included in *The New Negro* next to Schomburg's bibliography.[91] An important distinction related to Locke's title for his bibliography, "The Negro in Literature," is that his bibliography compiles books in which Black people, Blackness, and Black life are thematized regardless of the author's race; this approach of looking for Blackness "in literature" as a criteria plays out in singular ways in the first two subdivisions of Locke's bibliography. The first section titled "American Fiction before 1910" covers almost the same period as Schomburg's entire bibliography, but strikingly, there are only a handful of overlaps in the selection of authors or works due primarily to Locke's criteria that includes both Black and white authors; for example, some of the few overlaps in both bibliographies for Black books before 1910 are Brown's *Clotel* and Webb's *The Garies and Their Friends*. Interestingly, Locke's selections for this same period include some of Schomburg's omissions, such as Charles Chesnutt's *The Conjure Woman*; Dunbar's *The Sport of the Gods*; and Harper's *Iola Leroy*. As the title of Locke's section implies, the focus is not only on Black fiction but "American Fiction"; hence, Locke's bibliography includes fiction by white authors who thematized Black life, in both sympathetic and demeaning manner, such as Stephen Crane's *The Monster and Other Stories*; Thomas Dixon's *The Leopard's Spots*; William Dean Howells's *An Imperative Duty*; and Harriet Beecher

Stowe's *Uncle Tom's Cabin*. In both bibliographies, however, printed books of fiction by Black authors before 1910 represent only a handful of titles due primarily to the lack of publishing opportunities for Black authors up to this time. Schomburg resolves this absence by including other genres and forms of Black literary production in the form of slave narratives, pamphlets, and periodicals, while Locke tackles this gap by including books about Black life written by whites.

Subsequent subdivided sections in Locke's bibliography further show his distinct approaches to Black literature that diverge from Schomburg's in marked degrees, as Locke tries to make Black literature part of American literature and the larger Western literary tradition, while Schomburg's bibliography centers on Blackness and works written by Black and Black diasporic writers. Locke's bibliography continues with a section titled "American Fiction since 1910" that includes both Black and white authors but reflects the increasing number of Black books published by mainstream publishing houses; these contemporary Black authors include, for example, Jessie Fauset, James Weldon Johnson, Jean Toomer, and Walter White.[92] Locke's choice of dividing his "American Fiction" sections in two, pre- and post-1910, serves to showcase a particular moment in literary history when Black authors were published by mainstream publishing houses, which contributed to the literary output that became known as the Harlem Renaissance. Locke's bibliography engages almost exclusively with highbrow literature as he incorporates Black books with the work of established American and European authors. Locke, moreover, includes two subdivided sections titled "English Fiction" and "Continental Fiction." As in previous subdivisions, these compilations include mostly white authors who thematized Blackness with few exceptions; the "Continental Fiction" section consists mainly of French authors whose book titles are included in the original French, which relates to Locke's cosmopolitanism and background as a Rhodes Scholar studying in Europe.[93] Just as Schomburg's *Bibliographical Checklist* contains books written in French, it is likely that these bibliographies were intended primarily for a select group of experts rather than general readers. Both bibliographies, ultimately, fulfill their function as alternative texts that present competing interpretations regarding the Black literary past. It was Locke after all who included Schomburg's bibliography in *The New Negro* since each bibliography represented a distinct vision of Black cultural production that was susceptible to contestation and reinterpretation.

SCHOMBURG'S RECOVERY OF THE BLACK LITERARY PAST IN THE *NEW YORK AMSTERDAM NEWS*

Schomburg's writings on history, arts, and literature span the first three decades of the twentieth century in almost all the significant Black periodicals of that time inside and outside New York City. Among Schomburg's writings in Black periodicals, almost no critical attention has been given to his essays published in the *New York Amsterdam News*.[94] Part of the reason is that some of Schomburg's essays in the *Amsterdam News*, which are available at the Schomburg Center for Research in Black Culture, have not been published in book format.[95] The *Amsterdam News* emerged after World War I and the first migration of Black people to northern cities. Following the tradition of other Black newspapers, such as the *Chicago Defender*, the *Amsterdam News* not only focused on daily news but also printed fiction, poetry, book reviews, and essays by writers and scholars, including Du Bois, Hughes, and Carter G. Woodson, intended for a broad Black readership.[96] Schomburg wrote numerous articles for the *Amsterdam News* during the 1930s, including "Our Pioneers," a series of ten essays published from July 25 to September 26, 1936, related to Black historical and literary figures. As with Schomburg's essays in *Crisis* and *Opportunity* written in the 1910s and 1920s, his range of subjects and historical figures in his *Amsterdam News* pieces highlight Black figures from both the United States and the Black diaspora.[97] These essays exemplify the scope of Schomburg's scholarly and intellectual pursuits, as he theorized on the social, cultural, and artistic contributions and influence of Black diasporic subjects in the Americas for Black readers. Schomburg's use of the Black press as a form of literary production, moreover, followed the example of past writers and editors, such as Hamilton and Douglass, who maintained the legacy of Black authors by writing about them in their publications.

One of Schomburg's first essays for the *Amsterdam News* focuses on Jupiter Hammon, one of the first Black poets during the Colonial period, to bring attention to Hammon's early contributions to Black letters. Schomburg's piece, "Jupiter Hammon before the New York African Society" of January 22, 1930, investigates Hammon's social milieu, New York City during Colonial times, and the Black community in which Hammon lived "as a slave of the Lloyds family" who despite his bondage became a poet and orator. Schomburg's piece discusses some of the Black religious congregations in the city and their leaders such as Peter Williams Sr., the sexton and undertaker of John Street Methodist Church, to contextualize Hammon's poems printed in newspapers.[98] In his essay, Schomburg discusses one of the earliest instances of Black intertextuality, as he discovers that among Hammon's poems, "there is on record a poem to Phillis Wheatley soon as her pen took soaring wings."[99] Schomburg is referring here to Hammon's "An Address to Miss Phillis Wheatley" (1778), one of the earliest poems printed in a newspaper by a Black writer in the United States. While Hammon wrote poetry before Wheatley, he was only able to publish some of his poems in newspapers but not in book format as Wheatley did. In his essay, Schomburg reflects on the incompleteness of the Black archive at the time as he notes that the details of the life "of the first American poet of the Negro race [are] unknown."[100] Schomburg's recovery work, nonetheless, yields significant results as he discovers that Hammon "came before the New York African society and read a paper entitled 'An Address to the Negroes in the State of New York,'"[101] delivered in 1784 and printed in 1787. Part of Schomburg's knowledge of Hammon likely derives from the former's efforts as a collector of rare books. In "The Negro Digs Up His Past," Schomburg mentions that book collectors have recovered documents such as Hammon's *Address* of 1787;[102] his *Amsterdam News* essay, however, demonstrates that Schomburg's knowledge consisted of more than just those of a collector of rare manuscripts, as his writings critically contextualizes Hammon's literary legacy.

Schomburg's essay not only engages with Hammon as a writer and historical figure but also with the recovery of the Black literary past itself, as Schomburg discusses the lack of an academic infrastructure for the study of Black texts. Schomburg argues that Hammon is known as a historical figure but that not enough scholarship has been written or published about his work and laments, "Jupiter Hammon, almost unknown to the present generation, seems to have escaped the pen of most of the race writers."[103] In the 1930s, the academic infrastructure consisting of academic journals, university presses, scholarly monographs, and a readership consisting of scholars, professors, and students of Black texts was almost absent outside Schomburg's writing circles in New York City; nonetheless, the lack of critical engagement with Hammon's poetry continued in subsequent decades. As contemporary critic Cedrick May notes, while some of Hammon's poems "regularly appear in anthologies of American and African-American literature, there has not been a carefully edited edition of his works available for decades."[104] Schomburg's essay makes a case for more critical writing on Hammon to preserve his legacy, as Schomburg asks his readers, "[i]sn't it a pity that no efforts [have] been made to honor the memory of this apostle, earth's nobleman, the earliest poet of our freedom?"[105] In his essay, Schomburg discusses the publication history of an edition of Hammon's collected poems by Oscar Wegelin, published in 1915, and notes that unfortunately, "[a]s Negroes are reluctant or indifferent to purchase books that chronicle the worthy deeds of their own achievements, the Jupiter Hammon edition was limited to 97 copies.... The entire edition has long been out of print and not enough to go the rounds of the principal libraries of America."[106] Schomburg's effort to preserve Hammon's literary legacy exemplifies how as late as the 1930s some of the recovery of Black literary figures took place not only in printed books but also in the pages of Black newspapers.

Schomburg's article from "Our Pioneers" on the Black newspaper the *Freedom's Journal* stands as one of the earliest attempts to highlight the significance of the Black press and some of their earliest editors. In "Our Pioneers: 'Freedom's Journal'; Pioneer Negro Editors" of September 19, 1936, he focuses on the *Freedom's Journal*, the first Black newspaper in the United States and the influence of its co-editors, John B. Russwurm and Samuel E. Cornish, in creating publishing opportunities for Black writers. Schomburg's essay participates in archival recovery as he was writing at a time when the study of Black print culture had not been established as a field within Black literary studies. Schomburg explains, for example, that he has been able to corroborate that "[t]he earliest newspaper published by Negroes appears to be the 'Freedom's Journal,' bearing [the] date of March 16, 1827, and published . . . in New York City."[107] He analyzes the content of the issue and quotes from Russwurm and Cornish's editorial in which they delineate the newspaper's goal of serving as "a channel of communications between us and the public through which a single voice may be heard in defense of five hundred thousand free people of color. For often injustices had been heaped upon the race when our only defense was an appeal to [the] Almighty, but we believe that the time has now arrived when the calumnies of our enemies should be refuted by forcible argument."[108] Schomburg accentuates this moment in literary history when Black editors began to appropriate the means of literary production in the form of a printing press to create a newspaper as a venue to disseminate their ideas and those of other Black writers.

In her analysis of the newspaper, McHenry notes, "much of the content of *Freedom's Journal* was loyal to the editors' commitment to represent more fully the plight and achievements of black people and to document the white community's sympathetic response to unprejudiced representation of them."[109] In a similar way, Schomburg's interest in the *Freedom's Journal* is that it not only reported weekly news and events but, more importantly, it served as a platform for Black writers to enter social discourses in print, something that had been negated to them until that time.

Schomburg's scholarly knowledge and rhetorical strategies are reflected in "Our Pioneers: 'Freedom's Journal'; Pioneer Negro Editors" when he discusses the lives of Russwurm and Cornish, along with their ideological disagreements and subsequent split. Schomburg correctly situates Russwurm as "teaching in a colored school in Boston" from 1821 to 1824 and writes that "Russwurm matriculated at Bowdoin College, graduating with high honors in 1826."[110] Schomburg, however, acknowledges that his knowledge may be incomplete and cautions readers by stating that "[t]he question whether or not Russwurm was the first Negro to graduate from a northern college is a debatable question. We must leave that subject for another day in order to correct the pages of history."[111] As Winston James notes, Russwurm was indeed one of the first Black students to graduate from a U.S. college and the first from Bowdoin;[112] nonetheless, Schomburg's concession that he is unable to corroborate this fact seeks to build credibility among his readers. Similarly, he admits that "[t]he life story of Cornish seems not to have been written and must be buried in the early colored newspapers";[113] however, he is able to point out that Cornish was born in Virginia and that "[s]ome reports hold that he was a student of Princeton Theological Seminary, but I have been unable to locate any data that will nail down this fact."[114] Cornish came to New York City in 1821 and Russwurm in 1827; that same year they met and partnered to serve as co-editors of the *Freedom's Journal*. Cornish and Russwurm parted ways after six months due in part to ideological differences.[115] Schomburg mentions that Russwurm was involved in the Colonization Society while Cornish opposed it, and later the two became editors of other Black newspapers.

Schomburg's essay on the *Freedom's Journal* identifies the importance of the partnership between Russwurm and Cornish and their deliberate efforts to create a space for Black writers to publish their work. Schomburg writes that Cornish was "one of the ablest colored men of his day, ranking with

[Thomas] Hamilton of the *Anglo-African Magazine*...";[116] here, Schomburg explicitly makes the connection between two editors, Cornish and Hamilton, who were key in the development of not only the Black press but also the guardianship of the Black literary past. Schomburg identifies Hamilton's singular place in Black print culture in his role as editor of the *Anglo-African Magazine* in 1859, as Hamilton envisioned his periodical as a space for Black writers despite its short run. According to Ivy Wilson, "[w]hile African Americans could be found within the pages of white-edited periodicals, black periodicals pressed the call for self-representation as an urgent if not necessary responsibility."[117] Schomburg notes that the *Freedom's Journal* had a similar goal, and among the contributors to the *Freedom's Journal*, he identifies David Walker, the author of the *Appeal to the Colored Citizens of the World*; the Rev. Thomas Paul of the First Baptist Church of Boston; and Francis J. Webb, "the Philadelphia novelist."[118] The *Freedom's Journal* and the *Anglo-African Magazine* represent two early significant developments in Black print culture, and writers like Schomburg, through his articles in the *Amsterdam News* and other Black newspapers, kept alive the literary contributions of Cornish, Russwurm, and Hamilton. While Schomburg's recovering efforts and mapping of key moments in Black literary history were not unique, his contributions as a writer and deft researcher during the Harlem Renaissance have remained understudied. Schomburg's articles for the *Amsterdam News* appear as significant today as when they were written in the 1930s due to the ever-present struggles of Black writers for visibility and opportunities in a white-dominated newspaper and publishing industry.

Schomburg's *Amsterdam News* essays reflect his literary skills and knowledge but did not receive appropriate recognition due in part to the fact that they were not published in commonly associated print forms for academic inquiry, such as high-profile magazines, academic journals, and book monographs. Charles S. Johnson, who remained Schomburg's friend and corresponded with him during his later years, realized the significance of Schomburg's scholarly essays in the *Amsterdam News*; however, Johnson lamented that his friend had not made a more deliberate effort to publish his essays in a book format. Johnson wrote in a letter to Schomburg, "[s]ome of your interested friends and admirers of your erudition in the field of Afro-Americana are disturbed about the extremely partial and inadequate outlet for your chatty narratives about the early Negro great man in the *Amsterdam News*. Mind you, the *Amsterdam News* is a perfectly good paper, and better than most of the Negro papers for this purpose, but a newspaper is not enough."[119] Johnson suggests that Schomburg's articles "ought to be amplified and put into book form, and I am quite certain that a publisher could be found easily, and that they would find their way into use in the public schools."[120] Johnson's claim that "a publisher could be found easily" seems questionable since it relates precisely to Black writers' struggles from the start of the Black literary tradition to gain publishing opportunities, as most of them were often excluded from predominantly white mainstream publishers, newspapers, and magazines. Johnson's letter, nonetheless, correctly identifies the source of Schomburg's lack of recognition as a writer and an intellectual. Schomburg has been studied primarily a collector of rare books and manuscripts rather than an active contributor to the Harlem Renaissance since, contrary to most of his Black literary and intellectual counterparts, his essays were not collected or published in a book format.

Ultimately, it was Black print culture that gave countless writers of the Harlem Renaissance their start, and in the case of Schomburg, Black periodicals and newspapers are the primary repository of his legacy as a writer and scholar for present readers. His series of articles for the *Amsterdam News* were written two years before his death, but in some important respects, they stand as a synthesis of his Black diasporic project that, along with other historical writings, collections of books, and bibliographies, reflect Schomburg's identification of Black writers in the United States as forming part of his cultural identity. It was Bernardo Vega's remembrance of Schomburg that more succinctly speaks of this legacy. In his memoir, Vega credits Schomburg for having a deep interest in Black history and Black communities' role "in the history of our hemisphere..."[121] Vega also emphasizes two key points about Schomburg that are often overlooked; first, Vega does not refer to Schomburg only as a collector but also as "a prolific writer."[122] Second, Vega notes that while Schomburg came "as an immigrant" to New York City, he "bequeathed a wealth of accomplishments" not only to the Afro-Latinx diaspora in the United States but also "to North American blacks."[123] Schomburg contributed to the efforts of other Black writers, intellectuals, and scholars to recover and map the Black literary past in newspapers and periodicals just as other Black editors, writers, and intellectuals had done before him.

CHAPTER 3

LATINIDAD AND WORKING-CLASS SOLIDARITY IN JESÚS COLÓN'S SKETCHES

NEW YORK City at the turn of the twentieth century stood as the epicenter of Latinx writing and intellectual production through its network of Spanish-language newspapers and periodicals. Starting in the nineteenth century, Cuban writers in exile in the United States fighting for independence from Spain printed Spanish-language newspapers in New York City, such as *La Verdad*, started in 1848 and edited by Gaspar Betancourt Cisneros, and *El Mulato*, printed in 1854 and edited by Carlos de Colins.[1] Some of these newspaper editors were members of the Cuban social and economic elite in exile who, while embracing revolutionary ideas, also held major economic interests in Cuba, including stakes on the Cuban plantation economy.[2] The ongoing development of Spanish-language newspapers in New York City in subsequent decades is related to José Martí's formation of the Partido Revolucionario Cubano (Cuban Revolutionary Party) in 1892 and the continuing fight for Cuban and Puerto Rican independence. Spanish-language newspapers and periodicals published in New York City during this period include *Patria* and *La Doctrina de Martí*, and other periodicals with a middle-class and high-brow appeal, such as *La Revista Ilustrada de Nueva York*.[3] These newspapers were edited by Cuban and Puerto Rican writers and intellectuals, along with working-class and Afro-Caribbean writers, such as Sotero Figueroa, Rafael Serra, Francisco Gonzalo

"Pachín" Marín, and Martín Morúa Delgado.[4] In the early decades of the twentieth century, *La Prensa* of New York City, founded by José Camprubí in 1913, began with a readership consisting of Spanish and Cuban immigrants but subsequently grew by focusing on Spanish-speakers from Puerto Rico and other Latin American countries.[5] *La Prensa* printed a mix of U.S. and Latin American news with an emphasis on economic, social, and cultural events in New York City for a readership composed of not only Spanish-speakers residing in the United States but also for a "*Hispano-Americano*" (Hispanic American) community settled permanently in New York City. As a result, from the early decades of the twentieth century, Spanish-language print culture in New York City influenced early notions of identity formation and Latinidad in the United States.

Among the Spanish-language newspapers in New York City, *Gráfico* is representative of Spanish-language periodicals that covered the social and cultural life of a "Hispanic" community in the United States with transnational influences from Latin America. *Gráfico*, a New York City-based weekly founded in 1926 and first edited by Ramón La Villa and Alberto O'Farrill, focused on the arts while also promoting a "pan-Hispanism," or "Hispanic" identity, among different groups from Latin America living in the city.[6] *Gráfico* reflected New York City's demographics that encompassed people from the Caribbean who were directly affected by U.S. military interventions and economic influence. In the case of Puerto Rico, the Spanish-American War of 1898 and the Jones Act of 1917 increased the migration of Puerto Ricans to the United States, and primarily to New York City, as their chosen place for settlement on the mainland. The creation of Puerto Rican neighborhoods in Brooklyn, the Lower East Side, and East Harlem, as well as Puerto Rican cultural and social organizations in the city, emerged during the early decades of the twentieth century.[7] In 1927, Bernardo Vega became editor of *Gráfico* and continued its focus on Hispanic news, culture, and the arts in the city, in addition to his emphasis on Latin American literary and cultural production.[8] As John Alba Cutler has discussed, Spanish-language newspapers and periodicals printed in the United States, including *Gráfico*, reflected the transnational aspect of these publications, as the fiction and poetry of Latin American writers was widely reprinted in their pages.[9] Moreover, *Gráfico* included the writings of *cronistas* (chroniclers) who followed in the steps of Martí's style of newspaper writing consisting of a mix of news and social commentary.[10] Among *Gráfico*'s *cronistas*, Jesús Colón emerged as one of its more prominent writers, and after *Gráfico* ceased publication in 1931, due in large part to the Great Depression, Colón continued to write for Spanish-language and alternative newspapers, further developing an early notion of Latinidad that sought to unite different communities of Latin American background with shared traits in the United States.

In this chapter, I analyze Colón's sketches in Spanish-language newspapers, particularly in *Pueblos Hispanos* in the 1940s, and in communist publications in English such as the *Daily Worker* during the 1950s, along with those included in his book, *A Puerto Rican in New York and Other Sketches*, published by alternative press Masses and Mainstream in 1961. Colón's writings and engagement with alternative print publications in the form of labor and socialist newspapers and periodicals, along with his reading experiences that influenced the emergence of his working-class consciousness, remained key in shaping Colón's vision of Latinidad. Colón conceives of a Puerto Rican identity that, while maintaining an affinity to his country of origin and nationalist aspirations, also shared cultural, historical, and linguistic traits with other *Hispano* communities living in New York City that had the potential to unite them for social, labor, and political causes.[11] Literary scholars have focused on Colón's writings in the context of race in the United States due to his subjectivity as an Afro-Latinx in the United States;[12] likewise, these critical discussions have engaged with Colón's writings in relation to the marginalization of Black groups in the United States and the shared experiences between them and Afro-Latinxs. Another group of scholars have focused on Colón and other early *cronistas* of the diaspora in the context of Puerto Rican migration to New York City and the emergence of Puerto Rican social, cultural, and labor organizations in the early decades of the twentieth century.[13] My analysis builds on the foundational scholarship of Edna Acosta-Belén, Virginia Sánchez Korrol, and Edwin K. Padilla and their recovery of Colón's newspaper writings, as I concentrate on Colón's development as a writer and intellectual in the context of Spanish-language print culture in New York City.[14] Colón was able to evolve and continue his intellectual trajectory by transitioning from Spanish-language newspapers, such as *Pueblos Hispanos* in the 1940s, to writing for labor and communist publications in English, such as the *Daily Worker*, for a leftist and working-class readership for whom Colón's writings served as a window into the Puerto Rican and *Hispano* experience in New York City and as a corrective to their negative portrayals in U.S. mainstream media.

This chapter traces the development of a *Hispano* identity in Colón's sketches in Spanish-language and alternative newspapers and his collection of sketches published in book form. I began with an analysis of his Puerto Rican subjectivity as theorized in his sketches for *Pueblos Hispanos* during the 1940s. I then study some of Colón's sketches privileging their original publication in the *Daily Worker* as part of a series of sketches published in labor and socialist newspapers during the 1950s. I contextualize Colón's sketches in the *Daily Worker* and his engagement with labor and communist struggles through the experiences of Black writers, including W. E. B. Du Bois, Langston Hughes, and Richard Wright, who also published in communist publications to advance their social activism and writing careers. My analysis focuses on the publication of Colón's *A Puerto Rican in New York* by Masses and Mainstream in 1961 within the context of Latinx literature in the United States in the first half of the twentieth century and the role local and regional publishing houses played, as mainstream publishers almost systematically excluded Latinx authors. Colón's publication of *A Puerto Rican in New York* written in English connects him to the autobiographical narratives of some of his contemporary Black authors, such as Hughes's *The Big Sea* (1940) and Wright's *Black Boy* (1945). Colón's sketches written over the decades in *Pueblos Hispanos*, the *Daily Worker*, and *A Puerto Rican in New York*, depicting his own experiences and those of other *Hispanos* in New York City in the early decades of the twentieth century, reflect his search for a Latinidad, or an early iteration of a Latinx pan-ethnic group identification among distinct communities that shared not only a history of marginalization and racialization in the United States but also the potential to become a social and political force.

EARLY NOTIONS OF LATINIDAD IN COLÓN'S SKETCHES IN *PUEBLOS HISPANOS*

With the arrival of Puerto Ricans and other *Hispanos* to New York City and the development of Spanish-language print culture, *Pueblos Hispanos* is representative of New York City-based Spanish-language periodicals of the 1940s. Some of its predecessors focusing on society and culture were *Gráfico* and *La Revista de Artes y Letras* (Magazine of Arts and Letters).[15] *Pueblos Hispanos* started in 1943 with poet Juan Antonio Corretjer as editor and some of its assistant editors and contributors included Puerto Rican women writers, such as Consuelo Lee Tapia and Julia de Burgos.[16] The editorial line of *Pueblos Hispanos* reflected Corretjer's Puerto Rican nationalism and fight for independence while also printing the works of Latin American authors and other *Hispanos* in New York City.[17] Corretjer is representative of Puerto Rican New Yorkers invested in the nationalist struggle led by Pedro Albizu Campos.[18] Corretjer served as the General Secretary of the Nationalist Party of Puerto Rico, and some of his early editorials and articles for *Pueblos Hispanos* focus on Albizu Campos's fight for Puerto Rican independence.[19] At the same time, *Pueblos Hispanos* emphasized unity among *Hispano* communities in New York City; for instance, an early editorial in *Pueblos Hispanos* on February 20, 1943, encourages the identification of individuals from Latin American countries in New York City as *Hispanos*, a form of group solidarity based on shared traits. The editorial states that "los que hablamos en español, formamos . . . una familia" (those of us who speak Spanish . . . are part of a family).[20] According to the editorial, this *Hispano* Spanish-speaking "family" is also connected by race and ethnicity, as *Hispanos* represent mixes of the "español, negro o indio, o las tres cosas a la vez" (Spanish, Black, or Indian peoples, or the three combined).[21] *Pueblos Hispanos* not only attempted to unite *Hispanos* through their linguistic, ethnic, and racial ties but also as an emerging group in the United States with the potential to form coalitions to defend the rights of *Hispanos* in the United States.[22] Beyond *Pueblos Hispanos*' commitment to *Hispano* unity and group solidarity, Colón's sketches in the same publication further developed an early Latinidad consisting of *Hispanos*' potential to create social and political change in the United States.

By the time Colón's sketches appeared in *Pueblos Hispanos* in 1943, he had already developed a working-class consciousness through his social activism and labor organizing among Puerto Ricans in New York City and through his writings in labor and Spanish-language newspapers. Colón's understanding of class conflict was developed while growing up listening to *lectores* (readers) among *tabaqueros* (cigar makers) in Cayey, Puerto Rico.[23] When Colón moved to New York City in 1917, he worked as a laborer and completed high school in Brooklyn.[24] Colón was self-taught and shaped by his readings of books, newspapers, and periodicals; he became a community activist and organizer for Puerto Rican and labor causes during the 1920s and 1930s.[25] Colón participated in Puerto Rican community and labor organizations, such as the Alianza Obrera Puertorriqueña (Puerto Rican

Workers Alliance), in the 1920s.[26] Similar to Corretjer and Black writers of the period, including Du Bois and Hughes, Colón had been influenced by communism since his early years in New York City, becoming a member of the Communist Party of the USA (CPUSA) in 1933.[27] Part of Colón's intellectual development came as a writer for Spanish-language and labor newspapers. Colón wrote as a correspondent based in New York City for the newspaper *Justicia* of Puerto Rico in 1923.[28] He then became a contributor to Vega's *Gráfico* from 1927 to 1928. Using the pseudonym Miquis Tiquis, Colón wrote sketches for *Gráfico* in the vein of satirical social commentary popular in the Spanish-language press at the time.[29] His early sketches for *Gráfico* followed in the tradition of the *crónica* genre already popularized by Martí and other Latin American writers;[30] however, as Edwin K. Padilla correctly points out, a major difference between Colón's sketches and *crónicas* by "profesional *letrados*" (professional men of letters), who wrote *crónicas* as a hybrid genre that combined journalism and aesthetic elements, was that his sketches used more simple language and provided greater accessibility for working-class readers.[31]

Some of Colón's sketches in *Pueblos Hispanos* transition from Puerto Rican and nationalist concerns and themes, such as his support for Puerto Rican independence, toward an articulation of an early notion of Latinidad that consists of imagining Puerto Ricans as part of a larger *Hispano* community in New York City. In his sketch for *Pueblos Hispanos* titled "Puerto Rico es también una nación" (Puerto Rico Is also a Nation), published on July 17, 1943, Colón considers that Puerto Ricans are distinct from other U.S. citizens due to the island's colonial status. Rather than seeking assimilation, he believes that they should maintain their "puertorriqueñidad" (Puertoricanness) while fighting for independence and to preserve their history and cultural identity vis-à-vis U.S. hegemonic influence. Colón similarly theorizes about the essence of a Puerto Rican identity that has been truncated by American colonialism in Puerto Rico. According to Colón, Puerto Rico is a nation with its own territory, language, and culture but argues that although all Puerto Ricans are Puerto Ricans first rather than Americans, they cannot fully express their national pride since Puerto Rico is now a colony of the United States. An additional problem, he continues, is Puerto Ricans' "casi completo desconocimiento de nuestra historia y de nuestra cultura" (almost complete ignorance of our own history and culture) due to the U.S. colonial presence on the island.[32] In the same sketch, Colón cautions against Puerto Ricans' attempts to assimilate into U.S. society or what he calls "la corrosive influencia de una mal entendida americanización..." (the corrosive influence of a badly understood Americanization...).[33] In his attempt to delineate the Puerto Rican character, Colón goes as far as to overlook prevalent racial hierarchies in Latin America and Puerto Rico and affirms that an advantage for Puerto Ricans is "la complete ausencia de prejuicios raciales en nuestra personalidad como pueblo. El prejuicio racial que existe en Puerto Rico hoy, lo importaron los yanquis a Puerto Rico..." (the complete absence of racial prejudice as a feature of our people. The racial prejudice that exists in Puerto Rico today was brought to Puerto Rico by the Yankees...).[34] As a form of resistance, Colón proposed that Puerto Ricans express their "puertorriqueñidad" (Puertoricanness) and their "personalidad puertorriqueña" (Puerto Rican identity) to resist the island's status as a U.S. colony.[35]

In "Hacia una gran institución puertorriqueña" (Toward a Great Puerto Rican Institution) published in *Pueblos Hispanos* in July 24, 1943, Colón argues that Puerto Ricans in the mainland need to organize as a community since they face challenges different from those on the island, as the former confront racial and ethnic prejudice within mainstream white society and its institutions. He believes that since Puerto Ricans are a distinct group within the United States, "tenemos no tan sólo el derecho, sino el deber, de organizarnos en fuertes instituciones fraternales, sociales y políticas que expresen, defiendan y fortalezcan esta nacionalidad" (we have not only the right, but the duty, to organize in strong fraternal, social, and political institutions that express, defend, and strengthen our national group).[36] These social and civil organizations characterized early Puerto Rican migration to New York City, as they served as mutual aid societies and organizations to fight for workers' rights and political representation on the mainland. As Edna Acosta-Belén and Carlos Santiago observe, these organizations "facilitated the process of settlement and adaptation of a primarily working-class migrant community to a culturally different and largely unwelcoming environment."[37] Thus, Colón distinguishes between "puertorriqueños allá en la isla" (Puerto Ricans on the island) and Puerto Ricans "fuera de Puerto Rico" (outside of Puerto Rico) who have experienced processes of racialization and social exclusion due to their social position as a perceived non-white group within the prevailing U.S. racial hierarchies.[38] In a similar way, Colón's argument for Puerto Rican social and political representation on the mainland is connected to other *Hispanos* in the United States, or what he calls other "nacionalidades hispanas" (Hispanic nationalities), who include individuals from other backgrounds such as Cubans and Mexicans in New York City.[39] Colón notes that while these *Hispano* groups want to preserve their own ethnic identity within the United States as well, they have the potential to form a "colonia hispánica en Nueva York" (Hispanic community in New York) with shared goals as their numbers in the United States are increasing.[40] In a statement that uncannily foreshadows the position of Latinx people in the United States, he warns against adopting exclusionary and divisive practices between Puerto Ricans and other groups in the city since those divisions play into the hands of some local politicians.

Similarly, in other sketches for *Pueblos Hispanos* Colón connects panethnic unity among the growing number of Puerto Ricans and other *Hispanos* in New York City with the goal of political representation through voting. In his *Pueblos Hispanos* sketch "Inscríbete, regístrate y vota" (Sign up, Register, and Vote) of September 4, 1943, Colón tries to dispel the idea among some Puerto Ricans that engaging in the U.S. political system means giving up "[el] ideal de independencia" (the ideal of independence) for Puerto Rico; instead, he describes voting as a major step toward Puerto Rican political representation within the U.S. political system. According to Colón, Vito Marcantonio, a progressive Italian American congressman who represented East Harlem in Congress, employed this strategy; Marcantonio advocated for Puerto Rican independence, and in return, the Puerto Rican community "offered him their unlimited support, particularly through clubs and organizations."[41] Colón observes that legislation favorable to powerful economic interests has kept Puerto Rico as "la gran factoría de esclavos para la producción del azúcar..." (a great factory of slaves for the production of sugar...).[42] A way to challenge colonial exploitation, Colón explains, is through voting and political representation within the political system as Puerto Ricans must use "el arma del voto en Estados Unidos para llevar al Congreso y a todos los cuerpos legislativos en donde se nos dé el derecho de votar, a los verdaderos amigos para la causa de Puerto Rico..." (the vote as a weapon in the United States to get elected to Congress, and any other legislative bodies in which we have the right to vote, the true friends of the Puerto Rican cause).[43] He exhorts Puerto Ricans to become a political force through voting and asks that their "nacionalismo boricua se transforme en una poderosa fuerza en Estados Unidos... y en el Estado de Nueva York" (Puerto Rican nationalism becomes a powerful force in the United States . . . and in New York state).⁴⁴ In another sketch focusing on voting, Colón expands this political strategy to include a broader coalition of groups based not only on ethnic identity but also social class and race. He encourages readers to vote for New York representatives who can defend "los derechos del pueblo explotado, de las minorías raciales y de Puerto Rico . . ." (the rights of exploited peoples, racial minorities, and Puerto Rico).⁴⁵ This social, ethnic, and racial coalition, according to Colón, would have the potential to fight more effectively against discrimination and government neglect.

In other *Pueblos Hispanos* sketches, Colón advances the idea that the labor struggle is not only against capitalist interests oppressing working-class Puerto Ricans in the mainland but also against racial prejudice directed toward racialized groups. Colón's sketch "¡Cuidado, Harlem!" (Harlem, Watch Out!) of June 26, 1943, advocates for Puerto Ricans to build coalitions and to "[c]ontinuar luchando conjuntamente con las demás fuerzas sindicales y progresistas de Estados Unidos . . ." (continue fighting along with other unions and progressive forces in the United States . . .) while supporting candidates for Congress in the image of Marcantonio. In another sketch, "Los otros Estados Unidos" (The Other United States) of April 17, 1943, Colón describes the workers' struggle as a clash between progressives—composed of Puerto Ricans, *Hispanos*, minoritized groups, labor leaders, and socialists—and an antagonist group that includes capitalist interests and white supremacist groups such as the Ku Klux Klan. Colón's sketch emphasizes the enlightenment tradition of U.S. democratic, progressive, and labor forces that have historically served to counterbalance economic interests in the United States and Puerto Rico. This progressive tradition in U.S. politics, according to Colón, is exemplified by Wendell Willkie and F. D. Roosevelt who have fought for "la unificación de todas las fuerzas de progreso y libertad para el hombre . . ." (the unification of all progressive forces and freedom for men . . .).⁴⁶ Colón goes on to compare these progressive leaders with Puerto Rican independence figures such as Ramón Emeterio Betances and Albizu Campos. Colón, therefore, seeks to unite politically Puerto Ricans and *Hispanos* "con las grandes tradiciones revolucionarias y constructivamente democráticas del pueblo de los Estados Unidos" (with the great revolutionary and positively democratic traditions of the people of the United States) represented by figures such as Thomas

Paine, Elijah Lovejoy, and Eugene V. Debs.[47] Taking a pragmatic, rather than a revolutionary stance, Colón's sketch ends by exhorting Puerto Ricans and *Hispanos* to unite "en las luchas de estos hombres que forma los otros, los *verdaderos* Estados Unidos" (in the struggles of these men, who form part of the *true* United States).[48]

Part of Colón's developing Latinidad, or unity and solidarity among *Hispano* groups in the United States, is closely connected to Spanish-language publications such as *Pueblos Hispanos* as the venue to theorize about a shared identity among local *Hispano* communities in the United States. As Nicolás Kanellos observes, a characteristic of Spanish-language newspapers in the early twentieth century was "the defense of the community" as "[a]lmost all of the Hispanic immigrant newspapers announced their service in protection of the community in mastheads and/or in editorials..."[49] *Pueblos Hispanos* was not the exception, as each issue printed its nine-point mission that included "the unification of all of the Hispanic colonies in the United States..." and the defense of "the rights of all Hispanic minorities in the United States..."[50] Colón's sketch, "Éste es tu periódico" (This Is Your Newspaper) of March 27, 1943, argues that *Pueblos Hispanos* had contributed to the development of a *Hispano* identity and a sense of unity among *Hispanos* in New York, making the case that "[u]n periódico... como *Pueblos Hispanos*, debe ser parte de la carne y el espíritu de cada uno de nosotros los hispanos" (a newspaper... such as *Pueblos Hispanos* must be part of the flesh and spirit of each and every one of us *Hispanos*). Colón describes *Pueblos Hispanos* as a collective effort sustained by the support of the community not only as readers but also by physically bringing the newspaper to *Hispanos* across New York City. He explains that "[e]scribir, editar, imprimir y hacer circular un periódico no puede ser asunto de un pequeño grupo de individuos" (writing, editing, printing, and circulating a newspaper cannot be a task for a small group of individuals).[51] Colón argues that *Pueblos Hispanos*, and other Spanish-language newspapers in the United States for that matter, reflect their readers' aspirations and are even extensions of them, as he notes that "*tú*, lector, eres el periódico" (*you*, reader, are the newspaper).[52] Although *Pueblos Hispanos* as a publication was short-lived and stopped circulation in 1944, it contains the foundation of Colón's emerging notions of unity among *Hispanos* as a growing social and political force. He would continue to develop this notion of Latinidad in labor and communist print publications, particularly the *Daily Worker* during the 1950s.

THE WORKING-CLASS DIMENSION OF *HISPANOS* IN COLÓN'S SKETCHES FOR THE *DAILY WORKER*

Alternative print forms such as the labor press and periodicals affiliated with the Communist Party not only had an impact on Colón's writing and intellectual thought but also influenced and assisted some of the most important Black writers during the period between the world wars, such as Hughes and Wright.[53] The Harlem Renaissance represented the cultural moment when mainstream publishing houses began to publish the works of Black writers for the first time.[54] Early Black periodical editors and social activists at the turn of the twentieth century like Du Bois and Charles S. Johnson assisted not only as part of the force behind the intellectual and aesthetic articulations of the New Negro movement but also by putting in place the publishing infrastructure in the form of periodicals such as *Crisis* and *Opportunity*.[55] Some of the major Black authors who first published their fiction and poetry in these publications signed book contracts with mainstream New York publishers, exemplified by the case of Hughes's *The Weary Blues*, published by Alfred A. Knopf in 1925. The Great Depression, however, precipitated the decline of the Harlem Renaissance and the publication of Black authors with mainstream publishers. It also increased the interest in communism among Black writers who became involved with organizations and print publications affiliated with the CPUSA. As Lawrence Jackson suggests, "[o]nly recently have we begun to reckon fully with the import and prominence of the American Communist Party as an engine of intellectual and artistic development for black Americans who were committed to issues of social and economic justice."[56] In subsequent years, Hughes and Wright, among other Black writers and intellectuals, were influenced in significant ways by communist ideology, as they were supported and published by communist newspapers and magazines. Wright, for instance, wrote in 1937 for the *Daily Worker*, which was sponsored by the CPUSA, and in addition to Hughes's weekly column for the *Chicago Defender* starting in 1942, he also published poetry in *New Masses*, a literary magazine affiliated with the CPUSA.[57] These alternative print venues provided a source of income for these writers as they tried to gain or retain literary visibility.[58]

The *Daily Worker* reflects and parallels the rise and fall of the influence of the American Communist Party and demonstrates the importance of alternative newspapers for some writers of color, particularly from the 1930s to the 1950s. The *Daily Worker* traces its roots to the labor and abolitionist newspaper tradition in the United States that started in the early nineteenth century.[59] The rise of communism in the United States relates to the aftermath of the Russian Revolution of 1917 and the emergence of its communist and state-led economic system after World War I, starting in the 1920s. The *Daily Worker* began as the newspaper of the CPUSA in Chicago in 1924 and then transitioned to New York City in 1927.[60] While the *Daily Worker* was managed and edited by members of the CPUSA, the paper was not simply an outlet for communist propaganda; rather, it was a full-fledged daily newspaper in the tradition of leftist, radical, and labor press in the United States.[61] As an alternative print publication in New York City, the *Daily Worker* concentrated on working-class and labor issues, along with an emphasis on global and political news from a leftist perspective. As a result, the *Daily Worker* was one of the few daily newspapers that made a point of covering economic and social issues pertaining to Black people, women, and recent immigrants.[62] Morris Schappes, an early commentator of the legacy of the *Daily Worker*, explains that "no issue of the *Daily Worker* has ever appeared without news of the contributions and struggles for equality on the part of the Negro people themselves and of white workers and progressives who see this as the crucial problem that it is."[63] The *Daily Worker* served as an outlet for writers of color such as Wright and Colón and exemplifies the influence of alternative print venues, beyond the Black or Spanish-Language newspapers and periodicals, that published the work of writers of color, a marked contrast to mass-circulation newspapers that, until the 1970s, systematically excluded editors and writers of color from their ranks.[64]

Wright's involvement as editor and writer for the *Daily Worker* exemplifies the way leftist and communist publications during the period between the wars served as alternative venues for writers of color.[65] Wright's early writing career in the 1930s was launched with the assistance of communist organizations and their publications as he became a member of the American Communist Party in 1934 in Chicago and was involved in the John Reed Club, a cultural organization affiliated to the CPUSA. Some of Wright's early writing appeared in communist periodicals with ties to the CPUSA, such as *New Masses* and *Partisan Review*;[66] for instance, one of Wright's early short stories that thematizes communism, "Bright and Morning Star," was printed in *New Masses* in 1938.[67] Wright moved to New York City, where he became involved with the *Daily Worker* as a branch editor of its Harlem bureau.[68] Wright wrote more than a hundred articles for the *Daily Worker* in 1937, covering a range of Black and working-class news and everyday life events in New York City. As Earle Bryant argues, Wright's newspaper writings have received considerably less attention than his fiction; however, his articles for the *Daily Worker* "were written with close attention to detail and in disciplined, sculptured prose; they are for the most part models of diligent research and fluent writing, relentless in their probing and wide-ranging in their scope."[69] Wright left the *Daily Worker* to work in the Federal Writers' Project in New York City in 1937 but continued to write pieces for the *Daily Worker* until 1938. Years later, Wright would break with the Communist Party and write about his disillusionment in his well-known essay "I Tried to Be a Communist," published in the *Atlantic Monthly* in 1944. Starting in 1955, Colón wrote a weekly column for the *Daily Worker*, reflecting how communist publications supported the labor struggle and the fight for social, cultural, and political representation by people of color.

Colón's sketches in the *Daily Worker* are a continuation of his previous writings pertaining to Puerto Rico's colonial condition, U.S. imperialism, and his early articulation of Latinidad in *Pueblos Hispanos* that he sought to connect with the economic struggles of other working-class communities in the United States. During Colón's time between his writings for *Pueblos Hispanos* and the *Daily Worker*, he wrote for other publications, such as the Spanish-language weekly *Liberación*, published in New York City and edited by Aurelio Pérez. Colón similarly continued his activism within the Puerto Rican community in New York City and ran for political office without success.[70] Just as communist publications were key for some Black writers from the 1930s to 1950s, they were even more so for Colón, who is one of the few pre-1960 Puerto Rican writers who made a transition from Spanish-language print culture to writing in English for labor and communist publications. In this respect, Colón's sketches in the *Daily Worker* are closer to the newspaper writings of Black writers such as Wright and Hughes. Juan Flores, for instance, discusses how *Liberación* published Puerto Rican independentist writers living on or with ties to the mainland, including José Luis González, Bernardo Vega, César Andreu Iglesias, and Guillermo Cotto-Thorner;[71] however, these authors wrote primarily for Spanish-speaking audiences in the United States and Puerto Rico but did not transition to write in English for a broader labor or leftist readership.

It is important to note, nonetheless, that Colón's vision of working-class solidarity in his sketches for the *Daily Worker* sought a coalition between *Hispanos* and working-class communities regardless of race and ethnicity rather than a *Hispano* and Black solidarity.[72] Moreover, while Wright's articles for the *Daily Worker* complement aspects of his well-known fiction and nonfiction, Colón's writings for the same publication are an integral part of Colón's writing and intellectual legacy precisely because of the lack of publishing opportunities available for Puerto Rican authors in U.S. mass-circulation newspapers and periodicals. Part of Colón's literary legacy consists of his publications in alternative print forms such as his sketches for the *Daily Worker* that later became the basis for his book, *A Puerto Rican in New York*, consisting mostly of a collection of past writings previously published in the *Daily Worker*.

Some of Colón's early sketches in the *Daily Worker* add an economic critique to the colonial status of Puerto Ricans, as he argues that Puerto Ricans share a history of exploitation with U.S. workers on the mainland who have been oppressed by the same elites and economic interests that have exploited Puerto Rico. In his *Daily Worker* sketch "Columbus Discovers Puerto Rico" of November 21, 1955, Colón focuses on the conquest of the island on behalf of the Spanish crown for economic gain and how Christopher Columbus, with the stroke of a pen in 1493, took "possession of the island in the name of the king and queen of Spain." He identifies the economic conditions of Puerto Ricans in the 1950s, both on the island and on the mainland, as the aftermath of Columbus's first landing in the Americas. Colón frames Puerto Rico's struggle for independence in part as a struggle for economic self-determination against "400 years of Spanish bondage" and "over 50 years of American imperialism . . . that masquerade[s] today as 'The Puerto Rican Commonwealth' . . ."[73] According to Colón, the fight for Puerto Rican independence and the "fight for their full rights as first class citizens" are the first steps for a Puerto Rican "future of full economic, social and political freedom."[74] In another sketch, "How to Know the Puerto Ricans," published in the *Daily Worker* in January 23, 1956, Colón describes the territorial status of Puerto Rico not as a mutually agreed upon arrangement but rather an imposed political system based on U.S. military and economic control. He contends that "the Puerto Ricans have been exploited for hundreds of years. That strangers have been knocking at the door of the Puerto Rican nation for centuries always in search for something, to get something or to take away something from the Puerto Ricans."[75] Colón's "How to Know the Puerto Ricans" makes an appeal to the readers of the *Daily Worker* to understand and appreciate Puerto Rican history, culture, and to forge social solidarity among Puerto Ricans, white workers, and progressives, or more broadly, *Daily Worker* readers, since all of them have been "oppressed by the same forces."

In the pages of the *Daily Worker*, Colón fights historical distortions about Cuban and Caribbean history created by U.S. mainstream media that have kept U.S. audiences unaware of the effects of U.S. foreign policy and interventions in the Caribbean. Colón's sketch, "Hollywood Rewrites History," of September 4, 1956, discusses *Santiago*, a film produced by Warner Brothers studios in 1956 that misrepresents the life of José Martí, as the film depicts him living in opulence and as a slave owner. These distortions prompt Colón to use the pages of the *Daily Worker* to educate its readers on Caribbean history and the revolutionary legacy of Martí. Colón explains how the film omits the role of the Cuban Revolutionary Party created by Martí and other Cuban and Puerto Rican independentist leaders in the United States in 1892 and the way they tirelessly organized for the independence of both countries. Colón laments that the "heroic figures of Martí and [Antonio] Maceo, the heroic deeds of the Cuban people[,] and the Cuban and Puerto Rican patriots" are simply swept aside in this Hollywood version.[76] As a result, Colón describes *Santiago* as "the lowest point yet reached by Hollywood in ignorance and arrogance against Cuba and all Hispanic American culture."[77] In this and other sketches for the *Daily Worker*, Colón goes on to denounce the pernicious influence of U.S. mainstream media, in this case Hollywood movies, and how even "all the Cuban historians, writing for years in every language of the globe, will not be able to undo the damage done to Cuban history . . ."[78] Another Colón sketch, "If Instead of a Professor" of April 9, 1956, similarly criticizes mass-circulation newspapers such as the *New York Herald Tribune* that published pieces criminalizing Puerto Ricans but were often silent regarding the contributions of Puerto Ricans and other *Hispanos* to U.S. society. Colón concludes "Hollywood Rewrites History" by making a case for *Hispanos* to write their own narratives and fight "with our voices and our pens" in the print venues "still left in the people's hands . . ." Just as Colón advocated, the pages of the *Daily Worker* allowed him to delineate his own identity and rectify historical distortions about *Hispanos* in mass-circulation newspapers and films.

The *Daily Worker* remained under constant threat by the U.S. government, particularly in the form of McCarthyism and the Red Scare of the 1950s, which diminished the influence of the American Communist Party and silenced dissident voices fighting for equal rights in the United States.[79] In a sketch titled "And Fuchik Looked as Confident," of April 2, 1956, Colón recounts the government raid of the *Daily Worker* offices for alleged tax evasion that was primarily intended as an act of intimidation by the U.S. government attempting to suppress "free speech and [the] free press." He explains that "[h]iding the real motives under the pretext that the paper owed some taxes to the government[,] they came to suppress one of the clearest dissenting voices in the country against the shame of discrimination, exploitation and brink diplomacy."[80] The title of his sketch refers to a portrait in Colón's office of Julius Fuchik, a writer and leader of Czechoslovakia who died in a concentration camp in 1943 after being tortured by the Nazis. Colón looks at the portrait of Fuchik and imagines Fuchik telling him, "Jesús, it all has been done before. It has all been tried before. Remember?"[81] Colón superimposes the Third Reich as a totalitarian state with the surveillance and intimidation tactics of the F.B.I. and other government agencies against dissident voices. By looking at the portrait of Fuchik, Colón "became suddenly ever more confident of the final victory of the working class and its progressive peace loving allies in all other sectors of society."[82] Contrary to Colón's optimism, however, the *Daily Worker* became increasingly criticized by disillusioned communists and attacked by people who took part on the McCarthy anticommunist hysteria.[83] "And Fuchik Looked as Confident" ends with Colón looking at Fuchik's portrait that Colón imagines saying, "[h]asta Mañana" (see you tomorrow) and Colón confidently believing that the *Daily Worker* will continue to be published as it has been for the last thirty-two years. While it continued to be published for a few more years, the *Daily Worker* would cease as a daily newspaper but would continue to be published as a weekly due to the increasing hostility and attacks against communist sympathizers and organizations, in addition to the government's campaigns of intimidation and surveillance.

The influence of communism and the American Communist Party eventually diminished by the closing of the 1950s, and while prominent Black writers distanced themselves from the party due in part to the pernicious attacks by McCarthy and surveillance by government agencies, Colón remained a vocal advocate for communism. Du Bois, Hughes, and Wright, at different periods, moved away from communism due to government pressure, despite the influence that communist organizations and publications had had on their careers. For instance, McCarthyism and the F.B.I., which had Du Bois under surveillance since the 1940s, damaged Du Bois's career.[84] Hughes famously appeared at the Senate Permanent Sub-Committee on Investigations, led by Joseph McCarthy in Washington, D.C., in 1953 where he denied having communist ties.[85] Likewise, despite his success as a writer, Wright was denounced as a communist in the 1950s and remained under surveillance by the F.B.I. even after he moved to Europe where he remained isolated until his death in France in 1960.[86] Colón continued to write for publications affiliated with the CPUSA and to support the Soviet Union after 1956;[87] nonetheless, Colón also became isolated, as communism was attacked both on the mainland and by the Puerto Rican local government, which resulted in communism's steep decline on the island during the 1950s.[88] Colón's statement read at the Foley Square Courthouse in New York City on November 16, 1959, not only offers a forceful denunciation of McCarthyism but also presents a synthesis of some of Colón's major themes in his sketches for *Pueblos Hispanos* and the *Daily Worker*, such as the status of Puerto Rico as a colony, the dangers of U.S. cultural and economic imperialism, and the need for Puerto Rican and *Hispano* solidarity for political reform in the United States. In his statement, he denounces the members of the Committee on Un-American Activities as a persecutory body against "individuals who have dedicated long years of their lives in the defense of all that is free, true, and in the best traditions of democracy in the United States."[89] In a powerful articulation for *Hispano* solidarity, Colón states that "[t]here are millions of Latin Americans living in the United States. Cubans, Mexicans, Puerto Ricans, and many thousands from the other republics living here, who support . . . the progressive leaders and movements in this country. As in New York City with the Puerto Ricans . . . the Spanish-speaking people here are becoming a deciding force politically . . ."[90] Ultimately, Colón's unwavering support of communism and workers' struggles made possible the publication of his only published book during his lifetime.

COLÓN'S *A PUERTO RICAN IN NEW YORK* AND LATINX LITERATURE BEFORE 1960

Latinx authors of the 1940s and 1950s from the East Coast and the Southwest, and particularly from cities like New York City and San Antonio, shared in common their exclusion from mass-circulation newspapers and mainstream publishing houses with a few exceptions.[91] Most often, the experiences of early Latinx writers resemble those of Jovita González or Américo Paredes, who were unable to publish their fiction with New York publishers during the 1950s. Other Mexican American writers in the Southwest, such as José de la Luz Sáenz, Alonso Perales, Adela Sloss-Vento, and Elena Zamora O'Shea, published either their prose or fiction in local or regional Spanish-language newspapers and with regional publishing houses.[92] A similar publishing dynamic played out with Puerto Rican writers in New York City during the periods between the world wars. Julia de Burgos, for example, published essays and poems in *Pueblos Hispanos* in the 1940s and her poetry collections written in Spanish were published in Puerto Rico; however, Burgos and other Puerto Rican writers of the period living in New York City did not publish books with U.S. mainstream houses. Similar to the experience of Mexican American authors in the Southwest during the interwar period, Puerto Rican authors in New York City of the 1940s and 1950s published their books in Spanish with the support of local and independent publishers and targeted to a Spanish-speaking readership. Some of these authors and works include José Luis González's *El hombre en la calle* (1948), Guillermo Cotto-Thorner's *Trópico en Manhattan* (1951), René Marqués's *La carreta* (1953), Pedro Juan Soto's *Spiks* (1956), and Bernardo Vega's *Memorias* (written in the late 1940s but not published until 1977 in Spanish after his death).[93] Just as with their Mexican American counterparts in the Southwest, Puerto Rican authors in New York City engaged with their U.S. social and cultural context while writing in Spanish; nonetheless, these authors were not able to reach a broader readership and could not form literary connections with other Spanish-speaking writers in other regions of the United States. Lack of publishing opportunities were not only due to their relatively small population numbers and geographical locations but other contributing factors included the exclusionary practices of the U.S. mainstream publishing industry before the 1960s.

Colón's only published book during his lifetime, *A Puerto Rican in New York*, published by Masses and Mainstream in 1961, stands out among other books by Puerto Rican authors in the United States that preceded it. His engagement with the communist press, in the form of his writings for the *Daily Worker*, the *Worker* (the weekly that replaced the *Daily Worker*), and the periodical *Mainstream*, made it possible for him to republish some of his sketches in a book format for an English-speaking audience.[94] *Mainstream*, also known as *Masses and Mainstream*, was a monthly magazine started in 1948 resulting from the consolidation of two previous periodicals with communist ties, *New Masses* and *Mainstream*.[95] *Mainstream* and its editor Joseph Felshin also operated a book publishing imprint named Masses and Mainstream.[96] *A Puerto Rican in New York* consisted of a collection of sketches selected by Colón primarily from his previously published writings in the *Daily Worker*, along with a few pieces from *Mainstream* and original sketches. While the content of *A Puerto Rican in New York* differs in genre from other Puerto Rican books of the period, Colón's collection of newspaper writings in a book format resembles Hughes's collections of some of his *Chicago Defender* columns, subsequently published as *Simple Speaks His Mind* by Simon and Schuster in 1950.[97] *A Puerto Rican in New York* stood as the culmination of Colón's lifelong writing and intellectual journey attempting to reach English-speaking readers who identified with labor struggles and community activism beyond Puerto Rican or *Hispano* readers. *A Puerto Rican in New York* attempts to redress the distorted narrative of the Puerto Rican community in the city as depicted in the U.S. mainstream media. As Juan Flores correctly notes in his foreword to *A Puerto Rican in New York*, Colón's book written in English sought "to chip away at the formidable wall of stereotypes and bigotry which has long shrouded the image of all Puerto Ricans in the public eye."[98] While the reach of Colón's book was modest at the time of his publication, its engagement with his *Hispano* subjectivity makes it a foundational text in Latinx literature.

While *A Puerto Rican in New York* focuses primarily on the Puerto Rican community, some of its sketches chronicle Colón's intellectual journey through his reading of newspapers, books, and writings that characterize the autobiographies of some his contemporary Black authors. Most of the criticism focusing on *A Puerto Rican in New York* interprets Colón's book within the context of Puerto Ricans as an emerging diasporic community in the city and in relation to the stated goal in the book's preface of challenging the negative portrayals of Puerto Ricans in U.S. mainstream media.[99] Colón indeed criticizes mainstream newspapers, magazines, and books that misrepresent Puerto Ricans, which tend to focus on "what is superficial and sentimental, transient and ephemeral, or bizarre and grotesque in Puerto Rican life—and always out of context with the real history, culture and traditions of my people."[100] Moreover, *A Puerto Rican in New York* has been studied in relation to race and Colón's position as Afro-Latinx while denouncing the discrimination and second-class status of Afro-Puerto Ricans in New York City; Winston James, for example, discusses *A Puerto Rican in New York* in relation to Colón's position as Afro-Latinx and the way he emphasized Blackness in a revised second edition of *A Puerto Rican in New York* that was not published.[101] Equally important, some sketches included in *A Puerto Rican in New York* depict Colón's intellectual journey of self-discovery through his readings of newspapers and books and through his writing practice. His depiction of his self-education and his experiences as a recent arrival to the city form part of a long tradition of autobiographical writing by authors of color, particularly by some of his contemporaries, including Hughes's *The Big Sea* and Wright's *Black Boy*.

A Puerto Rican in New York chronicles Colón's literary and intellectual journey through his readings of newspapers, magazines, and books and his everyday life experiences as a laborer in New York City. The title of his book reflects the personal dimension of his narrative by using the singular noun, "a Puerto Rican" rather than the collective "the Puerto Rican." As David Vázquez correctly notes, Colón in *A Puerto Rican in New York* "remakes first-person personal narrative genres in terms of their multifaceted representations of individual subjectivity, community affirmation, and national belonging."[102] The opening sketch of the collection, "A Voice through the Window" thematizes the start of Colón's intellectual journey and the emergence of his social consciousness developed by listening to *tabaqueros* reading out loud newspapers and books among themselves. He recounts living close to a cigar factory in Cayey, Puerto Rico, and listening to "El Lector" (the lector) read books to *tabaqueros* making cigars at the factory. Colón wonders how working-class cigar makers "who hardly knew how to read and write" were able to discuss books and ideas from authors such as Émile Zola, Balzac, Hugo, and Cervantes that allowed them to develop a class consciousness.[103] Colón's learning from *tabaqueros* and *lectores* also signals the start of his individual and non-traditional educational path that would characterize his writing career in the United States. As Adalaine Holton correctly points out, "Colón acquired his political, literary, and philosophical education within the context of labor..."[104] While Colón concedes that the ideas discussed among *tabaqueros* were unintelligible to him during his youth, listening to "El Lector" made him "accustomed to hearing the repetition of certain words and phrases...," which Colón "came to understand more clearly" as he grew up.[105] One of his memories of Puerto Rico is that of *lectores* reading from memory with the book closed, which served as a literary inspiration for him, as he notes that those "feats of memory encouraged many workers and even boys like myself to try memorizing well-known passages like the introductory paragraph of *Don Quixote*, with which [he] started to like and then to love literature and the enlightened thinkers of mankind."[106] Years later living in New York City, Colón listened to people discussing ideas on the radio that reminded him of the *lectores*' voices. His early experiences related to reading newspapers and books in Puerto Rico represent the foundations of his interest in newspaper writing in subsequent years.

Colón's encounters with reading and books in the context of working-class labor within the modern city resemble Wright's own literary awakening in *Black Boy* when Wright arrives in Memphis as a teenager and makes sense of his experiences through newspapers and books. While working in Memphis after escaping poverty in rural Mississippi, Wright begins to read newspapers, borrows a library card from a Catholic coworker, and encounters for the first time the writing of H. L. Mencken in the newspapers, who in turn introduces Wright to other authors, such as Dostoevsky, Tolstoy, Twain, Zola, Balzac, and others.[107] At first, Wright is unable to discern the meaning in these texts, but he begins to "hunge[r] books" and discovers "new ways of looking and seeing" and "of being affected by something that made the look of the world different."[108] Based on this newly acquired knowledge, Wright begins to write and to reflect on the position of Black people in the Jim Crow South, which prompts him to move to Chicago. Wright's early reading experiences as a laborer in a modern city and his ability to interpret his reality through his readings of newspapers and books resembles Colón's early experiences in Cayey and New York City. Both, Wright in *Black Boy* and Colón in *A Puerto Rican in New York* grapple with economic hardship and struggles to remain afloat while both writers began journeys of self-instruction to supplement their lack of formal education. Their experiences contrast to those of Hughes, however, who in his autobiography also wrote about his intellectual journey. Hughes received a more traditional education that allowed him to attend Columbia University and then Lincoln University.[109] Wright and Colón both began their writing careers by writing for newspapers and magazines that were supported by labor and communist organizations, which proved key for Wright in Chicago and eventually launched his career as a fiction writer. In the case of Colón, it was first the

Puerto Rican labor press and subsequently Spanish-language newspapers and communist publications that made possible Colón's writing career.

The sketch "Kipling and I" continues Colón's theme of literary affinities in *A Puerto Rican in New York*, as he describes the influence that reading had on him when he arrived in New York City searching for work. Although he struggles financially, Colón possesses a "few books . . . in a soap box nailed to the wall," but his "most prized possession" is a framed print of Rudyard Kipling's poem "If."[110] In his analysis of "Kipling and I," Vázquez observes that Colón's reading of "If" "contrasts the ethos of liberal individualism with the lived experiences of working-class Puerto Ricans and African Americans in New York City."[111] In addition, the sketch similarly relates to Colón's own subjectivity as the poem has a special meaning to him beyond the communal experiences of Puerto Ricans in New York City. For Colón, "If" represents an aesthetic work that transcends everyday life and struggles. In Colón's view, Kipling's poem "seemed to summarize the wisdom of all the sages that ever lived in one poetical nutshell. It was what I was looking for, something to guide myself by, a way of life, a compendium of the wise, the true and the beautiful."[112] He hangs the framed poem on a wall near the entrance of his apartment and each morning as he leaves the apartment, he stands in "front of the poem and read[s] it over and over again, sometimes half a dozen times" letting the "sonorous music of the verse carry [him] away."[113] Colón's print of "If" also represents a memento as he carried "a handwritten copy as [he] stepped out every morning looking for work, repeating verses and stanzas from memory until the whole poem came to be part of [him]."[114] Kipling's poem stands for the potential of the intellect even in adversity; for instance, Colón recounts experiencing discrimination at work and clinging "to [the] poem as to a faith. Like a potent amulet . . ."[115] Poetry and aesthetic creation become forms of spiritual sustenance for him; however, his economic struggles in New York City clashing with his literary aspirations reflect two of the most prevalent tropes that permeate this and other sketches.

Colón's sketch "The Library Looks at the Puerto Ricans" connects two major themes not only in *A Puerto Rican in New York* but also in his previous sketches from *Pueblos Hispanos* and the *Daily Worker* pertaining to historical knowledge derived from books and the dearth of sources that objectively depict Puerto Rican history. The focus of his sketch is a pamphlet called the *Branch Library Book News* of February 1956, printed by the New York Public Library and distributed in the branch libraries, which contains a list of books on Puerto Rico. Colón assesses the book list and realizes it lacks current Puerto Rican publications, and some of the few that are published are not included in the list. Rather than discussing the list per se, Colón focuses on what he considers the glaring omissions in the list: the activities by Puerto Rican organizations that have taken place at those same New York City branch libraries, articles from labor newspapers and periodicals, and "numerous rare books and materials on Puerto Rico that [the New York Public Library] has on its shelves and in its vaults."[116] Moreover, Colón laments the lack of representation by Puerto Rican authors since the library list consists mostly of non-Puerto Rican writers. He is particularly distraught that the library pamphlet glaringly fails to mention the Schomburg Collection at the Harlem library branch, which is archived by the same institution that assembled the list. Colón notes that while the Schomburg collection is "dedicated to the Negro people and their history, there is a great amount of material on prominent Negro Puerto Ricans in its files."[117] Just as troubling for Colón, the list omits Arturo Schomburg himself, one of the most influential Puerto Rican literary figures in New York City.[118] As a result, his sketch decries the lack of literary and historical knowledge "in a library publication purporting to compile the most important books dealing with cultural developments and contributions of Puerto Rico and the Puerto Ricans in New York."[119] Colón's sketch reflects the depths of his knowledge and reading practices, as books and print culture informed his community activism and social engagement.

Other sketches in *A Puerto Rican in New York* thematize reading and learning in relation to some of Colón's acquaintances and the function of books and alternative newspapers within the Puerto Rican community. A recurrent theme in *A Puerto Rican in New York* is book reading and book borrowing, as he confesses that "[t]here is nothing so difficult as returning a book."[120] At times, he would fail to return a book; other times, friends would borrow books from him, and even on some occasions, visitors would take books from his bookshelves at home. Colón explains that "[b]ooks grow on you. They become part of you. Borrowed books intermingle with your own until they form a familiar pattern on the walls of your room."[121] In the sketch "Looking Just a Little Forward," Colón discusses reading among Puerto Ricans and how communist ideology can be studied through books. While discussing the idea of borrowing books, he recounts the case of one of his friends, José, who borrows Colón's copy of Edward Bellamy's *Looking Backward* written in Spanish.[122] Colón enjoys lending books to friends who can learn something from them. He uses Bellamy's novel to introduce friends to other novels such as Jack London's *The Iron Heel* and Maxim Gorky's *Mother*, and from there to pamphlets, and eventually "more serious theoretical works."[123] Similarly, Colón includes a discussion on the labor press and its role among Puerto Rican and working-class communities in effecting social change. In the same sketch, he compares his writings in the *Daily Worker* with one of the main premises in *Looking Backward*, the idea that "The Great Transformation" of the U.S. society and economic system will be carried out "by the working class."[124] Colón remembers dreaming that the *Daily Worker* shut down due to drop a in circulation but wakes up and finds solace in the fact that this was just a dream, since he considers the labor press an indispensable medium for social change. Books and newspapers were not only print forms used to spread labor and communist ideas, but they also formed an intricate part of Colón's own engagement with members of the Puerto Rican and *Hispano* communities.

Colón concludes his book with the sketch of the same name, "A Puerto Rican in New York," in which he synthesizes his vision of Latinidad already present in previous sketches from *Pueblos Hispanos* and the *Daily Worker*. In "A Puerto Rican in New York," Colón connects the settlement of the Puerto Rican community in New York City with his own individual story as he tries to answer the questions that people have asked him for the last forty years, "[w]hy did you come to New York?"[125] He believes it is due to the legacy of U.S. colonialism in the Caribbean. Colón grew up under the U.S. military occupation of Puerto Rico when the U.S. government controlled an entire nation with a population that some deemed as inferior. In school, Colón learned about U.S. history, historical figures, the Bill of Rights, and the constitution, as he was taught to see Puerto Ricans as part of "the people of the United States";[126] nonetheless, due to the process of racialization of non-whites prevalent in the United States at the time and transported to the Caribbean, one of his first memories at school was not being allowed to play checkers with one white American teacher because he was a Black student. Growing up, Colón began to reevaluate what he had learned in school and decided that "[i]n this 'we the people' phrase that I admired so much, were there first and secondary people? Were the other gradations and classifications not only because of race but because of money or social position?"¹²⁷ He reflects on Puerto Rico's colonial status through his readings and lived experiences, or what he calls "life itself," that consisted of discovering the existence of racial and social classifications both in the United States and Puerto Rico.¹²⁸ Colón, for instance, is "surprised to discover that the rich Puerto Rican sugar planter and the rich American investor belonged to the same clubs, played golf and danced and dined together."¹²⁹ In a similar way, he is disappointed to discover how the othering of Puerto Ricans and economic disparities created discrimination and class divisions by noting how "[r]ight by the big mansions of the sugar plantation owner or the comfortable houses of the overseer, [he] started noticing the hundreds of old crudely made peasant huts and slums of the worst kind, with thousands of people starving in them";¹³⁰ thus, Colón's identity and class consciousness is informed by his understanding of racial and social hierarchies enforced by white groups and economic interests both in Puerto Rico and in the United States.

The sketch "A Puerto Rican in New York" describes the emergence of Colón's *Hispano* identity and social consciousness as a direct result of his readings of newspapers and books that would lead to his advocacy for Puerto Ricans and *Hispanos* in New York City. Colón returns to his criticism of the negative portrayal of Puerto Ricans and *Hispanos* in mainstream publications and media, a theme already developed in some of his sketches in *Pueblos Hispanos* and the *Daily Worker*. He recounts that in his early memories about learning to read, he discovered "[a]s if [he] had never seen it before . . . that all [his] school books . . . were written in English" and contained a U.S.-centered interpretation of Puerto Rico and its people.¹³¹ In contrast, it was through the influence of *tabaqueros* and the pamphlets and labor newspapers they gave Colón to read that he learned that Puerto Rico was "a colony—a sort of storage house for cheap labor and a market for 'seconds' (cheap industrial goods)" and that Puerto Rico was only one country among a larger network of U.S. colonial possessions.¹³² As Colón began to read labor newspapers such as *Justicia* and *Unión Obrera*, he switched "from writing poor sonnets to reading good pamphlets."¹³³ Returning to the question of "why did you come to New York?" Colón concludes that "there was no future for a young man in Puerto Rico, but the future of the sugar cane field, with starvation wages. The future of an upward struggle with great odds against [working class Puerto Ricans]."¹³⁴ The economic conditions of those in Puerto Rico, however, were not drastically different from those of

Puerto Ricans arriving in New York City, as Colón discovers that the same corporations "were not only exploiting the Puerto Ricans in New York but the other various national minorities and workers . . ."[135] He argues that the shared economic struggles of Puerto Ricans in New York make them natural progressives who needed to come together through social and labor organizations and exercise their right to vote as U.S. citizens. His sketch concludes by warning that there are economic and political entities that consider Puerto Ricans a threat to U.S. society and have marginalized them through negative portrayals in mainstream media and mass-circulation newspapers. Colón wants the phrase "We the people" to achieve its true meaning as Puerto Ricans organize for a "progressive people's government" in the United States and for Puerto Rican independence that he believed imminent.[136]

Despite the critical depth of Colón's intellectual thinking, his vision of Latinidad was relegated to the archive due in part to the cultural marginalization of Latinx writers prior to the 1960s as his writings were only recovered by literary scholars decades later. Colón's writings center the experiences of Puerto Ricans and *Hispanos* in New York City and offer an early intellectual and theoretical framework for Latinidad among Latinx communities in the city for cultural, social, and political representation. Colón preceded the writings of the Nuyorican poets and the social platform of the Young Lords in New York City who, similar to the writers and leaders of the Chicanx Movement across the Southwest, articulated a racial and ethnic identity mostly without the knowledge of the cultural or literary antecedents who came before them.[137] One reason for this lack of literary and intellectual continuity was because *A Puerto Rican in New York* was published by an alternative press and was out of print shortly after its publication. It did not become available again until it was recovered by Juan Flores at the Center for Puerto Rican Studies at Hunter College, CUNY, who reprinted *A Puerto Rican in New York* in 1982 with International Publishers, another independent publishing house in New York City, for a new generation of Latinx readers. In subsequent years, Acosta-Belén and Sánchez Korrol published Colón's *The Way It Was and Other Writings* with Arte Público Press in 1993, a collection of his sketches previously published in the *Daily Worker* and the *Worker*, along with a critical analysis and detailed bibliography of Colón's sketches numbered in the hundreds and published in various alternative print publications. Subsequently, Edwin K.

Padilla edited a collection of Colón's sketches published in *Gráfico, Pueblos Hispanos*, and *Liberación* written in Spanish, *"Lo que el pueblo me dice..."* (What the People Tell Me...), published also by Arte Público Press in 2001. Colón's selected genre, the sketch, does not fit into a recognizable literary genre in American literary studies, which contributed to its literary neglect of previous decades. While Colón's literary legacy remained unavailable to Nuyorican authors and other Latinx writers in other regions at the time, Colón's writings are available to Latinx readers in the twenty-first century.

CHAPTER 4

IDENTITY AND INDIGENEITY IN JOSÉ DE LA LUZ SÁENZ'S WORLD WAR I DIARY

LATINX LITERARY production in the Southwest in the early decades of the twentieth century was developed by a robust network of Spanish-language newspapers and periodicals with a Mexican and Mexican American readership.[1] In Texas, one of the early and notable newspapers was *El Regidor* of San Antonio; its editor Pablo Cruz covered the trial of Gregorio Cortez, a Mexican American accused of shooting a sheriff in South Texas, whose influence in Mexican American cultural production was made famous by Américo Paredes decades later. Cruz assisted with raising funds for Cortez's trial in 1901 that resulted in his eventual release.[2] There was also *La Crónica* of Laredo, founded by Nicasio Idar in 1908, which was subsequently edited by some of Idar's progeny, including Eduardo, Clemente, and Jovita Idar. As a progressive publication, *La Crónica*, in addition to local news, promoted issues pertaining to Mexicans and Mexican Americans along the U.S.-Mexico border, such as labor organizing and the education of schoolchildren of Mexican origin.[3] In her newspaper columns, Jovita Idar wrote about the education of Mexican and Mexican American children and women's rights in the early decades of the twentieth century.[4] The Mexican Revolution influenced Spanish-language print culture in the Southwest through the exile of Mexican journalists who either avoided persecution or escaped the conflict by migrating to Texas. *Regeneración* of San Antonio, edited by Ricardo Flores Magón, is representative of the radical

Mexican press in exile in Texas during the Mexican Revolution. As Kelly Lytle Hernández explains, Magón influenced several Mexicans and Mexican Americans, who became known as the *magonistas*, and whose revolutionary and anti-capitalist ideology, often printed in the pages of *Regeneración*, planted the early seeds for revolution and social change on both sides of the U.S.-Mexico border.[5]

Amid the proliferation of Spanish-language newspapers and the growth of Mexican and Mexican American communities in Texas, *La Prensa* of San Antonio, edited by Ignacio E. Lozano, stands as one of the most important pre-1960 Spanish-language newspapers. *La Prensa* disseminated news, editorials, essays, and poetry that contributed to the development of Mexican American cultural, social, and political thought and emerging notions of a Mexican American identity. The formation of *La Prensa* in 1913, and its subsequent development as a leading Spanish-language newspaper in Texas, also relates to the migration of Mexican nationals during the Mexican Revolution. Originally from Mexico, Lozano moved to Texas and worked for Spanish-language publications before *La Prensa*, most notably in the weekly *El Imparcial de Texas*, printed in San Antonio and edited by Francisco A. Chapa. *La Prensa* began as a newspaper with a readership consisting primarily of Mexicans in exile communities in the United States, often referred to as *México de afuera* (a Mexican nation abroad). The first issue of *La Prensa* of February, 13, 1913, explains that its focus is on news "principalmente de México" (primarily from Mexico) and "la situación política de nuestra patria..." (and the political situation of our homeland), which meant Mexico.[6] *La Prensa* was characterized by a conservative editorial stance and an emphasis on Mexican nationalism and middle-class values;[7] however, as John Alba Cutler notes, *La Prensa* was far from a bourgeois publication, as it also covered working-class issues.[8] While *La Prensa* functioned as a transnational publication following closely the developments in Mexico, particularly the Mexican Revolution, Lozano's newspaper also covered local news for Tejanos; that is, Mexicans and Mexican Americans in Texas. *La Prensa*, for instance, printed articles on discrimination against people of Mexican origin, and over the decades, it published the writings of Mexican American writers, intellectuals, and civil rights activists, including José de la Luz Sáenz, Alonso S. Perales, Adela Sloss-Vento, Carlos E. Castañeda, and Américo Paredes. Spanish-language print culture in Texas, exemplified by *La Prensa*, was integral to the fight against segregation and the emergence of a Mexican American identity in the United States in the early decades of the twentieth century.

In this chapter, I analyze the development of José de la Luz Sáenz's articulations of his identity formation in print publications that was shaped by racialization, social oppression, and political disenfranchisement affecting the lives of Mexicans and Mexican Americans in Texas and across the Southwest. Despite the discrimination against Tejanos, Sáenz volunteered to serve in World War I and sent letters to *La Prensa* at critical moments during the war that offered current accounts of the service of Mexicans and Mexican Americans on the European front. Sáenz's letters about his war experiences published in *La Prensa* develop an argument for the inclusion of Mexican Americans using the tropes of patriotism, loyalty, and sacrifice, while at the same time downplaying the horrific effects of modern warfare on U.S. soldiers. Sáenz's newspaper writings during the war reflect the significance of his ideological stance in favor of U.S. values and ideals—despite their unequal treatment at home and the history of racial violence against those communities before the war—that parallel similar claims made in the Black press by some of the most prominent Black leaders and intellectuals, such as W. E. B. Du Bois, who encouraged Black men to join the army and prove their loyalty to the United States despite the pervasive segregation and racial violence against Black people not only in the South but also across the nation. Mexican American and Black soldiers, despite their service and claims for inclusion published in newspapers and periodicals, returned to the same segregated society and racial violence—including the appalling racial violence in the form of lynchings of Mexicans and Mexican Americans in Texas and Black people across the United States. Similar to Black activists and writers such as Du Bois, Sáenz and other Mexican Americans began to organize against racial discrimination and for civil rights after the war. Starting in 1924, Sáenz teamed up with fellow war veteran and activist Alonso S. Perales, and together they began a speaking tour in several cities in South Texas, emphasizing the need to end segregation and organize for civil rights, which led to the formation of the League of United Latin American Citizens (LULAC) in 1929.

Ideologically, early LULAC members of the 1930s, such as Sáenz and Perales, fought against segregation of people of Mexican origin in Texas primarily through their writings and activism, similar to the way Black writers and leaders fought to end segregation in the South. Nonetheless, in a marked contrast, LULAC leaders of the 1940s and 1950s sought to be classified legally as white in a search to gain the privileges of U.S. citizenship that would separate them as well from their Mexican counterparts in the United States. I argue that Sáenz's World War I diary titled *Los méxico-americanos en la gran guerra* (The Mexican-Americans during the Great War), published in San Antonio in 1933 by Artes Gráficas, presents a development in his articulating of a "Mexican-American" identity that emphasizes ethnic pride and Indigeneity while attempting to reconcile aspects of Sáenz's American, Mexican, and Indigenous backgrounds. Emilio Zamora and Ben Maya's foundational scholarship and translation of Sáenz's diary from Spanish to English in 2014 have significantly contributed to the study of Sáenz's war diary and his intellectual thought. While scholars of Mexican American history have studied Sáenz's diary, critics of Chicanx and Latinx literatures—not to mention critical studies focusing on American writers during World War I—have not given enough attention to the diary despite its significance in the development of Latinx literary and intellectual thought.⁹ I analyze Sáenz's narrative strategies in his diary that challenge the system of racial segregation in Texas and the racialization of non-whites in the army. Part of Sáenz's emphasis on his identity relates to his deep-seeded attachment to his Tejano community, referred to in Sáenz's writings as "*la raza*" (our people), which he envisions as a collective group with shared cultural and historical ties and social goals in the United States. In addition, I study Sáenz's articulation of his Indigenous background as an element of his Mexican American identity that allows him to interrogate the colonization of the American continent by Europeans and to create a sense of racial solidarity with Native peoples in the United States. While early LULAC leaders saw their fight for equal rights in communal terms by focusing on the end of racial discrimination against Tejanos, they did not see themselves as part of a larger coalition of non-white or racialized groups in the United States, particularly when it pertained to the racialization experienced by Black soldiers in the army and society at large.

RACIALIZATION IN TEXAS AND "TEXAS MEXICAN" SOLDIERS DURING WORLD WAR I

The social conditions in the early decades of the twentieth century in the United States pertaining Tejanos were influenced by racialization, exclusion, and racial violence. The racialization and racial violence against them in Texas began as early as the formation of the Republic of Texas and its subsequent entrance into the union as a slaveholding state in 1845. After Reconstruction, the racial order in Texas was enforced not only in the form of Jim Crow segregation of Black people but also by "Juan Crow" segregation of people of Mexican origin. The system of racial segregation in Texas was based on a racial hierarchy that influenced the social, political, economic, and educational opportunities of non-whites in the state. Laura E. Gómez has contextualized how, after the Treaty of Guadalupe Hidalgo, non-white inhabitants of the Southwest, primarily Mexicans and Indigenous groups, became racialized and excluded by law and in courts.[10] Historians have similarly studied the experiences of Mexican and Mexican Americans in Texas as characterized by racialization and racial violence in the form of lynchings that were common under Juan Crow.[11] The large exodus of Mexicans toward the Southwest caused by the Mexican Revolution increased the exclusion and repression of Mexicans and Mexican Americans in the United States; racial tensions reached a height with El Plan de San Diego (San Diego Plan) and the racial terror that was unleashed against Mexicans and Mexican Americans in Texas, particularly during the summer of 1915. As Monica Muñoz Martinez has documented, hundreds of Texans of Mexican origin were executed in an extrajudicial manner, primarily by members of the Texas Rangers, who were not held accountable since part of their role in the Borderlands was social control through racial intimidation and racial violence.[12]

Sáenz's early years as a schoolteacher in South Texas were influenced by the racialization and segregation of Mexican American schoolchildren in Texas at the turn of the twentieth century.[13] Sáenz experienced racial segregation firsthand, coming from a family of Mexican American laborers in South Texas living under Juan Crow segregation and economic exploitation.[14] In subsequent years, he received a distinct form of education in a Mexican community school, or *escuelita*, as these schools emerged in predominantly Mexican American communities in South Texas. Some of the *escuelitas'* subjects included Mexican history and Spanish, which played a role in the development of students' Mexican American identity.[15] Some of the *escuelitas* attended by students of Mexican origin were supported in part by journalists from Mexico who moved to Texas after the start of the Mexican Revolution. Sáenz met and was mentored by Eulalio Velázquez, the editor of the Spanish-language newspaper, *El Cosmopolita* of Alice, Texas.

Through Velázquez's guidance, Sáenz learned Spanish and Mexican history at a time when these subjects were not taught in traditional schools.[16] Sáenz became a schoolteacher in South Texas and wrote columns for Spanish-language newspapers, including *La Prensa*, starting in the 1910s, in which he brought attention to the issue of underfunded schools for schoolchildren of Mexican origin.[17] In a column titled "Del público: la nueva ley escolar obligatoria" (From the Public: The New Mandatory School Law) published in *La Prensa* on August 15, 1916, Sáenz discusses a new state law that would make school mandatory for children in the state of Texas and expects that it would not exclude schoolchildren of Mexican origin. His article emphasizes the importance of education for Tejanos, a cause that is present also in his subsequent social activism. Sáenz's piece for *La Prensa* reflects his initial emphasis on creating a sense of community and solidarity among Texans of Mexican origin, regardless of nationality, and their need to protect their rights in the United States. It also contains some of the concerns that would remain a constant in his writings, such as the importance of Spanish-language print culture in Texas to disseminate a message for social justice among Spanish-speaking readers.[18]

Woodrow Wilson's declaration of war presented to Congress on April 2, 1917, brought the United States and a substantial number of Mexicans and Mexican Americans in Texas, including Sáenz, into the mobilization period and the turmoil of war in Europe. As historian José Ramírez discusses in his excellent book *To the Line of Fire!*, the conscription strategy by the U.S. government from the start of the mobilization period was to frame civilian military service as based on loyalty to the country and patriotic duty rather than an imposition.[19] Similar to the way conscription worked across the country, a number of Tejanos responded to the first day of registration by joining the army on June 5, 1917.[20] Spanish-language newspapers in Texas, including *La Prensa*, echoed U.S. mass-circulation newspapers' call to join the war effort. According to José Ramírez, "[t]hroughout the course of the conflict overseas, most of the Spanish-language press maintained a steady drumbeat of patriotic messages."[21] Meaningful dissent after the U.S. declaration of war was absent due in part to the propaganda, surveillance, and censorship apparatus built around the war effort.[22] Most Tejanos volunteered or joined the army; however, a substantial number of Mexican Americans eligible to serve opted to evade the draft due in part to the United States' long history of mistreatment and exclusion.[23] Their resistance to serve was also related to episodes of racial violence in the form of extrajudicial killings and lynchings of Tejanos prior to the war, which increased due to the migration of Mexicans during the Revolution, the Plan de San Diego of 1915, and the militarization of the U.S.-Mexico border leading up to the United States' military participation in the war;[24] nonetheless, the reasons for Mexican Americans to evade the draft in Texas most likely involved a confluence of social, political, and economic motives, which in turn exacerbated animosity and racial violence toward them now labeled as "slackers."[25]

The dilemma for Tejanos regarding whether to serve was based in part on the segregation and racial violence against them, which resembles the experiences of Black people in the U.S. Black communities not only lived under Jim Crow in the South and de facto segregation in northern cities, but they also experienced anti-Blackness in the form of lynchings and white mob violence across the United States. Influential Black periodicals and newspapers during the early twentieth century, including Du Bois's *Crisis*, Robert Abbott's the *Chicago Defender*, and William Monroe Trotter's *Guardian*, denounced in their pages racial violence and the lynching of Black men.[26] Other Black writers, including Ida B. Wells, Walter White, James Weldon Johnson, and John Edward Bruce, became early civil rights activists in part by documenting and reporting on lynchings in Black newspapers and periodicals.[27] U.S. government propaganda and the Espionage Act, along with its censorship apparatus, also influenced the coverage of the war in the Black press. Although more ambivalent about the role of Black men in the war, the Black press, just like the Spanish-language newspapers in Texas, ultimately rallied around the war in various degrees;[28] for instance, Abbott supported the participation of Black men in the war but also continued his coverage of lynchings of Black people in the *Chicago Defender*, which was criticized by white Southerners as disloyal and detrimental to the war effort.[29] Other Black newspapers and periodicals continued their coverage of episodes of white mob violence and lynchings of Black people; nonetheless, this coverage remained closely monitored through the Espionage Act during the war.[30]

Some of Du Bois's writings related to the participation of Black men in the war, despite their racialized and segregated position in the United States, contextualize the dilemma shared with Mexican Americans regarding their war service and Sáenz's writings on the same topic.[31] Racial terror in the form of white mob violence and lynchings of Black men galvanized the formation of early civil rights organizations such as the National Association for the Advancement of Colored People (NAACP), along with its main publication, *Crisis*, one of the most widely circulating Black periodicals at the time. In his role as editor, Du Bois conceived *Crisis* as a means to disseminate his views and to organize against racial violence through social activism, which in its early years took the form of a "campaign against lynching and mob law ..."[32] Before the start of the mobilization period, Du Bois had written pieces in *Crisis* and other venues on whether Black men should serve in the army; in one often-quoted article titled "Awake America," published in *Crisis* in September 1917, Du Bois requests that the United States "enter this war for Liberty with clean hands" by acknowledging the lynchings of Black men and by "bow[ing] our shamed heads";[33] only then, according to Du Bois, "[could] we raise our weapons against the enemies of mankind, ... and pledge our sacred honor to make our own America a real land of the free."[34] Du Bois framed the participation of Black men in the war as a way to prove their loyalty to the United States in order to be granted full rights; he particularly linked Black men's service with "abolish[ing] Jim Crow ... ," ending the bias against Black people in the court system, and above all stopping the lynchings of Black men.[35] Part of Du Bois's argument consists of showing that Black men have contributed with their lives fighting for the United States since the formation of the country. Du Bois explains that in "five wars and now the sixth we black men have fought for freedom and honor. Whenever the American flag floats today, black hands have helped to plant it."[36] "Awake America" presents the dilemma and challenges of Black people as a racialized group in the United States when asked to serve despite the history of violence and disenfranchisement against them. Mexican Americans in Texas faced similar challenges, and in the case of Sáenz, he presents his war experience as evidence of belonging in the United States while setting aside the history of racialization of Tejanos, which prompted him to prove his loyalty in the first place.

Sáenz describes the contributions of Tejano soldiers during the war by writing letters related to his first-hand experiences serving on the European front that were published in *La Prensa* for a Spanish-speaking readership. While teaching in San Diego, Texas, in the summer of 1917, he received the news that he had been selected to serve in the army shortly after the United States entered World War I. Sáenz served in the army from February 1918, when he started training at Camp Travis in San Antonio, up to his return to the same city in June 1919. During his service as a member of the 360th Infantry Regiment of the 90th Division, Sáenz was part of the U.S. military force that participated in battles during the war in the months prior to the armistice of November 1918. Sáenz's military service would probably have been noted along with the tens of thousands of Tejano soldiers who fought in the war; however, one of his distinctions was that he meticulously kept a diary of his time in the army that he published years later.[37] In addition, Sáenz also wrote and sent letters to *La Prensa* during the war in which he recounts the actions of Tejano soldiers on the battlefield. Sáenz saw the war as an opportunity for Tejanos to serve and prove their loyalty to the United States by sacrificing their own lives, which parallels the way Du Bois framed Black solders' participation in the war. B. V. Olguín has described how Sáenz, and other Mexican American veterans from subsequent wars, displayed excessive patriotic and nationalistic attitudes while enacting an "empowering heroic performance . . ." during their service in U.S. military wars.[38] Moreover, Zamora has studied the way Sáenz used his war service to make an argument for equal rights for Mexican Americans based on their courage and sacrifice during the war;[39] however, Sáenz's articles published in *La Prensa* describing his war experiences while still in Europe show the ways in which he, and editors from *La Prensa*, employ the tropes of patriotism, courage, and sacrifice to make an argument for belonging while at the same time downplaying the horrors of the battlefield and remaining silent regarding the ongoing discrimination of Tejanos in the army and in South Texas communities.

Sáenz's first letter related to his war experience in Europe published in *La Prensa* is framed by an editorial commentary that aims to showcase him as a U.S. patriot and exemplary citizen while his narrative seeks to highlight the contributions of Tejanos to the war effort. Sáenz's piece, titled "Demostraremos que somos dignos de ocupar un sitio en estos campos donde se lucha por un noble ideal" (Let's Demonstrate We Deserve a Place in These Fields Fighting for a Noble Ideal), was published on August 12, 1918, while he was in the Marne region in France waiting to march to the front. In these war letters, Sáenz describes Mexican Americans as "*méxico-texanos*" (Texas Mexicans), which reflects his early attempts to draw a distinction between U.S. citizens of Mexican origin and Mexican nationals living in Texas.[40] At the same time, Sáenz's letter is printed under the subtitle: "Un soldado americano, de origen mexicano, nos habla con entusiasmo de Francia y de la cause que fué a defender" (An American soldier, of Mexican origin, shares his enthusiasm about the cause he went to defend in France), which emphasizes a national allegiance to the United States.[41] Likewise, Sáenz's letter reflects his embrace of the United States' democratic ideals, which he finds akin to those shared by people in France. The letter connects war combat with sacrifice as Sáenz acknowledges that this may not be the time to write about "la actuación de los muchachos méxico-texanos que siguen a la bandera americana" (the actions of the Texas Mexican youth who have followed the American flag) since the war is still ongoing;[42] however, both Sáenz and *La Prensa* editors argue that Texas Mexican soldiers are already performing their duty; he explains that several of them "han caído ya . . . defendiendo un ideal que los hijos de la libertad consideramos legítimo y sagrado" (have already fallen . . . defending an ideal that we, the sons of liberty, consider legitimate and sacred).[43] Sáenz's letter uses the tropes patriotism, sacrifice, and the belief in the United States' noble cause that echoes the rhetoric of the Wilson administration that described the U.S. involvement in the war as a fight for liberty and democratic ideas.[44] Sáenz's letter is framed by introductory and concluding paragraphs by *La Prensa* editors that portray him as unconditionally committed to "la justicia de la cause aliada . . ." (the noble justice of the allied cause),[45] which differs from Du Bois's concerns regarding the sacrifices asked of Black men in the pages of *Crisis*.

In a following letter published in *La Prensa*, Sáenz describes the role of Texas Mexican soldiers on the battlefield for the most part as a patriotic cause despite the brutality of the war, which he deems as heroic rather than dehumanizing. In "El diario de un soldado méxico-texano" (The Diary of a Texas Mexican soldier), published in *La Prensa* on October 27, 1918, Sáenz recounts the events of a few days in September 1918 as his unit prepared and carried an assault on the German trenches, culminating with his first experience in combat. Sáenz emphasizes soldiers' heroic ethos by describing them as getting ready for battle and anticipating "nuestro día glorioso, el gran día de triunfo de nuestra causa" (our glorious day; the great day of triumph of our cause).[46] While Sáenz's letter mentions war weapons in the form of U.S. artillery, machine guns, and grenades, which characterized the horrors of trench warfare in Europe, he focuses on the heroic aspect of the allied assault on German positions in which he participated over a few days period. Notably, Sáenz makes a brief reference to the "metralla y las granadas de gases asfixiantes [que] no los detenían y continuaban siempre sin cejar su avance ganando más y más terreno..." (machinegun fire and the asphyxiating gas grenades that did not stop them as they continued, always without stopping, to gain more and more ground . . .).[47] Sáenz, however, appears to drastically minimize the use of poison gas on soldiers, which he described in his diary in 1933 as "one of the most sad and horrible results of the war."[48] In his diary, he describes how, due to the effects of poison gas, soldiers became "resigned to die, and even welcome it when a shell hi[t] them and we [couldn't] stop the hemorrhage. On the other hand, dying slowly from the poison in our lungs and the loss of our minds [was] horrible."[49] Sáenz's original omission in his letter perhaps is explained by the larger goal of emphasizing how Texas Mexican soldiers engaged in warfare and contributed to the war effort with their lives. This could be seen in another section of the article subtitled "Otro hecho heroico" (another heroic deed), in which Sáenz describes an American sergeant and a Texas Mexican soldier taking on a German machine gun located at the top of a hill, ultimately sacrificing their lives to achieve "victory."[50] Sáenz's letter in *La Prensa* directed to his Spanish-speaking readership, nonetheless, emphatically situates Texas Mexican soldiers in the European trenches, proving their loyalty to the United States and paradoxically several of them paying with their lives.

Sáenz's letter, "Los últimos días en las trincheras" (The Last Days in the Trenches), published in *La Prensa* on February 2, 1919, recounts some of the deadliest days experienced by U.S. soldiers leading to the Armistice of November 11 seeking to document the presence of Texas Mexican soldiers at this historical moment. Sáenz recounts a particularly deadly night for U.S. troops when, as dark set in, he witnessed "el más horroroso bombardeo que habíamos visto . . ." (the most horrific bombardment we had seen).[51] In a fast-paced account of several days leading to the armistice, he depicts German soldiers attacking, and U.S. soldiers counterattacking the following day as they advanced and eventually forced whole companies of German soldiers to surrender; however, Sáenz omits in his letter several of the harrowing events that U.S. soldiers experienced, such as the lack of medical treatment for wounded soldiers and the loss of a great number of soldiers that he would recount in his diary.[52] Instead, Sáenz's letter published in *La Prensa* omits setbacks by U.S. soldiers, opting for a heroic rendering of those events that echoes the patriotic rhetoric of previous letters. "Los últimos días en las trincheras" omits the heavy casualties of the 90th division; instead, he states that in the early days of November "[a]quí fué cuando el heroísmo de nuestros 'doughboys' rayó en lo sublime..." (here is when the heroism of our doughboys bordered on the sublime...). The emphasis on the courage of U.S. and Texas Mexican soldiers relates to Sáenz's goal of highlighting the latter's service as loyal citizens as he writes, "[m]uy contentos debemos estar por lo alto que han puesto nuestro prestigio racial muchos de nuestros connacionales. Han sabido llenar a conciencia los deberes de un ciudadano cumplido" (we should be very glad by the way our racial pride has been elevated by many of our people. They have fulfilled the duties of a conscientious citizen).[53] Sáenz describes this battle prior to Armistice Day, in which Texas Mexican soldiers have been of great value to "la más sagrada de las causas" (the most sacred of causes), and thus depicting the end of the war as a glorious achievement in which Texas Mexican soldiers took part.[54]

In one of his last letters to *La Prensa* during the war, Sáenz seeks to further document the presence of Texas Mexican soldiers in Europe as active contributors to the war effort. After the armistice, he describes a gathering organized by Texas Mexican soldiers from the 360th Infantry Regiment at the France-Germany border in his piece, "Una fiesta de los soldados méxicotexanos que se encuentran en Alemania" (A Celebration of the Texas Mexican soldiers in Germany), published on March 3, 1919. In an important gesture, Sáenz includes in his letter a list of fifty-one names of Texas Mexican soldiers who served in the 360th Infantry Regiment, thus creating a public record of these soldiers' service. His letter also includes a speech he gave to his fellow soldiers that presents a synthesis of his letters published in *La Prensa*, as he explains that their service during the war will serve as proof of their loyalty to the United States. Sáenz tells the gathering, "es la legitima satisfacción de haber cumplido con nuestro deber... Nuestros hermanos que allá quedaron al otro lado del Atlántico, esperan mucho de nosotros y estoy segure que[,] en esta ocasión, no hemos defraudado sus esperanzas" (it is a legitimate satisfaction to have performed our duty... Our brothers, who remained on the other side of the Atlantic, expect a lot from us, and I am sure that on this occasion, we have not disappointed them).[55] As in previous letters, Sáenz emphasizes their patriotic duty, as he notes, "[u]na vez más han dado los nuestros una demostración de su estoicismo y de su desinterés a la vida, cuando se piensa tan solo en el cumplimiento del deber..." (once again, we have demonstrated our stoicism and disregard for our lives, when the only thing that matters is the fulfilment of our duty...).[56] Significantly, he had yet to explicitly connect his war service with his fight for equal rights.

Instead, Sáenz sets the foundation to establish a link between the sacrifice of Texan Mexican soldiers during the war and his subsequent fight for equal rights, as racial segregation in Texas remained in place after the war.

THE EARLY MEXICAN AMERICAN CIVIL RIGHTS MOVEMENT AND LULAC LEADERS' CLAIM TO WHITENESS

Sáenz and other Texas Mexican soldiers returned from the war in Europe to the same segregated society in Texas enforced through racial violence despite their war service. Adam Hochschild has described in detail how the postwar years gave rise to white nationalism, English-only laws, anti-immigrant legislation culminating with the Johnson-Reed Immigration Act of 1924, the resurgence of the Ku Klux Klan, white race riots, lynchings, and even lynchings of Black soldiers in uniform.[57] When they were in the army, Texas Mexican soldiers were used and tolerated, but once the war ended, most of them returned to their racialized position in society and their status as second-class citizens. Some Texas Mexican soldiers used their military service to secure employment and other Mexican nationals who served in the army gained U.S. citizenship, but most Texas Mexican soldiers returned to a society still characterized by racial prejudice.[58] Years later, in an essay titled "Racial Discrimination," Sáenz recounted the segregation that Texas Mexican veterans encountered when they returned home. First and foremost, he was disappointed by the lack of recognition of Texas Mexican soldiers after the war but also lamented the continuing segregation of schoolchildren of Mexican origin and Juan Crow laws in public accommodations.[59] According to Sáenz, just as damaging as racial segregation in school, "[w]orse still is the denial to serve us in public places such as barbershops, restaurants, and theaters, etc."[60] He believed that the sacrifice of Texas Mexican soldiers would change racial attitudes toward them in South Texas; however, his own account of their experiences after the war shows he had underestimated what John M. González describes as "the warp of whiteness," or the forces woven into the fabric of U.S. society that maintained a white supremacist social order.[61]

The continuing racial violence against Texas Mexicans that accompanied Juan Crow segregation, including the lynchings of Mexicans and Texas Mexicans in Texas after the war, was particularly disturbing for Sáenz.

According to José Ramírez, "anti-Mexican violence [after the war] remained rampant. Between 1919 and 1930, at least ten Mexicans fell victim to lynch mobs in the United States."[62] Racial violence against Mexican and Texas Mexicans was a constant threat, particularly in South Texas communities, and more broadly across the Southwest. Tejanos in the Southwest continued to experience episodes of racial violence and were lynched at a rate similar to that of Black men, starting after the U.S.-Mexican War up to the 1930s, as "the chances of a person of Mexican descent being lynched were comparable to, if not higher than, those of an African American in the South."[63] Sáenz specifically refers in "Racial Discrimination" to the lynchings of Mexicans and Texas Mexicans after the war, lamenting the "[n]umerous abuses [that] were perpetrated on members of our race such as lynchings [and] persecutions . . ."[64] Other Texas Mexican veterans who became civil rights leaders, such as Perales, would similarly denounce the lynchings of Mexican Americans, particularly the lynching of Elías Villareal Zárate in Weslaco, Texas, in 1922.[65] Sáenz and other Tejanos lived in a society that enforced racial hierarchies not only through racialized laws but also racial terror. Although Sáenz's war letters published in *La Prensa* do not mention this racial violence, his approach and writings after the war, however, resemble those used by Du Bois and other Black writers in subsequent years.

The constant threat of racial violence against Texas Mexicans represented a local manifestation of a larger system of racialized control through violence, particularly in the form of white mob violence and the lynchings of Black men that contributed to the creation or reinvigoration of Black civil rights organizations after the war. Reminiscing about the World War I years, Du Bois notes that the war brought "an extraordinary exacerbation of race hate and turmoil. Beginning with increased lynchings in 1915, . . . and finally in 1919 the worst experience of mob law and race hate that the United States had seen since Reconstruction."[66] The Red Summer of 1919 and the eruption of white race riots in major cities such as Washington, D.C., and Chicago were partly a consequence of the war, as Black veterans returned home seeking job opportunities in northern cities.[67] Du Bois notes that the war created the first great migration of Black people to northern cities, but it also marked the first time that white and Black workers competed for the same types of jobs. In "Returning Soldiers," an article published in *Crisis* in May 1919, Du Bois recounts that after the war, Black veterans were mistreated, and at times attacked, despite their war service. Du Bois argues that

Black men showed their loyalty and "fought gladly and to the last drop of bloo[d] for America and her highest ideals...";[68] however, America "gloats in lynching, disfranchisement, caste, brutality and devilish insult..." against Black men.[69] Du Bois maintains that the country, "despite all its better souls have done and dreamed, is yet a shameful land."[70] Why is the United States a shameful land? Du Bois asks rhetorically; because "[i]t *lynches*... [a]nd lynching is barbarism of a degree of contemptible nastiness unparalleled in human history. Yet for fifty years we have lynched two Negroes a week, and we have kept this up right through the war."[71] Rather than despair, however, Du Bois and other Black activists, such as James Weldon Johnson and Ida B. Wells, continued to write and organize for civil rights through the NAACP, in part because Du Bois believed that the United States was their "fatherland" and the "faults of *our* country are *our* faults."[72] Just as Du Bois chose to fight racial violence with civil rights activism, some Mexican Americans who served in the war took their fight against segregation and racial violence by organizing for civil rights in Texas.

Despite the specter of racial violence against non-whites in Texas, World War I veterans such as Sáenz, Perales, and John C. Solis, among others, began to organize for civil rights with the assistance of Spanish-language newspapers, including *La Prensa*, which would culminate in the formation of LULAC in 1929. Among these Mexican American activists, Perales stands out for his relentless social activism through social organizing, speeches, and writings, including articles for *La Prensa*, in which he articulates his Mexican American identity, which, similar to Sáenz, was connected to his fight for equal rights.[73] In the summer of 1924, Perales and Sáenz partnered for a speaking tour in towns in South Texas, including Corpus Christi, Kingsville, and others cities in the Lower Rio Grande Valley. At those rallies, Perales and Sáenz spoke against Juan Crow segregation and the need for Mexican Americans to organize; for instance, in a joined statement after their speaking tour, Perales and Sáenz declared, "[we] are now convinced of the urgent need to do whatever we can to improve our intellectual, economic, political[,] and social condition and insist that society respect our fundamental rights..."[74] Spanish-language newspapers such as *La Prensa* covered the speaking tour and assisted in the dissemination of their platform and principles.[75] While Mexican American civil rights organizations began to emerge in Texas in the 1920s, Perales and Sáenz envisioned a unified and more active organization.[76] In a letter to Perales in 1927, Sáenz writes that a statewide organization "es el remedio que hemos encontrado tú y yo para la enfermedad de desunión que sufrimos como raza" (is the remedy that you and I have found against the disease of disunion that we have suffered as people).[77] Around the same time, Sáenz also began his advocacy for erecting a monument in San Antonio that would honor the Texas Mexican soldiers who died in France during the war, a project that was supported by Perales and reported in *La Prensa*.[78] Sáenz, however, failed to raise the fifteen thousand dollars in public donations needed, and the monument did not materialize. During the following years, Sáenz and Perales continued to organize and succeeded in bringing together other Mexican American organizations into LULAC.

From its start, LULAC sought the improvement of Mexican American social and economic conditions by taking advantage of their U.S. citizenship and by emphasizing patriotism and loyalty to the United States, which resulted in the controversial exclusion of Mexican nationals from the organization. LULAC's founding leaders, particularly Perales, Sáenz, and José Tomás Canales, brought together previously formed Mexican American civil rights organizations in Texas.[79] Part of the impetus for a statewide organization, based on some of the correspondence and statements of Perales and Sáenz and the LULAC Constitution, was the need to fight against racial discrimination; for instance, Article Two of the LULAC Constitution called for the "eradication from our body politic all intents and tendencies to establish discriminatio[n] among our fellow-citizens on account of race, religion, or social position . . ."[80] As part of their strategy, LULAC leaders emphasized their U.S. citizenship, which resulted in the exclusion of Mexican nationals living in Texas, who were also considered Tejanos, from the organization.[81] Some of the correspondence and statements by Perales and Sáenz as they formulated LULAC's principles show that while they valued U.S. citizenship and civic duty, this emphasis was related in part to their goal of protecting the rights of people of Mexican origin in Texas "regardless of citizenship."[82] LULAC became a major force in the fight for Mexican American civil rights in the following decades, particularly in the period between the two world wars, not only in Texas but also across the Southwest; however, scholars of Mexican American history who came of age during the Mexican American civil rights movement of the 1960s and 1970s, such as Juan Gómez-Quiñones, interpreted LULAC leaders' fight against racial segregation through the prism of their "pro-assimilation tendenc[ies]."[83] Other scholars, however, have studied the formation and platform of LULAC and some of its early leaders, rather than their leaders of the 1940s and 1950s, offering a more nuanced portrait of the organization.[84]

Since its inception, however, LULAC indeed fought in courts for desegregation, particularly of schools, by using the legal strategy of claiming the classification of "white" for Mexican Americans; this strategy, however, had a long and complex legal history in the Southwest.[85] Laura E. Gómez's remarkable *Manifest Destinies* historicizes and analyzes the intricacies of the Treaty of Guadalupe Hidalgo and its provision to grant U.S. citizenship to Mexican nationals in the newly conquered territories of the Southwest, while at the same time excluding Indigenous peoples.[86] Nonetheless, ever since the U.S.-Mexican War, Mexican Americans have undergone a process of racialization through the court system that has sought to strip them of their full citizenship rights. As María Josefina Saldaña-Portillo notes, the "treaty set the terms for the incorporation of the annexed population by racializing annexed Mexicans in relation to Anglo-Americans . . ."[87] Moreover, "the racial logic of the treaty," according to Saldaña-Portillo, set in motion attempts by Mexican Americans to "repress or deny their indigenous and afromestizo heritage . . ."[88] In a legal sense, U.S. citizenship was connected to whiteness, and court cases in the Southwest at the turn of the twentieth century influenced the ability of Mexican Americans to gain U.S. citizenship based on racial classifications as court battles drew racial lines on citizenship and segregation based on race.[89] Thus, part of LULAC's early and subsequent strategy to fight school segregation in courts was to develop legal arguments to preserve a form of "white citizenship."[90] Perales, one of LULAC's founders, participated in court cases, particularly the *Del Rio ISD v. Salvatierra* case in 1930 that sought to end the segregation of Mexican American schoolchildren in Texas;[91] however, LULAC's attempt to claim whiteness for Mexican Americans implied an erasure of their Indigenous ancestry, in what Saldaña-Portillo describes as a "Faustian pact with whiteness" since, due to the prevailing racial dynamics outside the courts, Mexican Americans remained racialized and segregated in the United States.[92] However, not all the early LULAC leaders participated in these legal court cases or shared a vision U.S. citizenship closely tied to whiteness, as exemplified by Sáenz's World War I diary in which he theorizes about his identity consisting of Mexican, American, and Indigenous influences.

SÁENZ, MEXICAN AMERICAN IDENTITY, AND INDIGENEITY

Sáenz's World War I diary is the only known war diary written by a Mexican American, and its publication history reflects the challenges of Latinx writers prior to the 1960s while attempting to publish their works.[93] Large numbers of memoirs and nonfiction accounts about World War I were produced between 1918 and 1941;[94] nonetheless, Sáenz's diary has seldom been included in literary scholarship on World War I.[95] One of the few texts about the war by an author of color discussed in literary studies is Victor Daly's novel *Not Only War*, published in 1932.[96] Sáenz's diary titled *Los méxico-americanos en la gran guerra* (The Mexican-Americans in the Great War) was published in Spanish in San Antonio in 1933 by Artes Gráficas, a publishing house of Spanish-language books with a regional reach.[97] Artes Gráficas, however, was not a traditional publishing house in the modern sense with editorial and advertising departments; instead, it consisted primarily of a commercial printing press.[98] Just like other Latinx writers in the early decades of the twentieth century whose works were published either by independent, regional, or alternative publishing houses, Sáenz's diary failed to reach a broader readership, due in part to mainstream publishers' gatekeeping practices. Sáenz, for instance, tried to publish an English edition of his diary with New York City publishers but was unsuccessful.[99] In his diary, Sáenz relates the timing for its publication with the violence directed at veterans in Washington, D.C., in 1932, when they protested for benefits but were violently repressed.[100] His ideological motivation to publish the diary was to commemorate the sacrifice of Mexican Americans during the war, as he argued, "[i]t is only right that when the last glorious chapter of our National American History is written we do not forget that *Mexican Americans* have made a contribution with their blood."[101] According to Sáenz's own account, he was able to publish his diary "against all odds," as he had to first advertise the publication of his diary by advanced subscriptions in order to gather the funds to pay for its publication.[102] It is due to Sáenz's effort, and the exceptional recovery work of Zamora, who translated along with Ben Maya, edited, and published the English version of the diary in 2014, that contemporary readers are able to appreciate Sáenz's literary legacy.

Sáenz's diary presents a critical view of the discrimination in the U.S. Army that fought a war under the banner of a united nation; however, instances of discrimination permeated his experience in the army. Sáenz's diary does not thematize the discrimination he and countless other Mexican Americans encountered in the army as, contrary to Black soldiers, they served in integrated units. Instead, he minimizes most of these instances of discrimination as his intended goal is to highlight the sacrifice of Mexican American soldiers and make an argument for equal rights that was not yet developed in his letters published in *La Prensa* during the war. Also significantly, as the Spanish title of the diary implies, Sáenz now refers to Texas Mexicans as "Mexico-Americanos," an early iteration of the term "Mexican American," which reflects his evolving ethnic identity discussed at several instances in his diary.[103] Initially, Sáenz explains that serving in the army created a space in which discrimination and racial animosity were suppressed for the larger goal of winning the war. In some of his early experiences at Camp Travis, Sáenz recounts how even prejudiced whites of German origin now had to "march besid[e] [him] as [they met] the most exalted duty before man";[104] however, also from the start of the diary, he recounts episodes of discrimination in the army that he describes only in passing. Sáenz, for instance, refers to his life living under Juan Crow in South Texas and the "We don't serve Mexicans here" signs; nonetheless, he is thankful that those signs do not apply to him while in the army.[105] As the diary progresses, it is evident that discrimination is present in the army and its practices. When Sáenz begins to work as a typist for a captain while still at Camp Travis, one lieutenant asks him, "with the greatest sarcasm imaginable": "Is this letter written in Spanish or Mexican?"[106] Sáenz's superior perhaps is insinuating a distinction with racial and cultural connotations that associates the Spanish language with education and whiteness in contrast to his dark skin and Indigenous features. The same lieutenant exclaims out loud, "'You can't get a thing out of this kind of greaser.'"[107] Sáenz does not respond, but he recounts thinking about this "a great deal" and later regretted he "did not respond as [he] wished."[108] Sáenz excels at his typist job, thus challenging stereotypes of Mexican Americans as unskilled or uneducated; he explains, "[m]y white buddies have never seen a Mexican like me challenging them over a job like this and their pride does not allow them to accept it."[109] Thus, Sáenz's diary shows a tension between his goal of highlighting the contributions of Mexican American soldiers to the war effort while at the same time being racialized in the army.

Sáenz's diary similarly describes the lack of opportunities for educational advancement and promotion for Mexican Americans in the U.S. Army; despite the army's attempts to place soldiers from different ethnic groups in leadership positions, Sáenz never received an opportunity for advancement. Early in the diary, Sáenz hears that all soldiers are given the opportunity to apply for officer's school, but most soldiers in his unit do not believe this applies to Mexican Americans. He applies regardless, but he is not selected.[110] Sáenz's frustration is reflected in his narrative since the U.S. Army gave opportunities to immigrants and soldiers from various ethnic groups such as Germans, Italians, and Polish to become officers;[111] however, the army still racialized most Mexican American and Black soldiers. Sáenz secures a desk job because he is bilingual; then in France, he learns French by himself, which allows him to type messages for officers in English, Spanish, and French. After the armistice, Sáenz writes about U.S. officers on the European front leaving for the United States to attend university or to fill a better position available to them.[112] Despite his language skills, however, he confesses, "I had been denied the opportunity to study at a French or English university because I was a private."[113] Instead, while stationed in Germany after the armistice, the army selects him to teach English to Mexican American soldiers. After he applies to college in England for a second time, and he is again denied, a more resentful Sáenz explains that "[f]avoritism is at play; it is nothing more than a farce common to the military. Its unfairness, nevertheless, encourages me to fight for what is just without expecting anything from the government."[114]

Sáenz fights racialization by articulating a Mexican American identity that emphasizes ethnic pride and group solidarity as reflected by his use of the term "*la raza*" (our people), which acts as an affirmation of a group identity shared by people of Mexican origin in the United States.[115] In his diary, Sáenz specifically addresses his choice of "the term *raza*" since he acknowledges it encompasses a heterogenous community rather than a strict racial or ethnic category.[116] For Sáenz, "*la raza*" works as a group identification that unites Mexican American soldiers in group solidarity regardless of their race or ethnicity, as some of them could be considered white due to their Spanish or European background. His diary attempts to present Mexican American soldiers as part of one community united by shared social justice goals. For example, he is grateful that some Mexican Americans "have moved up the ranks to positions of honor. This speaks well for our *raza*."[117] After the armistice, Sáenz interprets the victory of the U.S. Army as a collective effort that included Mexican Americans who "held the name of our *raza* high."[118] Rather than arguing for the assimilation of people of Mexican origin into the United States through their army service,

Sáenz presents a distinct articulation of a Mexican American identity, as he argues that it was precisely their war service that allowed them to claim their rights in the United States as members of an ethnic group that is both Mexican and American. For instance, in a letter to his wife before his regiment moves to the front, Sáenz writes "[a]s long as the horrible and longstanding prejudice continues in Texas against our *raza*, our happiness will never be complete.... The fight for the rights of the oppressed gives us the opportunity to claim justice for the humiliations and difficulties we often face because we carry the indelible characteristics of our *raza*."[119] Nonetheless, Gabriela González correctly observes that in the early decades of the twentieth century, "la raza never was a unified entity but rather an imagined community..."[120] Indeed, Sáenz's diary reflects the complexity and tensions of affirming a Mexican American identity that can be both individually and collectively accepted.

An additional dimension of Sáenz's Mexican American identity developed in his diary relates to his embrace of his Indigenous ancestry.[121] Notably, it is primarily in his diary where he articulated this aspect of his identity. As Zamora observes, Sáenz "did not fully incorporate his indigenous identity into his discourse on Mexican rights";[122] nonetheless, this theorizing about his Indigeneity in his diary remains significant, as it complicates narratives regarding early LULAC leaders of the 1930s as seeking whiteness through the court system. Sáenz grew up learning about his Indigenous ancestry from his father, who believed their family traced his roots to Indigenous peoples from the Aztec civilization of central Mexico who migrated north up to Texas at the time of the conquest.[123] In an unpublished essay titled "Mi linaje Azteca" (My Aztec Lineage), Sáenz recounts a trip to Tamaulipas, Mexico, where a historiographer confirmed the story he heard from his father. Sáenz writes in "Mi linaje Azteca," "[e]ntonces veo que bien corrobora toda la parte de tradición que me narraba mi padre. Los aztecas de que yo desciendo entraron por el Golfo México, no al principio de la colonización del continente de sus primeros padres, sino cuando se derrumbó el Imperio de los Aztecas" (Then, I corroborated the story that my father told me. The Aztecs from whom I descend came from the Gulf of Mexico, not at the beginning of the colonization of the continent of the first forebearers, but rather after the Aztec empire crumbled).[124] Whether or not this account is rooted in historical accuracy, Sáenz embraces an Indigenous identity throughout his diary, as when he refers to himself as belonging to "the stoic Aztec race."[125] In another instance, he states, "I am Aztec through and through."¹²⁶ Sáenz's emphasis on his Indigenous ancestry also contains references to Mesoamerican historical figures; on one occasion during his time at the front, when shells are falling on him, and some Mexican American soldiers begin to falter, he notes that their dire circumstances "will test the mettle of the descendants of Xicotencatl and Cuauhtémoc," two of Mesoamerica's most prominent historical figures.¹²⁷

Among the Indigenous references and allusions in Sáenz's diary, none is more prevalent than the historical figure of Benito Juárez, a Mexican president of Indigenous background, who led the resistance against the French invasion of Mexico in 1861. According to Zamora, Sáenz deepened his knowledge of Mexican history due to the mentorship of newspaper editor Eulalio Velázquez who introduced Sáenz to the life of Juárez.¹²⁸ Sáenz held on to those lessons when he became an educator; for example, as a teacher in Texas before the war, Sáenz participated in a commemoration honoring Juárez, reported in *La Prensa* in 1915.¹²⁹ In the diary, Juárez stands as a towering historical figure of Indigenous background who ascended to the Mexican presidency in defiance of Mexico's own racial hierarchies, which had continued to racialize Indigenous people despite José Vasconcelos's formulation in the early decades of the twentieth century of Mexicans as part of *La raza cósmica* (the cosmic race) consisting of a mixing of races.¹³⁰ Sáenz refers to Juárez as "the model historical figure of our people" and as an anti-imperialist who fought and expelled the French when they tried to invade and rule Mexico.¹³¹ When referring to Juárez, Sáenz often mentions Juárez's hometown, San Pablo de Guelatao, in the state of Oaxaca, Mexico, to accentuate Juárez's Indigenous background, as Oaxaca remains one of Mexico's states most closely associated with Indigenous cultures and communities. In a gathering of Mexican American soldiers, Sáenz explains, "[a] few of us Aztecs . . . recalled the invincible Indian of San Pablo de Guelatao and his many sacrifices that are worth emulating."¹³² Moreover, Sáenz celebrates Juárez as a symbol of Indigenous resistance. Days before the start of his first combat experience at the front, he explains that this "should not frighten the descendants of the Indian from Guelatao who confronted the first cannon and flintlocks with slings and clubs."¹³³ Thus, Sáenz uses the idealized figure of Juárez to connect the war experiences of Mexican American soldiers with what Sáenz believed to be their Indigenous past.

Sáenz's emphasis on his Indigenous identity is distinct in relation to the history of racialization of the Southwest in which, from the start of the period of territorial expansion after the U.S.-Mexican War, members of the

Mexican American elite in those territories benefited from their recently acquired U.S. citizenship and "white" legal classification while rejecting or distancing themselves from the Indigenous elements of their Mexican identities.[134] Nonetheless, it is necessary to contend with the idea that Sáenz's emphasis on Indigeneity in his diary participates in the reconstruction and celebration of an Indigenous history and culture that remains inaccessible and is mainly idealized. Scholars of Latinx Indigeneity have studied the complex histories of Mexican Americans and Indigenous peoples in the Southwest since the region's formation and how these groups found themselves racialized in the U.S. context, while at the same time Mexican Americans attempted to climb U.S. racial hierarchies by reneging their Indigenous background and seeking whiteness through U.S. citizenship and the courts.[135] Based in part on this legacy of racialization in the Southwest, in which Mexican Americans also participated through the racialization of Indigenous groups, Sáenz seems to develop his own notion of Indigeneity to distinguish it from traditional notions of either Native peoples in the United States or Indigenous peoples in Mexico. In his essay "Racial Discrimination," published years later, Sáenz presents a version of Vasconcelos's cosmic race that sees all Mexicans as part Indigenous or mestizos but not necessarily "Indian." Sáenz explains, "[b]y Mexicans we mean all Indo-Americans or Amerindians regardless of whatever other blood may run now in their veins";[136] that is, he prefers the terms "Indo-Americans" and "Amerindians" rather than "Indians." This perhaps explains why at several times in his diary, Sáenz describes Mexican Americans as "Aztecs" rather than Indians; for example, in describing the state of mind of Mexican American soldiers, he explains that the "soldiers of my *raza*, the noble Aztec *raza*, do not falter";[137] in this and other instances, Sáenz's own mixing of his Mexican and Indigenous backgrounds may represent an idealized identification of Mexican Americans as sharing an Indigenous background; nonetheless, not all Mexican Americans fighting in the war considered themselves as having a shared Indigenous past.

In some of his writings, Sáenz seeks a historical lineage with early Indigenous people of Mesoamerica; however, he is less comfortable describing Mexican Americans as people of "Indian" ancestry. In his essay, "Racial Discrimination," Sáenz sheds light on his resistance to the term "Indian," as he dismissively suggests it is a misnomer since in "the so-called New World there were never INDIANS only Aborigines. . . . Any fifth grader knows that Columbus did not find India or the Indians he was looking for."[138] As Saldaña-Portillo notes, however, the term "Indian," more than a misnomer, had negative connotations among Mexicans and Mexican Americans due to the history of racialization and anti-Indigeneity on both sides of the U.S.-Mexico border.[139] Historically, according to Saldaña-Portillo, Mexican identity has consisted of openly distancing from any "Indian" ancestry, while at the same time embracing or celebrating an Indigenous past.[140] Moreover, Sáenz connects the term "Indian" to what he conceives as Indigenous peoples' history as colonized subjects from the start of the European conquest of the American continent. Sáenz, for instance, describes the early European colonization of the Americas as follows: "Spain destroyed the most advanced people and their civilization, took possession of their land, and killed countless members. Those who survived were brutally forced to labor for three hundred years; France exploited them likewise; the English, after grabbing their land, adopted the policy: 'The only good Indian is a dead Indian.'"[141] In an unpublished Spanish version of the same essay, Sáenz adds that from the beginning of the conquest of the Americas among European antagonists, "se fomentó el prejuicio y el odio salvaje hacia el elemento nativo" (prejudice grew along with a hideous hatred towards its Indigenous element);[142] therefore, his diary creates a counternarrative of Indigenous peoples as conquered and instead presents Mexican Americans of "Aztec" background as active participants of world conflicts. Whether Sáenz is purposely attempting not to describe himself as "Indian" or is proudly Indigenous, his embrace of a racial and ethnic mixing is distinct at a time when the racialization of non-whites, including Indigenous people in the Southwest, was maintained by both whites and Mexican American elites.

Sáenz's embrace of his Indigenous identity allowed him to develop a sense of ethnic solidarity with Native people in the United States through their shared social histories as racialized groups while fighting in the U.S. Army. Zamora has discussed Sáenz's attempts to create a connection between Native soldiers from Oklahoma during the war through what Sáenz perceived as a shared Indigenous ancestry.[143] While Sáenz in his diary calls Indigenous people in the United States "Indians," he connects Mexican American and Native soldiers from Oklahoma through their ancestral claims of the American continent as "the true Americans in our nation."[144] Significantly, Sáenz describes both Mexican American and Native soldiers as oppressed and marginalized groups in the United States fighting for basic rights. While at Camp Travis, he speaks with "Indians from Oklahoma" and discovers that they "are clear about the part they are to play in the Great War. It largely parallels our own. We, the Mexican Americans, are going to war fully conscious of our decision and cherishing in our hearts the hope for a better future for our people who have been unjustly treated and scorned for so long."[145] At another instance, Sáenz attends a performance after the armistice by "a group of 'Indians' from Oklahoma" that contains "scenes of the disappearing race and accurate depictions that tell us of their efforts to survive as the aboriginal *raza* of America.... Many of the Indians who are fighting for the nation are not treated like citizens, but they will demand it when they return."[146] Indeed, according to Ned Blackhawk, some Native activists demanded equal rights, specifically U.S. citizenship, "by evoking the heroism of Native soldiers" during World War I.[147] Moreover, the diary contains an instance when Sáenz initially mistakes Native soldiers for Mexican American soldiers. After sharing some of their experiences, he acknowledges the even more precarious position of Native peoples since they are not "being recognized as citizens" of the United States and concludes by noting that Mexican American, Native, and Black soldiers have assisted in the war effort.[148]

While Sáenz aptly connects the fight in Europe with the social position at home by both Mexican American and Native peoples in the United States, he fails to make the same connection when it comes to Black people, even when racialized practices and open discrimination, in different degrees, affected both Mexican American and Black soldiers in the army. Mexican American civil rights leaders of the 1930s were not exempted from racial prejudice; Perales, for instance, invoked the alleged hierarchy of races while denouncing segregation of Mexican Americans in Texas, conceding that while whites were at the top, Mexican Americans, given the same opportunities, could "surpass the descendants of other races..."[149] Sáenz and Perales, however, were not anti-Black.[150] These two early civil rights leaders made their lives' goal to fight against segregation and the unequal treatment of Mexican Americans rather than supporting or condoning racial hierarchies or the segregation of Black communities. In contrast, white segregationists in Texas in the 1930s attempted to segregate Mexican Americans along with Black people; this explains why Perales opposed in letters to state officials their attempt to classify Mexican Americans as "people of color" in Texas and instead wanted them to "classify Mexicans as White."[151] In the case of Sáenz, and his engagement with Black soldiers in the army, Black soldiers are absent from the diary for the most part due in part to their segregation in Texas and in the U.S. Army. While Sáenz mentions Black soldiers in his diary, they remain distant, and when they appear, it is mostly in their role as performers; for example, while at Camp Travis before sailing for Europe, he notes that a "band of black men" came from a nearby camp to perform, or toward the end of his deployment, when he attended a "minstrel show with song and dance by blacks from the south";[152] ultimately, his diary fails to engage with the plight of Black communities under Jim Crow and the segregation of Black soldiers in the army that Sáenz himself experienced in different degrees.

Sáenz's diary is significant not only for his deployment of Indigeneity to fight racialization but also as a conscious articulation of his Mexican American identity and ethnic pride in the early decades of the twentieth century. His diary is equally invaluable to Latinx literary history, as it reflects how a Mexican American writer, almost a hundred years ago, interpreted his Mexican American identity and attempted to define his multiple subjectivities in the United States. Although Sáenz's plan to create a monument to preserve the memory of Mexican American soldiers failed to materialize, his diary as a form of literary and intellectual achievement succeeds in preserving the sacrifices of Mexican American soldiers during the war in Europe. While Sáenz's writings did not achieve the heights of Du Bois's during their lifetimes, both of their writings allow for a critical appreciation of their shared strategies when demanding the end of segregation and racial violence based on the service of Black and Mexican American soldiers respectively during the war. Sáenz's print contributions, along with his social activism for the equal treatment of Mexican Americans, based in part on their war service, represent early attempts at articulating a Mexican American identity based on their historical and social conditions. Similar to Black print culture in the early decades of the twentieth century, which served as an integral aspect of the fight for civil rights by Black writers and intellectuals, Sáenz's newspapers writings for *La Prensa* and his diary demonstrate that early Latinx authors also employed various print cultures and literary genres to engage in intellectual debates in relation to their place as Latinx people in the United States. While Du Bois's writings, social activism, and intellectual legacy have been an indispensable part of the history of Black intellectual thought, Sáenz's contributions are just beginning to be incorporated into Latinx literary and intellectual history.

CHAPTER 5

ADELA SLOSS-VENTO'S ARCHIVAL PRACTICES AND MEXICAN AMERICAN CIVIL RIGHTS

THE STUDY of Latinx literary and intellectual history at the turn of the twentieth century has traditionally centered on Latinx male writers and intellectuals; however, some Latina writers, journalists, and editors were able to transcend social, educational, and publishing barriers between 1880 and 1960. Either in Texas or New York City, Jovita Idar, Alice Dickerson Montemayor, Elena Zamora O'Shea, Julia de Burgos, Consuelo Lee Tapia, and Josefina Silva de Cintrón entered literary and intellectual discourses by writing in nontraditional book formats and in Spanish-language newspapers and periodicals. They argued for their inclusion not only within U.S. society but also within early Latinx social and cultural organizations in which they were often granted only a second-class status or were altogether excluded.[1] Early Latina writers published outside U.S. mass-circulation newspapers and became writers, columnists, and editors in Spanish-language newspapers and periodicals at a time when Latinas were expected to fulfill traditional family and societal roles.[2] Jovita Idar's work as a writer and editor exemplifies the relationship between Spanish-language print culture and social activism in Texas; Idar wrote editorials for *La Crónica* of Laredo, Texas, a newspaper started by her father Nicasio Idar in 1909, focusing on women's rights and the improvement of educational opportunities for Mexican American children.[3] Jovita Idar was also active in organizing

La Liga Femenil Mexicanista (League of Mexican Women), a feminist organization created during El Primer Congreso Mexicanista (First Mexicanist Congress),[4] an early civil rights organization based in Laredo, Texas, that preceded the League of United Latin American Citizens (LULAC).[5] Montemayor, another Tejana, participated in Ladies LULAC, the women-only councils within LULAC, and was one of the first Mexican American women to write articles in the male-dominated organization's publication *LULAC News*, in which she published short fiction and essays on the lack of women representation in LULAC during the 1930s.[6] Zamora O'Shea, a schoolteacher by training, became what John M. González describes as a "vernacular historian."[7] Her literary and historical interests resulted in the publication of her novel *El Mesquite* (1935) with a local press in Dallas, which sought to recover the histories of Mexican Americans in the Southwest dating back centuries.

Puerto Rican women writers in New York City in the early decades of the twentieth century similarly contributed to the development of Latinx cultural production and early notions of Latinidad not only through books but also through their contributions as writers and editors of Spanish-language newspapers and periodicals. Burgos, one of the most important Latina poets of her period, lived and wrote in New York City at different times until her premature death in 1953. In addition to her volumes of poetry published in Puerto Rico, Burgos served as the art and cultural editor for *Pueblos Hispanos* in New York City and wrote essays for the same publication during the 1940s concerning the prejudices and exclusion faced by Puerto Ricans in the United States.[8] Lee Tapia also worked as an editor for *Pueblos Hispanos* and wrote columns for the same publication advocating for women's rights, was a member of the Communist Party, and a militant activist in New York City for Puerto Rican independence.[9] Silva de Cintrón founded and became editor of *Revista de Artes y Letras* (Magazine of Arts and Letters), one of the earliest Spanish-language monthly journals, published from 1933 to 1945 in New York City with a focus on culture and the dissemination of the work of *Hispano* and Latin American authors.[10] Similar to Bernardo Vega's *Gráfico*, another cultural magazine based in New York City, *Revista de Artes y Letras* focused on news, social issues, and cultural developments pertaining to Spanish-speaking readers in New York City. While scholars have made significant inroads in highlighting the contributions of early Latina writers, intellectuals, and social activists, their writings, both in Spanish-language and alternative print publications, they are yet to be fully incorporated within early Latinx literary and intellectual history.

In this chapter, I analyze the writings and archival practices of Adela Sloss-Vento as representative of the efforts of early Latinas in their roles as writers, chroniclers, and intellectuals despite their limited opportunities to enter literary and cultural debates but also within male-dominated Latinx communities, publications, and organizations. Sloss-Vento inserted herself into Latinx literary and intellectual history through her archival practices and writings, both in English and Spanish, in the form of newspaper writings, correspondence with the major male figures of the early Mexican American civil rights movement, and specifically through her *book-archive* on the movement's leader Alonso S. Perales, which chronicles, documents, and historicizes the rise of Mexican American civil rights activism in Texas from the 1920s after World War I to the passing of Perales in 1960. Sloss-Vento participated not only in the background as an archivist, amateur historian, and chronicler of the movement but also at the forefront writing letters and editorials for Spanish-language newspapers and publications, particularly for *La Prensa* of San Antonio, fighting against racial discrimination and the racialization of Mexican Americans in education, politics, and society in Texas.[11]

Due to the rigid gender roles ascribed to Mexican American women, Sloss-Vento did not participate as an organizer or as a member of Ladies LULAC; instead, her involvement revolved around her extensive correspondence on civil rights issues, particularly with the three main LULAC founders: Perales, José de la Luz Sáenz, and José Tomás Canales between 1927 and 1960. One of Sloss-Vento's most active periods relates to her participation, through her writings and correspondence, in the campaign against the Bracero Program, as it disproportionately affected Mexican Americans' economic prospects in South Texas. Sloss-Vento's archival practices are displayed at length in her book *Alonso S. Perales: His Struggle for the Rights of Mexican-Americans* (1977), a blend of biography, historical narrative, and archival recovery that I describe as a *book-archive*. Sloss-Vento uses the book format not only to chronicle and honor the legacy of early civil rights leaders but also, just as significant, as a figurative archive that seeks to recover, collect, and engage within her narrative with documents consisting of newspaper articles, columns, reviews, pamphlets, reports, and personal correspondence related to the movement. Her archival practices closely resemble similar efforts by pre-1960s Afro-Latinx and Black writers to preserve past histories for future generations.[12]

My analysis of Sloss-Vento's social activism and literary legacy builds on the works of Latina scholars who have recovered and studied pre-1960s Latina writers and intellectuals in the United States, especially in Texas and New York City.[13] This chapter is particularly indebted to the foundational scholarship of historian Cynthia Orozco and her studies on LULAC, its early leaders, and Sloss-Vento in particular, that have shed light on the social, political, and cultural legacy of the early Mexican American civil rights movement in Texas.[14] I began by studying Sloss-Vento's archival practices as described and implemented in her *book-archive* to argue for the singularity and significance of her work in her attempt to preserve the legacy of the movement and its leaders for subsequent generations. I argue that Sloss-Vento's *Alonso S. Perales* does not simply participate in the biography genre by focusing on Perales, but rather her book creates a space for Sloss-Vento to challenge U.S. historiography by accentuating the presence and exclusion of Mexican Americans in the Southwest through the historical figure of Juan N. Cortina, as mediated through Canales's pamphlet *Juan N. Cortina: Bandit or Patriot?* (1951). I then study how Sloss-Vento was not simply a chronicler of the movement working in the background but rather an engaged activist and participant in the movement through her various writings—including newspaper articles, correspondence, and a nontraditional book—and other activist roles that she sometimes emphasized in her book and at other times omitted. I explore one of Sloss-Vento's most active periods as a participant in the movement through her writings and correspondence during the campaign against the Bracero Program and its negative economic effects on Mexican Americans in South Texas; however, her critique also reflects some of her anti-immigrant views on undocumented Mexican workers. Her writings and opinions were imbued with the conservatism, Catholicism, and patriotism characteristic of Mexican American civil rights organizations and some of their leaders prior to the 1960s. Sloss-Vento's *book-archive* attempted to bridge the historical gap between the early movement and the emerging Chicanx Movement of the 1960s and 1970; while her efforts on this front were unsuccessful, Sloss-Vento's writings reveal that the fight against social, political, and cultural disenfranchisement by both movements was one and the same.

SLOSS-VENTO'S *BOOK-ARCHIVE* AND THE RECOVERY OF MEXICAN AMERICAN HISTORY

Latina writers, journalists, and social activists before the 1960s encountered significant obstacles to advancement due to the rigid social and gender roles ascribed to them, both within and outside their communities, and their lack of educational opportunities. Before the 1960s, segregation in Texas affected all aspects of Mexican Americans' lives including education; however, Mexican American women in South Texas were particularly constrained by their limited social and educational opportunities.[15] As a result, few Tejanas graduated from high school and even fewer of them went on to receive bachelor's degrees.[16] The reduced educational opportunities for Latinas limited their abilities to participate in social, cultural, and political discourses. As a result, Tejanas in the early decades of the twentieth century lacked publishing opportunities with mainstream and even local presses, as exemplified by the case of Leonor Villegas de Magnón, who was unable to publish her memoir, *The Rebel*, in her lifetime.[17] Likewise, Jovita González's novels were only published posthumously even though she had a master's degree and famously enlisted a white female co-author for the publication of her novel *Caballero* without success; another of her novels, *Dew on the Thorn*, remained unpublished in her lifetime.[18] A few Latina writers, such as Zamora O'Shea and Cleofas M. Jaramillo, were able to publish their books with local Texas presses. Similar dynamics influenced the publishing opportunities of Latina writers on the East Coast. Pre-1960s Puerto Rican women writers in New York City did not publish their books with mainstream U.S. publishers. Luisa Capetillo and Julia de Burgos, for instance, published their books in Puerto Rico in Spanish;[19] they did not publish books with U.S. mainstream publishers even after they became writers and activists on the mainland.

Sloss-Vento's social activism and writing career closely coincides with the emergence of the early Mexican American civil rights movement in South Texas. She was born in Karnes City, Texas, in 1901, and after a series of family relocations within the Rio Grande Valley, and due to the social and educational conditions for Mexican American women in Texas that impeded a traditional education, she wasn't able to graduate from high school until 1927. Around this time, a number of Mexican American soldiers who experienced the mobilization period during World War I had begun to organize social and civil rights organizations to improve the conditions of Mexican Americans in the state and to fight against racial discrimination. Sloss-Vento learned about the social activism of Perales and Sáenz from a newspaper article written by Perales and published in *El Fronterizo* of Rio Grande City in July 1927.[20] Despite societal and educational barriers, Sloss-Vento began corresponding with Perales beginning in 1927 about the importance of organizing for civil rights, and in the early 1930s, she wrote pieces in Spanish-language newspapers and periodicals on the importance of Mexican American social organizations and voting rights. She married Pedro C. Vento in 1935 and, after living in different cities in South Texas, the family settled in Edinburg, Texas, where she worked as a jail matron while still remaining active as a writer and activist.[21] As an author, Sloss-Vento remained at a disadvantage in relation to some of her Mexican American male counterparts who received teaching certificates, bachelor's, and law or graduate degrees.[22] Nonetheless, she continued to write on the same subjects for decades, reaching a high point with the publication of her book on Perales's legacy and the early Mexican American civil rights movement.

While Sloss-Vento's *Alonso S. Perales: His Struggle for the Rights of Mexican-Americans* makes Perales the central figure, her book does more than to serve as a biography of Perales; instead, her book functions also as a figurative depository or archive of collected printed sources regarding the history of the movement. As a nontraditional book, Sloss-Vento's *Alonso S. Perales* is distinct for various reasons; first, Perales died in 1960 at a time when he and Sloss-Vento were still corresponding, and she had already gathered a significant amount of archival material on Perales and the movement; however, her book was not published until years later in 1977 by Artes Gráficas, the same printing house located in San Antonio and used by Sáenz and Perales to publish their books.[23] Another element of her book is her admiration and emphasis on Perales that diminishes her own writings and participation in the movement. Part of these dynamics relates to the biography genre and its reliance on male historical figures overrepresented in mainstream publishing. Similarly, Sloss-Vento's focus on Perales conforms to the "great man" narrative, which according to Maylei Blackwell, also permeated the historiography of the Chicanx Movement.[24] Sloss-Vento's book, however, is more than a biography of Perales, as it posits collecting and archival practices at its center by not only engaging with primary sources but also embedding them throughout the text, as she reprints archival materials consisting, for example, of personal correspondence with local activists. Sloss-Vento's book serves at least three main intertwined functions: first, as its title implies, it is a biography, albeit incomplete, of Perales and his role as leader of the movement and founder of LULAC; second, the book seeks to document the contributions to other early leaders of the movement, not only Perales; and lastly, her book functions as a figurative archive of the early fight for Mexican American civil rights.

Sloss-Vento's *book-archive* consists of newspaper articles, columns, pamphlets, and letters incorporated into the body of her book with minimal framing or analysis seeking to preserve and serve as a depository of the legacy of Perales and the movement. Her book includes a "selected bibliography" consisting of books, newspaper articles, correspondence and other primary sources that appear standard judged by today's publishing and academic practices; however, in the 1970s, Sloss-Vento was one of the few writers participating in the collection and preservation of primary sources pertaining to Mexican American history.[25] Orozco has discussed Sloss-Vento's "role as archivist," since the sources she used for her book were known to her due to her intimate knowledge as a participant in the movement; some of those sources were part of her own archive since university libraries at the time lacked Mexican American collections.[26] Sloss-Vento's collecting and recovering practices in the early decades of the twentieth century resemble those of Arturo Schomburg and other Black collectors, as they sought to preserve books, newspapers, periodicals, and pamphlets pertaining to the Black literary and historical past that had been neglected or excluded from cultural institutions and university libraries.[27] Similar to the way the archival practices of Schomburg created what Adalaine Holton aptly describes as a "counter-archive,"[28] Sloss-Vento's *book-archive* sought to counteract mainstream historical narratives about the history of Mexican Americans in the Southwest. Schomburg and Sloss-Vento were early pioneers of the field of Latinx archival research, but while Schomburg made the recovery of the Black diasporic past one of his main focuses in his lifetime, his collection serving as the basis for one of the most important research centers of Black studies in the United States, her collecting practices are of a more modest scale since, as Orozco notes, she was a "grassroots archivist without training in library science or professional archival practices."[29] Nonetheless, Sloss-Vento thought of herself as a documentarian whose efforts resulted in a personal archive that constitutes what María Cotera describes as a "composite text" that contains an "unwritten history of intellectual labor" and challenges the gaps in the official archive.[30] Thus, Sloss-Vento's collecting and archival practices embedded in her book are not secondary; rather, they are the book's raison d'être.

The structure, composition, and chapters' content of Sloss-Vento's *Alonso S. Perales* present a mix of primary print sources framed by her narrative, reflecting its nontraditional form representative of some early Latinx books. Sloss-Vento, for instance, quotes extensively from her correspondence with Perales and other male leaders throughout the book, seeking to emphasize the function of her book as a depository of collected documents. In the preface to her book, she states that the documents and sources used belong to her own archive as she "has gathered materials, such as newspaper clippings, articles, correspondence, [and] books of the hard and long struggle of the three leaders, especially that of Alonso S. Perales who dedicated his life in the struggle for the rights, advancement and justice of the Mexican-Americans."[31] Sloss-Vento similarly notes early in the book that in writing about Perales, she is relying on her personal correspondence with him from 1927 until his death in 1960.[32] The book's distinct structure and organization relates in part to Sloss-Vento's hesitancy to fully claim her role as writer due to her lack of credentials not only vis-à-vis a white publishing industry but also in relation to the male-dominated Spanish-language print culture at the time.[33] In addition to the book's preface, Sloss-Vento also wrote a prologue that was deleted in which she states, "[t]his author asks the forgiveness of the reader in view she is not a writer."[34] Ultimately, rather than a traditional analysis or historical narrative, her book reads in part as a compilation of primary sources included in the body of the text with minimal framing or contextualization. In doing so, Sloss-Vento perhaps sought to emulate Perales's own practice in his books, particularly the first volume of *In Defense of My People*, of compiling his previously published newspaper writings, personal correspondence, and other public documents. As a result, Sloss-Vento participates in nontraditional publishing dynamics similar to other early Latinx writers such as Perales and Jesús Colón.

Sloss-Vento's archival practices emphasize the importance of Spanish-language newspapers published in Texas before 1960 not only as documentation for her book but also because she was one of the early Mexican American writers who theorized about the significance of Spanish-language print culture in preserving the Mexican American past in Texas. In her book's preface and in other sections, Sloss-Vento argues that Spanish-language newspapers were integral to the early fight for Mexican American civil rights; she mentions a number of Spanish-language publications from Texas and credits two of their editors, Ignacio E. Lozano of *La Prensa* of San Antonio and Santos de la Paz, the editor of *La Verdad* of Corpus Christi.[35] Sloss-Vento acknowledges *La Prensa* for publicizing the leaders' meetings, public speeches, and particularly for serving as an outlet for their letters and editorials; she describes *La Prensa* as "our right arm, carrying the message, the needed inspiration for the struggle of our people."[36] In making this point, Sloss-Vento emphasizes the bias against and erasure of Mexican Americans in English-language newspapers in Texas. She quotes Perales, who asserts that not a single English-language newspaper in Texas focused on the concerns and the discrimination against Mexican Americans in Texas at the time; he observes that with the exception of the *McAllen Monitor* and *The Daily Texan*, the latter published by students at the University of Texas, he has "never read or known of any newspapers or Anglo-American editorials that have condemned the problem of race discrimination against the people of Mexican [o]rigin in the State of Texas."[37] While Sloss-Vento aptly gives credit to *La Prensa* for its role in the movement, she does not mention that some of her own letters and writings were published in this and other newspapers, particularly after the creation of LULAC in the early 1930s.

Sloss-Vento's *Alonso S. Perales* recovers the history of Mexican Americans in the Southwest, particularly by reinterpreting the historical figure of Juan N. Cortina based on Canales's pamphlet. Early sections in her book trace Mexican Americans' struggle against racial discrimination to the history of exclusion and racialization by white settlers during the decades following the U.S.-Mexican War. Sloss-Vento's engagement with the historical Cortina is significant since in Canales's account, Cortina is transformed from a Borderlands "bandit," as portrayed in mainstream historical narratives, to a figure of resistance of mythical proportions for Mexican Americans in Texas. According to Sloss-Vento, Cortina encapsulates the history of "racial and cultural discrimination, exploitation, and injustice" toward Mexican Americans and their land dispossession after the Treaty of Guadalupe Hidalgo.[38] In relation to Sloss-Vento's archival practices in her book, she bases her discussion of Cortina on Canales's pamphlet *Juan N. Cortina: Bandit or Patriot?*, published in 1951 by Artes Gráficas.[39] In relation to the nontraditional aspect of her book, she bases her account on Cortina from Canales's pamphlet by quoting entire paragraphs; thus, allotting most of the chapter's space to Canales. Sloss-Vento quotes from Canales's pamphlet extensively to show the racialization of Mexican Americans through laws and the courts system. Canales's pamphlet, for instance, contains quotes from Walter Prescott Webb's *The Texas Rangers* (1935) to document that, at the time of Cortina's actions, "[o]ne law applied to [Mexican Americans] and another, far less rigorous, to the political leaders and to the prominent Americans."[40] After the Treaty of Guadalupe Hidalgo, Mexican Americans of every class, according to Canales, were looking for a leader "who would throw off American domination, redress grievances, and punish their enemies," and they found him in Cortina.[41] Sloss-Vento concludes her chapter by arguing that Cortina's story "is proof of the persecution against Mexican-Americans, and the courage of individuals as Cortina to fight for the injustices of the underdog";[42] thus, her engagement with Canales's pamphlet reflects the ways in which her book both recovers and challenges the prevalent, white-dominated history of the Southwest.

Sloss-Vento rehabilitates the historical figure of Cortina, as Canales did before her, since Cortina offered an opportunity to challenge the historiography of the Texas Borderlands that emerged during the early decades of the twentieth century, as she presents Mexican Americans as active participants in Texas history. John M. González has characterized the cultural, literary, and intellectual production of Mexican American writers in the early decades of the twentieth century as a "Border Renaissance" and a counternarrative to "pervasive anti-Mexican discourses that had historically circulated throughout Anglo-Texas."[43] While Canales was not a trained historian, his compelling rendering of Cortina's actions in his pamphlet resembles the scholarly work of Américo Paredes and his recovery of the historical figure of Gregorio Cortez in *"With His Pistol in His Hand,"* also written in the 1950s.[44] Aaron Sánchez argues that Canales's engagement with Cortina follows a pattern by Mexican American writers who recovered historical characters and transformed them into figures of resistance to challenge mainstream historical narratives.[45] In the case of Cortina, Zamora O'Shea also wrote a pamphlet on Cortina that Sáenz translated but which remained unpublished.[46] These writers and intellectuals reclaimed the figure of Cortina for its symbolic power for Mexican Americans, just as other Mexican American communities and writers across the Southwest have reinterpreted the lives and actions of other "bandits" and "outlaws," such as Joaquín Murrieta and Tiburcio Vásquez.

Sloss-Vento's *Alonso S. Perales* interprets Cortina's resistance against white settlers as an antecedent of the same fight for Mexican American rights that gained momentum after World War I and was led by activists like Canales. Sloss-Vento in her book refers to Canales's efforts to "denounce[e] the Texas Rangers for [the] crimes they committed along the border" against Mexicans and Mexican Americans in the aftermath of El Plan de San Diego.[47] Before his involvement as one of the LULAC founders, Canales served in the Texas State legislature in 1919, when he called for an investigation on the indiscriminate murders of Mexicans and Mexican Americans at the hands of the Texas Rangers.[48] Sloss-Vento is one of the early Mexican American writers who wrote about the significance of Canales's courageous acts, as he initiated an investigation that included a series of hearings at the Texas State Legislature in which he was the sole legislator who presented evidence against the Texas Rangers for their racial violence and extrajudicial killings of Mexicans and Mexican Americans.[49] The trait that Sloss-Vento emphasizes about Canales is his courage in the face of great danger after publicly denouncing white state officials; she notes that "[a]fter having taken those actions, the life of [Canales] became in danger. Often, he had to sleep in jails for security."[50] Sloss-Vento's discussion of Canales's writings and his actions as state legislator, however, omits references to his extensive social activism; she simply includes an anecdote from one of their conversations when she asked Canales why he continued to write and speak about Cortina after his "persecution," to which he simply responded, "[f]or the privilege of stating the truth."[51] Sloss-Vento's extensive use of quotes from Canales's pamphlet in her narrative without contextualizing his writings and social activism is representative of the structure of her book, as it is based on extensive use of primary documents, in this case Canales's pamphlet, that covers most of the chapter with minimal intervention by Sloss-Vento.

SLOSS-VENTO INSERTS HERSELF INTO THE HISTORY FOR CIVIL RIGHTS

Sloss-Vento describes the emergence of the early civil rights movement led by Perales, Sáenz, and Canales during the 1920s and 1930s as a continuation of the fight against discrimination and racialization exemplified by

Cortina but also as a struggle in which she becomes an active participant. She posits racial discrimination at the center of the movement as she states, "[o]ne of the greatest obstacles of the people of Mexican descent and against Mexican-Americans, was racism, especially cultural and economic discrimination."[52] Sloss-Vento's *Alonso S. Perales* chronicles the events that led Mexican American social activists, some of them World War I veterans, to organize after the war for a state-wide civil rights organization resulting in the formation of LULAC in 1929. Sloss-Vento adds that early leaders united on behalf of Mexican Americans in Texas who have "suffered humiliation, exploitation, and other injustices..."[53] As a result, her *book-archive* recovers this history by focusing on the three main leaders that made it possible—Perales, Sáenz, and Canales—since according to Sloss-Vento, they sought to "unite our people, to urge them to fight for their rights in an effort to end the abuses, the injustices, the humiliations";[54] however, her book is not a detached account of this history, but instead it contains the personal account of her own participation in the movement and her correspondence with these three leaders from 1927 to 1960.

The structure of Sloss-Vento's nontraditional book allows her to insert herself into this history as an active participant and writer during the movement. Critical assessments of her book have both overlooked and circumspectly engaged with her placement in the narrative; for instance, Arnoldo Vento's introduction to his mother's book does not mention the extent to which she positions herself as a participant within its history; instead, Vento praises her portrayal of Perales and presents the book as a study that "provides a glimpse into the real social, economic and cultural conditions affecting the Mexican-American people of Texas."[55] In contrast, Donna Kabalen de Bichara has identified autobiographical elements in Sloss-Vento's book.[56] Indeed, Sloss-Vento portrays Perales as the most significant leader of the movement, as several of her book's chapters build upon this premise, and historians such as Orozco have similarly established Perales's indisputable role as the leader of the early fight for civil rights in Texas;[57] however, in the first paragraph of the book, Sloss-Vento inserts herself first by using the first person, "I," which is more apt for the memoir genre, to denote her own involvement in the movement and personal acquaintance with Perales; for example, she writes, "[i]t was 1927, when I became an enthusiastic corroborator [*sic*] on behalf of the cause of the Mexican American."[58] While the word "corroborator" may denote her involvement merely as a chronicler, this is most likely a typo since in the next paragraph, Sloss-Vento states that her involvement consisted of a "collaboration" with Perales,[59] and subsequent sections throughout the book suggest that she was more than a peripheral participant since the early years of the movement.

While the genre of Sloss-Vento's *Alonso S. Perales* most closely resembles the biography of a "great man," it also documents the extent of her participation. In the deleted prologue, she states that "[s]he has been a collaborator for the Mexican American cause and through the years has defended that same cause as directed" by Perales, Sáenz, and Canales.[60] While this statement minimizes her involvement and suggests that her role is one of subordination to male leaders waiting to receive their orders, as her narrative progresses, it is possible to discern the degree to which Sloss-Vento inserted herself into her narrative on Perales, not only as a chronicler, or as "collecting data,"[61] but as an active participant even before the formation of LULAC. In the book's third chapter, Sloss-Vento continues to use the personal pronoun "I" when she states, "[t]his writer met [Perales], his best friend Prof. J. Luz Sáenz, and Mrs. Marta Engracia Pérez de Perales in 1927. This was the year I had just finished high school."[62] Sloss-Vento similarly describes the details of their encounter and how she read an editorial written by Perales in *El Fronterizo* of Rio Grande City "concerning the racial discrimination that existed against the Spanish-speaking people" in Texas.[63] She recounts writing to Perales and receiving an invitation to visit him at his law office in McAllen where she meets Perales, Sáenz, and Marta Perales; according to Sloss-Vento, "[i]t was at this meeting that I became inspired to collaborate with our leaders in favor of our cause."[64]

Sloss-Vento's involvement during the early years of the movement gave her first-hand knowledge regarding events that led to the formation of LULAC, which in turn she used to act as a documentarian of the movement. Based on her collecting of Spanish-language newspapers as evidence and her own testimony, Sloss-Vento's book establishes Perales as the indisputable leader of the movement based on his role during the formation of the League of United Latin Americans, an early predecessor of LULAC, in Harlingen, Texas, in 1927.[65] According to Sloss-Vento, all started with Perales, who was then joined by Canales and Sáenz; Perales then called for a "reunion at Harlingen" and invited Bernardo "Ben" Garza of Corpus Christi who led the Sons of America and the Kings of America, two other Mexican American organizations that preceded LULAC.[66] According to

Sloss-Vento, "[t]hese three leaders constantly made trips and worked among our people with regard to their rights. They held meetings, reunions, wrote to the different newspapers. They spoke before the law and defended our people from all kinds of injustices."[67] Moreover, Sloss-Vento inserts herself into this history by including her correspondence with Perales regarding these events; likewise, she includes an article from *La Prensa* from May 20, 1931, in which she praises Perales for his efforts, which in turn she includes as evidence and as part of her archive.[68] At the end of her chapter appropriately titled "Documentation on the Founding of LULAC," Sloss-Vento alludes to Perales's own attempts to document through correspondence the origin of LULAC toward the end of *In Defense of My People*; she paraphrases Perales stating, "my records are at the disposal of anyone who wishes to examine them in regard to the truth that I have stated."[69] Thus, the structure, content, and intent of Sloss-Vento's genre-defying book situates her as both chronicler and active participant in the movement.

Sloss-Vento's *Alonso S. Perales* contains a narrative tension related to her authorial voice, as she at times presents herself as a participant in the movement primarily through her archival practices and correspondence with leaders, but at other times, she minimizes, and at times omits, her involvement as activist and writer. One of LULAC's top priorities during its early years was education through its fight against the segregation of Mexican American schoolchildren. Perales, Sáenz, and Sloss-Vento agreed on the need to improve educational opportunities for Mexican American schoolchildren in South Texas;[70] for instance, Sloss-Vento, along with Sáenz and others, participated in a committee created in Mission, Texas, in 1930 that sought to contest "la segregación de esos escolares de las aulas públicas" (the segregation of those schoolchildren in public schools).[71] In addition to her activism against school segregation, Sloss-Vento notes in her book, "I wrote several times in the newspaper [*La Prensa*,] which at the time was our right arm in informing and organizing the Mexican-Americans toward solutions of our many problems."[72] But rather than including her newspaper writings of the 1930s, Sloss-Vento minimizes her involvement by simply mentioning these events in the abstract; moreover, among the several letters and pieces she wrote for Spanish-language newspapers, she only mentions one published in *La Prensa* on May 20, 1931, in which she praises Perales.[73] The basis of this article is a letter Sloss-Vento sent to *La Prensa*; the published article portrays her both as a supporter and active participant in the movement, as it concludes by stating, "[Sloss-Vento] aboga por que todos los ciudadanos de descendencia Mexicana se unan fuertemente y materialicen acertadamente el noble ideal del autor de la Liga de Ciudadanos Unidos Latino-Americanos" (Sloss-Vento advocates that all citizens of Mexican descent create a strong bond and strive to achieve the noble ideal of the creator of the League of United Latin American Citizens).[74] *La Prensa*'s description of Sloss-Vento is one of a committed activist in the fight for civil rights, writing and urging Mexican Americans to join the movement; however, this version of herself is absent for the most part in her book.

During the next few years following the formation of LULAC, Sloss-Vento continued to write letters to newspapers and editorials pertaining to voting rights and the place of Mexican American women in a male-dominated society, which are absent in her book. Her reticence to discuss her contribution to the movement seems puzzling, especially because she is one of the few Tejanas who wrote essays, editorials, and opinion pieces in Spanish-language newspapers since, as Orozco observes, "Mexican American women had limited access to getting published in the press."[75] Sloss-Vento, for example, wrote a letter to *La Prensa* that was partially printed in the article titled "La Política del Mexico-Americano" (The Politics of the Mexican American) in May 7, 1932, a piece that exhorts Mexican Americans in South Texas to vote and gain representation in local government. Sloss-Vento is quoted encouraging Mexican Americans to learn about the U.S. political system and exercise their rights; according to the article, "[l]a autora de estas opiniones considera que uno de los principales pasos que deben dar los votantes méxico-americanos para adquirir mayor prestigio y fuerza y estar capacitados para el ejercicio de sus deberes cívicos, es instruirse lo más que pueden sobre ciencia política . . ." (the author of these opinions believes that one of the most important steps that Mexican American voters can take, in order to gain recognition and strength, and be able to exercise their civic duties, is to educate themselves in political science as much as possible . . .).[76] Subsequently, Sloss-Vento published opinion pieces for *La Prensa* on similar topics, including Mexican American voting rights and civic duty. In her *La Prensa* article titled, "Sobre el votante latinoamericano" (On the Voter of Latin American Origin), of September 13, 1934, Sloss-Vento criticizes political patronage and the buying of votes by politicians in exchange for favors; her editorial seeks to educate Mexican Americans on the importance of voting as a civic duty as when she states, "[n]osotros como ciudadanos Latino-americanos guardamos el orgullo de considerarnos primeros ciudadanos de estos lugares, y como primeros ciudadanos deberíamos estar más aventajados en el deber de cumplir como ciudadanos aptos y bien preparados" (We, as citizens of Latin American descent, pride ourselves on being the first citizens of these lands, and as such, we should be more conscientious about our duties as well-informed citizens).[77]

During LULAC's early years, Sloss-Vento remained a major supporter of the organization's political goals despite its male-centered structure since the basis for her support can be discerned based on one of the few articles she wrote for *LULAC News* in March 1934, which, although it focuses on women's dissatisfaction in their marriages, upholds men's position of authority within their families.[78] As Orozco notes, Sloss-Vento did not join LULAC through a Ladies LULAC council, the gender-segregated groups for women in LULAC.[79] Sloss-Vento's LULAC piece titled, "Why There is no True Happiness in Many Latino Homes," focuses on the conditions of women within Mexican American families, which offers insights into her gender views and the role of women within Mexican American communities. Scholars have correctly interpreted Sloss-Vento's *LULAC News* article as a piece arguing for Mexican American women's rights;[80] nonetheless, her piece does not sufficiently challenge gender hierarchies, as it maintains men's position as the head of the household. Sloss-Vento begins her article by noting that "[s]ince childhood," Mexican American women are "imprisoned" because of customs and live in a society where Mexican American men have "all the privileges and rights."[81] According to Sloss-Vento, Mexican American men at the start of a relationship are encouraged to court women, but after marriage, men's attitudes toward them change. She argues that the husband "should beautify the home with loyalty and good intentions receiving her with joy and contentment; instead[,] he converts it into a prison for her. The result is that the wife begins to feel lonely and disappointed."[82] Sloss-Vento considers whether Mexican Americans should emulate the white household since it offers more freedom to women and goes as far to argue that in the white household, a woman is a man's "companion and not a slave."[83] A white woman in marriage, according to Sloss-Vento, "enjoys equal privileges and the husband is careful not to offend her with bad behavior."[84] Despite overstating the position of white women in their households, Sloss-Vento makes a compelling case for the position of Mexican American wives; her message, however, is not for women's empowerment but for men to improve their marriages by seeking to "be more honorable, good and kind" to their wives.[85] Sloss-Vento's interpretation of women's role in marriage, and within the community at large, aligns with her social activism practices and writings; she corresponded with and supported male leaders from the sidelines rather challenging the gender hierarchies within the movement, a dynamic clearly present during Sloss-Vento's collaboration with male leaders.

SLOSS-VENTO AND THE CAMPAIGN AGAINST THE BRACERO PROGRAM

Sloss-Vento's involvement during the movement increased during her years-long campaign against the Bracero Program during the late 1940s and early 1950s and reached its apex during the public meeting to protest the so-called "wetback pamphlet," which she organizes along Perales and Sáenz. Sloss-Vento devotes an extensive part of *Alonso S. Perales* to the Bracero Program in part because Perales led the effort against it in Texas, but also because she was an active participant in the campaign. The Bracero Program represented the U.S. solution to the shortage of laborers and farmworkers created by World War II; the program began in 1942 and continued after the war until 1964. During the early years of the program, hundreds of thousands of Mexican nationals came to work in the United States, primarily in the Southwest.[86] From the U.S. perspective, the Bracero Program provided an almost unlimited supply of Mexican laborers coming to the United States to work primarily in agricultural fields, which created winners and losers; the winners were the U.S. government and agribusinesses that relied on a low-wage labor force for their own economic profit, which explains why the program remained in place after the war. The losers were mostly Mexican American farmworkers in the Southwest. Sloss-Vento, along with Perales and Sáenz, was against the Bracero Program because it deprived Mexican Americans of economic opportunities, as they were forced to compete for the same low-wage agricultural jobs. According to Sloss-Vento, the "Bracero contracts as well as the heavy influx of thousands of aliens, served to displace American workers of Mexican descent along the Texas border, as well as other parts of Texas and other States."[87] Nonetheless, in their attempt to protect Mexican American workers, civil rights organizations, such as LULAC and the GI Forum, were not only against the Bracero Program, but they also targeted their critiques on undocumented Mexican workers who also came to work in the United States during those same years.

The late 1940s and early 1950s stands as the period when Sloss-Vento and Perales worked most closely and corresponded more regularly, as they found common ground in their critique of the Bracero Program. As early as 1947, Sloss-Vento was corresponding with Perales and other concerned parties describing in detail the negative effects of the Bracero Program on Mexican Americans in Texas.[88] Her knowledge of the Bracero Program was derived from her personal experiences living in the Borderlands region in Edinburg, Texas, her readings of Spanish-language newspapers, and her deep-rooted desire to improve the conditions of Mexican Americans. Around that same period, for example, Sloss-Vento wrote to Perales sharing how her desire to assist Mexican Americans contrasted to her husband's lack of enthusiasm for civil rights causes, as she confesses, "tengo un esposo que . . . no habla en favor de nuestros derechos" (I have a husband who . . . does not speak up for our rights).[89] When describing her opposition to the Bracero Program, Sloss-Vento includes in the body of her book entire letters that Perales sent to religious leaders on "the labor problem."[90] Also in her book, she recounts sending Perales newspaper articles on the Bracero Program, and Perales writing her back expressing his concerns on the "problem."[91] Sloss-Vento even recounts writing to President Dwight Eisenhower in 1954 on the same topic and receiving a letter from Perales encouraging her actions by stating, "I congratulate you for having sent valuable information upon the subject to President Eisenhower."[92] When it came to the campaign against the Bracero Program, Sloss-Vento was no longer the passive chronicler of the movement that she sought to portray herself as in the earlier sections of her book; instead, she was a participant in the economic and political debates to end the program.

An unsettling aspect of Sloss-Vento's public campaign against the Bracero Program is her parallel critique of undocumented Mexican workers coming to the United States, whom she considers just as detrimental to Mexican Americans' economic prospects as braceros, or even more. Sloss-Vento, Perales, and Sáenz, were not only against braceros but also considered undocumented workers "illegal[s]" and a "problem" for the United States.[93] While scholars have discussed Sloss-Vento's contradictions regarding her views on immigration, there is a tendency to minimize her writings and negative views on this topic.[94] Donna Kabalen de Bichara, however, has engaged with Sloss-Vento's "conflicting views" on the Bracero Program and undocumented workers and has quoted from her correspondence to acknowledge her involvement in "a discourse that labels Mexican citizens as undesirables."[95] During the period of Juan Crow segregation in Texas, Sloss-Vento considered undocumented Mexican workers an additional social burden for Mexican Americans; she believes that they "added to the already existing racial discrimination and prevented an expeditious solution to our economic, social and political problems and to the general welfare of the Mexican-Americans."[96] Some of her writings on this topic during this period contain instances of anti-immigrant rhetoric and acceptance of anti-immigrant tropes, such as the belief that undocumented workers have brought "problemas como son los robos y crímenes" (problems such as robberies and crimes) to Texas towns.[97] Likewise, in an unpublished essay titled "Problems in the Lands [sic] of America: the Wetback Problem," Sloss-Vento describes in a nuanced way the exploitation of undocumented workers by agribusinesses and the low wages they receive that affect all farmworkers in South Texas; nonetheless, in the same essay, Sloss-Vento attempts to prove that undocumented Mexican workers account for the increased number of murders and crime in the region.[98]

Just as Sloss-Vento saw undocumented workers as a "problem," some of her writings make an argument that the real culprits for the lack of economic opportunities for Mexican Americans are the agribusinesses and employers who benefit from the exploitation of farmworkers whether they are Mexican Americans, braceros, or undocumented workers. In her book, Sloss-Vento acknowledges that U.S. agribusinesses were primarily responsible for the increase of undocumented workers since they used the shortage of workers during the war years as an excuse to continue the Bracero Program, but the reality was that they "were growing rich by exploiting the illegal Mexican workers as well as Braceros."[99] Moreover, in some of her writings of the period, she advocates for stiff penalties and fines for the businesses and employers who benefit from the low wages in agricultural regions in the Southwest. In an unpublished essay, "The Wetback Problem: A Harmful and Costly Problem," Sloss-Vento contends that it "is absolutely necessary that stricter laws be passed imposing heavy penalties to farmers, packing shed owners and other places that profit and exploit the undocumented worker."[100] In other instances, Sloss-Vento shows a more empathetic view of undocumented families; while denouncing the deplorable housing conditions which unscrupulous employers provide to braceros, she writes about a sick child of an undocumented worker she tries to help.¹⁰¹ Despite her negative views on undocumented workers, Sloss-Vento considers the possible benefits for Mexican Americans once undocumented Mexican workers increase in numbers in the United States; she notes that "new generations of Mexican descent [children] will come out from the illegal migration who no longer will be aliens but American [c]itizens. Our minority in the future will constitute the majority. Apparently we say in Spanish[:] 'No hay mal que por bien no venga' [every cloud has a silver lining]; a saying of a long suffering and patient people."¹⁰²

Their shared critique of the Bracero Program created an exchange of ideas between Sloss-Vento and Perales; however, it was their correspondence regarding the public meeting to protest the so-called "wetback pamphlet" of 1951 that further inserts her into the movement. In *Alonso S. Perales*, Sloss-Vento uses a substantial amount of space discussing the "wetback pamphlet," the name used at the time for the study titled *The Wetback in the Lower Rio Grande Valley of Texas* by Lyle Saunders and Olen Leonard that contained a foreword by George I. Sánchez, published by the University of Texas in 1951. As one of the few Mexican American faculty members at the University of Texas at the time, and a former LULAC President, Sánchez similarly contributed to the campaign against the Bracero Program and undocumented workers; Sanchez's foreword to the pamphlet starts by arguing that "[o]ne of the most serious problems facing the people of Texas is the presence . . . of wetbacks—illegal aliens who cross the border from Mexico mainly in search of agricultural employment but who are to be found in many cities of the state in many non-agricultural jobs."¹⁰³ Sánchez's biographer, Carlos Blanton, notes that Mexican American leaders in Texas at the time, including Sánchez, "lived in a world of contradictions" regarding their views on immigration and undocumented workers.¹⁰⁴ Sánchez's promotion of the pamphlet, according to Blanton, was derived from his agreement with the conclusions of the pamphlet's authors that sought to "uncove[r] an embarrassing wealth of racism toward Mexican people by Valley Anglos, racism that cut across class, profession, and education."¹⁰⁵ When Sloss-Vento learned about the content of the pamphlet in newspapers, she strongly denounced it not because it claimed to be a study on "illegal aliens" coming to the United States from Mexico, but to her dismay, the pamphlet contained "countless insults degrading all people of Mexican descent, Mexican-Americans and the Mexican people in general."[106] While seemingly overlooking her own views on undocumented workers, Sloss-Vento argues in her book that the pamphlet propagated stereotypes about Mexicans and Mexican Americans that increased whites' resentment and hatred toward them.[107] One of the most troubling aspects of the pamphlet for Sloss-Vento was that Sánchez, LULAC itself, and other Mexican American organizations, such as the GI Forum, led by Hector P. García, endorsed it.[108] By the 1950s, the early leaders of LULAC had left their roles in the organization, and as a result, Perales and Sáenz publicly denounced the pamphlet and Sánchez himself in letters and editorials in newspapers.[109]

The campaign against the pamphlet, which included Sloss-Vento as one of its leaders, represents one of the most compelling instances of her active participation in the movement. The meeting in Mission, Texas, on March 9, 1952, stands as the culmination of the campaign when Sáenz, Canales, and other leaders converged for a public gathering. Sloss-Vento omits in her book that she corresponded with Perales and Sáenz regarding the organization of the Mission meeting and acted as a major organizing force behind the scenes; Perales wrote a letter to Sloss-Vento encouraging her to contact Sáenz, who is also active in the protest against the pamphlet, and to work together since Sáenz needs "apoyo y ayuda" (help and support).[110] In another letter a few days later, Sloss-Vento writes to Perales saying she is willing to "ayudar con dinero" (help with money) and continue to work "undercover" in whatever is needed to make the protest a reality.[111] In her book, Sloss-Vento simply mentions that "she was ready to help with money and with publicity" for the protest;[112] however, she is the person who writes to Sáenz asking him to create a committee during the meeting when she suggests, "[n]o cree ud. que a medida que el pueblo se informe se debe formar un [c]omité o que se dirijan a ud. sobre que es lo qué se debe hacer" (don't you think that as our people learn [about these events], a committee should be formed or people should contact you about what is to be done?).[113] Her letters reflect the degree to which she often had to defer to male activists due to gender constraints that relegated her social activism to the sidelines. Sloss-Vento writes in her book that the protest in Mission, Texas, was a success and that a report was adopted at the meeting refuting in detail the pamphlet's findings and censuring the University of Texas, and Sánchez himself, for sponsoring the pamphlet; the report also concludes with a request that a copy is sent to the President of the University of Texas and its Board of Regents.[114]

While Sloss-Vento attempted to minimize her role in the organization of the Mission meeting in her book, reports about the meeting in newspapers and correspondence between her and some male leaders acknowledged her organizing efforts. In her book, Sloss-Vento identifies Sáenz and Canales as the principal speakers during the Mission meeting since Perales was not able to attend.[115] Sloss-Vento minimizes her participation even as one of the protest's participants describes her as their Doña Josefa Ortiz de Domínguez, a historical Mexican figure known for her contributions during the Mexican war for independence, which Sloss-Vento considers "a title [she] was far from deserving";[116] however, an article in *La Prensa* mentions her as one of the organizers.[117] In a similar manner, Canales in a letter to Sloss-Vento of June 1, 1952, expresses his admiration for her organizing efforts and uses the allusion she included in her book, "You are the true Doña [Josefa] Ortiz de Domínguez (the famous Corregidor of Texas). You have done more and are doing more to help the Latin Americans than any other person."[118] Sloss-Vento's sustained reticence to claim her leadership role in this campaign relates to her views that women needed to act within the parameters imposed by male figures in Mexican American communities at the time.

SLOSS-VENTO'S CATHOLIC HERITAGE, CONSERVATISM, AND THE POST-1960 CHICANX MOVEMENT

Catholicism, and more specifically Mexican Americans' Catholic heritage in Texas, enters the latter sections of Sloss-Vento's book and some of her other writings during the 1950s when she returns to her discussion on the historical presence of Mexican Americans in the Southwest dating back centuries. *Alonso S. Perales* engages with the scholarship of Carlos E. Castañeda, a Mexican American academic and intellectual at the University of Texas at the time.[119] Sloss-Vento's book discusses Castañeda's recovery of Mexican American history in the Southwest in the form of his multi-volume book, *Our Catholic Heritage in Texas: 1519–1936* (1936–1950);[120] in his book, Castañeda argues that the Southwest was first Spanish, then formed part of Mexico, and only much later became part of the United States. While

Sloss-Vento was attracted to Canales's recovery of the figure of Juan Cortina for his historical significance to Mexican Americans, Castañeda's scholarship on Mexican Americans' Catholic past represents for her another form of reclaiming Mexican Americans' rightful place in the Southwest. Sections of Sloss-Vento's book focus on some of Castañeda's historical writings and public lectures mediated by Perales in his *La Prensa* weekly column titled, "Arquitectos de nuestros propios destinos" (Architects of Our Own Destinies), published during the month of December in 1952.[121] According to Sloss-Vento, the goal of Perales's dissemination of Castañeda's scholarship for a general readership was to show "that our forefathers were the first settlers, the first Texans, and the first Americans in Texas, New Mexico, and many other places in this country";[122] however, she quotes Perales lamenting that Mexican Americans living in Texas at the moment, despite having "fought for liberty and helped Texas gain independence, . . . they have been made to feel like strangers in their own native lands."[123] Sloss-Vento believes that if Mexican Americans would become familiar with Castañeda's writings, "they would be well informed and prepared to respond to anyone who might think our ancestors came only yesterday."[124] As in previous sections of her book, Sloss-Vento quotes entire paragraphs in the body of her narrative from Perales's newspaper columns discussing Castañeda's work, thus deferring to Perales as a male authority on academic matters. At the same time, she inserts herself in the narrative only by mentioning her own experience attending one of Castañeda's lectures in Mission, Texas, in 1952;[125] however, this is a passing reference, which relegates her own experience listening to Castañeda's lecture to the background.

It is important to note that historical accounts on the presence of Mexican Americans in Texas made by Castañeda, Perales, and Sloss-Vento excluded Indigenous peoples and recent Mexican immigrants from Texas history, which is connected in part to claims to "whiteness" made by pre-1960s Mexican American civil rights leaders, including Sloss-Vento. Scholars have discussed how some Mexican American communities in the Borderlands at the turn of the twentieth century were attracted not only to their Catholic heritage derived from their Spanish background and ancestry but also by notions of cultural superiority and racial hierarchies in relation to Indigenous groups who also inhabited the Southwest.[126] In the case of Sloss-Vento, she considered herself a white person of Mexican descent; in an early newspaper article published in *La Prensa*, of January 8, 1928, Sloss-Vento is adamant about her belief that Mexican Americans are not "people of color" but white.[127] In the case of Perales, he seems more ambivalent in his columns on Castañeda's writings about the racial composition of these early Mexican American inhabitants of Texas, opting for a view of *mestizaje*, or racial mixing, as descending from "Catholic Kings" of Spain and "the invincible Cuauhtémoc," adding that it "was the mixture of these two great races, the fusion of their generous blood that formed a new Mexican people."[128] Sloss-Vento's interpretation of their Catholic heritage, however, disregards the Indigenous presence in the Southwest; for instance, she considers Castañeda's *Our Catholic Heritage* a book that refers to "the persecution of our people as well as to the traditions of our ancestors, who were the first to open the wilderness of Texas, New Mexico, and other states . . ."[129] Sloss-Vento's description of the Southwest before Spanish and Mexican settlers as a "wilderness," echoes Manifest Destiny historiography, and in part Castañeda's own historical narrative, which participates in the conception of territories west of the Mississippi as either empty grounds, or a wilderness with Indigenous populations who needed to be civilized.[130]

Catholicism influenced other aspects of Sloss-Vento's writings related to her interactions with male leaders of the movement and her views on the place of women in a male-dominated society. Mexican Americans' Catholic heritage was not just a historical lesson for Sloss-Vento; rather, Catholicism held a major sway on her and other early Mexican American civil rights activists.[131] Mario T. García has argued that Catholicism played a major role in pre-1960s Mexican American social movements, but those influences have not sufficiently been studied.[132] Sloss-Vento's *Alonso S. Perales* emphasizes at different moments that the fight against racial discrimination carried by Perales, Sáenz, and Canales emerged from their religious beliefs and was driven by God; for instance, she writes that the "great leaders like [Perales] have been called upon by God for such struggle. Although the struggle is like a [crucifixion], they know in their hearts that it is the only course that can free any people from exploitation and [oppression]."[133] In another of her discussions on the same topic, Sloss-Vento mentions the presence of a higher power guiding their fight for justice for Mexican Americans; she notes, "[t]hese leaders were persecuted by the enemies of our cause but nothing seemed to stop them . . . They seemed to be moved by an invisible spirit."[134] In her remembrance of Sáenz after his death in 1953 included in her book, Sloss-Vento writes that he was "able to put aside all his obstacles" since there was "no doubt that he was chosen by God to solve our problems."[135] Sloss-Vento's use of religious imagery in her writings in the form of a crucifixion, persecution, enemies, and a savior of long-lasting suffering people are used in reference to the actions of male leaders, which aligns with her deference to them throughout most of her narrative.

Sloss-Vento's writings are similarly influenced by the ideal of respectability, anti-communist attitudes, and an emphasis on American patriotism, which combined are reflective of her deep-seated conservatism.[136] Gabriela González argues that the ideal of "respectability" among Mexican American communities in the Southwest before the 1960s was essential to Mexican Americans who adhered to middle-class values such as respect for institutions and ideas of economic progress that included "an ideal of female domesticity and male breadwinners."[137] Sloss-Vento's writings reflect a conservatism that is informed by Catholicism and the idea of respectability that sheds light on some of her beliefs, shared by other Mexican Americans in Texas who were part of the middle class of white and Spanish descent, and are related to historical claims of the Southwest that excluded recent Mexican immigrants who were working class and more racially diverse. Likewise, respectability informed Sloss-Vento's views on feminism, communism, and patriotism that were also shared with early civil rights leaders;[138] for instance, in an unpublished essay titled "Two Evils from Within," Sloss-Vento warns that racial discrimination and economic exploitation represent "two powerful evils that are helping the Communists to weaken, to disunite and to destroy us from within."[139] The patriotic zeal of early leaders such as Perales and Sáenz, according to Aaron Sánchez, derived in part from their organizational strategy of tightening community ties and embracing a Mexican American identity that would differentiate them from *México de afuera* (a Mexican nation abroad) or Mexican exiles in Texas.[140] Sloss-Vento, for instance, uses at times the term, "Americans of Mexican descent";[141] that is, people who consider themselves "Americans" first who happened to be of "Mexican descent." At other times, when she praises the early leaders of the movement, she notes that "[t]heir patriotism and their faith in our democratic principles are ample proof of their true Americanism."[142]

Towards the end of Sloss-Vento's *Alonso S. Perales*, she argues that the early fight against racial discrimination and for civil rights in Texas led by Perales and other leaders was a precursor of the fight for Mexican American civil rights of the 1960s and 1970s. Sloss-Vento had at least two main motivations for publishing her book in the 1970s mostly at her own expense; first, she sought to document Perales's indisputable role as the main leader of the movement and founder of LULAC since after his death in 1960, she had to emphasize this point in different venues and publications using her archive and personal letters to prove it.[143] An additional reason for publishing her book was Sloss-Vento's emphasis on preserving the legacy of Perales and other early leaders for the new generation of social activists emerging in the late 1960s and early 1970s. As Orozco notes, Sloss-Vento is one of the few Mexican American writers who was able to bridge the generational divide between early leaders of the movement and an upcoming generation of Chicanx activists.[144] On her remembrance of Sáenz after his death included in her book, Sloss-Vento argues that "[i]t is necessary to note the sacrifices and constant struggles of the early civil rights leaders.... [Perales, Canales, and Sáenz] were the first three to fight, and we owe them our great step forward towards the progress and well-being of the Mexican-American people."[145] Likewise, Sloss-Vento's book contains a sustained argument for preserving Perales's legacy for a new generation of activists; she describes Perales as "a man of high moral ethics and principles who ... [r]ather than taking the easy road to financial and political success, he chose ... to struggle for the rights and advancement [of his people] during his lifetime..."[146] She believed that these early leaders had made great sacrifices and had risked their lives during the fight for civil rights, and she was one of the first writers who made a case for their legacies since Mexican Americans, according to Sloss-Vento, owed them "a great debt."[147]

Despite Sloss-Vento's various attempts to bridge the divide between the two generations of activists, she achieved modest success and encountered resistance as emerging leaders of the Chicanx Movement opposed the conservatism, patriotism, and claim to whiteness espoused by pre-1960s civil rights leaders and politicians in Texas. Orozco observes that after its publication in 1977, Sloss-Vento's book was modestly reviewed in Spanish-language newspapers, and she did not receive a response from José Angel Gutiérrez, one of the young leaders of the Chicanx Movement and founder of the Raza Unida Party in Texas in 1970, after she sent him a copy of her book.[148] Clearly, there was not only a generational divide but also a major ideological chasm between the conservatism of early leaders and the militant politics of the Chicanx Movement. For instance, Sloss-Vento was extremely circumspect in the way she questioned or challenged women's role in male-dominated Mexican American communities and particularly while inserting herself in the history of the movement; also, the role of Mexican American women in the movement are conspicuously absent in most of her writings. The contrast between Sloss-Vento, a Mexican American activist of the pre-1960s decades, and Chicana feminists and activists of the 1960s and 1970s cannot be more stark; Chicanx activists such as Anna Nieto-Gómez, for instance, openly challenged gender roles and the marginalized position of women in the Chicanx Movement;[149] likewise, Martha Cotera in her book *Diosa y Hembra* (1976) centers the histories of women in Mexican American history.

There is a conservative streak that runs through Sloss-Vento's writings pertaining to the role of women in a male-dominated society, undocumented workers, and middle-class respectability, which was precisely the type of conservative attitudes and political positions that Gutiérrez and other young Chicana activists resisted; nonetheless, Sloss-Vento's legacy as a writer, chronicler, archivist and civil rights leader remains indispensable. After decades of involvement in the movement, Sloss-Vento began to receive some recognition along with the early male leaders; for instance, a few years before his passing, Perales in his *La Prensa* column of July 18, 1957, acknowledges Sloss-Vento as "una gran líder de nuestro pueblo en el Valle Bajo de Rio Grande . . ." (a great leader of our people in the Lower Rio Grande Valley).[150] Sloss-Vento's writings reflect the forces that sought to relegate her to the background due to the position of women in a male-centered society while at the same time accurately reveal her place at the forefront of the fight against discrimination in Texas. Sloss-Vento's writings were not transgressive but very much aligned with the conservative ideologies and values characteristic of the early movement. Sloss-Vento, however, was unequivocally right when she argued in her book that the fight against racial discrimination and racialization taken upon by early civil rights leaders, including herself, was the same as the one taken by Chicanx activists; it is through her collecting, archival work, and writings that contemporary readers can appreciate those commonalities.

CHAPTER 6

RACIALIZATION AND THE U.S. OCCUPATION OF JAPAN IN AMÉRICO PAREDES'S WRITINGS

THE EMERGENCE of Latinx scholarship in the United States in the form of a book monograph is connected to the history of university presses and the long history of systematic exclusion of students and faculty of color dating back to the formation of the oldest universities in the United States.[1] The beginning of U.S. university presses mirrored exclusionary practices in the U.S. publishing industry that lacked representation of writers of color. Due to the way knowledge production emerged in the U.S. academy, scholars of color, including Latinx scholars, seldom entered academic discourses through the publication of academic monographs from university presses until recent decades. University presses were first established in the late nineteenth century with Cornell University Press (1869) and Johns Hopkins University Press (1878); other university presses, including the University of Chicago Press (1891), the University of California Press (1893), Columbia University Press (1893), and Yale University Press (1908), followed in subsequent decades.[2] University presses, as Kathleen Fitzpatrick states, "have as the cornerstone of their missions the publication of the products of scholarly research, for use by scholars in further research, bringing intellectual distinction to their institutions through their contributions to the advancement of knowledge in key academic fields."[3] These institutions and their fields of study, however, were Western-oriented and Eurocentric, and consequently knowledge production in the humanities by university presses reflected this ideological bent with few exceptions. Before the 1960s, there were few scholars of color and even fewer opportunities for them to publish their work with university presses. For example, Cornell, a university with a publishing infrastructure, hired its first Black tenure-track faculty member, J. Saunders Redding, in 1970. In addition, books by university presses included a peer-review process that added an additional hurdle for scholars of color that differed from the challenges present in commercial publishing. Thus, prior to the 1960s and the series of student-led protests that gave rise to the creation of Black and ethnic studies at colleges and universities, university presses for the most part served as gatekeepers that lacked incentives to publish scholars of color.

The historical dearth of academic monographs by Latinx scholars can be contextualized through the experiences of Black scholars prior to 1960. Historically Black Colleges and Universities (HBCUs) and their academic infrastructure remained the primary venue for Black scholars to publish and disseminate their work.[4] The group of Black scholars connected to the Harlem Renaissance during the 1920s and 1930s, including W. E. B. Du Bois, Alain Locke, Carter G. Woodson, Charles S. Johnson, and Sterling Brown, taught at HBCUs and, despite their exceptional academic credentials, did not publish books with university presses. Most Black scholars of the second generation of the 1940s and 1950s, such as Ralph Bunch and Lawrence D. Reddick, taught at HBCUs for most of their academic careers; however, a few of them became professors at selective universities, such as J. Saunders Redding, first at Brown and then Cornell, and W. Allison Davis at the University of Chicago.[5] Like in most cases of literary marginalization of authors of color, the exclusion of Black scholars from university presses contains a few exceptions, as in the case of W. Allison Davis. As a PhD from University of Chicago, Davis began his academic career at the same university and holds the distinction of being the first Black faculty member to earn tenure at the Predominately White Institution (PWI) in 1947. Davis was also one of the few Black scholars who published with an academic press.[6] Davis's book *Deep South* was published by University of Chicago Press in 1941; however, his monograph was co-authored with two white scholars who received most of the credit.[7] Despite his decades-long career, Davis did not publish another book with a university press. A more common experience for Black scholars is exemplified by Nick Aaron Ford, an English PhD from

Iowa State University, who taught at Morgan State University in the 1950s. As Lawrence Jackson recounts in his exceptional book *The Indignant Generation*, Ford tried to get his work published by an academic press for almost a decade. After a series of slights and racially charged reader responses and rejections by several editors of academic presses, Ford ultimately gave up.[8]

A few Mexican American writers and scholars before the 1960s worked primarily at PWIs in the Southwest and some of them were able to publish with university presses. In the early twentieth century, some Mexican Americans earned graduate degrees at PWIs, as in the case of Carlos E. Castañeda and Jovita González who earned MAs at the University of Texas, Arthur L. Campa who received a PhD from Columbia University, and George I. Sánchez who graduated with a PhD from University of California-Berkeley. As Emma Pérez notes, the writings and scholarly output of these writers were key in the development of a Chicanx consciousness in the 1960s and the study of Chicanx intellectual history in subsequent decades.[9] While most of these scholars had academic careers at PWIs, most of their academic works were published in academic journals or regional outlets with few exceptions.[10] Sánchez was able to publish *Forgotten People: A Study of New Mexicans* with the University of New Mexico Press in 1940; nonetheless, Sánchez, just as Black scholars of the same period, only published one book with a university press despite their long academic careers.[11] While larger factors were at play in the publication of academic books, such as student demographics, the small number of faculty of color, and the lack of an academic infrastructure for scholars of color, academic publishers were part of the broader pattern of literary exclusion of writers of color before the 1960s. University presses did make choices when scholars of color submitted their book manuscripts. Consequently, the publication of Américo Paredes's *"With His Pistol in His Hand"* in 1958 by the University of Texas Press had major ramifications for Paredes's academic and literary career and for the development of the Latinx literature and intellectual thought.

In this chapter, I focus on Paredes's engagement with the racialization of Mexican Americans in the Southwest and Asians in the Pacific as developed in some of his early poetry, writings for a U.S.-sponsored newspaper, short fiction, and scholarship. I argue that Paredes's gradual development of his Mexican American identity was particularly marked not only by the racialization of Mexican Americans in the Southwest but also by the racialization of Asian people by U.S. soldiers during the occupation of Japan, which permeated his writings over decades. Some of Paredes's early poems published in Spanish-language newspapers during the 1930s reflect the influence of racialization and racial violence toward Mexican Americans that is present also in Paredes's fiction written in the years leading to World War II. His writings during his time in Asia, particularly his articles for the U.S. Army newspaper *Pacific Stars and Stripes*, and especially those related to his coverage of the Tokyo war crimes trial in 1946, as well as his short stories set in the Pacific, show the ways in which the racialization of Japanese soldiers and civilians during the war influenced Paredes's evolving notions of his Mexican American identity that also is present in *"With His Pistol."* Ramón Saldívar's foundational book *The Borderlands of Culture* offers the most thorough synthesis of Paredes's writings and intellectual thought, including analyses of his writings in newspapers and short stories set in the Pacific. My analysis builds on the work of Ramón Saldívar and other scholars who have studied different aspects of Paredes's fiction and scholarly writings.[12] Moreover, I employ an Asian American studies theoretical framework that contextualizes the long history of the racialization of Asian subjects in the United States that existed before the war in the Pacific between the United States and Japan, and the subsequent U.S. occupation of Japan after the war.

I begin by analyzing Paredes's early poetry written in Spanish, including poems such as the "The Mexico-Texan" (1935), "Alma Pocha" (1936), "A México" (1937), and "México, la ilusión del continente" (1937), that reflect the articulation of a Texas Mexican identity that was influenced by racialization and racial violence as it embraces a Mexican heritage while attempting to reject its U.S. influences. Paredes's early poetry seeks to forge an identity that, while still Mexican American, emphasizes Mexican influences due to the social exclusion of Texas Mexicans in the Borderlands. I then explore a similar tension present in *George Washington Gómez*, a novel completed in 1939 and revised as a final draft in 1940.[13] My analysis focuses on moments of convergence between Paredes's coverage for *Pacific Stars and Stripes* of early developments in the Tokyo war crimes trial and his series of short stories pertaining with the war in the Pacific. Paredes grappled with the racialization of Japanese soldiers, leaders, and civilians as he himself was not only a racialized subject in the Southwest but was part of the U.S. Army forces that fought and occupied Japan. I then connect Paredes's experience in Asia with the epilogue of *"With His Pistol"* and its depiction of Mexican American cultural production in the Borderlands and racial violence through the life and legend of Gregorio Cortez. Paredes's writings reflect an evolving identity from "Texas Mexican" as described in his early poetry and fiction toward "Mexican American," as presented in his epilogue that was influenced in part by Paredes's time in Asia. Ramón Saldívar has convincingly argued that Paredes's experiences in Asia were crucial to Paredes's thinking and interpretation of the Borderlands and its cultural production;[14] nonetheless, processes of racialization and the seeming contradictions they created in relation to Paredes's development of his identity represent a constant theme throughout some of his most representative writings, which has been hard to discern chronologically since some of his writings remained unpublished for decades.

My analysis of Paredes relates to the alternative print forms and genres that influenced and contributed to the development of Paredes's literary and intellectual output. Some of Paredes's early poems appeared in Spanish-language newspapers in Texas, such as the *Brownsville Herald* of Brownsville and *La Prensa* of San Antonio, which served as spaces to disseminate Mexican American cultural production for Spanish-speaking readers during the early decades of the twentieth century. For instance, the review in *La Prensa* of Paredes's early poetry collection, *Cantos de adolescencia* (Songs of Youth), published in 1937, highlights the role of Spanish-language regional publishing houses in Texas. Around the same time, Paredes wrote *George Washington Gómez*, in which he further thematizes aspects of his Texas Mexican identity, but his novel remained unpublished until 1990. Moreover, his writings for the U.S. government publication *Pacific Stars and Stripes* highlights the role of alternative print forms in the development of his critique on the treatment of Japanese soldiers and civilians during the war. During the 1950s, Paredes tried to publish some of his early short fiction, particularly "Over the Waves Is Out" and "A Cold Night," with mainstream magazines, including *Partisan Review, The New Yorker*, and *Harper's Magazine*, without success. My analysis suggests that the publication of *"With His Pistol"* represents the single most important publishing event in Paredes's career. Before the publication of his scholarly monograph with the University of Texas Press in 1958, Paredes had published only one short story in *The New Mexico Quarterly*, a university-sponsored publication. The publication history of various Paredes's works exemplifies the literary marginalization of a broader group of Latinx scholars and writers by mass-circulation magazines, mainstream publishing houses, and academic presses; at the same time, it also reveals the seized opportunities that allowed for the development of Latinx literary and intellectual tradition before the 1960s.

RACIALIZATION AND IDENTITY IN PAREDES'S EARLY POETRY AND FICTION

Some of Paredes's poems of the 1930s reflect the tension between his allegiance to either Mexico or the United States and the embrace of a Texas Mexican identity that emphasizes Mexican historical and cultural influences to counteract the history of segregation, racial violence, and racialization that affected Tejanos in the U.S.-Mexico Borderlands.[15] Paredes's early poems published in *La Prensa* in the 1930s, such as "L'Amour" (Love), "Al cumplir veintiún años" (On Reaching Twenty-One Years), and "Mis tres novias" (My Three Girlfriends), were written in Spanish and depicted romantic love and youth aspirations;[16] however, other poems revolve around his identity and themes of social protest. Paredes's poem, "The Mexico-Texan," written in October 1935 but not published in the *Brownsville Herald* until October 17, 1937, represents one of his early manifestations of his Texas Mexican identity. As José López Morín correctly points out, "The Mexico-Texan" illustrates Paredes's "dilemma of an in-between existence" in the U.S.-Mexico border.[17] Paredes's "The Mexico-Texan" stands as a precursor of Mexican American cultural production that contains social protest elements and a denunciation of the racialized position of Texas Mexicans north of the border. As the title of the poem conveys, a "Mexico-Texan," which is Paredes's term for "Texas Mexican," describes a subject with divided allegiances but also one who is racialized and dispossessed. Notably, the subject in the poem seeks to affirm his Mexican heritage due to his exclusion from U.S. mainstream society and culture. Paredes's poem not only thematizes social exclusion but also challenges U.S. cultural production and poetry conventions through his emphasis on everyday language, or what Alicia Schmidt Camacho calls "border vernacular," as a counterhegemonic poetic form.[18] As the poem's speaker states, his Mexican identity "ru[n]s ... deep down [i]n h[is] heart," but he is dispossessed and does "no[t] [have] lan[d]"; the speaker is also racialized as whites "call h[i]m da Mexican Grease[r]."[19] Moreover, the "Mexico-Texan" is a cultural outsider in his own land as "[t]he dam[n] gringo lingo he no cannot spik," but he is also alienated on the south of the border.[20] The poem's speaker is "Mexican-born" but when he is in Mexico, he hears "Go back to da Gringo! Go leecka hees boot!"²¹ Ultimately, the "Mexico-Texan" remains marginalized and torn between two societies, as the poem concludes with the narrator celebrating "[b]oth September da Sixteen and Fourth of July."²²

While *La Prensa* published Paredes's poems that were more aligned to classical poetry conventions and romantic themes, its editor, Ignacio E. Lozano, objected to Paredes's poetry that engaged with social protest, racial violence in the Borderlands, or the theme of divided allegiances between Mexico and the United States. As Paredes recounted years later, he unsuccessfully attempted to publish in *La Prensa* his poem "Alma Pocha" (Pocho Soul) in 1936.²³ "Alma Pocha" thematizes the gradual land dispossession of Texas Mexicans in the Southwest, and of equal significance, it engages with episodes of racial violence against Texas Mexicans by including the image of a lynching. The poem's title includes the term "Pocho," usually a derogatory term used by Mexicans to refer to a Mexican living in the United States. In the poem, the speaker recounts the early dispossession of his family's land after the formation of the state of Texas by white settlers who the narrator calls "invasores" (invaders).²⁴ The poem's narrator connects Texas independence with the racialization of Texas Mexicans by stating, "[e]n tu propio terruño serás extranjero / por la ley del fusil y la ley del acero" (You will be a foreigner in your own homeland / by the law of the musket and the sword).²⁵ Moreover, the speaker of "Alma Pocha" mentions his father's murder and land dispossession, along with episodes of racialized violence in the form of his brother's lynching as he states, "verás a tu hermano colgado de un leño / por el crimen mortal de haber sido trigueño" (you'll see your brother hanged from a tree / for the mortal crime of being black-skinned).²⁶ "Alma Pocha" reflects the speaker's deep-seated resentment as he states, "[y] si vives, acaso, será sin orgullo, / con recuerdos amargos de todo lo tuyo" (and if you happen to survive, it will be without pride, / with bitter memories of everything that was yours).²⁷ The lasting image of the poem is of a dispossessed Texas Mexican as the narrator states, "donde fueras el amo serás el sirviente" (where you once ruled, you'll become the servant).²⁸ Although Paredes's poem consists of only four stanzas, it forcefully conveys the history of racial violence in the Borderlands and its consequences for Texas Mexicans.

While "Alma Pocha" was rejected by *La Prensa*, the newspaper promoted Paredes's poetry collection, *Cantos de adolescencia*, published in 1937 by

Librería Española, a local San Antonio press, that contains poems celebrating a Mexican identity more aligned to *La Prensa*'s ideological stance. Some of the poems included in *Canto de adolescencia* were printed in *La Prensa*'s section "Lunes literarios de *La Prensa*" (*La Prensa*'s Literary Mondays) on October 18, 1937, along with a review by Enrique Ortega. While *Cantos de adolescencia* combines lyrical poetry using classical meter and rhyme schemes with themes of love, romance, and nature, the first four poems under the subtitle "La lira patriótica" (The Patriotic Harp) present Mexico as an idealized place in contrast to the realities north of the border. Of these four poems, *La Prensa* published two, "A México" (To Mexico) and "México, la ilusión del continente" (Mexico, the Illusion of the Continent).[29] These two poems set the tone thematically for the entire collection; thus, creating an aesthetic work that seeks to affirm a Mexican identity in the context of the U.S.-Mexico Borderlands. In "A México," the speaker establishes in the first stanza that he is purposefully using Spanish and dedicating the first poem to Mexico: "mi primera poesía en nuestra lengua / fué, patria, para ti" (my first poem in our language / was, homeland, for you). The poem's speaker acknowledges that Mexico is not without blemishes, but his love for Mexico is unconditional: "Conozco bien, mi patria, tus defectos / y porque los conozco, yo te quiero" (I know my homeland well, your blemishes / and because I know them, I love you).[30] In the second poem, "México, la ilusión del continente," Paredes returns to the theme of conflicted allegiances as Mexican and American as the speaker states, "[y]o paso mis veinte años desgraciados / confuso en lo sajón y lo latino" (I've spent my unhappy twenty years / confused between the Saxon and the Latino). Even when the poem attempts to assert the speaker's Mexican identity, he acknowledges his tenuous claim to his Mexican sense of belonging as he confesses, "me he llamado sin serlo mexicano / pues he dudado de mi propia raza" (I've called myself Mexican without being one / since I've doubted my own identity).[31] The speaker wants Mexico to guide him and offer strength as Mexico becomes, "¡La ilusión del alma mía!" (The illusion of my soul!);[32] thus, these poems assert a Mexican identity in part as a reaction to Texas Mexicans' exclusion north of the border.

The tension in some of Paredes's early poems regarding his Texas Mexican identity is articulated in his prologue to *Cantos de adolescencia* where he affirms his Mexican heritage and the use of the Spanish language. Paredes's prologue to *Cantos de adolescencia* states that the verses included in the collection are by "un adolescente méxico-texano" (a Texas Mexican youth).³³ By describing himself as a Texas Mexican, Paredes seeks to define and advance a mixed identity culturally and aesthetically through poetry as he delves into the meaning of "méxico-texano," which represents a "[f]enómeno sociológico, planta de tiesto, hombre sin terruño propio y verdadero, que no es ni mexicano ni yanqui" (sociological phenomenon, anchored tree, man without land, who is neither Mexican nor Yankee).³⁴ He discusses his mixed identity during his youth when he felt "un momento netamente mexicano y al otro puro yanqui" (at one moment completely Mexican and at another a whole Yankee).³⁵ Moreover, Paredes writes about his intention to write in Spanish despite "la influencia de una escuela en inglés y de muy pocos libros en la lengua de Cervantes. En verdad, todavía me siento más seguro de mí mismo en la lengua de Shakespeare que en la mía" (the influence of my education in English and the few books in the language of Cervantes. However, I still feel more comfortable in the language of Shakespeare than in my own).³⁶ His embrace of the Spanish language reflects Paredes's yearning to connect to his Mexican cultural heritage. He ends his prologue with the resolution of "ya no escribir más verso en la lengua sajona" (no longer write more verse in English).³⁷ His commitment to the Spanish language stands as part of his in-between space as both Mexican and American.

While Paredes's prologue does not explicitly engage with racial prejudice or racial violence, the subtext of some of his poems in *Cantos de adolescencia* relates in part to the racialization and second-class citizen status of Texas Mexicans that is identified by Ortega in his review of Paredes's poetry collection. In his review of *Cantos de Adolescencia* for *La Prensa* of October 18, 1937, Ortega interprets Paredes's poetry as partly engaging with social protest through cultural production by Texas Mexicans. Ortega emphasizes the significance of Paredes's poetry collection since there is a need for books focusing on Texas Mexicans as Ortega states, "[l]a producción literaria de los méxico-texanos, es casi nula, manifiestamente insignificante, si se tiene en cuenta la importancia en números de la población de origen mexicano en el Estado de Texas" (the literary production by Texas Mexicans is almost nonexistent, clearly insufficient, if one takes into consideration the number of people of Mexican origin in the State of Texas).³⁸ Ortega correctly interprets Paredes's poetry as participating in Texas Mexicans' cultural and literary production as Paredes at the same time was also influenced by

Spanish-language newspapers in Texas such as *La Prensa*, which according to Paredes, "attempted to create a bilingual culture for Mexican Americans."[39] Ortega similarly connects some of the protest themes in *Cantos de adolescencia* with "las causas denunciadas por el abogado Alonso S. Perales en su obra 'En Defensa de mi Raza', [las] mismas que llenan de profunda amargura los labios del joven poeta Paredes . . . en sus 'Cantos de Adolescencia' . . ." (the issues denounced by the lawyer Alonso S. Perales in his book *In Defense of My People*, the same ones that fill with deep bitterness the lips of the young poet Paredes . . . in his *Songs of Youth* . . .).[40] Ortega's astute claim identifies Perales as one of Paredes's intellectual influences as the latter was aware of *In Defense of My People* and considered Perales a "protest writer."[41] Other writers such as Carlos E. Castañeda wrote to congratulate Paredes on the publication of *Cantos de adolescencia* and similarly to Ortega, Castañeda interprets Paredes's poetry collection as representative of emerging cultural production by one of their own who will "redimir en parte la inopia literatura de los méxico-tejanos" (redeem in part the literary vacuum among Texas Mexicans).[42]

Paredes's fiction of this period, particularly *George Washington Gómez*, offers an in-depth historical exploration of the violent history of the Borderlands and the racialization of Texas Mexicans;[43] however, Paredes's novel reveals an evolution in his Texas Mexican identity from his early poetry. The novel's subtitle, *A Mexicotexan Novel*, reflects the social and cultural context of the 1930s as the historical period when Paredes articulated his identity as a "méxico-texano." While the connections between Paredes's early poetry and fiction in relation to themes of identity, racial violence, and social justice have not always been discernable due in part to the publication history of his early work, he reminded readers of these connections. Decades later, in a letter to Nicolás Kanellos, Paredes explained that "[t]here were a lot of us *mejicanos* writing verse and prose in the 30s and 40s; I belonged to a little group of such writers on the Lower Border. But as far as I know, I was the only one who attempted to address the social and political problems of our people through literature."[44] *George Washington Gómez* engages more fully with the history of racial violence toward Texas Mexicans, particularly by the Texas Rangers, and the aftermath of El Plan de San Diego.[45] The sense of alienation in one's own country present in his poetry is also thematized in his novel through its main character, Guálinto Gómez, a Texas Mexican, who is "[b]orn a foreigner in his native land," and although he was born in Texas, he "consider[s] himself a Mexican."[46] Due in part to his position as a racialized subject in the Borderlands, one of Guálinto's wishes when he grows up is to fight white settlers "like Gregorio Cortez and [Juan] Cortin[a] . . ." did before him.[47] Paredes's confrontational narrative regarding the dispossession of land and racial violence toward Texas Mexicans clashes with Guálinto's process of assimilation through the U.S. school system for most of the narrative that also reflects an in-between space in Paredes's identity as in his poetry. Nonetheless, it is important to note that in *Cantos de adolescencia*, Paredes vows to continue writing in Spanish, but *George Washington Gómez*'s final 1940 draft was written in English, which reflects a switch in language with the explicit goal of reaching a broader readership beyond his Texas Mexican community.[48]

Paredes's engagement with his Texas Mexican identity in *George Washington Gómez* began to conflate in unexpected ways with the position of other non-white groups such as Asian Americans and Native peoples within the prevailing racial hierarchies in the Southwest at the time. Paredes's novel written in the 1930s already describes a society in South Texas composed of other non-white groups beyond Texans of Mexican origin. This is exemplified in the scene when Guálinto is not allowed to enter the restaurant and dance hall where his classmates plan to celebrate their graduation; Paredes's novel thematizes racialization and discrimination against Texas Mexicans, as Guálinto is stopped at the restaurant's door and questioned about whether he is of Mexican origin. The narrator suggests that Guálinto could have said that he was "Spaniard," hence of European descent, since his skin is "white" but chooses to identity as "Mexican" and is denied entrance.[49] The novel, nonetheless, highlights the presence of racial hierarchies as just before Guálinto is denied access, two Japanese American brothers, Jimmy and Bob Shigemara, who are Guálinto's classmates, are allowed to enter the restaurant.[50] The scene brings attention to the enforcement of racial hierarchies in Texas with whites and immigrants of European background at the top, followed by Asian Americans and non-white Texans of Mexican origin below them. Just as unsettling, Paredes's novel situates the even more precarious position of Indigenous peoples in this racial hierarchy, which has been identified by literary scholars as a problematic aspect of *George Washington Gómez*.[51] In perhaps the most well-known and controversial aspect of Paredes's novel when Guálinto returns to his hometown after college and becomes a spy for the U.S. Army, he remembers when he used to daydream about his "great-grandfather's time" in the Borderlands after

Mexico's independence, organizing "*rancheros* into a fighting militia and train[ing] them . . . to exterminate the Comanches."⁵² In Paredes's novel, the Southwest is represented as a contested territory where racial hierarchies have existed for centuries ever since the first European settlers. These racial dynamics in the Borderlands will become global as Paredes grapples with his own racialization in the U.S. Army and its involvement in Asia during and after World War II.

RACIALIZED AND RACIALIZER IN PAREDES'S NEWSPAPER ARTICLES AND SHORT FICTION

Asian Americans on the West Coast were racialized during the nineteenth century and decades before the U.S. Army entered the war in the Pacific after Pearl Harbor. As scholars of Asian American history have noted, prior to Pearl Harbor, the United States had systematically excluded through legislation most immigrants from Asia, including Japanese immigrants, based primarily on the racialized premise that Asians were inferior peoples.⁵³ The Chinese Exclusion Act of 1882 was the most visible of a series of legislations that by the 1930s had barred most Asian immigrants from legally residing in the United States and becoming U.S. citizens.⁵⁴ The Johnson-Reed Act of 1924, according to Erika Lee, "was the result of decades of activism on the part of nativists who lobbied for immigration restrictions as a way to 'stem the tide' of undesirable foreigners."⁵⁵ Parallel to the U.S. military response after Pearl Harbor, the U.S. government initiated the systematic internment of most of the Japanese population in the United States based primarily on racialization premises even when many of them were U.S. citizens. As Iyko Day suggests, Pearl Harbor was not the sole motive for the internment of civilians of Japanese descent, as it was also the result of anti-Asian racism and the prospects of economic gain for white landowners in California.⁵⁶ The 1944 U.S. Supreme Court case *Korematsu v. United States* upheld the internment of U.S. citizens of Japanese descent and created a legal precedent for the U.S. government to detain people based on ethnic origin if deemed a threat regardless of their U.S. citizenship.⁵⁷ By most accounts, the war in the Pacific was different from the European front, in part because it was a racialized war characterized by the dehumanizing treatment of POWs by both Japanese and U.S. soldiers.⁵⁸ Moreover, perhaps one of the most disturbing aspects of World War II was the bombing of German and Japanese cities and civilians that caused almost unimaginable damage and suffering to hundreds of thousands of people, which culminated with the U.S. Army's use of atomic weapons for the first time in human history on Japanese but not on German civilians.[59]

Paredes joined the military and served in World War II in 1944. While he did not see combat, he became part of the U.S. occupation forces in Japan where he experienced firsthand the racialization of the Japanese population. During his time in Japan, Paredes served as an editor and staff writer for the army publication *Pacific Stars and Stripes* for which he covered the early proceedings of the Tokyo war crimes trial and wrote a series of newspaper articles based on the early stages of trial procedures from April to June 1946 before Paredes was discharged from his assignment with the U.S. Army.[60] Ramón Saldívar's *Borderlands of Culture* contains the most extensive analysis of Paredes's reporting in Asia for *Pacific Stars and Stripes* and *El Universal* of Mexico on various topics including Japanese culture, society, and politics.[61] Paredes's newspaper writings for *Pacific Stars and Stripes* are intrinsically linked to his role as a member of the U.S. occupation force and the medium, a daily newspaper funded and controlled by the U.S. Army with an intended audience of U.S. forces in Japan and Korea, that if not propaganda, it sought to highlight a triumphalist interpretation of the U.S. occupation of a formerly sovereign country.[62] The leading defendant during the Tokyo trial was former Japanese prime minister, Hideki Tojo, along with twenty-seven other high-ranking officers who, as Paredes reports on April 30, 1946, had been "charged with planning, preparing, initiating and waging wars of aggression in violation of international law and treaties" in addition to the charges of "crimes against humanity."[63] The Tokyo trial defendants were found guilty on November 1948 and Hideki Tojo, along with most defendants, were executed in December 1948. While the Tokyo war crimes trial sought to prosecute and judge Japanese high-ranking military leaders for crimes committed during the war, the legality and moral certainty of the trial was also questioned from the moment it began. According to Yukiko Koshiro, the Tokyo trial was "criticized even by members of the Allied nations as a forum for vengeance, vindication, and propaganda."[64] As a member of the U.S. military who was also covering the trial, Paredes similarly struggled with the legality and legitimacy of the trial, and this ambivalence is reflected in his coverage.

While Paredes's coverage of the trial reflects the U.S. Army's contention that Tojo and other defendants were responsible for war crimes, Paredes attempts to balance his reporting by presenting competing arguments at different junctures during the early stages of the trial. A major question regarding the validity of the Tokyo trial was the conspicuous absence of Emperor Hirohito as one of the defendants since the United States needed him to pacify and stabilize Japanese society and economy after the war.[65] Paredes, for example, reports on May 1, 1946, that for the Japanese press, the indictment and charges against Tojo seem justifiable but "American newspapers on the other hand, commented that the list of Japanese war criminal suspects should be larger, including Hirohito himself."[66] The absence of Hirohito remained a controversial aspect of the Tokyo trial that Paredes, rather than dismissing it, acknowledged in his coverage. Moreover, his reporting engaged with some of the defense's main arguments, such as the claim that the actions of the Japanese military did not fall outside the lines of traditional warfare and neither did they target a specific ethnic group as the Germans did. Paredes quotes Dr. Tadashi Hanai, who served as Tojo's defense lawyer, saying that "Tojo and other war crimes suspects may be found guilty of breaking the peace, but they are not guilty of the charge of murder..."[67] Likewise, Paredes in his reporting allows Tojo's defense to challenge the comparison between the Nuremberg trials where Nazi officials were similarly tried for war crimes from 1945 to 1946 and the Tokyo trial. Paredes acknowledges Hanai's contention "that in the Nuremberg trials, the Nazis are being tried for ordering wholesale killings of Jews and others. Japanese military leaders never gave such orders..."[68] As a result, Paredes's reporting reflects his attempts to balance his coverage despite serving as a correspondent for a U.S. Army publication.

Paredes's coverage of the Tokyo war crimes trial combines at times sensationalist elements along with hard questions pertaining to the impartiality of the trial. As Ramón Saldívar correctly observes, there is an element of the "voyeuris[tic]" in Paredes's reporting on the major indictment session during the trials.[69] Rather than focusing on the substance of the charges, Paredes writes about the slap that Tojo received from one of the co-defendants, Shumei Okawa, that becomes the center of Paredes's coverage in the first page of *Pacific Stars and Stripes* on May 4, 1946. The article's header reads: "Co-Defendant Slaps Tojo on Head during Session: 47 Indictment Counts Read." His coverage begins with the following statement, "[w]ar crimes defendant Hideki Tojo was slapped smartly on his bald pate twice during his arraignment and that of 27 co-defendants before the Military Tribunal for the Far East at the War Ministry building in Tokyo Friday."[70] Paredes explains that "[t]he slapper was neurotic Shumei Okawa, one of the defendants and self-appointed star performer of the proceedings."[71] His coverage of the indictment session, however, takes a serious tone when he describes tribunal president William F. Webb who "opened the proceedings with a statement in which he said that the coming trial was as important as any criminal trial in all history."[72] Paredes also refers to the alleged impartiality of a judicial system controlled by a military power over a defeated belligerent country as he quotes Webb, "[t]o our great task we bring open minds both on the acts and on the law . . . The onus will be on the prosecution to establish guilt beyond a reasonable doubt."[73] In addition, his article includes the argument made by other members of the defense counsel opposing the trials on procedural terms due in part to the "substantial errors" in the Japanese translations of the indictments.[74]

One of Paredes's last articles covering the Tokyo war crimes trial relates to its moral justification and the argument that the Japanese army was not the only army engaged in war crimes. José Limón, for instance, interprets Paredes's coverage of the trial in part as Paredes's attempt "to defend Tojo against various charges of war crimes."[75] If not an open defense of Tojo by Paredes, there is a moral ambivalence in Paredes's coverage that brings attention at different moments to the actions of the U.S. Army during the war. His article of May 15, 1946, focuses on defense counsel U.S. Army Major Ben Bruce Blakeney seeking the "dismissal of the 55-count indictment" arguing that "under the present indictment, there will be trials of the losers after every war."[76] Paredes then describes in detail Blakeney's critique of the trial as setting a pernicious precedent for future wars, as victors would be able to judge members of the losing army "[w]hether a war be aggressive or defensive," and in these types of tribunals "all killings by victors would be lawful, while all killings by losers would be murder."[77] Significantly, Paredes's article focuses on one of the most controversial aspects of the war in the form of the dropping of the atomic bomb on Japanese civilians; he quotes Blakeney arguing that "[i]f the killing of admiral [Isaac] Kidd in the Pearl Harbor bombing was murder . . . we know the name of the very man whose hand [loosened] the atomic bomb on Hiroshima and the names of the men who planned this bombing. Is murder on their conscience?"[78] Paredes quotes another member of the defense, Capt. George Furness, who argues that the trial "can neither be fair, legal or impartial under the circumstances of its appointment, and therefore has no jurisdiction."[79] Moreover, Paredes includes a counterargument presented by the chief prosecutor, Joseph B. Keenan, who states that the dropping of the atomic bomb in Hiroshima "needed no more apology than the act of a man who shoots an outlaw in self[-]defense."[80] In relation to the charge against the partiality of a military court set by the victorious army, Paredes quotes Keenan acknowledging the impossibility of an unbiased trial, as "[i]t would be necessary to bring men from Mars ... to get a neutral court in this case."[81] Ultimately, Paredes's coverage of the Tokyo trial reflects his own struggle grappling not only with the partiality of the trial but also with the role of the U.S. military during and after the war.

Paredes's short fiction written and set in Asia, which remained unpublished until decades later, closely engages with some of the questions raised in his coverage of the Tokyo war criminal trial once he was released of his role as a reporter. Paredes's understanding of the effects of the war on Japanese civilians depicted in his newspaper writings and short fiction in Asia was informed by his observations and reporting on the ground after the war's end rather than by experiencing the war as a combat soldier. As Steven Rosales notes, several Mexican American soldiers who served in combat units in the Pacific during World War II were physically and psychologically wounded due to the brutal conditions of warfare.[82] Paredes was discharged from the U.S. Army in late 1946 but stayed in the Pacific working as a member of the American Red Cross. During this period, Paredes wrote at least eight short stories set in the Pacific written between 1945 and 1950 that were included in his short story collection, *The Hammon and the Beans and Other Stories*, published decades later in 1994 by Arte Público Press.[83] Due to the time lapse between their creation and publication, Paredes's stories set in Asia could be interpreted as part of what Elizabeth McHenry describes as unpublished fiction by Black authors that constitutes a distinct form of literary production. As McHenry suggests, the unpublished short fiction of some Black writers, which can be applied to the experiences of other writers like Paredes, "encourages us to rethink what success, failure, and even publication meant in the historical moment in which [these authors] lived."[84] Like other authors of color who were unable to publish their works before the 1960s due in part to their literary exclusion from mainstream publications and publishers, Paredes tried to publish his short fiction in the 1950s in mainstream periodicals such as *Partisan Review*, *The New Yorker*, and *Harper's Magazine*, among several others, but was rejected without exception.[85] Although Paredes's stories set in Asia remained unpublished for decades, they contain key elements of his thinking pertaining to the rightfulness of the U.S. war in the Pacific, along with the role that U.S. soldiers of color played in the racialization of the Japanese during the war.

Paredes's short story "The Gift" revolves around the torture and indiscriminate killings of POWs by Japanese soldiers fueled by mutual racial animosity.[86] "The Gift" is set in a Japanese POW camp on an unidentified location during the war. This markedly grim story focuses on a group of U.S. soldiers trying to stay alive during their imprisonment as Japanese soldiers show no qualms about torturing and executing them in disregard of international laws that regulate the treatment of war prisoners. According to Yoneyuki Sugita, "Japanese and Americans had demonstrated vehement racial hatred toward one another during the war, much of the enmity having been inculcated through the formal channels of state propaganda."[87] In Paredes's story, U.S. soldiers trying to escape are executed and when Lt. Commander Young, the highest-ranking U.S. prisoner, kills a Japanese sergeant, Young and all the remaining POWs in the hut are executed. The treatment and torture of POWs by both Japanese and U.S. soldiers during World War II represents one of the most disturbing characteristics of the war in the Pacific.[88] Japan challenged and waged an open war against European colonialist powers in Asia, including the United States and its former colonial territory, the Philippines, as Japan sought colonial hegemony in Asia based on its own racial hierarchies. As Yukiko Koshiro explains, "[w]hen Japan expanded its colonial empire, . . . racial superiority became an ideological force to legitimate Japan's rule over non-Japanese people in Asia."[89] "The Gift" similarly focuses on the GIs' racial hatred of the Japanese soldiers even as the GIs have reasons to fear their Japanese captors as they are being tortured and executed. The story's Mexican American narrator, simply identified as "Mex," explains that during their captivity, "[w]e were all afraid—of being beaten or killed some day."[90] The GIs, however, are also prone to dehumanize their Japanese captors; for instance, the narrator calls the Japanese sergeant, "Monkeyface";[91] likewise, the narrator uses the derogatory and widely used term "Japs" to refer to the Japanese soldiers.[92] Rather than ascribing blame to one side, Paredes's story accentuates the inhumanity and brutality of the treatment of POWs based on shared racial contempt.

"The Gift" thematizes the nature of war conflicts, particularly the war in the Pacific, as acts of unspeakable violence that fell on individual soldiers. In Paredes's story, it is a group of GIs that plots to kill Young, a fellow soldier, to protect the remaining members of the group. During a harrowing attempt to survive, the narrator says, "[s]o we started making plans to kill Young" while another POW says, "one of us must sacrifice himself to save the rest,"[93] which parallels the logic of the war in the Pacific where U.S. soldiers were fighting a war to defeat Japan after its attack on Pearl Harbor. The U.S. Army's all-out war in the Pacific was characterized by ruthlessness against Japanese soldiers, the bombing of cities and civilians, and ultimately, the use of atomic bombs to end the war. "The Gift" presents soldiers of color in the U.S. Army who not only racialized the Japanese soldiers but at the same time were racialized at home and in the army. In Paredes's story, "Mex" is tasked with killing Young by the drawing of sticks. The irony of this event is not lost on the Mexican American soldier who says, "I got the short one. I knew it would happen; all my life I've got the short end of the stick,"[94] a clear reference to his position as a racialized subject in U.S. society who is now fighting a war for the same country that has marginalized him. "The Gift" also highlights the value of human connections when soldiers are confronted with the violence of war. When the narrator is uncertain about whether he will be tortured, he realizes "how Young felt and why he ratted on us all the time. I felt sorry for him, too."[95] If the POW camp stands for a microcosm of the larger war in the Pacific, rather than racial hatred or revenge, the Mexican American soldier laments the difficult choices soldiers had to make during armed conflicts. Paredes's story ends with the narrator witnessing the execution of his former groupmates as he explains, "[b]y the time Young's turn came, I was sick of watching heads half-chopped off. I'm sure the Jap lieutenant in charge of the execution felt the same way I did."[96] At the end of the story, "Mex" receives a small bag with a child's tooth as a "gift"; however, the more consequential "gift" is surviving the war, which allows him to tell the story.

Paredes, influenced in part by his coverage of the Tokyo war crimes trial, turns the tables in his short story "Ichiro Kikuchi," as the GIs become the executioners of Japanese POWs during the war in the Pacific, suggesting that war crimes were committed by both sides. Paredes's story is narrated by Ichiro Kikuchi, a Japanese Mexican soldier, who came to Japan from Mexico just before the start of the war. Kikuchi is recruited by the Japanese army and sent for combat to the Philippines; he is captured along with a group of Japanese soldiers who are asked to dig a ditch that will serve as their grave. Decades later, in a letter to Ramón Saldívar, Paredes directly connected the Tokyo war crimes trial to "Ichiro Kikuchi," explaining that "[t]here were plenty of 'war crimes' committed by the U.S. forces long before Vietnam and My Lai. Yet we executed the Japanese leaders as war criminals because Japanese soldiers also committed the same kind of atrocities."[97] Similar to "The Gift," Paredes's "Ichiro Kikuchi" contains an even more significant moment of human connection amid war violence.[98] While in "The Gift," a Mexican American soldier takes part in the dehumanization of Japanese soldiers, in "Ichiro Kikuchi" another Mexican American soldier, Sergeant Melguizo, spares Kikuchi's life when the former sees Kikuchi's Virgen de Guadalupe medallion hanging on his neck, which evokes their shared ethnic, religious, and linguistic ties, as both are of Mexican descent, Catholic, and speak Spanish. After it is implied that Melguizo spared Kikuchi's life, the latter confesses, "[i]t is because of her, the dark Virgin, that I am alive today."[99] The medallion also creates a tie between two racialized subjects. As Ramón Saldívar notes, Melguizo spares Kikuchi's life because the former sees "himself partially in the demonized Japanese Other";[100] however, instead of acknowledging this act of ethnic solidarity when Kikuchi and Melguizo crossed paths in Tokyo after the war ends, Melguizo claims not to recognize him, which prompts Kikuchi to wonder, "[i]s he ashamed of what he did for me?"[101] Melguizo's reaction speaks of the troubled assessment of the United States' war in the Pacific by Mexican American soldiers who were racialized in the United States and at the same time were asked to fight a racialized war against the Japanese.

Just as the killings of POWs on both sides remain morally unjustifiable, "Ichiro Kikuchi" engages with another questionable aspect of the war in the form of the bombing of Japanese cities and civilians by the United States toward the end of the war. "Ichiro Kikuchi" does not end with the encounter between Melguizo and Kikuchi in the streets of Tokyo, as critical interpretations of the story would suggest;[102] instead, Paredes's story thematizes the U.S. aerial bombardment of Tokyo and other Japanese cities. Historians have discussed how Japan was forced to surrender through the bombing of its population and cities.[103] According to Niall Ferguson, towards the conclusion of the war and "[w]ithin five months, roughly two-fifths of the built-up areas of nearly every major city [in Japan] had been laid waste, killing nearly a quarter of a million people, injuring more than 300,000 and turning eight million into refugees."[104] In Paredes's story, Kikuchi plans to return to Mexico after the war, but his father, Keigo Kikuchi, is also in Japan recovering from lung damage. Kikuchi explains that his father "was an air-raid warden during the fire bombings. The section of town just downhill from where we live was set afire before dawn one day."[105] During that bombing, Kikuchi recounts the story of a woman with three children who ran out of their burning house, but whose oldest daughter was not able to escape. Ichiro's father attempted to rescue the child but was only able to recover the dead body, and during the attempted rescue, he inhaled the fumes that damaged his lungs. Kikuchi then is not only a survivor of the actual war, but his father is a survivor of the bombing. Kikuchi recalls that his father "was very brave, going into that burning house. My mother says the neighbors called him a hero. But that was before the war ended. There are no heroes now."[106] The ending of "Ichiro Kikuchi" renders most of the Japanese population defeated and demoralized due to the aerial bombings; however, as Paredes pondered after the Tokyo trial, it was only the Japanese military leaders who were found guilty of waging a war of destruction.

In "The Terrible High Cost" Paredes develops in more detail the theme of the war's economic, social, and psychological impact on Japanese civilians that is often overlooked within the larger narrative of Japanese demilitarization and eventual economic recovery after World War II. Paredes's story is narrated by Peter Richards, a professor from Texas just back from Japan after spending time there during the occupation. Richards recounts how he got a rare copy of a Hiroshige print that involves Kunio Yoshida, a Japanese professor of literature before the war, who was relegated to the position of janitor at Richards's workplace after the war and who is barely able to sustain his family when they first meet. Yoshida's story is told from Richards's perspective to emphasize the story's white gaze and how narratives about the U.S. occupation of Japan and its aftermath are usually mediated by U.S. historians and through the larger narratives of U.S. military victories in the Pacific. Richards appears indifferent to Japanese civilians' suffering even as he tries to empathize with Yoshida's plight. Richards believes that Japanese "all looked so much alike, shabby and sad-looking, always bowing at every American in sight."[107] It does not occur to Richards that the war and the bombing of civilian populations have diminished their economic and social conditions. Richards meets Yoshida's family and describes their neighborhood as "a depressing place, a desolate scene of burned out buildings dotting large areas where nothing else stood."[108] While the desolate appearance of Yoshida's neighborhood was caused by "the Allied fire bombings of the city,"[109] Richards feels no regrets or responsibility for this destruction or the suffering of Japanese civilians. Instead, Richards believes Yoshida and other Japanese should not be "offended" by the U.S. assistance in the country's reconstruction since "[a]fter all, the Japanese had lost the war."[110] As Christine Hong correctly observes, "[h]aving defeated the foe, the U.S. war machine shifted gears to reengineer [Japanese] civil society."[111] Consequently, Richards considers himself a detached observer whose presence in Japan is the result of the actions of its military leaders in which the U.S. occupation army acts as a benevolent force.

"The Terrible High Cost" explores the economic and psychological toll of the war and the U.S. occupation of Japan on civilians through Yoshida's experiences and those of his family. Yoshida comes from a prosperous Japanese family who can send him to the United States to get a "doctorate in American literature from an Ivy League school . . ." and then return to Japan.[112] When war with the United States starts after the attack on Pearl Harbor, Yoshida is in his forties and avoids the draft, but he loses almost everything during the war except the "few valuables" he was able to bury "before the fire bombing began in earnest . . ."[113] For Yoshida's father the "war was especially hard on him . . . He lost his wife, [Yoshida's] mother, and he has not yet recovered,"[114] which is one of the sources of sorrow and emptiness that permeates the story. At one point, Yoshida's father laments, "I should die like a samurai, but how can I do so? First His Majesty's government commands that I give up my swords to the army. Then the Americans bomb my garden. How can I die an honorable death?"[115] Yoshida's father responds by jumping off a cliff in the town of Otani, which is referred to in the story as "the suicide capital of Japan."[116] While Yoshida's father personifies the Japanese people's enduring desolation created by the war and the occupation, Paredes's story also contains several ironies that renders it almost a satire. When Richards learns about the tragedy, he assists Yoshida with money and by securing a position as a teaching assistant at a two-year college for GIs. Yoshida, however, is imprisoned by the mayor of Otani when Yoshida is unable to pay for the "expenses incurred by the town because of his father's suicide."[117] The ending of "The Terrible High Cost" adds an ironic twist to the story's title as it relates not only to the suicide of

Yoshida's father but also to his daughter's suicide, which at "least this time [Yoshida] can afford..."[118]

Among Paredes's short stories set in Asia, "Sugamo" returns more deliberately to the questions of moral justice raised during his coverage of the Tokyo war crimes trial and the racialization of not only the Japanese but other Asian peoples during subsequent U.S. interventionist wars in Asia. "Sugamo" chronicles the fate of Private Jewel C. Jones, a Black soldier who is in prison waiting to be court-martialed for the killing of a Japanese bar manager in Tokyo while Jones was on leave from the Korean front during the Korean War. Paredes's story is recounted through flashback scenes while Jones is in prison and during his military courtroom appearance. While on the Korean front, Jones is asked to take a Korean POW to headquarters and "[b]e back in fifteen minutes,"[119] which is a euphemism for the summary execution of POWs. The actions of U.S. soldiers in "Sugamo" are troubling, particularly in relation to the racialization of Korean soldiers during the war and the U.S. military criminal system. "Sugamo," however, engages more purposely with the idea of the racialization of Asian populations by U.S. soldiers of color during U.S. wars in the Pacific.[120] A central conflict in the story is Jones's killing of a Korean POW without a trial; however, as Paredes himself recounted, Japanese military leaders during the Tokyo trial were the ones found guilty of war crimes even when extrajudicial killings were committed by both sides.[121] Korea as the setting of the story is significant as it places the U.S. military at the center of an expansionist project in the Pacific, a similar interventionist military approach that was condemned on the part of the Japanese military during the Tokyo trial. The execution of a Black soldier within the U.S. Army further questions the impartiality of a U.S. military judicial system still operating within the background of Jim Crow segregation and its disproportionally high number of court-martialed and executed Black soldiers during World War II.[122]

"Sugamo," more than other Paredes's stories set in Asia, engages with the racialized treatment of soldiers of color in the U.S. Army and the racialization of Asian subjects by U.S. soldiers of color, which render them both racialized and racializers. As Julia Lee suggests, Black and Asian interracial encounters in fiction at times engaged in "multiple logics of exclusion [that] are being constructed and mobilized in order to marginalize not only their own group but the other as well."[123] "Sugamo" participates in these "logics of exclusion," as it returns to Paredes's theme introduced in "The Gift" in which it is not only white U.S. soldiers but also soldiers of color who dehumanize Japanese soldiers. In "Sugamo," Jones looks through his cell and sees "a crowd of gooks play ball" and wonders, "[h]ow different they are... nothing like Americans at all."[124] Jones's own racial views lead him to consider Koreans "just a race of kids that never grew up."[125] The white MPs guarding Jones not only hold a racial contempt for the Koreans, but they are even more vicious with their racial hatred toward Jones, their Black fellow soldier. One of the MPs pits Jones against the Koreans by asking Jones, "[h]ow about you, Sambo? You don't like them either, do you?"[126] Jones does not respond and looks down at his boots. As Ramón Saldívar notes, Paredes's story engages with the "double jeopardy of racism, its destructive force whether one expresses it or receives it..."[127] The scene at the bar, which doubles as a prostitution house, is also racially charged at different levels. Jones attacks the Japanese bar manager when he is not allowed to see a Japanese dancer presumably because he does not have a "ticket" or because he is a Black man.[128] It is likely that Jones's race also played a role since in representations of Black soldiers in Japanese fiction during the postwar, as Michael Molasky notes, "whites as well as blacks constitute racial others for the Japanese" but "blackness represents a more radical alterity—a darker shade of difference."[129] At another level, Jones's killing of the manager perpetuates the stereotype of Black men as violent. The narrative, however, suggests that Jones's attack is due to the psychological trigger of their constant use of the phrase "thank you," as the manager's actions bring back the memory of the Korean soldier killed by Jones.[130] Ultimately, Jones and other soldiers of color went to fight a war for a country that excluded and racialized them and in turn saw their adversaries in similar ways.

ECHOES OF WORLD WAR II IN *"WITH HIS PISTOL IN HIS HAND"*

The publication of *"With His Pistol in His Hand"* by the University of Texas Press in 1958 stands as one of the most consequential events in Paredes's writing career, as it resulted in academic and literary recognition in the decades that followed, which in turned allowed for the publication of his unpublished poetry and fiction. Paredes married his second wife, Amelia Shidzu Nagamine, of Japanese and Uruguayan descent, in Japan and returned to Texas in 1950 to study at UT-Austin with the assistance of the

GI Bill.[131] Only after his wife was able to reside in the United States due to changes in immigration laws that permitted the entrance of people of Japanese descent into the United States, was Paredes able to continue graduate studies at UT-Austin. Before the publication of *"With His Pistol,"* Paredes's poetry had been printed in Spanish-language newspapers and by Librería Española, a local publishing house with a limited regional reach. Likewise, he wrote fiction, including *George Washington Gómez*, the short stories that will become part of *The Hammon and the Beans and Other Stories*, and *The Shadow*;[132] however, despite multiple attempts to publish these works with mainstream magazines and publishing houses, Paredes was able to publish just a single short story, "Over the Waves Is Out," in 1953 in the *New Mexico Quarterly*, a local publication sponsored by the University of New Mexico. Paredes's publication record up to this point speaks of the literary marginalization of Latinx writers before the 1960s, but it also accentuates the crucial importance of the publication of his revised PhD dissertation as an academic book. Manuel Medrano, one of Paredes's biographers, notes that the publication of *"With His Pistol"* was key for his academic career, as he was teaching at Texas Western College in El Paso before his book was published.[133] Paredes's move to UT-Austin as a professor of English in 1958 may not have occurred without the acceptance of his manuscript by the University of Texas Press.

The publication history of *"With His Pistol,"* recounted by scholars and Paredes himself, centers on the idea that he wrestled with the University of Texas Press to publish the book, since the press wanted to suppress the negative references to the Texas Rangers;[134] however, the correspondence between the Director of the University of Texas Press, Frank H. Wardlaw, and Paredes shows that Wardlaw did not falter on his enthusiastic support of Paredes's manuscript at any of the different editorial stages during the manuscript review process. Wardlaw believed that Paredes's manuscript was filling a void in the scholarship regarding the cultural production of Mexican Americans in the Southwest. While Mexican American scholars such as Arthur L. Campa and George I. Sánchez were able to publish books with academic presses prior to Paredes, *"With His Pistol"* is the first academic book that counters the overwhelming number of Manifest Destiny historical narratives regarding the formation of Texas.[135] *"With His Pistol"* famously engaged with the leading scholarship on the history of Texas represented by Walter Prescott Webb's *The Great Plains* (1931) and *The Texas*

Rangers (1935), and J. Frank Dobie's *The Flavor of Texas* (1936).[136] While university presses historically excluded scholars of color for the most part, the topic of Paredes's manuscript correlated with the emphasis of regional history by the University of Texas Press that its new director, Frank H. Wardlaw, sought when the press was reorganized in 1950.[137] An important aspect that is at times overlooked in the publication history of *"With His Pistol"* is that Paredes had the backing of stellar white scholars at UT-Austin who saw his scholarship not as radical reinterpretation of cultural production in the Borderlands, but rather as one competing narrative within the larger Manifest Destiny historiography of Texas that would remain almost unchallenged even after the publication of Paredes's work.[138] After Paredes completed his dissertation, Stith Thompson recommended the manuscript to the University of Texas Press.[139] Decades later, Paredes himself would emphasize Wardlaw's attempt to remove from the manuscript "the derogatory comments about the Texas Rangers" and about Webb,[140] but their exchanges during the manuscript review process reflects a less contentious ideological clash.

The correspondence between Paredes and Wardlaw relating to the publication of *"With His Pistol"* shows that, rather than a story of academic exclusion or suppression, it was an unusual story about an academic press editor showing rare unwavering support for publishing the work of a Mexican American scholar. Paredes sent his manuscript to the University of Texas Press on May 1956 knowing that the topic of his dissertation, the life of Gregorio Cortez and the Mexican American culture and ballads developed in the Borderlands, was scholarly viable. In addition, he was aware of the social dimension of his work as he considered Cortez a "symbol to most méxico-texanos, especially on the Border, of their struggle to secure equal rights."[141] Paredes's statement relates to his emphasis in his early poetry and fiction on the social conditions of Texas Mexicans in the Borderlands before World War II. Wardlaw sent Paredes a five-page report of his manuscript on January 1957.[142] While Wardlaw's overall reaction is positive, his main concern revolves around the manuscript's organization, as he envisions a book not only for experts but also one that could appeal to the general public. Paredes's critique of the Texas Rangers is not the main point of Wardlaw's suggestions for revision; instead, Wardlaw writes that "Dr. Walter Prescott Webb, who is chairman of our faculty advisory board, says that this particular service is long overdue, although he ruefully finds himself the villain of the piece at several points."[143] Wardlaw adds that "Dr. Webb has enthusiastically recommended your book for publication . . ."[144] Wardlaw asks Paredes to avoid bias not because of Paredes's critique of Webb or the Texas Rangers but because it weakens the manuscript's main claims. This differs from the story of suppression regarding Paredes's book manuscript due to his critique of the Texas Rangers or Webb. Wardlaw ends his letter focusing on the manuscript's structure stating that he "feel[s] quite strongly that the book must be reorganized with the general reader in mind if it is to achieve its full potentialities."[145] Paredes replied to Wardlaw stating that he does not think he can revise the manuscript to the satisfaction of the press's advisory board and asked for his manuscript.[146] However, if Paredes would have been right about Wardlaw's charge of bias toward Webb and the Texas Rangers, Wardlaw would have simply returned the manuscript to Paredes just as countless other editors had done before him, but he did not.

Instead, Wardlaw replied to Paredes's letter pleading with him to reconsider his manuscript withdrawal; Wardlaw "believe[s] that [Paredes] can" revise the manuscript and assures him that "[n]one of us here want your point of view or your arguments 'watered down' in the least."[147] Reiterating his previous comments in relation to Webb's involvement in the decision to publish the manuscript, Wardlaw tries to reassure Paredes that "[o]ne of the great values of your work lies in the fact that it depicts, for the first time in print, the true attitude of the Border people toward the Texas Rangers. Dr. Webb was particularly impressed with this, and said that it was long overdue."[148] Wardlaw ends his letters asking Paredes to reconsider rescinding his manuscript from the press. Paredes acquiesced and wrote to Wardlaw explaining that while he is not "certain whether [he] can revise the manuscript in a manner that would be satisfactory[,]" he has "decided that it is a good idea to rewrite the whole thing in a more publishable form anyway."[149] Paredes then went on to revise, shorten, and reorganize the manuscript's structure based on Wardlaw's suggestions, who in turn considered the revised manuscript "splendid."[150] The topic of bias or the treatment of the Texas Rangers did not appear in subsequent correspondence between Paredes and Wardlaw leading to the book publication. Even after the monograph was published, Wardlaw was proud of its publication by the University of Texas Press. In a letter to George I. Sánchez, Wardlaw states that *"With His Pistol"* "is an unusually fine book and [I] am proud that we had a part in it. It will no doubt infuriate some Texans, notably the Ranger worshippers, but it should add to the understanding of many more."¹⁵¹ However, the publication of *"With His Pistol"* did not mean that other university presses, or even University of Texas Press, increased the publication of works by Mexican American scholars. The exclusion of scholars of colors by academic presses only began to shift after student protests for ethnic studies at colleges and universities in the 1960s and 1970s.

"With His Pistol" contains echoes of World War II along with the struggle between the Mexican and American in Paredes's identity after his experiences during the U.S. occupation of Japan. Despite the critique in *"With His Pistol"* of Texas historiography and the racial violence carried out by Texas Rangers against Texas Mexicans, Paredes's book contains a critical evolution of his Mexican and American identity. Rather than an ideological return to his 1930s poems and *George Washington Gómez* when Paredes's writings asserted a Mexican heritage as a counterbalance to the exclusion of Texas Mexicans, *"With His Pistol"* and the figure of Gregorio Cortez are reflections of an evolving "Mexican American" identity based in part on his experiences in Asia.¹⁵² As Ramón Saldívar correctly notes, "the marks of Asia are visible throughout *With His Pistol in His Hand.*"¹⁵³ Paredes indeed connects his experiences in the Borderlands as a racialized subject before the war with his experiences in Asia and the racialization of Asian people in the Pacific; however, rather than focusing on the logic of racialization that both affected and influenced Mexican American soldiers, *"With His Pistol"* engages with how Mexican American soldiers were able to carve a space within American mainstream society. In the epilogue section of *"With His Pistol,"* after investigating the life and legend of Gregorio Cortez, Paredes discusses Cortez's legacy that Paredes connects to World War II by arguing that the war changed Texas Mexicans in the Borderlands. He argues that before World War II, especially during the period of Aniceto Pizaña's uprising in 1915, economic changes pushed Texas Mexicans "into the depressed class, both economically and politically."¹⁵⁴ Paredes notes that "[u]ntil the rise of Hitler in Germany and the beginning of World War II, a majority of Border Mexicans continued to think of themselves as people apart."¹⁵⁵ Texas Mexicans before the war were economically isolated from the larger U.S. economy and society, and this isolation allowed them to preserve their cultural ties with Mexico. According to Paredes, they "directed their energies not toward being accepted into the majority but toward maintaining their own individual rights as members of an aloof enclave struggling to keep its

own identity."[156] As a result, the war and their army deployment changed their perception of themselves vis-à-vis U.S. mainstream society.

Paredes argues in *"With His Pistol"* that World War II changed the Texas Mexicans' cultural production of the Borderlands, as they came to see themselves as Americans due to their war experiences.[157] In the book's epilogue, Paredes notes that Cortez's sons served in World War II; one of Cortez's sons, Gregorio, "fought the Germans with his rifle in his hand," and another son, Louis, "belonged to the air unit that dropped the atomic bomb on Japan."[158] Rather than finding racialized kindred subjects between the Japanese and Mexican American soldiers, Paredes connects Cortez's family to the U.S. military force just as Paredes was part of the U.S. occupation army in Japan. Paredes argues that after the war, Texas Mexicans developed a culture and identity that was in dialogue with the people and cultures outside the Borderlands, as he notes, "with the advent of World War II greater members of north-bank Borderers began to think of themselves seriously as Americans."[159] *"With His Pistol"* not only engages with Mexican American ballads or the preservation of a Borderlands cultural identity; instead, he envisions the postwar Borderlands as an "in-between" space composed of both Mexican and American cultural and ideological influences. Paredes notes that Texas Mexicans from the Borderlands, just like himself, were "surprised to find that the peoples of Europe and the Pacific thought of [them] as just another American."[160] This major shift in relation to Paredes's identity is clearly exemplified by the symbolism of the Alamo both in *George Washington Gómez* and *"With His Pistol."* In Paredes's novel, there is a scene in which some white students are proud that their ancestors "fought at the Alamo," but Guálinto is proud that his ancestors "killed Gringos at the Alamo."[161] *"With His Pistol"* connects the histories of both white Americans and Mexican Americans through World War II by stating, "[i]n the Pacific, [the] Texas-Mexican and Anglo-Texan fought side by side against an enemy that made for himself an Alamo out of every bunker and every cave."[162] Paredes concludes the epilogue noting that the "Brownsville's World War II hero ... was not the hero of the Border folk but of the American People."[163] Paredes's epilogue reflects how his experiences as part of the U.S. Army that occupied Japan and racialized Asian populations in the Pacific seem to have brought him closer to his American identity, even as most Mexican Americans remained racialized in Texas before and after the war.

Paredes's Texas Mexican identity developed while growing up in the racialized Borderlands, as reflected in his early poetry and fiction, including *Cantos de adolescencia* and *George Washington Gómez*. World War II, the U.S. occupation of Japan, and the start of the Korean War influenced Paredes by showing how racialization traveled beyond Texas, as the United States contributed to the racialization of Japanese soldiers and civilians. His newspaper articles for *Pacific Stars and Stripes* on the Tokyo war crimes trial, along with his short fiction set in Asia, reflect the contradictions within a military structure that racialized its enemies but also soldiers of color within its ranks. The publication of *"With His Pistol"* by the University of Texas Press illustrates the influence academic presses had on scholars of color and the impact such publications could have on their careers. While university presses were notorious for their gatekeeping practices before the 1970s, the publication of *"With His Pistol"* in 1958 represented an exception rather than a trend among university presses at the time. *"With His Pistol"* became a foundational text for Mexican American writers and scholars who came of age intellectually during the 1960s and subsequent decades. In contrast to Sloss-Vento, who unsuccessfully sought to connect the legacy of early Mexican American civil rights leaders with emerging activists of the Chicanx Movement, Paredes in his position as an academic was able to influence early scholars such as Juan Gómez-Quiñones and José Limón,[164] thus making Paredes an intellectual contributor to the Mexican American civil rights movement of the 1960s and 1970s. The fight for the inclusion of writers of color did not only originate with students' demands for ethnic studies on college campuses during the 1960s and 1970s, but also was influenced by the efforts from scholars, writers, and civil rights leaders of previous decades who fought for literary, scholarly, and intellectual recognition.

CONCLUSION

PUBLISHING LATINIDAD PAST AND PRESENT

THE PERIOD between 1880 and 1960 in Latinx literary and intellectual history includes a relatively small number of books published by U.S. mainstream publishers that have become part of the Latinx literary tradition, such as Ruiz de Burton's *The Squatter and the Don*, Niggli's *Mexican Village*, and Villarreal's *Pocho*. A substantial number of books, including Díaz Guerra's *Lucas Guevara*, Espinoza's *Under the Texas Sun*, and Perales's *In Defense of My People*, were published in Spanish by local publishing houses with an intended Spanish-speaking readership either on the East Coast or in the Southwest; nonetheless, due in part to their local or regional reach, these texts did not break into mainstream literary or intellectual discourses in the United States after their publication. Pre-1960s Latinx writers published their works in specific U.S. regions, were concerned with distinct historical events, and represented groups from Latin America in the United States or members of other groups such as Mexican Americans who in most cases did not identify as part of a pan-ethnic group. These and other characteristics have raised questions related to canonization, periodization, and historization in the formation of the Latinx literary and intellectual tradition. Scholars of Latinx literary history have advanced different methodologies to incorporate these texts and writers into a unified Latinx literary history and more broadly within the larger American literary tradition.¹ Moreover, critical studies have focused on important questions in the analyses of Latinx literary and intellectual history regarding processes of identity formation among some of these authors while accounting for their distinct backgrounds, geographies, and regional or transnational visions.² Early Latinx authors often wrote about their own conceptualizations regarding their racial or ethnic identities vis-à-vis the white majority in a specific U.S. region. Latinx literary and intellectual production provided the outlet where these authors theorized about their own identities, or what in contemporary analyses is often described as Latinidad.

In the preceding chapters, I interpreted the development of the Latinx literary and intellectual tradition from 1880 to 1960 as a process enriched by the study and analysis beyond single-authored books of fiction or poetry as the primary markers of literary or intellectual value. Due in part to the limited opportunities for Latinx authors to publish their writings with U.S. mainstream publishers, the development of Latinx literary history did not only occur through the production of books of fiction or poetry but also through alternative print forms and genres that until recently have remained on the periphery when mapping the tradition. Indeed, most authors studied in the previous chapters achieved either literary or intellectual recognition since they were able to publish books with either regional, alternative, or academic presses, as in the case of Sloss-Vento, Colón, and Paredes respectively; however, some of these and other authors also attempted to publish their works with New York City publishers without success. Thus, I have argued that due in part to these limited publishing opportunities with U.S. mainstream publishers, early Latinx literary and intellectual production occurred in local Spanish-language newspapers, the labor press, U.S. government publications, or as in the case of Martí, in Latin American newspapers. While my study focused on the publication histories of these writers, particularly in relation to the publication of their nontraditional books, there is still more to study in relation to the exclusion of Latinx writers and journalists from mass-circulation newspapers and periodicals before the 1970s.³ Writers like Sloss-Vento and Colón used Spanish-language newspapers and periodicals in San Antonio and New York City respectively as opportunities to enter public debates and advocate for their respective communities that otherwise would not have been afforded to them.

In *Publishing Latinidad*, I focused on how Latinx literary and intellectual production occurred in alternative print forms and genres in addition to books and Spanish-language publications. Alternative print forms, such as translations, paratexts, bibliographies, and sketches, to name a few, have remained for the most part on the margins of critical studies that seek to comprehensively map the Latinx literary and intellectual tradition. Early Latinx writers and intellectuals engaged with other forms of print and genres, as in the case of Martí's translations, Schomburg's prefaces and bibliographies, and Colón's sketches published in the labor press. When early Latinx authors published books with regional or alternative presses, these books took the form of nontraditional genres not commonly associated with literary and intellectual production, as in the case of Sáenz's diary, Sloss-Vento's biography, and Colón's collection of newspaper writings. Martí was an already established poet when he arrived in New York City; however, some of his publishing projects in the United States involved translations of books written in English. In one of the most significant instances that highlights the influence of nontraditional literary genres prior to the 1960s, Paredes was able to publish his scholarly monograph with a university press, which allowed him to become a published fiction writer; however, Paredes's monograph also highlights the scarcity of such publishing opportunities for other Latinx scholars in previous and subsequent years. Latinx authors for the most part did not have access to mainstream publications and publishers; nonetheless, this does not mean that Latinx writers did not engage in public debates, particularly when it came to challenging the marginalized position of their respective communities within U.S. society; these writings were made possible largely by alternative print forms. Rather than just a complement, these and other print forms and nontraditional books represent an integral part of this period in Latinx literary and intellectual history.

Rather than superimposing contemporary articulations of Latinidad on these alternative print forms and genres in Latinx literature, I emphasize that it was early Latinx writers who theorized about their racial and ethnic identities and the place of their local communities in relation to the larger U.S. white majority. Authors that comprise chapter-length case studies in *Publishing Latinidad*, with perhaps the exception of Martí, challenged in their writings the racialization of their respective communities that took the form of exclusion, disenfranchisement, and segregation through legislation and the judicial system and, in some cases, through extrajudicial methods and racial violence. Their theorizing about aspects of their racial and ethnic identities, in various print forms have contributed to the formation of a pan-ethnic vision of Latinidad and group solidarity among different groups who are currently encompassed under a "Latinx" category. Moreover, for some early Latinx writers, their own racial and ethnic identities were not fixed but evolved as in the case of Sáenz, Perales, and Colón, as shown by their writings in different print publications. I have argued that writers who are the focus of my study, except for Martí, wrote with an awareness of their racialization by the white majority that at every turn kept them on the margins of society since the early periods of U.S. territorial expansion in the Southwest and the Caribbean. As a result of their racialized position in U.S. society, they remained excluded from mass-circulation newspapers, high-profile periodicals, and mainstream publishing houses. While early Latinx authors identified as members of distinct groups in local geographical regions in the United States, these authors shared histories of racialization, marginalization, and exclusion from U.S. society. These shared traits are what has led to my interpretation of how these authors engaged with early notions of Latinidad, an emphasis on either ethnic, cultural, or linguistic characteristics, and a set of histories from different regions in the United States, which has contributed to the contemporary "Latinx" pan-ethnic identification in academic discourses and has allowed for the mapping of a "Latinx" literary tradition.

A major claim in *Publishing Latinidad* is that early Latinx writers entered public discourses through alternative print forms and developed racial and ethnic identities by focusing not only on processes of racialization affecting their own communities but also other non-white groups in the United States. The histories of their communities (Mexican Americans, Puerto Ricans, Cuban Americans) relate to the histories of other non-white groups (Black, Indigenous, and Asian Americans) due in a large part to the way racialization occurred in the United States since the start of the country's formation. An analysis of early Latinx writing through various print cultures shows that these authors and intellectuals at times theorized about their position as racialized subjects by writing about the experiences of other non-white groups. Sáenz's diary, for instance, compares the fight for civil rights by Mexican Americans in the early decades of the twentieth century with the struggles of Native people in the United States. While some authors like Martí and Schomburg sought to develop transnational or diasporic networks and alliances against U.S. expansionism, they also interpreted their struggle by writing about processes of racialization in the United States, as in the case of Martí's analysis of Indigenous people's land dispossession and Schomburg's recovery of Black texts that were relegated to the margins in mainstream historical accounts. Literary critics have identified instances of cross-racial commonalities among Latinxs and other minoritized groups. Juan Flores in his foreword to Colón's *A Puerto Rican in New York*, for instance, explains that the experiences of Afro-Latinxs were tied to those of Black people and other marginalized groups in New York City.[4] In my study, I developed a chronological narrative that traces instances where Latinx authors, perhaps with the exception of Martí, wrote about the shared racialized experiences with other non-white groups during some of the most significant historical periods in U.S. history (Indian removal, the Spanish-American War, and the two world wars). Indeed, the emerging field of comparative ethnic literatures has allowed for the interpretation of early Latinx writers and intellectuals as some of the early ethnic comparativists.

Publishing Latinidad seeks to contribute to the increasing number of critical studies on Latinx literary history that have offered analyses on pre-1960s Latinx writers and intellectuals in different geographies and temporalities. While there has been an increasing number of studies in the past two decades since Kirsten Silva Gruesz argued that the Latinx literary canon, as represented by the *Norton Anthology of Latino Literature* (2011), was still "a body of literature that doesn't yet have a literary history,"[5] the field still offers exciting possibilities for further development.[6] There is a need for additional studies that contextualize the contributions of early Latinx writers like Luisa Capetillo, Leonor Villegas de Magnón, José Tomás Canales, Juan Antonio Corretjer, Elena Zamora O'Shea, and Josefina Silva de Cintrón since these authors are yet to be more fully incorporated in Latinx literary studies. Additional book-length studies would continue to study the publishing practices of early twentieth-century Spanish-language newspapers and periodicals and their editors, including Jovita Idar, Sotero Figueroa, Alberto O'Farrill, Bernardo Vega, Ignacio E. Lozano, and Consuelo Lee Tapia. Possible avenues for investigation would employ a comparative ethnic studies framework to focus on the newspaper writings and editorial practices of early Latina editors and their Black counterparts, such as Gertrude Bustill Mossell, Pauline Hopkins, Alice Dunbar Nelson, Ida B. Wells, Jessie Fauset, and Dorothy West.

The access to publishing venues for Latinx writers changed with the student-led protests at college campuses during the 1960s and 1970s that allowed for the emergence of an academic infrastructure and the study of Latinx authors, and other writers of color, who were previously excluded from the curriculum. While mainstream publishing houses increased the number of the authors of color they published, Latinx literary production also occurred in alternative print forms and through the emergence of Latinx publishing houses. Latinx periodicals and journals such as *El Grito*, *Caracol*, *Aztlán*, and *Revista Chicano-Riqueña* emerged as outlets for Latinx writers and scholars to publish their works. Just as important, independent Latinx presses such as Third Woman Press, led by Norma Alarcón, and Quito Sol Publications, started by Octavio I. Romano, served as some of the early publishing venues for some of the most acclaimed post-1960s Latinx writers. Among these efforts, Arte Público Press under the leadership of Nicolás Kanellos stands out as it has functioned as the most important Latinx publishing house since its creation in 1979. Arte Público Press often offered the first publishing opportunity to now-canonical Latinx authors during the 1980s who then went on to publish other works with mainstream publishers. In a similar way, Arte Público Press has played an unparalleled role in recovering and publishing early Latinx texts that otherwise would have remained in the Latinx archive. Kanellos, in his role as "senior editor" of Latinx literature through Arte Público Press, has remained for almost the last fifty years the most important publisher of early and contemporary Latinx books.[7] Similarly, academic presses have served a significant role in the publication and recovery of the Latinx literary and intellectual past.[8] Notably, the University of New Mexico Press and its series Pasó Por Aquí has republished early *Nuevomexicano* texts from the Southwest. The University of Arizona Press series Camino del Sol, for instance, is dedicated to publishing the work of contemporary Latinx writers and poets. While efforts by Latinx and university presses are crucial, Latinx writers are yet to receive meaningful publishing opportunities from mainstream houses.

More than half a century after the first efforts of Latinx authors to publish with mainstream publishing houses, the literary marginalization of Latinx writers, and other authors of color, continues in the twenty-first century, and the need for greater literary representation and structural change in U.S. publishing remains as pressing as it has been in the past. Increasingly, literary scholars have begun to interrogate the influence of the mainstream publishing industry on U.S. cultural production—an industry that is more than ninety-percent white and has systematically "redlined" authors of color.[9] Literary critics have similarly focused on the effects of publishing conglomeration, the increasing emphasis on commercial bestsellers in the past decades, and the homogenization of fiction through the emergence of online publishing platforms.[10] The U.S. publishing industry plays a predominant role when it comes to readers' preferences and, historically, has almost systematically excluded writers and editors of color, as white editors make the majority of acquisition decisions.[11] It is worth interrogating the practices of some contemporary mainstream publishers that still direct the weight of their marketing departments to the same Latinx writers whose books they first published almost forty years ago. While publishing books represents a business that acts in accordance with profits and losses, market demands, demographics, and readership trends, book publishers and editors have often prided themselves on the premise that their profession is not only driven by monetary gains but also contributes and influences U.S. cultural production.[12] There is a need to envision, develop, and implement strategies for Latinx representation and structural change in mainstream publishing since Latinxs have remained for the most part invisible in mainstream literary publications and in leadership positions at publishing houses.[13] This is exemplified by the extremely low number of Latinx editors in mainstream publishing and by the absence of Latinx writers for the most part in mainstream publications, such as the *New York Times*, *New Yorker*, *Paris Review*, and *New York Reviews of Books*, for the past several decades. This invisibility is not the result of lack of resources, education, or talent on the part of Latinx writers and editors; rather, it reflects a continuing lack of access. The almost invisibility of Latinx writers in mainstream publications and publishing did not occur by happenstance; it has been the result of centuries of social, economic, and cultural marginalization.

There have been changes in the past few years in the mainstream publishing industry in its attempt to include Latinx authors, but as is often the case, it is still unclear if these relatively minor and slow steps represent meaningful inclusion or structural lasting change. The pages of current mainstream newspapers now showcase more than one Latinx author in their list of upcoming novels; likewise, contemporary Latinx authors can write narratives beyond the expected performance of Latinidad for non-Latinx readers. Latinx authors have started to gain visibility in literary organizations and awards such as the Pulitzers and the National Book Awards. It is noteworthy that mainstream publishers have begun to address glaring disparities when it comes to representation in editorial positions. While these are encouraging signs, Latinx writers, publishers, scholars, and activists should continue to advocate for meaningful and sustainable change in mainstream publications and publishing. One of the most significant and enduring lessons of the period of the student-led protests at college campuses during the 1960s and 1970s is that access to historical, cultural, and literary experiences for students of color was seldom given without having to fight for it.

NOTES

Introduction

1. The recovery and publication of pre-1960s Latinx literary text from multiple geographies and authors from different backgrounds by Arte Público Press constitutes one of the most significant developments in the formation of the Latinx literary tradition. See Castañeda and C. Lomas, *Writing/Righting History*.
2. I employ the term "Latinx" when referring to what has also been conceived as "Latina/o" literary studies due to its possibilities in allowing the conceptualization of the literary and intellectual production that today constitutes the largest minoritized group in the U.S. At times, Latinidad in the context of Latinx literature has been theorized in relation to race and ethnicity and for its possibilities for pan-ethnic and racial, cultural, social, and political solidarity; see Caminero-Santangelo, *On Latinidad*. Moreover, within the realm of literary studies, Latinidad and the rubric "Latinx" have the potential to stand for something beyond ethnic and racial identification. As Kirsten Silva Gruesz states, "LatinX is not a demographic label but a conceptual frame, one that downgrades ethnicity as the principal rationale of the category." Gruesz, *Cotton Mather*, 229. Terms such as "Latinx," "Afro-Latinx," and Latinidad have historically remained in constant flux. Throughout my study the terms "Latinx" and "Latinidad" acknowledge women, Black, Indigenous, and other communities who have traditionally remained on the margins during the early conceptualization of a Latino identity formation in the U.S. See Morales, *Latinx*. Moreover, I use the term "Latinx" retroactively to describe authors from different Latin American backgrounds who either grew up or resided in the U.S. before 1960. For a cogent discussion of the term "Latinx" to denote nineteenth century authors of Latin American and Caribbean descent writing in Spanish in the U.S., see Lamas, *Latino Continuum*, 4–11.

3. See Kanellos, *Latinos and Nationhood*, 27; and Cutler, "Latinx Historicisms," 105.
4. I use the term "racialization" as it is theorized by Charles W. Mills in *The Racial Contract* and Latinx scholars such as Ian Haney López, Martha Menchaca, and Laura E. Gómez, who have studied white supremacy as a system of social and economic control, the function of racial hierarchies, and the exclusion of non-white groups through laws and the judicial system during the formation of the U.S. and its territorial expansion, particularly in the Southwest and the Caribbean.
5. See, for instance, Tebbel, *History of Book Publishing in the United States* (4 Vols.); Amory and Hall, *History of the Book in America* (5 Vols.); Tebbel, *Between Covers*; Radway, *Feeling for Books*; and Silverman, *Time of Their Lives*.
6. Jackson, "Talking Book," 254.
7. Jackson, "Talking Book," 254.
8. Rezek, "Racialization of Print," 418.
9. Other scholars who have built upon Bourdieu's theorizations on class distinction and cultural capital include Guillory, *Cultural Capital*; English, *Economy of Prestige*; and Thompson, *Merchants of Culture*.
10. Bourdieu, *Distinction*, 120.
11. Guillory, *Cultural Capital*, ix.
12. For critics of Black literature who have focused on the creation, production, distribution, and reception of books by Black writers, particularly from the early decades of the twentieth century, see Hutchinson, *Harlem Renaissance*; Young, *Black Writers, White Publishers*; Hutchinson and Young, *Publishing Blackness*; Edwards, *Practice of Diaspora*; Jackson, *Indignant Generation*; and Bernard, *Carl Van Vechten*.
13. Hutchinson and Young, *Publishing Blackness*, 4.
14. See White, *Tastemaker*, 165–96; and Claridge, *Lady with the Borzoi*, 115–25.
15. Jean-Christophe Cloutier's *Shadow Archives* studies the large number of pre-1960s Black texts now located at university archival collections that were not printed during the authors' lifetimes.
16. So, *Redlining Culture*, 22.
17. Young, *Black Writers, White Publishers*, 19.
18. Young, *Black Writers, White Publishers*, 17.
19. The study of nineteenth-century Spanish-language print culture in the U.S. constitutes one of the most important developments in Latinx literary studies. In recent decades, there has been an increase in scholarship of Spanish-language print culture in the U.S. represented by critics such as Nicolás Kanellos, A. Gabriel Meléndez, Kirsten Silva Gruesz, Rodrigo Lazo, Jesse Alemán, John M. González, Ramón Saldívar, Laura Lomas, John Alba Cutler, Carmen Lamas, Vanessa Fonseca-Chávez, and José Aranda.
20. Kanellos and Martell, *Hispanic Periodicals*, 7.
21. One of the most important developments in the study of Spanish-language print culture has been the digitalization of Spanish-language newspapers and periodicals in the form of the Readex Hispanic American Newspapers, 1808–1980 database, a project developed in collaboration with the Recovering the U.S. Hispanic Literary

22. Lazo, *Letters from Filadelfia*, 19.
23. Gruesz, *Ambassadors of Culture*, xvi. See also Coronado, *World Not to Come*, xv; and Aranda, *Places of Modernity*, 28.
24. See Gruesz, *Ambassadors of Culture*; Lazo, *Writing to Cuba*; Lamas, *Latino Continuum*; and Cutler, "Latinx Modernism."
25. See Ernest, *Liberation Historiography*; Gardner, *Black Print Unbound*; Rusert, *Fugitive Science*; and Spires, *Practice of Citizenship*.
26. Spires, *Practice of Citizenship*, 7.
27. See, for example, Nerone, "Newspapers and the Public Sphere"; and Kaestle and Radway, "History of Publishing."
28. Tebbel, *Book Publishing*, 9–10.
29. Scholars have studied the proliferation of various *Nuevomexicano* literary forms such as poetry, fiction, and essays produced prior to 1960 in Spanish-language newspapers and periodicals beyond the printed book. See Gonzales-Berry, *Critical Essays on the New Mexican Literary Tradition*; Torres, *World of Early Chicano Poetry*; A. Meléndez, *So All Is Not Lost*; and A. Meléndez and Lomelí, *Writings of Eusebio Chacón*.
30. See G. Padilla, *My History, Not Yours*; Coronado, *World Not to Come*; Varon, *Before Chicano*; Lamas, *Latino Continuum*; Aranda, *Places of Modernity*; Lazo, *Letters from Filadelfia*; Spires, *Practice of Citizenship*; and Jackson, *Indignant Generation*.
31. Coronado, *World Not to Come*, 393.
32. McHenry, *Negro Literature*, 21.
33. McHenry, *Negro Literature*, 5.
34. See Coronado, *World Not to Come*; Lazo, *Letters from Filadelfia*; and Lamas, *Latino Continuum*.
35. See M. García, *Mexican Americans*; Gómez-Quiñones, *Roots of Chicano Politics*; Torres-Saillant, *Intellectual History of the Caribbean*; J. M. González, *Border Renaissance*; A. Sánchez, *Homeland*; and Kanellos, *Latinos and Nationhood*.
36. Coronado, *World Not to Come*, 30.
37. Paul Frymer in *Building an American Empire* explains that since its beginnings, the U.S. government policy during westward expansion consisted of removing and displacing non-whites and replacing them with white settlers, and when Indigenous, Black, and other non-white communities could not be further removed, they were excluded through legislation and the courts system. Frymer, *American Empire*, 20.

Chapter 1

1. Some of these scholars include Nicolás Kanellos, A. Gabriel Meléndez, Francisco A. Lomelí, Rodrigo Lazo, Jesse Alemán, Kirsten Silva Gruesz, José Aranda, Laura Lomas, and Carmen Lamas.
2. Cutler, "Latinx Modernism," 572.

3. I follow the lead of scholars who have used the term "Latinx" retroactively to encompass the various print cultures and archives from Spanish-speaking writers from different backgrounds who lived and wrote in the U.S. In the context of Spanish-language print culture and Latinx literary history, Cutler argues that "[t]he *x* in *Latinx* indexes the fragmentation and fugitivity of the archive, gesturing toward everything missing, everything we do not know and may never know about the periodicals, their editors, and contributors." Cutler, "Latinx Modernism," 575. See also Varon, "Archival Excess in Latinx Print Culture."
4. See Lazo, *Writing to Cuba*; Luis-Brown, *Waves of Decolonization*; Hoffnung-Garskof, *Racial Migrations*; and Lamas, *Latino Continuum*.
5. Lamas, *Latino Continuum*, 8.
6. Cutler, "Latinx Modernism," 575.
7. Guerra, *Myth of José Martí*, 6. For historical analyses on Martí's role in the movement for Cuban independence and his revolutionary writings, see also Ferrer, *Insurgent Cuba*, 112–38; E. Meléndez, *Patria*, 64–80; and L. Pérez, *Sugar, Cigars, and Revolution*, 270–99.
8. See Belnap and Fernández, *José Martí's "Our America"*; Allen, *José Martí Selected Writings*; Rotker, *American Chronicles of José Martí*; and Ramos, *Divergent Modernities*.
9. My analysis builds on the work of literary scholars who have studied Martí's writings on U.S. Indigenous people and his translation of *Ramona*. See Gillman, "*Ramona*"; L. Lomas, *Translating Empire*; Camacho, *José Martí*; Fountain, *José Martí*; and Lamas, *Latino Continuum*.
10. Critical discussions of Martí and U.S. Indigenous people are yet to grapple with the imposition of U.S. laws and its court system on Native groups who already possessed their own modes of sovereignty as historicized and theorized by scholars such as Audra Simpson, Jodi Byrd, Glen Sean Coulthard, María Josefina Saldaña-Portillo, and Mark Rifkin.
11. Martí, *Obras Completas*, 11: 264. Martí's 26-volume *Obras Completas* (Complete Works), published by Editorial Nacional de Cuba and mostly written in Spanish, has not been translated into English; only a handful of his newspaper writings have been translated, particularly in *José Martí Selected Writings*, edited and translated by Esther Allen. Unless otherwise noted, this and subsequent translations in this and the following chapters are mine. In a few instances, I included missing accents in words, particularly in Spanish-language newspapers' titles.
12. Camacho, *José Martí*, 46–47.
13. For an analysis of Mexico's racial hierarchies, see Menchaca, *Recovering History*, 49–66.
14. Martí, *Obras Completas*, 6: 283.
15. Martí, *Obras Completas*, 6: 283.
16. Camacho, *José Martí*, 143–44.
17. Kaestle and Radway discuss technological developments such as the telegraph, the telephone, and the typewriter that allowed news and events to travel across

18. Sundquist, *Empire and Slavery*, 78.
19. Benjamin Madley observes that readers' interest in the plight of Indigenous groups and their land dispossession coincided with positive portrayals published in books. Madley, *American Genocide*, 357. Some of these nonfiction works include Thomas Henry Tibbles's *The Ponca Chiefs: An Indian's Attempt to Appeal from the Tomahawk to the Courts* (1879); George W. Manypenny's *Our Indian Wards* (1880); and Sarah Winnemucca Hopkins's *Life among the Piutes: Their Wrongs and Claims* (1883).
20. Mathes, *Jackson*, 25–26.
21. On Jackson's early newspaper writings on Indigenous people prior to *A Century of Dishonor*, see Mathes, *Jackson*, 21–37. For an analysis of Jackson's articles in *Century* magazine, see Holbo, "Industrial & Picturesque Narrative."
22. Critics such as Rotker, Ramos, L. Lomas, and Allen have focused on Martí as a New York City-based writer engaging in U.S. social and political debates through his writings in newspapers and periodicals.
23. Collins, "Pure Feelings," 13. Some of Martí's early newspaper writings in New York City are written from the perspective of a traveler-observer and his privileged position as intellectual, or *letrado*, who was conversant with European culture, literature, and art. Collins, "Pure Feelings," 17.
24. Rotker, *American Chronicles*, 33–34. New technologies such as the telegraph along with the increase of international relations and commerce helped newspapers at the time, such as *La Nación*, to facilitate the translation and serialization of European novels within their pages. Rotker, *American Chronicles*, 33.
25. Ramos, *Divergent Modernities*, 86.
26. For discussions on the *crónica* as a genre in Latin America and Martí's use of it, see Rotker, *American Chronicles*, 57–59; and Ramos, *Divergent Modernities*, 112–18.
27. Rotker has identified at least two distinct stages in Martí's *crónicas* during his New York City years, beginning from 1881 to 1884 with his initial encounter with U.S. social, political, and cultural life as a "dazzled spectator," moving to his "critical radicalization" from 1884 to 1892. Rotker, "Exile Gaze," 69.
28. For discussions on the rise of nationally distributed magazines in the U.S. such as *Harper's* and *Century* magazine, see Kaestle and Radway, "History of Publishing," 13–14. *Century* magazine, for instance, was the venue where writers such as Edward Eggleston and Jackson wrote about Indigenous people. See Jackson, "Father Junipero and His Work"; and Eggleston, "The Aborigines and the Colonists," both published in *Century* in 1883.
29. L. Lomas, *Translating Empire*, 98–99.
30. Martí's *La América: Revista de Agricultura, Industria y Comercio* (America: A Magazine on Agriculture, Industry, and Business) was the first periodical Martí edited in the U.S. from December 1883 to July 1884. L. Lomas, *Translating Empire*, 86. In an article published in the January 1884 issue of *La América*, Martí describes his

ideal readership for his publication as Spanish-speaking readers with cultural or commercial ties to both the U.S. and Latin America who wish to understand "la mente de los Estados Unidos del Norte" (North American thought) and as a venue to exchange "intereses y pensamientos" (interests and thoughts) among people in North and South America. Martí, *Obras Completas*, 8:266.
31. Martí, *Obras Completas*, 13: 430.
32. Martí, *Obras Completas*, 13: 437.
33. Ramos, *Divergent Modernities*, 83.
34. See, for example, "They Must Go. The Crow Indians Have Rich Lands and They Must Move Off," *Kansas City Star*, February 8, 1882.
35. Indigenous resistance against U.S. military campaigns of aggression, based on the latter deployment of deadly technologies improved during the Civil War, has been misleadingly framed in historical memory as "Indian Wars." Madley, *American Genocide*, 12.
36. Martí, *Obras Completas*, 9: 297.
37. Rifkin, *Beyond Settler Time*, xi.
38. Martí, *Obras Completas*, 9: 297.
39. See "Coveting the Crow Lands," *Cherokee Advocate*, March 24, 1882.
40. Martí, *Obras Completas*, 9: 297.
41. Dunbar-Ortiz, *Indigenous Peoples' History*, 146.
42. Martí, *Obras Completas*, 9: 297.
43. Rifkin, *Beyond Settler Time*, 60.
44. Rifkin, *Beyond Settler Time*, 52.
45. Byrd, *Transit of Empire*, xii.
46. Jackson, *Century of Dishonor*, 95.
47. Martí, *Obras Completas*, 9: 298.
48. Jackson, *Century of Dishonor*, 95–96.
49. Rifkin, *Beyond Settler Time*, 52.
50. Wood's piece for *Century* chronicles the history of past interactions between the Nez Perce and the U.S. government prior and during the military campaign against the former led by the U.S. cavalry that culminated with the "capture" of their leader Joseph in 1877. Wood, "Chief Joseph," 141.
51. Martí, *Obras Completas*, 13: 447.
52. Dunbar-Ortiz, *Indigenous Peoples' History*, 149. Camacho observes that Martí's *crónica* omits the names of Generals Howard and Miles from the *Century* piece since Martí had praised Miles in his previous *crónica* on the Cheyenne. Camacho, *José Martí*, 96.
53. Martí, *Obras Completas*, 13: 449.
54. Martí, *Obras Completas*, 13: 447.
55. Martí, *Obras Completas*, 13: 449.
56. Martí, *Obras Completas*, 13: 449.
57. Jackson, *Century of Dishonor*, 133.
58. Martí, *Obras Completas*, 13: 449.
59. Camacho, *José Martí*, 97, 100.

60. Martí, *Obras Completas*, 10: 321. During the conference's opening session, attendees were similarly critical of the U.S. government and its treaty policy that had rendered Native groups as "outside our institutions and the protection of our laws." *Proceedings*, 11.
61. Fletcher began her ethnographic and anthropological work in 1880 studying with Frederic Ward Putnam at the Peabody Museum at Harvard; in subsequent years, Fletcher traveled and lived among different Native groups including the Sioux, Omahas, and the Nez Perce. Mark, *Stranger in Her Native Land*, xiii.
62. Martí, *Obras Completas*, 10: 323.
63. Fletcher traveled and visited Indigenous lands and witnessed firsthand the interactions among Native peoples, merchants, and government officials. In her address at the Mohonk Conference, Fletcher focuses on the annuities owned by the U.S. government marked for food and clothing that failed to reach those communities, which as a consequence "tend[ed] to pauperize the Indian." *Proceedings*, 46.
64. Martí, *Obras Completas*, 10: 323.
65. Martí, *Obras Completas*, 10: 323.
66. Rifkin, *Beyond Settler Time*, viii.
67. During the 1885 Lake Mohonk Conference, a series of resolutions were passed honoring Jackson's recent death by some of the conference's most prominent attendees such as Erastus Brooks and Fletcher who praised Jackson for her reform efforts on behalf of Native peoples. *Proceedings*, 68–71.
68. Martí, *Obras Completas*, 10: 322.
69. Martí, *Obras Completas*, 10: 322.
70. Martí, *Obras Completas*, 10: 322.
71. Jackson, *Century of Dishonor*, 27.
72. Jackson, *Century of Dishonor*, 30.
73. Jackson, *Century of Dishonor*, 341.
74. Martí, *Obras Completas*, 10: 327.
75. Simpson, "Ethnographic Refusal," 67.
76. Coulthard, for instance, argues that the recognition of Native groups by the U.S. government as members of its political structure sought to "entice Indigenous people to *identify*, either implicitly or explicitly, with the profoundly *asymmetrical* and *nonreciprocal* forms of recognition either imposed on or granted to them by the settler state and society." Coulthard, *Red Skin, White Masks*, 25.
77. Simpson, *Mohawk Interruptus*, 7–8.
78. Madley, *American Genocide*, 220–21.
79. Lamas, *Latino Continuum*, 18.
80. Lamas, *Latino Continuum*, 8.
81. Lamas, for instance, analyzes the extent to which Tolón's *Compendio de la historia de los Estados Unidos ó república de América* (1853), a translation of Emma Willard's *Abridged History of the United States or Republic of America*, made multiples changes in his translation, including "textual interventions," that challenged Willard's historical account. Lamas, *Latino Continuum*, 79.
82. L. Lomas, *Translating Empire*, 84.

83. Ramos, *Divergent Modernities*, 83. For a thorough analysis of Martí's economic realities in New York City related to his writings, see Ramos, *Divergent Modernities*, 83–91.
84. L. Lomas, *Translating Empire*, 264.
85. Vallejo, "José Martí," 781.
86. Mathes, foreword, xvi. In 1883, after reporting on Indigenous communities in southern California, Jackson famously wrote to the editor of the *Atlantic Monthly* stating, "[i]f I could write a story that would do for the Indians a thousandth part that *Uncle Tom's Cabin* did for the negro, I would be thankful the rest of my life." Quoted in Mathes, foreword, xvi.
87. Phillips, *Jackson*, 260.
88. Phillips, *Jackson*, 260.
89. See Luis-Brown, "Arrogant Mestiza," 822–25; Alemán, "Historical Amnesia," 74–79; J. M. González, "Warp of Whiteness," 441–47; L. Lomas, *Translating Empire*, 264–71; Gillman, "*Ramona* in 'Our America,'" 103–8; Vallejo, "José Martí," 779–83; and Lamas, *Latino Continuum*, 142–53.
90. L. Lomas, *Translating Empire*, 264.
91. Camacho, *José Martí*, 119.
92. Martí, *Obras Completas*, 24: 204. Gillman analyzes in detail the connection between Stowe's *Uncle Tom's Children* and Jackson's *Ramona* to argue for Martí's translation of *Ramona* as an attempt to connect the mistreatment and struggles of Black and Native peoples in the U.S. Gillman, "*Ramona* in 'Our America,'" 91–92.
93. Martí, *Obras Completas*, 24: 203.
94. Quoted in Mathes, afterword, 399.
95. Martí's novel, *Amistad funesta* (Fatal Friendship) published in the New York City-based magazine *El Latino-Americano* in 1885, contains a romantic plot infused with Latin American modernist tendencies but does not openly engage with social or political topics. For discussions of *Amistad funesta* in the context of *latinoamericanismo* and in relation to his translation of *Ramona*, see Luis-Brown, *Waves of Decolonization*, 88–95; and Lamas, *Latino Continuum*, 141–53.
96. Martí, *Obras Completas*, 24: 40.
97. After the U.S.-Mexican War, California Indigenous groups were displaced and some forced into bondage or indentured servitude when white settlers began to arrive in California. As Menchaca notes, "most of the Indians living among the settlers lost their homes, [and] the legal infrastructure was created to convert them into indentured slaves." Menchaca, *Recovering History*, 257. See also Reséndez, *Other Slavery*, 306–8.
98. Aranda, *Places of Modernity*, 111.
99. Jackson, *Ramona*, 189.
100. Martí, *Obras Completas*, 24: 351.
101. Menchaca, *Recovering History*, 258–59.
102. Menchaca, *Recovering History*, 263.
103. In their report on the conditions of California Indigenous people, Jackson and Kinney write about the lack of legal recourse in state and U.S. courts for Native indi-

viduals to claim their lands through litigation and how they were simply unaware of any legal recourse or learned about their land being taken only when a sheriff arrived. Jackson and Kinney, "Report," 470–71.
104. Jackson, *Ramona*, 191.
105. Martí, *Obras Completas*, 24: 352.
106. In their report, Jackson and Kinney give the example of a San Ysidro Native group who were removed from their land, tried to survive on the outskirts of their former lands but lacked water, and how some of them died of hunger. Jackson and Kinney, "Report," 488–90.
107. Madley, *American Genocide*, 146.
108. See Jackson, *Ramona*, 349–90; and Martí, *Obras Completas*, 24: 477–503.
109. Jackson and Kinney, "Report," 471.
110. Madley, *American Genocide*, 354.
111. Jackson, *Ramona*, 340.
112. Martí, *Obras Completas*, 24: 469.
113. Byrd, *Transit of Empire*, 223.
114. Jackson, *Ramona*, 347.
115. Martí, *Obras Completas*, 24: 474.
116. Jackson, *Ramona*, 347.
117. Martí, *Obras Completas*, 24: 474–75.
118. The killing of Alessandro was based on the murder of a Cahuilla Indigenous person, Juan Diego, who was shot by Sam Temple for stealing a horse that was similarly ruled a "justifiable homicide." Mathes, afterword, 397.
119. J. M. González, "Warp of Whiteness," 454.
120. Jackson, *Century of Dishonor*, 340. For an analysis of Jackson's views on U.S. citizenship for Native peoples and its connection to land redistribution and ownership in California, see P. Ramirez, "Inherited Obligations," 152–57.
121. Quoted in Madley, *American Genocide*, 186.
122. Madley, *American Genocide*, 8. In 2019, the Governor of California, Gavin Newsom, formally acknowledged and apologized for the devastating consequences of the dispossession of California Native peoples by white settlers assisted by state and federal authorities, which Newson described as a "genocide" since there is "[n]o other way to describe it. And that's the way it needs to be described in the history books." Quoted in Cowan, "It's Called Genocide."
123. Limerick, *Legacy of Conquest*, 197.
124. Madley, *American Genocide*, 187.
125. Dawes, "Solving the Indian Problem," 28–29.
126. Martí, *Obras Completas*, 11: 133.
127. Martí, *Obras Completas*, 11: 134.
128. Saldaña-Portillo, *Indian Given*, 14.
129. For discussions on the racialization of non-white groups, including Indigenous groups and Mexican Americans, after the U.S. military conquest of California in 1848, see Almaguer, *Racial Fault Lines*, 4–12; and Menchaca, *Recovering History*, 215–37.

130. Frymer, *American Empire*, 17.
131. Martí, *Obras Completas*, 11: 263–64.
132. Martí, *Obras Completas*, 11: 264.
133. Byrd, *Transit of Empire*, xxiii.
134. Martí, *Obras Completas*, 11: 264.
135. Rifkin, *Beyond Settler Time*, 95.
136. Rifkin, *Beyond Settler Time*, 95.
137. Martí, *Obras Completas*, 12: 206.
138. Martí, *Obras Completas*, 12: 206.
139. For a compelling analysis of "Cómo se crea un pueblo nuevo en los Estados Unidos," see Camacho, *José Martí*, 186–202.
140. For discussions on Martí and his writings in U.S.-based print venues around the 1890s such as *La Revista Ilustrada de Nueva York* (New York Illustrated Magazine); *La edad de oro* (The Golden Age), a magazine for children published during 1889; and *Patria*, published between 1892 and 1894, see Kreitz, "American Alternatives"; Schultz de Mantovani, prologue, 9–33; and E. Meléndez, *Patria*, 81–96.
141. Lamas, *Latino Continuum*, 175–76.

Chapter 2

1. Ernest, *Chaotic Justice*, 17.
2. Some of these books include William Cooper Nell, *The Colored Patriots of the American Revolution* (1855); William Wells Brown, *The Black Man: His Antecedents, His Genius, and His Achievements* (1863); and George Washington Williams, *History of the Negro Race in America from 1619 to 1880* (1883). Ernest, *Chaotic Justice*, 13.
3. McHenry, *Forgotten Readers*, 86.
4. Representative of this trend is the publication of Martin Delany's *Blake* that was serialized in Hamilton's *Anglo-African Magazine* in 1859. For discussions on Hamilton and the *Anglo-African Magazine*, see McHenry, *Forgotten Readers*, 129–40; and Wilson, "Brief Wondrous Life."
5. For discussions on Black print culture during the early decades of the twentieth century, see Hutchinson, *Harlem Renaissance*; Edwards, *Practice of Diaspora*; and Jackson, *Indignant Generation*.
6. See Gates and Jarrett, *New Negro*.
7. See, for example, Tillman, "Afro-American Women and Their Work." *A.M.E. Church Review*, April 1895; Braithwaite, "Negro in Literature." *Crisis*, September 1924; and Du Bois, "Criteria of Negro Art." *Crisis*, October 1926.
8. Schomburg, "Negro Digs Up His Past," 235.
9. Sinnette, *Black Bibliophile*, 32.
10. McHenry, *Negro Literature*, 6. For discussions on alternative forms of Black literary production, see Ernest, *Chaotic Justice*, 14–15; Gardner, "Literary Reconstructions," 433–34; McHenry, *Forgotten Readers*, 12–13; Helton, "Making Lists," 82–88; and Spires, "Liberation Bibliography," 2–20.

11. Sinnette, *Black Bibliophile*, 107.
12. For other scholars who have studied Schomburg's contributions to the recovery of Black history and cultural heritage from a transnational and diasporic perspective, see Sánchez González, *Boricua Literature*; Hoffnung-Garskof, "Migrations"; Valdés, *Diasporic Blackness*; and García Peña, *Translating Blackness*.
13. Valdés, *Diasporic Blackness*, 7, 23.
14. Valdés, *Diasporic Blackness*, 4.
15. Hoffnung-Garskof, "Migrations," 37.
16. In their discussion on the emerging approaches to the study of Schomburg's contributions to Black intellectual thought, Laura Helton and Rafia Zafar point out that despite the considerable number of Schomburg's published and unpublished writings that exist, most of these works remain unexplored. Helton and Zafar, "Schomburg," 9.
17. For a detailed discussion on Schomburg's role in Las Dos Antillas and Schomburg's position during the Spanish-American War, see Hoffnung-Garskof, "Migrations," 9–19.
18. Mirabal, *Suspect Freedoms*, 112.
19. When Figueroa arrived in New York City, he established a printing press under the name América where he printed books and newspapers and served as editor of *La Revista Ilustrada de Nueva York* from 1890 to 1892. Kanellos, "Sotero Figueroa," 330.
20. Kanellos, "Sotero Figueroa," 330.
21. Valdés, *Diasporic Blackness*, 40.
22. Kanellos, *Latinos and Nationhood*, 70. See Figueroa's *Ensayo biográfico de los que más han contribuido al progreso de Puerto Rico* (Bibliographical Essay of Those Who Have Contributed to the Progress of Puerto Rico) published in 1888 and *La verdad de la historia* (The Truth about History), a collection of essays originally published in *Patria* in 1892.
23. Sinnette, *Black Bibliophile*, 75.
24. See Sinnette, *Black Bibliophile*, 28–31; Hoffnung-Garskof, "Migrations," 22–25; and Valdés, *Diasporic Blackness*, 64–68. Schomburg, for instance, dedicated to Bruce his well-known lecture "Racial Integrity: A Plea for the Establishment of a Chair of Negro History in Our Schools and Colleges" (1913).
25. Bruce, for example, was a recognized amateur historian with several contacts in the Black press and wrote for Black newspapers as a contributor for publications such as the *Cleveland Gazette*. Crowder, *Bruce*, 96, 113.
26. Locke, *New Negro*, 415.
27. Schomburg, for example, first met Du Bois when the former was accepted into the American Negro Academy for whom Du Bois and Bruce were founding members, and in time, Du Bois and Schomburg corresponded on historical and literary matters. Sinnette, *Black Bibliophile*, 51–53.
28. When discussing their acquaintance, Sinnette points out that "[b]y no stretch of the imagination, however, did Du Bois consider Schomburg a genuine historian or scholar." Sinnette, *Black Bibliophile*, 53. While there may be evidence in the archive

to support this claim, some of their correspondence shows that Du Bois valued Schomburg's historical writings; for instance, after accepting one of Schomburg's essays for *Crisis* in 1927, Du Bois eagerly asked Schomburg in a letter if he would write another article on the history of Black artists in Seville based on Schomburg's recent trip to Spain. Du Bois to Schomburg, May 6, 1927. Schomburg replied that his piece on this topic had already been sent to Charles Johnson to be published in *Opportunity*. Schomburg to Du Bois, May 21, 1927.

29. For a thorough discussion on Du Bois's pioneering work in *Crisis*, see Hutchinson, *Harlem Renaissance*, 142–69.
30. Valdés's analysis is representative of interpretations of Schomburg's writings in Black periodicals during the early decades of the twentieth century that center around his interest on historical figures of the Black diaspora. Valdés, *Diasporic Blackness*, 72–79.
31. García Peña, *Translating Blackness*, 81.
32. Mirabal, *Suspect Freedoms*, 163–64. As scholars have noted, Schomburg's essay on Estenoz ends with the often-quoted phrase: "The Negro has done much for Cuba; Cuba has done nothing for the Negro," as Schomburg also considers Black people in Cuba almost better off under the previous Spanish colonial rule than under U.S. military and economic influence. Schomburg, "Estenoz," 144. For an analysis of Schomburg's piece on Estenoz, see Valdés, *Diasporic Blackness*, 75–78.
33. See Schomburg, "Negro Brotherhood of Sevilla," *Opportunity*, June 1927; and "Negroes in Sevilla," *Opportunity*, March 1928. See also, Holton, "Archival Encounters in Spain."
34. McHenry, *Negro Literature*, 6.
35. Schomburg, "Racial Integrity," 7–8. Among other early contributions by Black authors, Schomburg mentions in his lecture Frances E. W. Harper, David Walker, and Frederick Douglass. Schomburg, "Racial Integrity," 10–12.
36. Gates, *Phillis Wheatley*, 31. Tara Bynum's analysis of Wheatley disrupts this common interpretation of Wheatley as "the 'first' Black woman to publish a book of poetry" and as an early representative of a "linear and deeply racialized tradition that moved with ease from her poems to the narratives of Frederick Douglass and Harriet Jacobs and then on to the fiction of Toni Morrison." Bynum, *Reading Pleasures*, 29. Instead, Bynum's analysis of Wheatley focuses on her interiority and her community of readers.
37. Schomburg and Heartman shared an interest in collecting Wheatley's books, letters, and poems. Schomburg's book collection included at least four copies of Wheatley's works in 1912. Sinnette, *Black Bibliophile*, 89.
38. For discussions on the poetry of Hammon and Wheatley as representative of recovery efforts during the nineteenth century, see Cavitch, "Phillis Wheatley"; Gates, *Phillis Wheatley*; and Spires, "Faithful Reflection."
39. McHenry, *Forgotten Readers*, 97.
40. Heartman, *Phillis Wheatley*, 8.
41. Du Bois to Heartman, July 30, 1915.

42. Genette explains that elements that form part of the internal structure of a text such as forewords, prefaces, and afterwords allow readers "either stepping inside or turning back" from a text and serve to produce "a better reception for the text and a more pertinent reading of it." Genette, *Paratexts*, 2.
43. Genette, *Paratexts*, 210.
44. Schomburg, "Appreciation," 7.
45. Schomburg, "Appreciation," 8.
46. Schomburg, "Appreciation," 9–10.
47. See Gates, *Phillis Wheatley*, 5–16; Carretta, *Phillis Wheatley*, 111–13; and Waldstreicher, *Odyssey of Phillis Wheatley*, 41–45.
48. Lossing, *Eminent Americans*, 250.
49. Schomburg, "Appreciation," 12.
50. Charles Mills explains that Enlightenment writers such as John Locke, Immanuel Kant, and others postulated theories regarding political freedom and egalitarianism that applied to "*white* men" only, while non-whites were "designated as born *un*free and *un*equal." Mills, *Racial Contract*, 16.
51. Gates, *Phillis Wheatley*, 25.
52. Hartman, *Scenes of Subjection*, 304.
53. Schomburg, "Appreciation," 9.
54. Schomburg, "Appreciation," 9.
55. Schomburg, "Appreciation," 9.
56. See Brown, *Black Man*, 138–42; Gates, *Phillis Wheatley*, 74; and Du Bois, "Phillis Wheatley," 337.
57. Schomburg's "Appreciation" includes the often-discussed quote from Jefferson's *Notes on the State of Virginia* (1784): "Religion had produced a Phillis Whately [sic], but it could not produce a poet," adding that "her poems were below the dignity of criticism." Schomburg, "Appreciation," 14. Writing around the same time as Schomburg, James Weldon Johnson used the same quote from Jefferson in his 1922 preface to his *Book of American Negro Poetry*. Johnson, *Negro Poetry*, xxiii.
58. Schomburg, "Appreciation," 14.
59. Schomburg, "Appreciation," 14.
60. Schomburg, "Appreciation," 15. Grégoire's book in English *An Enquiry Concerning the Intellectual and Moral Faculties, and Literature of Negroes* was translated by David Bailie Warden in 1810; however, it is likely that Schomburg is quoting from the French version as he was able to correspond in French as part of his job as a clerk at the Bankers' Trust Company. Hoffnung-Garskof, "Migrations," 36.
61. Schomburg, "Appreciation," 15.
62. Clarkson, *Slavery and Commerce*, 184. Contemporary scholars of Wheatley such as Carretta continue to point toward Clarkson's use of Wheatley's poetry as it speaks of the reach of her poetry. Carretta, introduction, xxxvi.
63. Schomburg, "Appreciation," 15.
64. McHenry, *Negro Literature*, 78.
65. McHenry, *Negro Literature*, 79.

66. Helton, "Making Lists," 85.
67. Valdés, *Diasporic Blackness*, 103.
68. McHenry studies bibliographies at the turn of the twentieth century included in manuals such as *Progress of the Race* (1897) as well as bibliographies compiled by Daniel Murray for the 1900 Paris Exposition and the Library of Congress, and Du Bois's series of bibliographies while a professor at Atlanta University starting in 1900. McHenry, *Negro Literature*, 16–17, 110–11.
69. Sinnette, *Black Bibliophile*, 32.
70. Porter, *Early Negro Writing*, 4.
71. Schomburg, *Bibliographical Checklist*, 15–19.
72. Manuel Martín-Rodríguez has suggested how different editions or reprints of early Chicanx texts could be studied as not only following a chronological order but also "as a process of changes in critical and popular reception" based on readership practices. Martín-Rodríguez, *Life in Search of Readers*, 54.
73. Schomburg, *Bibliographical Checklist*, 23–25. Before Schomburg, Horton's poetry and legacy remained almost unacknowledged with few exceptions such as William G. Allen's 1849 pamphlet that included poems by Wheatley and Horton. Cavitch, "Phillis Wheatley," 220. Several decades later, J. Saunders Redding wrote in 1939 about Horton's poetry in relation to the poetry of Wheatley and Hammon. Sherman, introduction, 32.
74. Edwards, *Practice of Diaspora*, 4.
75. For an analysis of Porter's career and her legacy in the field of Black bibliography, see Spires, "Order and Access."
76. Porter, *Negro Poets*, 5.
77. Porter, "Black Antiquarians," 5.
78. Porter, "Black Antiquarians," 15.
79. Porter, *Negro Poets*, 5.
80. Porter, *Negro Poets*, 5.
81. Porter, *Negro Poets*, 5.
82. Schomburg, *Bibliographical Checklist*, 15–19.
83. Porter, *Negro Poets*, 30–35.
84. Porter, *Negro Poets*, 82. In relation to the academic infrastructure that assisted Porter in her bibliographical work, she includes at the end of her bibliography a list of "Selected References on the History and Criticism of Negro Poetry," which includes some of the previous recovery efforts by early scholars such as Oscar Wegelin, Sterling A. Brown, and J. Saunders Redding. Porter, *Negro Poets*, 88–90.
85. Porter, *Negro Poets*, 6.
86. See McHenry, *Negro Literature*, 82–87; Nwankwo, "McKay and Guillén," 112–13; and Danky, "African American Print Culture," 350.
87. Rampersad, introduction, xiii. Locke's anthology was published by a mainstream publisher, Albert & Charles Boni, an up-and-coming New York City-based publishing house. Originally, *The New Negro* was a follow-up to Locke's special issue titled "Harlem: Mecca of the New Negro," published in the magazine *Survey Graphic*

in 1925. Based on the success of the *Survey Graphic* issue, Albert Boni envisioned a similar anthology of Black authors in book format that could "sell for $4.50 and which [Boni] hopes would be taken by every college and library in the country." Stewart, *New Negro*, 483.

88. Schomburg, "Select List," 423.
89. See McHenry, *Negro Literature*, 81.
90. Schomburg, "Select List," 422.
91. McHenry uses a comparative approach to analyze Du Bois's series of bibliographies published as part of the Atlanta University Studies publications for which Du Bois served as director. McHenry, *Negro Literature*, 110–11.
92. Locke, "Negro in Literature," 428–29.
93. During his studies in England, Locke traveled to continental Europe and visited "Paris, Berlin, and Rome, cities associated with a new artistic modernism and avant-garde of pre-World War Europe." Stewart, *New Negro*, 115. Schomburg first traveled to Europe in 1927 with the proceeds from the sale of his collection; however, Schomburg's bibliography, in contrast to Locke's cosmopolitan emphasis, reflects a Black diasporic vision of the Americas.
94. Sinnette, Valdés, and García Peña have analyzed and engaged with Schomburg's essays in Black newspapers and periodicals but not specifically with his essays in the *Amsterdam News*.
95. Flor Piñeiro de Rivera's compilation of Schomburg's writings contains a representative sample of his work, but none of his articles from the *Amsterdam News* are included. As she notes, these essays had not been recovered at the time of her book publication in 1989. Piñeiro de Rivera, *Schomburg*, 12.
96. Woodson, for example, wrote dozens of essays intended for various Black newspapers across the country. Morris, *Woodson*, 48–49. One of these newspapers was the *Amsterdam News*. In his preface to *The Weary Blues* (1925), Hughes indicates that some of his poetry has been published in the *Amsterdam News*.
97. Schomburg's *Amsterdam News* essays, for example, focus on Antônio Carlos Gomes, a Black opera composer. "Antonio Carlos Gomes," August 30, 1933; Crispus Attucks, the first Black man killed during the American Revolution. "Crispus Attucks," August 24, 1935; and Robert Brown Elliot, an Afro-Caribbean who became South Carolina Attorney General during Reconstruction. "Statesmen from Jamaica," August 29, 1936.
98. See also Schomburg, "Our Pioneers: Saga of Peter Williams," *Amsterdam News*, July 25, 1936.
99. Schomburg, "Jupiter Hammon."
100. Schomburg, "Jupiter Hammon."
101. Schomburg, "Jupiter Hammon."
102. Schomburg, "Negro Digs Up His Past," 232.
103. Schomburg, "Jupiter Hammon."
104. May, preface, xiii.
105. Schomburg, "Jupiter Hammon."

106. Schomburg, "Jupiter Hammon." For a discussion on the role of Wegelin, a collector of Black books, in the recovery of Hammon's poems through the edited publication of his poems, see May, preface, xii-xv.
107. Schomburg, 'Freedom's Journal.'
108. Schomburg, 'Freedom's Journal.'
109. McHenry, *Forgotten Readers*, 91. For a discussion of the *Freedom's Journal* and its function as a literacy tool in Black communities, and as a New York City-based newspaper that reached Black readers in other states, see McHenry, *Forgotten Readers*, 88–102.
110. Schomburg, 'Freedom's Journal.'
111. Schomburg, 'Freedom's Journal.'
112. James, *Russwurm*, 16.
113. Schomburg, 'Freedom's Journal.'
114. Schomburg, 'Freedom's Journal.'
115. Winston James, however, refutes the idea that Cornish resigned over differences related to Russwurm's colonization ideas as "all evidence indicates that the two men parted on amicable terms . . ." James, *Russwurm*, 32.
116. Schomburg, 'Freedom's Journal.'
117. Wilson, "Brief Wondrous Life," 20.
118. Schomburg, 'Freedom's Journal.'
119. C. Johnson to Schomburg, October 12, 1936.
120. C. Johnson to Schomburg, October 12, 1936. Around the same time, Johnson had suggested to Schomburg that he secure money through external sources to fund his research. The Rosenwald Fund financially supported part of Johnson's scholarly work at Fisk University. Gilpin and Gasman, *Charles S. Johnson*, 34. In another letter to Schomburg, Johnson encourages Schomburg to apply for a Rosenwald grant since "[t]hey have great respect for you, and believe you know completely your field . . ." C. Johnson to Schomburg, November 28, 1935.
121. Vega, *Memoirs*, 196.
122. Vega, *Memoirs*, 196.
123. Vega, *Memoirs*, 196.

Chapter 3

1. For discussions of Spanish-language newspapers in New York City during the second half of the nineteenth century, see Lazo, *Writing to Cuba*; Lamas, *Latino Continuum*; and Mirabal, *Suspect Freedoms*.
2. Mirabal, *Suspect Freedoms*, 40.
3. For analysis of Spanish-language print culture in New York City in the late nineteenth century, see Hoffnung-Garskof, *Racial Migrations*; E. Meléndez, *Patria*; and Kreitz, "American Alternatives."
4. On Spanish-language newspapers in New York City and Afro-Latinx writers, see Acosta-Belén and Santiago, *Puerto Ricans*, 170–84; Mirabal, *Suspect Freedoms*, 97–

105; Kanellos, "Sotero Figueroa"; Kreitz, "Sotero Figueroa"; and Lamas, *Latino Continuum*, 153–62.
5. Kanellos and Martell, *Hispanic Periodicals*, 58.
6. Kanellos and Martell, *Hispanic Periodicals*, 53–54. On the influence of *Gráfico* on "Hispanic" cultural life in New York City, see Sánchez Korrol, *Colonia to Community*, 71–77; Luis, *Two Cultures*, 108–10; López, *Unbecoming Blackness*, 31–47; and Cutler, "Latinx Modernism," 573–74.
7. On the history and cultural production of Puerto Ricans in New York City, see Vega, *Memoirs*; J. Flores, *Divided Borders*; Sánchez Korrol, *Colonia to Community*; Mirabal, *Suspect Freedoms*; and Whalen, "Colonialism."
8. For an analysis of Vega as a chronicler of early Puerto Rican migration to New York City in the early decades of the twentieth century, see Luis, *Two Cultures*, 99–120.
9. See Cutler, "Rubén Darío" and "Latinx Modernism."
10. Kanellos and Martell, *Hispanic Periodicals*, 54.
11. I employ the term *Hispano* as used in the context of Spanish-language print culture in New York City in the early decades of the twentieth century and Colón's use of the term in his Spanish-language sketches for *Pueblos Hispanos*.
12. See J. Flores, *Divided Borders*, 135–41; Luis, *Two Cultures*, 121–29; and James, *Banner of Ethiopia*, 195–231.
13. See Sánchez Korrol, *Colonia to Community*; Acosta-Belén, "Building of a Community"; and E. Padilla, "Jesús Colón."
14. See *The Way It Was and Other Writings* by Jesús Colón, edited by Acosta-Belén and Sánchez Korrol; and *"Lo que el pueblo me dice . . ."* by Jesús Colón, edited by E. Padilla.
15. *Revista de Artes y Letras*, published from 1933 to 1945, was founded and edited by Josefina Silva de Cintrón and focused on social, cultural, and political topics pertaining to *Hispanos* in the U.S. Sánchez Korrol, *Colonia to Community*, 74. See also Schlau, "Cultural Leader."
16. Kanellos and Martell, *Hispanic Periodicals*, 111. See also Pérez Rosario, *Julia de Burgos*, 69–93.
17. See Kanellos and Martell, *Hispanic Periodicals*, 110–11; and Cutler's "Rubén Darío," 72–73, 83–85.
18. For discussions on Albizu Campos and the struggle for Puerto Rican independence, see Denis, *War Against All Puerto Ricans*; and Morales, *Fantasy Island*, 32–48.
19. See, for example, Corretjer, "Este es Albizu Campos," *Pueblos Hispanos*, February 20, 1943.
20. "Hombro a hombro" (Shoulder to Shoulder).
21. "Hombro a hombro."
22. According to the same editorial, the social and political basis for this union required *Hispanos* working together "en la defense de todos los derechos de las minorías hispanas en Estados Unidos—puertorriqueños, filipinos, mexicanos, españoles, etc. . . ." (to defend the rights of all the Hispanic minorities in the U.S.—Puerto Ricans, Filipinos, Mexicans, Spaniards, etc. . . .) "Hombro a hombro."

23. Bernardo Vega was one of the early writers who chronicled the educational function of *lectores* among Caribbean cigar makers in cities such as New York City and Tampa, Florida, and their financial support for the fight for Cuban and Puerto Rican independence. See Vega, *Memoirs*, 111–18; and Sánchez Korrol, *Colonia to Community*, 137–42.
24. Kanellos and Martell, *Hispanic Periodicals*, 112. In relation to Colón's education, Vega discusses the creation of the *Ateneo Obrero*, an alternative night school for workers in 1926, in which Vega was the president and Colón was a member. Vega, *Memoirs*, 144. Classes at the *Ateneo Obrero* were led by "socialist professors who volunteered their services." Vega, *Memoirs*, 147.
25. Linda Delgado observes that Colón led during his lifetime "more than thirty-three lodges and community organizations throughout New York City." Delgado, "Jesús Colón," 71.
26. J. Flores, *Divided Borders*, 136.
27. Kanellos and Martell, *Hispanic Periodicals*, 113.
28. Kanellos and Martell, *Hispanic Periodicals*, 112.
29. Colón's "Un jíbaro en New York" and a series of sketches under the header "El Neoyorkino," published in *Gráfico* in 1927 combine social commentary with his experiences as a recent arrival to the U.S. As Edwin K. Padilla correctly notes, "[n]o existe, en estos primeros artículos en español la lucha por los derechos civiles, los prejuicios sociales o las preocupaciones económicas que años más tarde Colón caracterizó su producción en inglés" (does not exist, in these early articles in Spanish, the struggle for civil rights, social prejudices or economic concerns that would characterize Colón's writing output in English). E. Padilla, "Jesús Colón," 372.
30. For discussions on Colón's sketches as following the *crónica* tradition in Spanish-language newspapers in the U.S., see Kanellos, "Cronistas and Satire"; E. Padilla, "Jesús Colón"; and Holton, "Little Things Are Big."
31. E. Padilla, introduction, xxxix.
32. Colón, "Puerto Rico."
33. Colón, "Puerto Rico."
34. Colón, "Puerto Rico."
35. Colón, "Puerto Rico."
36. Colón, "Hacia una gran institución."
37. Acosta-Belén and Santiago, *Puerto Ricans*, 57.
38. Colón, "Hacia una gran institución."
39. Colón, "Hacia una gran institución."
40. Colón, "Hacia una gran institución."
41. Sánchez Korrol, *Colonia to Community*, 189–90.
42. Colón, "Inscríbete."
43. Colón, "Inscríbete."
44. Colón, "Inscríbete."
45. Colón, "Te lo recordamos."
46. Colón, "Estados Unidos."

47. Colón, "Estados Unidos."
48. Colón, "Estados Unidos."
49. Kanellos, "Recovering," 439.
50. Kanellos and Martell, *Hispanic Periodicals*, 110.
51. Colón, "Éste es tu periódico."
52. Colón, "Éste es tu periódico."
53. For analyses on the influence of communism on Black writers during the decades after the Great Depression, see Maxwell, *New Negro, Old Left*; Baldwin, *Beyond the Color Line*; and Jackson, *Indignant Generation*.
54. On the publishing dynamics between mainstream publishers and Black writers during the Harlem Renaissance, see Hutchinson, *Harlem Renaissance*; Young, *Black Writers, White Publishers*; and Jackson, *Indignant Generation*.
55. Jackson, *Indignant Generation*, 21–22.
56. Jackson, *Indignant Generation*, 12.
57. Jackson, *Indignant Generation*, 27–29.
58. According to Arnold Rampersad, Hughes in 1940, after twenty years writing for magazines and publishing several books with Knopf, lacked financial stability as he became "a poor man's literary Titan, without a best-seller." Rampersad, *Sing America*, 380. See also De Santis, *Langston Hughes*, 13–15.
59. Some of these early labor newspapers include the *Farmers' and Mechanics' Advocate* of Charlestown, Indiana; *The Liberalist* of New Orleans; the *Working Man's Advocate* of Boston; and the *Working Men's Bulletin* of Buffalo, New York. Schappes, *Daily Worker*, 9. Late-nineteenth- and early-twentieth-century Spanish-language labor newspapers in New York City included *El Despertar*; *Cultura Proletaria*; and *Brazo y Cerebro*. Kanellos, *Hispanic*, 47.
60. Bryant, *Byline*, 5.
61. Some of the *Daily Worker*'s early editors included J. Louis Engdahl and William F. Dunne who had previous editorial experiences at other socialist and leftist newspapers. Schappes, *Daily Worker*, 22.
62. Schappes, *Daily Worker*, 19.
63. Schappes, *Daily Worker*, 26.
64. For an analysis on the systematic exclusion of writers of color from the U.S. news publishing industry up to the 1970s, see González and Torres, *News for All the People*, 301–39.
65. For an overview of Wright's editorial work and writings in the *Daily Worker*, with articles counted in the hundreds, see Bryant, *Byline*.
66. Wright's poem "Between the World and Me" that describes the lynching of a Black man was published in *Partisan Review* in 1935, a leftist publication that had its origins in the New York City chapter of the John Reed Club. Jackson, *Indignant Generation*, 28. For a discussion on *New Masses* and Black writers such as Hughes and Claude McKay, see Hemingway, *Artists*, 7–13.
67. For a discussion of "Bright and Morning Star" and its communist influences, see Maxwell, *New Negro, Old Left*, 182–83.

68. Bryant, *Byline*, 7.
69. Bryant, *Byline*, x.
70. Acosta-Belén and Sánchez Korrol, introduction, 23.
71. J. Flores, foreword, xiii.
72. Similarly, some of Colón's sketches for the *Daily Worker* that would become part of *A Puerto Rican in New York* do not theorize about possible coalitions between *Hispano* and Black communities. As William Luis notes, while "race appears as a subtext throughout his sketches . . . , Colón is ambivalent about the significance of race." Luis, *Two Cultures*, 122.
73. Colón, "Columbus."
74. Colón, "Columbus."
75. Colón, "How to Know."
76. Colón, "Hollywood."
77. Colón, "Hollywood."
78. Colón, "Hollywood."
79. For discussions on the intimidation tactics used by the government during McCarthyism and the Red Scare, see Maxwell, "Editorial Federalism"; and Morgan, *McCarthyism*, 374–424.
80. Colón, "Fuchik."
81. Colón, "Fuchik."
82. Colón, "Fuchik."
83. In a sketch, "Red Roses for Me," of November 20, 1956, Colón recounts receiving hate mail due to his writings in the *Daily Worker*. He attempts to find the silver lining in these attacks by thinking that the "reactionary elements in our midst are being hurt and are concerned about our paper's message to the people."
84. As Maxwell notes, Du Bois's F.B.I. file was 756 pages long. Maxwell, "Editorial Federalism," 136. For discussions on Du Bois and communism, see Lewis, *Du Bois*, 554–71; and Van Wienen, *American Socialist*, 270–78. While Du Bois was not a member of the Communist Party, he could write with admiration about Stalin as in his piece "On Stalin" (1953). Du Bois was critical of McCarthyism and the Red Scare and its damage on Black figures such as Paul Robeson. Du Bois, "Real Reason," 798. In later years, Du Bois continued to write favorably about the Soviet Union. Du Bois, *Autobiography*, 34–35.
85. For a detailed discussion of Hughes's Senate hearing, see Rampersad, *I Dream a World*, 209–22.
86. For the extensive surveillance by the F.B.I. of Du Bois, Hughes, Wright, and many other Black writers that lasted for over half a century (1919–1972), see Maxwell, "Editorial Federalism."
87. After Colón's sketches for the *Daily Worker*, he wrote for its weekly version the *Worker* from 1958 to 1968. When the *Worker* became the *Daily World* in 1968, he continued to write for this publication from 1968 to 1971. Acosta-Belén and Sánchez Korrol, introduction, 111–21.
88. For a discussion on the attacks on communists in Puerto Rico by local officials and the decline of communism in Puerto Rico, see Paralitici, *Historia*, 164–169.

89. Colón, *Way It Was*, 100.
90. Colón, *Way It Was*, 101.
91. Some of these exceptions include María Cristina Mena's short fiction published in mainstream periodicals such as *American Magazine* and *Century* in the 1910s; Josefina Niggli's *Step Down, Elder Brother* published by Rinehart & Co. in 1947; and José Antonio Villarreal's *Pocho* published by Doubleday in 1959.
92. Sáenz, Perales, and Sloss-Vento wrote newspaper pieces in *La Prensa* of San Antonio and published nonfiction books with Artes Gráficas, a regional Spanish-language press in San Antonio. Matthis Publishing Co., a local publishing press in Dallas, published Zamora O'Shea's novel *El Mesquite* in 1935.
93. J. Flores, *Divided Borders*, 145. For discussions on the development of Puerto Rican literature in New York City before the 1960s, see Flores, *Divided Borders* and *Diaspora Strikes Back*; Luis, *Two Cultures*; Sánchez González, *Boricua Literature*; and Kanellos, *Hispanic*.
94. The writing of *A Puerto Rican in New York* in English also relates to Colón's lifelong efforts to become proficient in English in order to influence labor, leftists, and progressive readers and as part of his literary and intellectual journey. Melissa Coss Aquino discusses some of Colón's letters to his wife, Concha Colón, in which he shares his desire to write in English and make a living as a writer. Aquino, "Concha Colón," 68–70.
95. Hemingway, *Artists*, 214–15.
96. The publishing arm of *Mainstream*, Mainstream Publishers, lasted from 1948 to 1963. Replying to a reprinting request, Colón names the publisher of his book, "Mainstream Publishers," which he explains went out of business by 1965. Colón to Kraus, July 30, 1965.
97. Hughes compiled and published other collections of his *Chicago Defender* columns focusing on the fictional character Jesse B. Simple such as *Simple Takes a Wife* (1953), *Simple Stakes a Claim* (1957), and *The Best of Simple* (1961). For a discussion of Hughes's Simple columns, see Rampersad, *I Dream a World*, 64–67.
98. Flores, foreword, xvi.
99. See Flores, foreword, ix–xvii; Luis, *Two Cultures*, 122–29; James, *Banner of Ethiopia*, 214–31; Vázquez, *Triangulations*, 50–60; and Holton, "Little Things Are Big," 5–18.
100. Colón, *Puerto Rican*, 9.
101. James notes that the reprinting of *A Puerto Rican in New York* in 1982 was based on the first 1961 edition; however, there is a revised version of the book by Colón archived at the Jesús Colón Papers at the Center for Puerto Rican Studies. James, *Banner of Ethiopia*, 221–22.
102. Vázquez, *Triangulations*, 53.
103. Colón, *Puerto Rican*, 11.
104. Holton, "Little Things Are Big," 8.
105. Colón, *Puerto Rican*, 12.
106. Colón, *Puerto Rican*, 13.
107. Wright, *Black Boy*, 249.

108. Wright, *Black Boy*, 249.
109. For a discussion of Hughes's academic experiences, see Hughes, *Big Sea*, 81–85, 278–84.
110. Colón, *Puerto Rican*, 39.
111. Vázquez, *Triangulations*, 56.
112. Colón, *Puerto Rican*, 39.
113. Colón, *Puerto Rican*, 40.
114. Colón, *Puerto Rican*, 40.
115. Colón, *Puerto Rican*, 41.
116. Colón, *Puerto Rican*, 139.
117. Colón, *Puerto Rican*, 140.
118. Colón admired Schomburg and even emulated some of the latter's archival habits as he collected newsletters, clippings, and journals that would become important in the study of the Puerto Rican community in New York City. Acosta-Belén and Sánchez Korrol, introduction, 25–26.
119. Colón, *Puerto Rican*, 140.
120. Colón, *Puerto Rican*, 159.
121. Colón, *Puerto Rican*, 161.
122. Bellamy's *Looking Backward* (1888), a utopian novel set in the U.S. in the year 2000, had a major impact on the popularization of socialist ideas in the U.S. at the turn of the twentieth century and became one of the most widely read books in the U.S. Beaumont, introduction, vii.
123. Colón, *Puerto Rican*, 187.
124. Colón, *Puerto Rican*, 188.
125. Colón, *Puerto Rican*, 197.
126. Colón, *Puerto Rican*, 197–98.
127. Colón, *Puerto Rican*, 198.
128. Colón, *Puerto Rican*, 198.
129. Colón, *Puerto Rican*, 198–99.
130. Colón, *Puerto Rican*, 199.
131. Colón, *Puerto Rican*, 199.
132. Colón, *Puerto Rican*, 199.
133. Colón, *Puerto Rican*, 199.
134. Colón, *Puerto Rican*, 200.
135. Colón, *Puerto Rican*, 200.
136. Colón, *Puerto Rican*, 201.
137. On the social and cultural connections between the Young Lords and the Nuyorican poets, see Luis, *Two Cultures*, 42–52.

Chapter 4

1. For discussion on the number of printing presses and the development of Spanish-language newspapers in other parts of the Southwest such as California, New Mex-

ico, and Colorado, see Kanellos, "Recovering"; Kanellos and Martell, *Hispanic Periodicals*; and A. Meléndez, *So All Is Not Lost*.

2. Kanellos and Martell, *Hispanic Periodicals*, 99.
3. Kanellos and Martell, *Hispanic Periodicals*, 100.
4. For analyses of the Idar family's journalism, social activism, and *La Crónica*, see G. González, *Redeeming La Raza*, 19–40; and Masarik, "Por la Raza, Para la Raza."
5. K. Hernández, *Bad Mexicans*, 6–7. G. González discusses the contrast between the *magonistas*' radical platform disseminated in *Regeneración* and more moderate newspapers such as Nicasio Idar's *La Crónica*. G. González, *Redeeming La Raza*, 59–66.
6. "A *La Prensa*."
7. See Cutler, "Rubén Darío," 77–81; J. M. González, *Border Renaissance*, 132–33; and Aranda, *Places of Modernity*, 156–57.
8. Cutler, "Rubén Darío," 79.
9. See Zamora, "Fighting"; B. Johnson's "Cosmic Race in Texas"; and J. Ramírez, *To the Line of Fire!*
10. Gómez, *Manifest Destinies*, 123.
11. See Menchaca, *Recovering History*; Orozco, *No Mexicans*; G. González, *Redeeming la Raza*; and Martinez, *Injustice*.
12. Martinez, *Injustice*, 21. See also B. Johnson, *Revolution in Texas*; and S. Hernández and J. M. González, *Reverberations of Racial Violence*.
13. For discussions on the segregation of schoolchildren of Mexican origin in Texas at the turn of the twentieth century, see Barragán Goetz, *Reading*, 49–68; and Blanton, *Strange Career*, 42–55.
14. For an overview of Sáenz's family background and early educational experiences in South Texas, see Sáenz's autobiographical essay, "I by Myself"; and Zamora, "José de la Luz Sáenz." During his early years in an underfunded school in Alice, Texas, Sáenz recounts being underappreciated by some white teachers but also encouraged by others. Sáenz, "I by Myself," 4.
15. Barragán Goetz, *Reading*, 128.
16. Zamora, "Experiences," 32.
17. Sáenz wrote pieces for other Spanish-language newspapers including the *McAllen Evening Monitor*, *La Verdad*, *La Voz*, and the *Texas Outlook*. Zamora, "Experiences," 34.
18. Sáenz acknowledges the importance of Spanish-language print culture in his efforts to fight school segregation in a letter printed in *La Prensa* on January 26, 1917, when he thanks Lozano for his support. Sáenz, "Una carta del Profesor."
19. J. Ramírez, *Line of Fire!*, 22.
20. J. Ramírez, *Line of Fire!*, 22–23.
21. J. Ramírez, *Line of Fire!*, 73. The Spanish-language press in Texas supported the war effort; however, Ricardo Flores Magón was arrested for publishing an anti-capitalist manifesto in *Regeneración* during the war, which was printed in California after Magón left Texas, and was sentenced to twenty years in prison. J. Ramírez, *Line of Fire!*, 45–46.

22. See J. Ramírez, *Line of Fire!*, 39–56; P. James, "Propaganda: Martialing Media"; and Hochschild, *American Midnight*, 55–70.
23. J. Ramírez, *Line of Fire!*, 31.
24. See B. Johnson, *Revolution in Texas*, 71–107; and Martinez, *Injustice*, 10–22.
25. J. Ramírez, *Line of Fire!*, 33.
26. See Jordan, *Black Newspapers*, 14–16; and Greenidge, *Black Radical*, 77–82.
27. See Jordan, *Black Newspapers*, 39–48; and Lentz-Smith, *Freedom Struggles*, 69–79.
28. Notable critics of the participation of Black men in the war include the editors of the *Messenger*, Chandler Owen and A. Philip Randolph. See, for example, Owen, "Failure of Negro Leadership," *Messenger*, January 1918.
29. Jordan, *Black Newspapers*, 33.
30. Hochschild, *American Midnight*, 117.
31. For a detailed study of Du Bois and World War I, see Chad Williams, *Wounded World*. The basis of Williams's analysis is Du Bois's unpublished book manuscript about the war, "The Black Man and the Wounded World," which Du Bois was unable to revise and publish with the mainstream publishing house Harcourt Brace & Co. Williams, *Wounded World*, 346–50.
32. Du Bois, *Dusk of Dawn*, 114.
33. Du Bois, "Awake America," 379.
34. Du Bois, "Awake America," 379.
35. Du Bois, "Awake America," 379.
36. Du Bois, "Awake America," 379.
37. Zamora, *Diary*, 16.
38. Olguín, *Violentologies*, 30.
39. Zamora, "Fighting," 215.
40. Sáenz, and other authors in their newspaper writings, use at times this alternative spelling "*méxico-texanos*" when referring to "*méxico-tejanos*."
41. Sáenz, "Demostraremos."
42. Sáenz, "Demostraremos."
43. Sáenz, "Demostraremos."
44. Hochschild, *American Midnight*, 32–33.
45. Sáenz, "Demostraremos."
46. Sáenz, "El diario."
47. Sáenz, "El diario."
48. Zamora, *Diary*, 203. This and other quotes from Sáenz's diary originally written in Spanish are taken from Zamora's translation, *The World War I Diary of José de la Luz Sáenz*.
49. Zamora, *Diary*, 203.
50. Sáenz, "El diario."
51. Sáenz, "Los últimos días."
52. Sáenz's letter for *La Prensa* covers the days leading to the armistice starting on October 26 to November 11; however, he includes a more thorough and expanded version of those days and events in his diary. Zamora, *Diary*, 246–285.

53. Sáenz, "Los últimos días."
54. Sáenz, "Los últimos días."
55. Sáenz, "Una fiesta."
56. Sáenz, "Una fiesta."
57. Hochschild, *American Midnight*, 201–32.
58. J. Ramírez, *Line of Fire!*, 117, 120–21.
59. Sáenz, "Racial Discrimination," 32.
60. Sáenz, "Racial Discrimination," 33.
61. J. M. González, "Warp of Whiteness," 437.
62. J. Ramírez, *Line of Fire!*, 121.
63. J. Ramírez, *Line of Fire!*, 121.
64. Sáenz, "Racial Discrimination," 32.
65. Perales, *In Defense*, 74.
66. Du Bois, *Dusk of Dawn*, 123.
67. See Davis, "Not Only War is Hell"; and Hochschild, *American Midnight*, 247–258. For a firsthand account of the white mob violence in Chicago, otherwise known as the "Chicago race riots," of July 1919, see Carl Sandburg, *The Chicago Race Riots*, a series of newspaper articles written for the *Chicago Daily News* in 1919.
68. Du Bois, "Returning Soldiers," 380.
69. Du Bois, "Returning Soldiers," 380.
70. Du Bois, "Returning Soldiers," 380.
71. Du Bois, "Returning Soldiers," 380.
72. Du Bois, "Returning Soldiers," 381.
73. For a thorough analysis of Perales's legacy as a civil rights leader, see Orozco, *Pioneer of Mexican-American Civil Rights*. For a discussion of Perales's writings and intellectual legacy, see R. Garcia, "Alonso S. Perales."
74. Perales, *In Defense*, 27.
75. See, for example, "Continúan su jira de conferencias A. S. Perales y J. L. Sáenz," *La Prensa*, August 24, 1924; and "Termino una jira de conferencias," *La Prensa*, August 31, 1924.
76. World War I veterans John C. Solis, Pablo Cruz, and Leo Longoria founded the Order of the Sons of America (OSA) in 1921. There were other organizations such as the Order of the Sons of Texas and the Order of the Kings of America that subsequently joined LULAC. J. Ramírez, *Line of Fire!*, 123. For discussions of the emergence of civil rights organizations coalescing into LULAC, see Orozco, *No Mexicans*, 151–80; and Perales, "True Origin of [LULAC]," an essay included in Perales, *In Defense*, 256–76.
77. Sáenz to Perales, May 26, 1927.
78. See "Se levantará en San Antonio un monumento a los méxico-texanos que murieron en Francia," *La Prensa*, May 27, 1928.
79. For discussions on the formation of LULAC, see M. García, *Mexican Americans*, 25–38; Gómez-Quiñones, *Roots of Chicano Politics*, 365–76; and Orozco, *No Mexicans*, 151–173.

80. Orozco, *No Mexicans*, 237.
81. A major criticism of LULAC has been the exclusion of Mexican nationals from LULAC membership. Zamora, "Fighting," 228. According to Natalia Molina, LULAC was formed by leaders who "pursued an agenda of assimilation, excluding from membership Mexicans who were not U.S. citizens." Molina, *How Race Is Made*, 41. Nonetheless, the motives of this exclusion were complex; Aaron Sánchez, for instance, has contextualized the tensions between Mexican exiles in Texas after the Mexican Revolution and U.S. citizens of Mexican origin who were at odds socially and culturally. A. Sánchez, *Homeland*, 48–52.
82. Perales, *In Defense*, 27.
83. Gómez-Quiñones, *Roots of Chicano Politics*, 367.
84. See, for example, Orozco, *No Mexicans*; Zamora, "Fighting"; and B. Johnson, "Cosmic Race in Texas."
85. Ian Haney López's *White by Law* develops a compelling analysis of how, historically, the U.S. legal system and its courts have worked through racialization as a system of control and to guard the boundaries of whiteness, or who is considered white in legal terms, which also included Mexican Americans.
86. Gómez, *Manifest Destinies*, 5–6. For a cogent analysis of the history of racialization of Mexican Americans in the Southwest after the Treaty of Guadalupe Hidalgo, legislation debates about immigration of the 1920s, and the role of LULAC, see Molina, *How Race Is Made*, 24–42.
87. Saldaña-Portillo, *Indian Given*, 133.
88. Saldaña-Portillo, *Indian Given*, 134.
89. Saldaña-Portillo, for example, discusses the case of Ricardo Rodriguez, a Mexican national who lived in San Antonio and whose application for U.S. citizenship was denied in Texas courts in 1893 since he was neither a white nor Black man but was of "self-evident Indian ancestry." Saldaña-Portillo, *Indian Given*, 156–57.
90. Saldaña-Portillo, *Indian Given*, 155.
91. The Salvatierras were the parents who sued the Del Rio school district. Similar to subsequent court challenges against desegregation involving LULAC, part of the plaintiffs' legal argument was that Mexican Americans should be considered "white." For analyses of the case, see Orozco, "Del Rio ISD v. Salvatierra"; and Menchaca, *Mexican American Experience*, 113–119.
92. Saldaña-Portillo, *Indian Given*, 161. See also Salinas, "Legally White, Socially Brown"; and A. Sánchez, *Homeland*, 44–67.
93. Genaro Padilla's *My History, Not Yours* studies the long tradition of nineteenth-century Mexican American authors in the Southwest who wrote about their war experiences using the autobiography genre such as Juan Seguín's *Personal Memoirs* (1858), Mariano Guadalupe Vallejo's "Recuerdos históricos y personales tocante á la alta California" (1875), and Rafael Chacón's "Memorias" about his service during the Civil War (1912).
94. Isherwood, "Memoirs," 110.

95. See, for example, Rennie, *American Writers and World War I*; Gandal, *Gun and the Pen*; and Dayton and Wienen, *Literature and Culture of the First World War*.
96. An alternative press, Christopher Publishing House, published *Not Only War*. Daly's novel was written with the goal of presenting the double struggle of Black people, fighting for democracy abroad and for civil rights at home. Davis, introduction, xiv. For discussions of Daly's novel, see J. James, *Freedom Bought with Blood*, 170–87; and Gandal, *War Isn't the Only Hell*, 172–99.
97. Kanellos, "Recovering," 442–43.
98. Starting at least in 1930, Artes Gráficas was advertised by its owner, José C. Ramírez, in *La Prensa* as a "imprenta" (printing press) at "precios razonables" (reasonable prices). See "Revista," *La Prensa*, December 18, 1930. In subsequent years, Artes Gráficas most likely grew and its business expanded beyond printing. When Artes Gráficas published the second volume of Perales's *En defensa de mi raza* in 1937, for example, it advertised the book in *La Prensa*. "Segundo tomo" (Second volume), July 11, 1937.
99. Zamora, *Diary*, 7. The José de la Luz Sáenz Papers at the Nettie Lee Benson Library contain correspondence between Sáenz and New York City publishing houses such as Little, Brown & Company and William Morrow, regarding a possible publication of his diary in English that did not materialize. See, for instance, F. Phillips to Sáenz, August 20, 1945.
100. Sáenz, *Diary*, 469.
101. Sáenz, *Diary*, 467.
102. Sáenz, *Diary*, 470. Part of the publication history of Sáenz's diary is described at the end of the diary when he thanks all the individuals who gave money in advance through a subscription method. Sáenz calls people who contributed "collaborators because this publication would not have been possible without their help." Sáenz, *Diary*, 473.
103. My analysis of Sáenz's diary uses the current term "Mexican American" when referring to its hyphenated equivalent "Mexican-American" used in his diary.
104. Sáenz, *Diary*, 40.
105. Sáenz, *Diary*, 41.
106. Sáenz, *Diary*, 72.
107. Sáenz, *Diary*, 72.
108. Sáenz, *Diary*, 72.
109. Sáenz, *Diary*, 73.
110. Sáenz, *Diary*, 87.
111. Gandal, *Gun and the Pen*, 78–79.
112. Sáenz, *Diary*, 341.
113. Sáenz, *Diary*, 345.
114. Sáenz, *Diary*, 363.
115. Sáenz's pieces in *La Prensa* from the 1910s already included the term "*raza*," a widely used term in newspapers and publications as in the case of Perales's book

title in Spanish *En defensa de mi raza* (In Defense of My People) published in 1936. The word *"raza"* also translates or refers to "race" or "ethnicity." In the Spanish version of the diary, for example, Sáenz in the dedication page refers to Mexican American soldiers as "soldados americanos de raza Mexicana" (American soldiers of Mexican origin). Sáenz, *Los méxico-americanos*, 6. While *raza* denotes a group identification based on race, Gabriela González explains that *la raza* as used by Mexican American political activists in the 1930s and 1940s denotes more than racial identification as the term "sought to foster ethnic pride and unity across the axes of gender, class, and national differences . . ." G. González, *Redeeming la Raza*, xv.

116. Sáenz, *Diary*, 40.
117. Sáenz, *Diary*, 79.
118. Sáenz, *Diary*, 306.
119. Sáenz, *Diary*, 179.
120. G. González, *Redeeming la Raza*, 193.
121. For historians who have discussed Sáenz's engagement with his Indigeneity in his diary, see B. Johnson, "Cosmic Race in Texas," 416; and Zamora, "Fighting," 227.
122. Zamora, "Fighting," 225.
123. For an overview of the rise of the Aztecs, also referred as Mexicas, among other Mesoamerican Indigenous groups prior to the Spanish conquest, see Menchaca, *Recovering History*, 33–36.
124. Sáenz also wrote an unpublished autobiographical essay, "I by Myself," about his father's "personal pride" when his father used to tell Sáenz: "I am an Aztec." Sáenz, "I by Myself," 2.
125. Sáenz, *Diary*, 25.
126. Sáenz, *Diary*, 98.
127. Sáenz, *Diary*, 251.
128. Zamora, "Experiences," 32.
129. See "Conmemoraron el aniversario de la muerte de Juárez los vecinos de Moore, Texas," *La Prensa*, July 24, 1915.
130. For an analysis of Vasconcelos's cosmic race in the context of emerging Mexican American civil rights organizations in Texas, including LULAC, see B. Johnson, "Cosmic Race in Texas."
131. Sáenz, *Diary*, 386.
132. Sáenz, *Diary*, 160.
133. Sáenz, *Diary*, 185.
134. For a detailed analysis of how Mexican American elites in the Southwest after the U.S.-Mexican War tried to maintain their "fragile claim to whiteness" and how this involved the rejection of their Indigenous heritage, see Gómez, *Manifest Destinies*, 85–103.
135. See Saldaña-Portillo, *Indian Given*; M. Cotera and Saldaña-Portillo, "Indigenous but Not Indian?"; Blackwell, Boj Lopez, and Urrieta, "Critical Latinx Indigeneities"; and Trujillo, *Land Uprising*.
136. Sáenz, "Racial Discrimination," 29.

137. Sáenz, *Diary*, 152.
138. Sáenz, "Racial Discrimination," 29.
139. Saldaña-Portillo, *Indian Given*, 8.
140. Saldaña-Portillo, *Indian Given*, 8.
141. Sáenz, "Racial Discrimination," 31.
142. Sáenz, "Discriminación racial."
143. Zamora, "Fighting," 225.
144. Sáenz, *Diary*, 291.
145. Sáenz, *Diary*, 60.
146. Sáenz, *Diary*, 385.
147. Blackhawk, *Rediscovery of America*, 383.
148. Sáenz, *Diary*, 395.
149. Perales, *In Defense*, 26.
150. As Tanya Katerí Hernández has shown, anti-Blackness has historically permeated Latinx communities' attitudes toward Black and Afro-Latinx people. T. Hernández, *Racial Innocence*, 14–25. Nonetheless, as Zamora notes, rather than upholding anti-Black views, Perales attempted to fight segregation and the possibility of making Mexican Americans "a permanent underclass" in Texas. Zamora, *In Defense*, xxvi.
151. Perales, *In Defense*, 178.
152. Sáenz, *Diary*, 62, 442.

Chapter 5

1. There were other regions in the Southwest such as New Mexico with a long tradition of pre-1960s Latina writers that included Nina Otero-Warren, Cleofas M. Jaramillo, and Fabiola Cabeza de Baca. See Rebolledo, *Women Singing in the Snow*.
2. For analyses of early Latina writers and Spanish-language print culture, see Kabalen Vanek and Mijares Cervantes, *Women and Print Culture*; and Feu and Y. Padilla, *Latina Histories and Cultures*.
3. Kanellos and Martell, *Hispanic Periodicals*, 100.
4. G. González, *Redeeming la Raza*, 41.
5. For discussions of Jovita Idar's journalism and activism, see G. González, *Redeeming la Raza*, 19–43; and Barragán Goetz, *Reading*, 69–80.
6. Montemayor's influence grew within LULAC as attested by her work as associate editor of *LULAC News* in 1940. Orozco, "Montemayor," 67. See also J. M. González, *Border Renaissance*, 163–69.
7. J. M. González, *Border Renaissance*, 85.
8. Pérez Rosario, *Julia de Burgos*, 74, 83.
9. Kanellos and Martell, *Hispanic Periodicals*, 111. See, for example, Lee Tapia, "Día internacional de la mujer Brooklyn," *Pueblos Hispanos*, April 3, 1943.
10. Sánchez Korrol, *Colonia to Community*, 74. See also Schlau, "Cultural Leader."
11. For discussions on racialization and the marginalization of Mexican Americans in Texas in the context of their fight for civil rights in the early decades of the twentieth century, see M. García, "Alonso S. Perales," 151–54; and Orozco, *Pioneer*, xxix-xxx.

12. As Cloutier notes, "[t]he archive is never an end in itself... but rather a speculative means to possible futures, including unknowable teleologies guided by unborn hands." Cloutier, *Shadow Archives*, 3. For an overview of critical discussions related to the function of the archive and Black writers such as Wright, Petry, and Ellison, who conceived of their work in part as an archival practice, see Cloutier, *Shadow Archives*, 5–14.
13. Some of these Latina scholars include Vicki Ruiz, Virginia Sánchez Korrol, Rosaura Sánchez, Beatrice Pita, Tey Diana Rebolledo, Clara Lomas, María Cotera, Donna M. Kabalen Vanek, and Lisa Sánchez González.
14. See Orozco, *No Mexicans, Women, or Dogs Allowed; Pioneer of Mexican-American Civil Rights*; and *Agent of Change*.
15. Orozco, *Agent of Change*, 26. For discussions on the lack of educational opportunities for Puerto Rican women in New York City before the 1960s and the activism of Pura Belpré and Antonia Pantoja to improve those conditions, see Sánchez González, *Stories I Read to the Children*, and Sánchez Korrol, "Antonia Pantoja."
16. Orozco, *Agent of Change*, 26.
17. C. Lomas, introduction, xlv.
18. M. Cotera, "Jovita," 136, 131.
19. Walker, introduction, vi.
20. Orozco, *Agent of Change*, 29.
21. While Sloss-Vento used different versions of her last name during her writing career, I follow the lead of her biographer, Cynthia Orozco, who uses the hyphenated version.
22. Orozco, *Agent of Change*, 141.
23. Since Artes Gráficas was not a traditional publishing house in the modern sense but consisted primarily of a printing press, Orozco notes that Sloss-Vento had to pay thousands of dollars at the time to publish her book. Orozco, *Agent of Change*, 93.
24. Blackwell, *¡Chicana Power!*, 28.
25. In addition to Spanish-language newspaper articles and a few of her correspondences with Perales, Sloss-Vento's bibliography included books with limited circulation at the time such as Canales's *Juan N. Cortina: Bandit or Patriot?*; Castañeda's articles based on his book *Our Catholic Heritage in Texas*; and Perales's two major works, *In Defense of My People*, and *Are We Good Neighbors?*
26. Orozco, *Agent of Change*, 34–35.
27. See Kanellos, "Sotero Figueroa" and *Latinos and Nationhood*, 69–83; Valdés, *Diasporic Blackness*, 91–107; and Sánchez González, "Decolonizing Schomburg."
28. Holton, "Decolonizing History," 220.
29. Orozco, *Agent of Change*, 33.
30. M. Cotera, "Unpacking," 300.
31. Sloss-Vento, *Perales*, vii.
32. Sloss-Vento, *Perales*, 6. Orozco emphasizes Sloss-Vento's unique position as a woman who was able to correspond as an equal with male Mexican American civil rights

33. Orozco, *Agent of Change*, 135.
34. Vento, *Writer*, 130. Sloss-Vento's son, Arnoldo Vento, wrote a study of his mother's work, *Adela Sloss-Vento: Writer, Political Activist, and Civil Rights Pioneer*, published in 2017 that contains more than a hundred primary sources in their entirety written by Adela Sloss-Vento, transcribed and in most cases translated from Spanish to English by Arnoldo Vento. These documents form part of the private Adela Sloss-Vento archive in possession of the family.
35. Sloss-Vento, *Perales*, vii–viii. Sloss-Vento mentions other Spanish-language newspapers printed in Texas that contributed to the movement including *El Comercio* of Harlingen, *La Avispa* of Del Rio, *El Fronterizo* of Rio Grande City, *The Monitor* and *Diogenes* both of McAllen, and *Las Noticias* of Laredo. Sloss-Vento, *Perales*, viii.
36. Sloss-Vento, *Perales*, 1.
37. Quoted in Sloss-Vento, *Perales*, 16.
38. Sloss-Vento, *Perales*, 3.
39. Canales's *Juan N. Cortina: Bandit or Patriot?* consists of an address delivered by Canales at the Lower Rio Grande Valley Historical Association in San Benito, Texas, in 1951. Canales recounts Cortina's history and family background and mentions that he is "related to Cortina." Canales, *Cortina*, 3. Canales's pamphlet discusses the arrival of white settlers to Texas, Cortina's land dispossession, his attempted raid of Brownsville in 1859, and his eventual exile in Mexico.
40. Quoted in Sloss-Vento, *Perales*, 4. While Canales uses Webb's *The Texas Rangers* as an historical source to make a case for Cortina, Américo Paredes in *"With His Pistol in His Hand"* famously challenged Webb's historical account for its depiction of Mexican Americans. Paredes, *"With His Pistol,"* 17–18.
41. Quoted in Sloss-Vento, *Perales*, 4.
42. Sloss-Vento, *Perales*, 5.
43. J. M. González, *Border Renaissance*, 6.
44. Orozco discusses Canales as a person of multiple talents and affiliations; in addition to his work as attorney, legislator, and civil rights activist, Canales was also interested in Mexican American history. Orozco, "J. T. Canales," 179.
45. A. Sánchez, "*Mendigos*," 111.
46. Zamora O'Shea's pamphlet on Cortina similarly presents him as a wealthy rancher wronged by white settlers, taking justice into his own hands with the "assistance of friends who had suffered at the hands of the newcomers . . ." Zamora O'Shea, "Cortina," 7. For a discussion of Zamora O'Shea's recovery of the Mexican American past in her novel *El Mesquite*, see J. M. González, *Border Renaissance*, 80–94.
47. Sloss-Vento, *Perales*, 8.
48. For a compelling book-length collection of critical essays of the Canales investigation of the Texas Rangers in 1919, see S. Hernández and J. M. González, *Reverberations of Racial Violence*.
49. Martinez, *Injustice*, 183–84.

50. Sloss-Vento, *Perales*, 8.
51. Sloss-Vento, *Perales*, 8.
52. Sloss-Vento, *Perales*, 2.
53. Sloss-Vento, *Perales*, 2.
54. Sloss-Vento, *Perales*, 2.
55. Vento, introduction, ix.
56. Kabalen de Bichara, "Self-Writing," 252.
57. Orozco, *Pioneer*, xvii.
58. Sloss-Vento, *Perales*, 1.
59. Sloss-Vento, *Perales*, 1.
60. Vento, *Writer*, 130.
61. Vento, *Writer*, 130.
62. Sloss-Vento, *Perales*, 6.
63. Sloss-Vento, *Perales*, 6.
64. Sloss-Vento, *Perales*, 7. Sloss-Vento initially wrote to Perales, and he wrote her back inviting her to meet in his McAllen law office. Perales to Sloss-Vento, November 7, 1927.
65. Sloss-Vento documents the events that led to the formation of the League of United Latin Americans at the Harlingen meeting in minute detail using Spanish-language newspapers such as *La Avispa* of Del Rio, *El Comercio* of Harlingen, and *Diogenes* of McAllen that reported on these events, including those who participated at the meeting. Sloss-Vento, *Perales*, 25–26.
66. Sloss-Vento, *Perales*, 18. For an overview on the role of these leaders in LULAC, see Orozco, *No Mexicans*, 151–73; and Perales's own account in "True Origin of [LULAC]," the essay that concludes *In Defense of My People*, 256–76.
67. Sloss-Vento, *Perales*, 18.
68. Sloss-Vento, *Perales*, 22–23.
69. Sloss-Vento, *Perales*, 24.
70. See, for example, Perales's "To the Mexican Youth" originally published in *La Prensa* in 1929. Perales, *In Defense*, 61–65. See also Sáenz, "Del público: la nueva ley escolar obligatoria," *La Prensa*, August 15, 1916.
71. "Importantes trabajos," *La Prensa*, December 14, 1930.
72. Sloss-Vento, *Perales*, 22.
73. Sloss-Vento, *Perales*, 22–23. See also Sloss-Vento, "Es Encomiada La Labor del Lic. Perales," *La Prensa*, May 20, 1931.
74. Sloss-Vento, "Es Encomiada."
75. Orozco, *Agent of Change*, 135.
76. Sloss-Vento, "La Política."
77. Sloss-Vento, "Sobre el votante." Sloss-Vento ends her piece stating that the right to vote is key for Mexican Americans and just as important, organizations that protect those rights such as LULAC, are needed to improve some of the social and economic conditions "que afectan al pueblo Latino-americano" (that affect the people of Latin American descent). Sloss-Vento, "Sobre el votante."

78. In a piece titled "Importancia de la Liga de Ciudadanos Unidos Latino-Americanos," published in *La Prensa* in October 19, 1932, Sloss-Vento considers the creation of LULAC "uno de los pasos más trascendentales que se han dado en pro del mejoramiento intelectual del elemento americano de origen latino" (one of the most transformative steps taken to improve the welfare of Americans of Latin origin).
79. Orozco, *Agent of Change*, 46.
80. See J. M. González, *Border Renaissance*, 169–71; and Orozco, *Agent of Change*, 50–51.
81. Vento, *Writer*, 89. The following quotes from this piece are from Arnoldo Vento's translation of Sloss-Vento's original article written in Spanish, "Por qué en muchos hogares Latinos no existe verdadera felicidad," published in *LULAC News*, 1 March 1934.
82. Vento, *Writer*, 90.
83. Vento, *Writer*, 90.
84. Vento, *Writer*, 90.
85. Vento, *Writer*, 90.
86. L. Flores, *Grounds for Dreaming*, 73. For in-depth analyses of the Bracero Program, see Rosas, *Abrazando el Espíritu*; and L. Flores, *Grounds for Dreaming*.
87. Sloss-Vento, *Perales*, 32.
88. Sloss-Vento to Perales, September 8, 1947.
89. Sloss-Vento to Perales, December 6, 1947. Despite sharing this piece of personal information, Orozco has dispelled any suggestions that the relationship and correspondence between Sloss-Vento and Perales went beyond their collaboration on civil rights. Orozco, *Agent of Change*, 115–16.
90. Sloss-Vento, *Perales*, 34–36.
91. Sloss-Vento, *Perales*, 36–37.
92. Quoted in Sloss-Vento, *Perales*, 36.
93. Sloss-Vento, *Perales*, 38.
94. See Vento, *Writer*, 43–52; and Orozco, *Agent of Change*, 69–76.
95. Kabalen de Bichara, "Expressions," 200.
96. Sloss-Vento, *Perales*, 33.
97. Sloss-Vento to Perales, September 8, 1947.
98. Vento, *Writer*, 100.
99. Sloss-Vento, *Perales*, 32.
100. Vento, *Writer*, 121.
101. Sloss-Vento to Perales, November 12, 1947.
102. Sloss-Vento, *Perales*, 37.
103. G. Sánchez, foreword, 3.
104. Blanton, *Long Fight*, 156.
105. Blanton, *Long Fight*, 150.
106. Sloss-Vento, *Perales*, 38.
107. Sloss-Vento, *Perales*, 38–39.

108. Sloss-Vento, *Perales*, 45. Sloss-Vento wrote a letter to García on December 17, 1951, protesting the GI Forum's endorsement of the pamphlet; she writes, "I am surprised Dr. García, a person like yourself knowing full well who our executioners are and where the problem lies, that you are willing to solve the situation by supporting those that denigrate people of Mexican descent. There are no Mexicans [who] are cowards, inferior, or filthy. It is only those that exploit [them] who create this picture." Vento, *Writer*, 152.
109. Sloss-Vento reprints almost in its entirely in the body of her book Sáenz's denunciation of the pamphlet in his article titled "The Wetback Pamphlet," published in the *McAllen Monitor* on November 20, 1951. Sloss-Vento, *Perales*, 48–50. For a detailed discussion on Sánchez and his acrimonious public exchanges with Perales and Sáenz, see Blanton, *Long Fight*, 145–56.
110. Perales to Sloss-Vento, December 14, 1951.
111. Sloss-Vento to Perales, December 17, 1951.
112. Sloss-Vento, *Perales*, 39.
113. Sloss-Vento to Sáenz, January 3, 1952.
114. Sloss-Vento, *Perales*, 45.
115. Sloss-Vento, *Perales*, 41.
116. Sloss-Vento, *Perales*, 39.
117. See "Importante reunión en Mission, Texas," *La Prensa*, March 14, 1952.
118. Vento, *Writer*, 182.
119. For discussions on Castañeda's writings on Mexican Americans and Catholicism, see Almaráz, *Knight without Armor*; and M. García, *Mexican Americans*, 231–251.
120. For an insightful discussion on the publication history of Castañeda's *Our Catholic Heritage*, see Almaráz, *Knight without Armor*, 32–40.
121. Some of Perales's original newspaper columns used by Sloss-Vento in her book include "¿Quiénes son los mexicanos que residen en Texas?" *La Prensa*, December 7, 1952, and "¿Quiénes son los mexicanos que residen en Texas?" *La Prensa*, December 12, 1952.
122. Sloss-Vento, *Perales*, 50–51.
123. Quoted in Sloss-Vento, *Perales*, 57.
124. Sloss-Vento, *Perales*, 55.
125. Sloss-Vento, *Perales*, 55.
126. See Saldaña-Portillo, *Indian Given*, 108–132; Gómez, *Manifest Destinies*, 85–103; and Fonseca-Chávez, *Colonial Legacies*, 24–41.
127. Rodolfo Uranga, the author of the newspaper article states, "La señorita Sloss no quiere que a los mexicanos nos llamen 'gente de color,' como sucede con frecuencia. Dice que México y los pueblos latinoamericanos están considerados como blancos" (Miss Sloss does not want Mexicans to be called "people of color," as is often the case. She says Mexico and other Latin American countries are predominantly white). Uranga, "Glosario del día."
128. Quoted in Sloss-Vento, *Perales*, 51. Perales at other times, similar to Sloss-Vento, argued that Mexican Americans should not be considered "people of color." Perales, *In Defense*, 185.

129. Sloss-Vento, *Perales*, 5.
130. Castañeda's *Our Catholic Heritage* adopts anti-Indigenous views as it describes Native peoples in the Southwest as either subjugated "mission Indians" or groups in a state of "barbarism" as in the case of the Comanche. Castañeda, *Our Catholic Heritage*, 323–25.
131. Orozco has identified Christianity as a major influence in Sloss-Vento. Orozco, *Agent of Change*, 33. Mario T. García has studied the "central role" that Catholicism played in Perales's "personal, social, and political formation and mind set." M. García, "Perales," 152.
132. M. García, *Católicos*, 12.
133. Sloss-Vento, *Perales*, 6.
134. Sloss-Vento, *Perales*, 18.
135. Sloss-Vento, *Perales*, 62.
136. Similar to Sloss-Vento, Ella Baker worked for civil rights behind the scenes for decades and their legacies have remained in the shadows of male leaders. Sloss-Vento and Baker, however, differ in distinct ways ideologically as the latter remained critical of patriarchal institutions such as the church and was attracted to communism. See West, *Black Prophetic Fire*, 89–108.
137. G. González, *Redeeming la Raza*, 18.
138. During the denunciation of the "wetback pamphlet," Sáenz wrote a newspaper editorial reprinted in Sloss-Vento's book in which he fears that their protest against the pamphlet may portray them as "Communists or as disloyal Americans"; however, he adds that it is precisely because they are "genuine Americans" that they are raising their voices in protest. Sloss-Vento, *Perales*, 50. In other words, communism for Sáenz was antithetical to their American patriotism.
139. Vento, *Writer*, 118.
140. A. Sánchez, *Homeland*, 12. Sloss-Vento similarly discusses in her book this tension between Mexican Americans and Mexicans in exile in Texas. Sloss-Vento, *Perales*, 26–28.
141. Sloss-Vento, *Perales*, 11.
142. Sloss-Vento, *Perales*, 12.
143. See Sloss-Vento to Benitez, June 20, 1974; Sloss-Vento's unpublished "Alonso S. Perales: Precursor and Founder of LULAC," October 1978; and Sloss-Vento to Pérez de Perales, June 2, 1980.
144. Orozco, *Agent of Change*, 85–86.
145. Sloss-Vento, *Perales*, 64.
146. Sloss-Vento, *Perales*, 77. See also Sloss-Vento to J. T. Canales, March 29, 1961. In this letter, she writes to Canales regarding the need to commemorate Perales as the rightful founder of LULAC.
147. Sloss-Vento, *Perales*, 12.
148. Orozco, *Agent of Change*, 96–97. In Gutiérrez's book, *The Making of a Chicano Militant*, he specifically positions his social and political activism in opposition to the conservative politics of Mexican American leaders and politicians in Texas of previous decades. Gutiérrez, *Making*, 11–12.

149. Blackwell, ¡Chicana Power!, 50.
150. Perales, "Continua el entusiasmo." In another newspaper column, Perales includes Sloss-Vento's name along with the names of Canales, Sáenz, and Castañeda as "líderes de nuestro pueblo por el progreso y el bienestar de nuestro pueblo en este país" (leaders for the progress and wellbeing of our people in this country). Perales, "Ha muerto," *La Prensa*, November 6, 1958.

Chapter 6

1. Craig Wilder's *Ebony and Ivy* discusses the emergence of the first colleges and universities in the U.S. as white-only institutions with deep ties to European colonialism, profits from the transatlantic slave trade, and the exploitation of Black bodies during slavery.
2. Mudditt, "University Presses," 330–31.
3. Fitzpatrick, *Planned Obsolescence*, 158.
4. Lovett, *Historically Black Colleges*, 111–12.
5. Slater, "First Black Faculty," 99. Academia, however, served as a major intellectual and creative space for Black scholars and writers that was essential for the development of Black literary and intellectual production. For an analysis of how academia served as a home for Black writers prior to the 1960s, see L. Porter, *The Blackademic Life*.
6. A handful of university presses published the work of Black writers or scholars as in the case of Margaret Walker's *For My People* (Yale University Press, 1942), and Eric Williams's *Capitalism and Slavery* (University of North Carolina Press, 1944).
7. Varel, *Lost Black Scholar*, 9.
8. For a detailed discussion on Nick Aaron Ford's manuscript and its rejection by different editors from university presses, see Jackson, *Indignant Generation*, 333–41.
9. E. Pérez, *Decolonial Imaginary*, 9–10.
10. Some of the exceptions include Josefina Niggli's *Mexican Village* (University of North Carolina Press, 1945), and Arthur L. Campa's *Spanish-Folk Poetry in New Mexico* (University of New Mexico Press, 1946).
11. Sánchez, for instance, also wrote *"The People": A Study of the Navajos* in 1948, a project commissioned by the United States Indian Service and supported by the University of New Mexico, which was not published by its press.
12. Representative analyses of *George Washington Gómez* include R. Saldívar, *Borderlands of Culture*, 145–89; J. M. González, *Border Renaissance*, 127–56; Limón, *Américo Paredes*, 9–34; and Cutler, *Ends of Assimilation*, 35–44. Critical discussions on Paredes's *"With His Pistol"* in relation to his treatment of the history of the U.S.-Mexico Borderlands include R. Saldívar, *Chicano Narrative*, 26–48; Limón, *Dancing with the Devil*, 76–94; and J. Saldívar, *Border Matters*, 36–56.
13. For an overview of the publication history of *George Washington Gómez*, see Rolando Hinojosa's introduction to the novel first published in 1990 by Arte Público Press. In a letter to Sharon Reynolds, Paredes also discusses in detail the early drafting of the novel and his subsequent decision not to alter the text for the

1990 edition. Paredes to Reynolds, August 7, 1992. See also R. Saldívar, *Borderlands*, 123–24.
14. R. Saldívar, "Asian Américo," 584.
15. On the racialization and segregation of Tejanos, or Mexicans and Texans of Mexican origin at the turn of the twentieth century, see Orozco, *No Mexicans*, 17–39; and Menchaca, *Mexican American Experience*, 75–112.
16. See "L'Amour," *La Prensa*, April 13, 1936; "Al cumplir veintiún años," *La Prensa*, November 16, 1936; and "Mis tres novias," *La Prensa*, July 8, 1940.
17. Morín, "Early Works," 13.
18. Schmidt Camacho, *Migrant Imaginaries*, 41. For an analysis of "The Mexico-Texan" in relation to its poetic form, vernacular speech, and its theme of social justice, see Schmidt Camacho, *Migrant Imaginaries*, 43–49.
19. Paredes, "Mexico-Texan."
20. Paredes, "Mexico-Texan."
21. Paredes, "Mexico-Texan."
22. Paredes, "Mexico-Texan."
23. J. M. González, *Border Renaissance*, 132. González discusses "Alma Pocha" as a poem that Paredes wrote in commemoration of the Texas Centennial celebration in 1936. J. M. González, *Border Renaissance*, 132–35. "Alma Pocha" remained unpublished for decades and was only published in 1991 by Arte Público Press as part of Paredes's poetry collection *Between Two Worlds*.
24. Paredes, *Two Worlds*, 35.
25. Paredes, *Two Worlds*, 35.
26. Paredes, *Two Worlds*, 35.
27. Paredes, *Two Worlds*, 35.
28. Paredes, *Two Worlds*, 35.
29. For analyses of *Cantos de adolescencia*, see Olguín and Vásquez Barbosa, introduction, xxiii-lxiii; and R. Saldívar, *Borderlands*, 247–63.
30. Paredes, "A México."
31. Paredes, "México, la ilusión."
32. Paredes, "México, la ilusión."
33. Paredes, *Cantos*, 3.
34. Paredes, *Cantos*, 3.
35. Paredes, *Cantos*, 3.
36. Paredes, *Cantos*, 3.
37. Paredes, *Cantos*, 4.
38. Ortega, "El Diario."
39. R. Saldívar, *Borderlands*, 125.
40. Ortega, "El Diario."
41. R. Saldívar, *Borderlands*, 141.
42. Castañeda to Paredes, October 25, 1937. Gregorio Garza, editor of the newspaper *El Regional* of Matamoros, Mexico, similarly praised *Cantos de adolescencia* after Paredes sent him a copy. Garza to Paredes, August 25, 1937.

43. For book-length analyses on the history of racial violence against Mexicans and Mexican Americans in the Borderlands in the early decades of the twentieth century, see B. Johnson, *Revolution in Texas*; and Martinez, *The Injustice Never Leaves You*.
44. Paredes to Kanellos, June 23, 1989.
45. Paredes himself described his intent to engage in his novel with the history of the Texas Rangers, *los sediciosos*, El Plan de San Diego, *los magonistas*, and the ways these historical events and figures were incorporated into *George Washington Gómez*. R. Saldívar, *Borderlands*, 116–24.
46. Paredes, *GWG*, 15, 147.
47. Paredes, *GWG*, 103.
48. Paredes mentions that he wrote the novel in English to reach a broader audience in contrast to Perales who wrote *En defensa de mi raza* in Spanish but was only able to reach a Spanish-speaking readership. R. Saldívar, *Borderlands*, 141.
49. Paredes, *GWG*, 173.
50. Paredes, *GWG*, 172.
51. For critiques of Paredes's novel and its disavowing of Indigeneity, or as containing a vision of settler colonialism by Mexicans and Mexican Americans in the Southwest, see Saldaña-Portillo, *Indian Given*, 149–53; Olguín, *Violentologies*, 54–58; and Aranda, *Places of Modernity*, 126–31.
52. Paredes, *GWG*, 282. As Limón explains, Paredes came from a family that traced its roots to a Spanish settlement in South Texas whose economic model was based on ranching and where Indigenous communities were either "subdued or integrated" into this agricultural economy. Limón, *Américo Paredes*, 3.
53. See E. Lee, *Making*, 109–136 and *America*, 75–111; and Lew-Williams, *The Chinese Must Go*, 53–88.
54. E. Lee, *America*, 110–11.
55. E. Lee, *Making*, 134. For discussion on the effects of the U.S. Immigration Act of 1924, also known as the Johnson-Reed Act, that halted Japanese immigration to the U.S., see Koshiro, *Trans-Pacific Racisms*, 20–21; and E. Lee, *Making*, 134–35.
56. Day, *Alien Capital*, 119–21.
57. E. Lee, *Making*, 235.
58. Ferguson, *War of the World*, 544–45.
59. Ferguson, *War of the World*, 572–73.
60. For a thorough and compelling analysis on the background and legacy of the Tokyo war crimes trial, see Bass, *Judgment at Tokyo*, 6–29.
61. See R. Saldívar, *Borderlands*, 344–75. For other analyses of Paredes's writings in Asia, see J. Saldívar, *Trans-Americanity*, 123–36; and Limón, *Américo Paredes*, 36–56.
62. In an interview with Calderón and López-Morín decades later, Paredes questioned the impartiality of the news coming from U.S. military authorities in Japan based on his field reporting and hearing stories from Japanese farmers and their economic struggles that differed from the stories reported by the U.S. occupation force. Calderón and López-Morín, "Interview," 211.

63. Paredes, "Tojo Heads List."
64. Koshiro, *Trans-Pacific Racisms*, 19.
65. Sugita, *Pitfall or Panacea*, 9.
66. Paredes, "Defense Head."
67. Paredes, "Defense Head."
68. Paredes, "Defense Head."
69. R. Saldívar, *Borderlands*, 382.
70. Paredes, "Co-Defendant."
71. Paredes, "Co-Defendant." Paredes recounted decades later being reprimanded by an army lieutenant who misunderstood the word "neurotic" for "psychotic," which he used to describe Shumei Okawa and accused Paredes "of being an apologist for the Japanese criminals." Paredes to R. Saldívar, December 13, 1993.
72. Paredes, "Co-Defendant."
73. Paredes, "Co-Defendant."
74. Paredes, "Co-Defendant."
75. Limón, *Américo Paredes*, 39.
76. Paredes, "Tojo's Defense."
77. Paredes, "Tojo's Defense."
78. Paredes, "Tojo's Defense."
79. Paredes, "Tojo's Defense."
80. Paredes, "Tojo's Defense."
81. Paredes, "Tojo's Defense."
82. Rosales, *Soldados Razos*, 165.
83. For a genesis of the publication of Paredes's short story collection in 1994, see Paredes to R. Saldívar, October 2, 1991.
84. McHenry, *Negro Literature*, 192.
85. Paredes received multiple rejection slips from mainstream magazines after submitting some of his short stories including "Sugamo," *Partisan Review*, March 3, 1953; "Over the Waves Is Out," *The New Yorker*, February 1953; and "A Cold Night," *Harper's Magazine*, February 1953. After learning about Arturo Islas's inability to publish his novel *The Rain God* (1984) with a New York publisher despite multiple attempts, Paredes shared in a letter to José David Saldívar similar struggles "having some of [his] short stories taken seriously by magazine and journal editors." Paredes to J. Saldívar, February 7, 1992.
86. R. Saldívar has offered the most thorough analysis of Paredes's short stories set in the Pacific. See R. Saldívar, introduction, xxxiii-li, and *Borderlands*, 321–43. See also Limón, *Américo Paredes*, 56–71.
87. Sugita, *Pitfall or Panacea*, 5.
88. Ferguson, *War of the World*, 544–45.
89. Koshiro, *Trans-Pacific Racisms*, 7.
90. Paredes, *Hammon*, 119.
91. Paredes, *Hammon*, 119.
92. Paredes, *Hammon*, 121.

93. Paredes, *Hammon*, 122.
94. Paredes, *Hammon*, 122.
95. Paredes, *Hammon*, 123.
96. Paredes, *Hammon*, 124.
97. Paredes to R. Saldívar, December 13, 1992.
98. For a compelling analysis of "Ichiro Kikuchi" as a "cross-racial encounter" between a Japanese Mexican and a Mexican American soldier in the context of the emergence of "Chicanx political agency," see Gonzales Sae-Saue, *Southwest Asia*, 52–57.
99. Paredes, *Hammon*, 151.
100. R. Saldívar, introduction, xl.
101. Paredes, *Hammon*, 157.
102. See R. Saldívar's *Borderlands*, 331; and Gonzales Sae-Saue, *Southwest Asia*, 56–57.
103. See Ferguson, *War of the World*, 571–76; and Bass, *Judgment at Tokyo*, 55–58.
104. Ferguson, *War of the World*, 573. Ferguson also writes about one air raid in Tokyo that claimed about 80,000 to 100,000 lives on March 9, 1945. Ferguson, *War of the World*, 573.
105. Paredes, *Hammon*, 157.
106. Paredes, *Hammon*, 159.
107. Paredes, *Hammon*, 172.
108. Paredes, *Hammon*, 174.
109. Paredes, *Hammon*, 174.
110. Paredes, *Hammon*, 182.
111. Hong, *Violent Peace*, 55.
112. Paredes, *Hammon*, 173.
113. Paredes, *Hammon*, 175.
114. Paredes, *Hammon*, 176.
115. Paredes, *Hammon*, 178.
116. Paredes, *Hammon*, 177. Paredes discussed that while in Japan after the war, he read in the newspapers about the city of Atami, "Japan's suicide capital" that served as the basis for the story. Paredes to R. Saldívar, December 13, 1992.
117. Paredes, *Hammon*, 179.
118. Paredes, *Hammon*, 184.
119. Paredes, *Hammon*, 161.
120. After Paredes wrote an early draft of "Sugamo," he revised the story and made two key changes; he changed the main character's race from white to Black and moved the story from Japan to Korea. Paredes to R. Saldívar, December 13, 1992. Limón incisively observes that some of Paredes's writings from Asia suggest that he harbored different views about Asian populations as he privileged Japanese over Chinese and Korean nationals. Limón, *Américo Paredes*, 42.
121. In a letter to R. Saldívar, Paredes connects "Sugamo" to the Tokyo war crimes trial; Paredes remembers a colonel telling him during his coverage of the war trials, "[i]f we want revenge of these Japs, we should just take them out and shoot them. What

their soldiers did, our GIs did the same thing. I know it." Paredes also makes a specific connection between "Sugamo" and the Tokyo trial by using as the story's title the name of the prison where Hideki Tojo was held, trialed, and executed. Paredes to R. Saldívar, December 13, 1992.
122. Delmont, *Half American*, 166–71.
123. J. Lee, *Interracial Encounters*, 5.
124. Paredes, *Hammon*, 160.
125. Paredes, *Hammon*, 160–61.
126. Paredes, *Hammon*, 163.
127. R. Saldívar's *Borderlands*, 333.
128. Paredes, *Hammon*, 165.
129. Molasky, *American Occupation*, 73, 74.
130. Paredes, *Hammon*, 166, 167.
131. For discussions on the GI Bill and how it influenced social mobility for Mexican American veterans who were able to receive benefits, see Rodríguez, Heilig, and Prochnow, "Higher Education," 59–74; and Rosales, *Soldados Razos*, 137–47.
132. Paredes tried multiple times to publish *The Shadow*, written in the 1950s, with a mainstream publisher without success. See Evan Thomas's letter to Paredes declining to publish *The Shadow* with Harper & Brothers. Thomas to Paredes, July 3, 1957. *The Shadow* was not published until 1998 by Arte Público Press. See also R. Saldívar, *Borderlands*, 139–40, 395–97.
133. For an overview of Paredes's time at UT-Austin as a graduate student and his return as a professor, see Medrano, *In His Own Words*, 53–60.
134. For discussions on the publication history of *"With His Pistol,"* see R. Saldívar's *Borderlands*, 110–15; Medrano, *In His Own Words*, 53–57; and Martinez, *Injustice*, 264–65.
135. See E. Pérez, *Decolonial Imaginary*, 15; Saldaña-Portillo, *Indian Given*, 10, 144–45; and Martinez, *Injustice*, 23–24, 240–46.
136. For an analysis of Webb's *The Texas Rangers*, see J. M. González, *Border Renaissance*, 53–66. For a discussion on J. Frank Dobie, see Limón, *Dancing with the Devil*, 43–59.
137. The University of Texas Press started in 1922 but published only a few books before 1950. Wardlaw became the director after he founded and directed the University of South Carolina Press. Wardlaw's interest is representative of the trend among university presses to focus on regional topics; in the case of the University of Texas Press, its focus was the Southwest, Texas history, and Latin America. Hawes, *Advance Knowledge*, 44–45.
138. Robert Stephenson, Professor of English at UT-Austin, became Paredes's advisor and PhD dissertation director, and other members of Paredes's doctoral committee included Mody Boatright and Stith Thompson who were considered "the most respected folklorists [at] the time." R. Saldívar, *Borderlands*, 109, 113.
139. R. Saldívar, *Borderlands*, 113.

140. R. Saldívar, *Borderlands*, 113.
141. While conducting research for his dissertation, Paredes contacted relatives of Gregorio Cortez; see, for example, Paredes to L. Cortez, May 23, 1955.
142. Wardlaw wrote to Paredes, "[t]here are several main elements in this work which are of great value and interest to the general reader. One of these is your exceedingly penetrating analysis of the border country and its people." Wardlaw to Paredes, January 14, 195[7]. Wardlaw's letter is dated January 14, 1956, but the sequence of other letters related to his manuscript suggests it should be dated January 14, 1957. Paredes replies to Wardlaw regarding the content of this letter on February 21, 1957.
143. Wardlaw to Paredes, January 14, 195[7].
144. Wardlaw to Paredes, January 14, 195[7].
145. Wardlaw to Paredes, January 14, 195[7].
146. Paredes to Wardlaw, February 21, 1957.
147. Wardlaw to Paredes, February 25, 1957.
148. Wardlaw to Paredes, February 25, 1957.
149. Paredes to Wardlaw, March 4, 1957.
150. Wardlaw to Paredes, July 18, 1857.
151. Wardlaw to G. Sánchez, May 12, 1959.
152. For discussions on the degree to which World War II and Asia influenced Paredes, see Limón, "Imagining the Imaginary"; and R. Saldívar's "Asian Américo."
153. R. Saldívar, "Asian Américo," 592.
154. Paredes, *"With His Pistol,"* 105. Zamora discusses in detail Mexican Americans' "seemingly permanent condition of racialized occupational inequality" in Texas between 1930 and 1960. Zamora, *Claiming*, 5.
155. Paredes, *"With His Pistol,"* 106.
156. Paredes, *"With His Pistol,"* 106.
157. As Luis Alvarez explains, the identities of Latinx servicemen during World War II "were at least partially produced outside" of the U.S. "and in relation to a range of non-American people and cultures, in the context of total war that served American imperialism." Alvarez, "Transnational Latino," 76. See also Gonzales Sae-Saue, *Southwest Asia*, 48–51.
158. Paredes, *"With His Pistol,"* 105.
159. Paredes, *"With His Pistol,"* 106.
160. Paredes, *"With His Pistol,"* 106.
161. Paredes, *GWG*, 148.
162. Paredes, *"With His Pistol,"* 107.
163. Paredes, *"With His Pistol,"* 107.
164. Limón, *Américo Paredes*, 119–20.

Conclusion

1. See Martín-Rodríguez, *Life in Search of Readers*, 139–70; Gruesz, "What Was Latino Literature?"; and Cutler, "Latinx Historicisms."

2. See, for example, J. M. González, *Border Renaissance*; Varon, *Before Chicano*; Aranda, *Places of Modernity*; and Lamas, *Latino Continuum*.
3. Juan González and Joseph Torres have documented the almost systematic exclusion of writers of color since the inception of U.S. newspapers and newsrooms that continued until the 1970s. González and Torres, *News for All the People*, 301–24.
4. J. Flores, foreword, xii. See also Luis, *Two Cultures*; and Jiménez Román and Flores, *The Afro-Latin@ Reader*.
5. Gruesz, "What Was Latino Literature?," 336.
6. *The Latino Nineteenth Century* edited by Jesse Alemán and Rodrigo Lazo and *The Cambridge Companion to Latina/o American Literature* edited by John M. González represent recent examples of collaborative efforts by groups of scholars that have mapped and contextualized the Latinx literary tradition.
7. Kanellos, *Latinos and Nationhood*, 27.
8. A few examples of republications of early Latinx texts include Cleofas M. Jaramillo's *Romance of a Little Village Girl* by the University of New Mexico Press; Elena Zamora O'Shea's *El Mesquite* by Texas A&M University Press; and Jovita González's *Life along the Border* also by Texas A&M University Press.
9. See So, *Redlining Culture*.
10. See Sinykin, *Big Fiction*; and McGurl, *Everything and Less*.
11. So, *Redlining Culture*, 8–9.
12. See Ginna, *What Editors Do*, 4–5.
13. Arlene Dávila's excellent *Latinx Art* thoroughly documents similar dynamics playing out in U.S. museums, galleries, organizations, and cultural institutions as Latinx artists and creators remain invisible in those spaces.

BIBLIOGRAPHY

Acosta-Belén, Edna. "The Building of a Community: Puerto Rican Writers and Activists in New York City (1890s-1960s)." In *Recovering the U.S. Hispanic Literary Heritage. Vol. I*, edited by Ramón Gutiérrez and Genaro Padilla, 179–95. Houston: Arte Público Press, 1993.

Acosta-Belén, Edna, and Carlos E. Santiago. *Puerto Ricans in the United States: A Contemporary Portrait*. Boulder: Lynne Rienner, 2006.

Acosta-Belén, Edna, and Virginia Sánchez Korrol. Introduction to *The Way It Was and Other Writings*, by Jesús Colón, edited by Edna Acosta-Belén and Virginia Sánchez Korrol, 13–30. Houston: Arte Público Press, 1993.

"A *La Prensa*, a nuestros amigos y al público." *La Prensa*, February 19, 1913.

Alemán, Jesse. "Historical Amnesia and the Vanishing Mestiza: The Problem of Race in *The Squatter and the Don* and *Ramona*." *Aztlán* 27, no. 1 (2002): 59–93.

Allen, Esther. "Translating the Local: New York's Micro-Cosmopolitan Media, from José Martí to the Hyperlocal Hub." In *Avenues of Translation: The City in Iberian and Latin American Writing*, edited by Regina Galasso and Evelyn Scaramella, 112–32. Lewisburg: Bucknell University Press, 2019.

Almaguer, Tomás. *Racial Fault Lines: The Historical Origins of White Supremacy in California*. Berkeley: University of California Press, 1994.

Almaráz, Félix D. *Knight without Armor: Carlos Eduardo Castañeda, 1896–1958*. College Station: Texas A&M University Press, 1999.

Alvarez, Luis. "Transnational Latino Soldering: Military Service and Ethnic Politics during World War II." In *Latina/os and World War II: Mobility, Agency and Ideology*, edited by Maggie Rivas-Rodríguez and B. V. Olguín, 75–93. Austin: University of Texas Press, 2014.

Amory, Hugh, and David D. Hall, eds. *A History of the Book in America. Vol. I: The Colonial Book in the Atlantic World*. Chapel Hill: University of North Carolina Press, 2007.

Aquino, Melissa Coss. "Jesús y Concha Colón: A Puerto Rican Story of Love, Tradition, Migration and Modernity in Early 20th Century New York." *Centro* 29, no. 2 (2017): 62–87.

Aranda, José F. *The Places of Modernity in Early Mexican American Literature, 1848–1948*. Lincoln: University of Nebraska Press, 2022.

Baldwin, Kate A. *Beyond the Color Line and the Iron Curtain: Reading Encounters between Black and Red, 1922–1963*. Durham: Duke University Press, 2002.

Barragán Goetz, Philis M. *Reading, Writing, and Revolution: Escuelitas and the Emergence of a Mexican American Identity in Texas*. Austin: University of Texas Press, 2022.

Bass, Gary J. *Judgment at Tokyo: World War II on Trial and the Making of Modern Asia*. New York: Knopf, 2023.

Beaumont, Matthew. Introduction to *Looking Backward 2000–1887*, by Edward Bellamy, vii–xxx. New York: Oxford, 2007.

Belnap, Jeffrey, and Raúl Fernández, eds. *José Martí's "Our America": From National to Hemispheric Cultural Studies*. Durham: Duke University Press, 1998.

Bernard, Emily. *Carl Van Vechten and the Harlem Renaissance: A Portrait in Black and White*. New Haven: Yale University Press, 2012.

Blackhawk, Ned. *The Rediscovery of America: Native Peoples and the Unmaking of U.S. History*. New Haven: Yale University Press, 2023.

Blackwell, Maylei. *¡Chicana Power! Contested Histories of Feminism in the Chicano Movement*. Austin: University of Texas Press, 2011.

Blackwell, Maylei, Floridalma Boj Lopez, and Luis Urrieta Jr. "Special Issue: Critical Latinx Indigeneities." *Latino Studies* 15, no. 1 (2017): 126–37.

Blanton, Carlos K. *George I. Sánchez: The Long Fight for Mexican American Integration*. New Haven: Yale University Press, 2014.

Blanton, Carlos K. *The Strange Career of Bilingual Education in Texas, 1836–1981*. College Station: Texas A&M University Press, 2004.

Bourdieu, Pierre. *Distinction: A Social Critique of the Judgement of Taste*. Translated by Richard Nice. Cambridge, MA: Harvard University Press, 1984.

Braithwaite, William Stanley. "The Negro in Literature." *Crisis*, September 1924. In *The New Negro: Readings on Race, Representation, and African American Culture, 1892–1938*, edited by Henry L. Gates and Gene Andrew Jarrett, 182–90. Princeton: Princeton University Press, 2007.

Brown, William Wells. *The Black Man, His Antecedents, His Genius, and His Achievements*. New York: Thomas Hamilton, 1863.

Bryant, Earle V., ed. *Byline, Richard Wright: Articles from the Daily Worker and New Masses*. Columbia: University of Missouri Press, 2015.

Bynum, Tara A. *Reading Pleasures: Everyday Black Living in Early America*. Champaign: University of Illinois Press, 2023.

Byrd, Jodi A. *The Transit of Empire: Indigenous Critiques of Colonialism*. Minneapolis: University of Minnesota Press, 2011.

Calderón, Héctor, and José Rósbel López-Morín. "Interview with Américo Paredes." *Nepantla* 1, no. 1 (2000): 197–228.

Camacho, Jorge. *Etnografía política y poder a finales del siglo XIX: José Martí y la cuestión indígena*. Chapel Hill: University of North Carolina Press, 2013.

Caminero-Santangelo, Marta. *On Latinidad: U.S. Latino Literature and the Construction of Ethnicity*. Gainesville: University of Florida Press, 2007.

Canales, José Tomás. *Juan N. Cortina: Bandit or Patriot?* San Antonio: Artes Gráficas, 1951.

Carretta, Vincent. *Phillis Wheatley: Biography of a Genius in Bondage*. Athens: University of Georgia Press, 2011.

Carretta, Vincent. Introduction to *Phillis Wheatley Complete Writings*, edited by Vincent Carretta, xiii-xxxvii. New York: Penguin, 2001.

Castañeda, Carlos E. *Our Catholic Heritage in Texas: 1519–1936: Transition Period: The Fight for Freedom 1810–1836. Vol. VI*. New York: Arno Press, 1976.

Castañeda, Carlos E. Letter to Américo Paredes, October 25, 1937. Américo Paredes Papers. Nettie Lee Benson Latin American Collection. University of Texas at Austin. Box 18, folder 8.

Castañeda, Antonia, and Clara Lomas, eds. *Writing/Righting History: Twenty-Five Years of Recovering the US Hispanic Literary Heritage*. Houston: Arte Público Press, 2019.

Cavitch, Max. "The Poetry of Phillis Wheatley in Slavery's Recollective Economies, 1773 to the Present." In *Race, Ethnicity and Publishing in America*, edited by Cécile Cottenet, 210–30. New York: Palgrave, 2014.

Claridge, Laura. *The Lady with the Borzoi: Blanche Knopf, Literary Tastemaker Extraordinaire*. New York: Farrar, Straus, and Giroux, 2016.

Clarkson, Thomas. *An Essay on the Slavery and Commerce of the Human Species, Particularly the African*. Philadelphia: Nathaniel Wiley, 1804.

Cloutier, Jean-Christophe. *Shadow Archives: The Lifecycles of African American Literature*. New York: Columbia University Press, 2019.

Collins, Michael. "'Pure Feelings, Noble Aspirations and Generous Ideas': The Martí-Dana Friendship and the Cuban War of Independence." *Radical Americas* 1, no. 1 (2016): 1–24.

Colón, Jesús. "Columbus Discovers Puerto Rico." *Daily Worker*, November 21, 1955.

Colón, Jesús. "¡Cuidado, Harlem!" *Pueblos Hispanos*, June 26, 1943.

Colón, Jesús. "Éste es tu periódico." *Pueblos Hispanos*, March 27, 1943.

Colón, Jesús. "And Fuchik Looked as Confident." *Daily Worker*, April 2, 1956.

Colón, Jesús. "Hacia una gran institución Puertorriqueña." *Pueblos Hispanos*, July 24, 1943.

Colón, Jesús. "Hollywood Rewrites History." *Daily Worker*, September 4, 1956.

Colón, Jesús. "How to Know the Puerto Ricans." *Daily Worker*, January 23, 1956.

Colón, Jesús. "If Instead of a Professor." *Daily Worker*, April 9, 1956.

Colón, Jesús. "Inscríbete, regístrate y vota." *Pueblos Hispanos*, September 4, 1943.

Colón, Jesús. "Un jíbaro en Nueva York." *Gráfico*. August 21, 1927.

Colón, Jesús. Letter to Michael Kraus, July 30, 1965. Jesús Colón Papers. Center for Puerto Rican Studies Library & Archives, Hunter College, CUNY.

Colón, Jesús. "El Neoyorkino." *Gráfico*, August 28, 1927.

Colón, Jesús. "Los otros Estados Unidos." *Pueblos Hispanos*, April 17, 1943.

Colón, Jesús. *"Lo que el pueblo me dice...": Crónicas de la colonia Puertorriqueña en Nueva York*, edited by Edwin K. Padilla. Houston: Arte Público Press, 2001.

Colón, Jesús. "Puerto Rico es también una nación." *Pueblos Hispanos*, July 17, 1943.

Colón, Jesús. *A Puerto Rican in New York and Other Sketches*. New York: International Publishers, 1982.

Colón, Jesús. "Red Roses for Me." *Daily Worker*, November 20, 1956.

Colón, Jesús. "Te lo recordamos otra vez." *Pueblos Hispanos*, September 25, 1943.

Colón, Jesús. *The Way It Was and Other Writings*. Edited by Edna Acosta-Belén and Virginia Sánchez Korrol. Houston: Arte Público Press, 1993.

"Conmemoraron el aniversario de la muerte de Juárez los vecinos de Moore, Texas." *La Prensa*, July 24, 1915.

"Continúan su jira de conferencias A. S. Perales y J. Luz Sáenz." *La Prensa*, August 24, 1924.

Coronado, Raúl. *A World Not to Come: A History of Latino Writing and Print Culture*. Cambridge, MA: Harvard University Press, 2013.

Corretjer, Juan Antonio. "Este es Albizu Campos." *Pueblos Hispanos*, February 20, 1943.

Cotera, María E. Introduction to *Life along the Border: A Landmark Tejana Thesis* by Jovita González, edited by María Cotera, 3–33. College Station: Texas A&M University Press, 2006.

Cotera, María E. "Jovita González Mireles: Texas Folklorist, Historian, Educator." In *Leaders of the Mexican American Generation: Biographical Essays*, edited by Anthony Quiroz, 119–39. Denver: University Press of Colorado, 2015.

Cotera, María E. "Unpacking Our Mother's Libraries: Practices of Chicana Memory before and after the Digital Turn." In *Chicana Movidas: New Narratives of Activism and Feminism in the Movement Era*, edited by Dionne Espinoza, María E. Cotera, and Maylei Blackwell, 299–316. Austin: University of Texas Press, 2018.

Cotera, María E., and María Josefina Saldaña-Portillo. "Indigenous but not Indian? Chicana/os and the Politics of Indigeneity." In *The World of Indigenous North America*, edited by Robert Warrior, 549–68. New York: Routledge, 2015.

Cotera, Martha P. *Diosa y Hembra: The History and Heritage of Chicanas in the U.S.* Austin: Information System Development, 1976.

Coulthard, Glen Sean. *Red Skin, White Masks: Rejecting the Colonial Politics of Recognition*. Minneapolis: University of Minnesota Press, 2014.

"Coveting the Crow Lands." *Cherokee Advocate*, March 24, 1882.

Cowan, Jill. "'It's Called Genocide': Newson Apologizes to the State's Native Americans." *New York Times*, June 19, 2019. https://www.nytimes.com/2019/06/19/us/newsom-native-american-apology.html.

Crowder, Ralph L. *John Edward Bruce: Politician, Journalist, and Self-Trained Historian of the African Diaspora*. New York: New York University Press, 2004.

Cutler, John A. *Ends of Assimilation: The Formation of Chicano Literature*. New York: Oxford University Press, 2015.

Cutler, John A. "Latinx Historicisms in the Present." *American Literary History* 34, no. 1 (2022): 102–12.

Cutler, John A. "Latinx Modernism and the Spirit of Latinoamericanismo." *American Literary History* 33, no. 3 (2021): 571–87.

Cutler, John A. "Rubén Darío, Latino Poet." *English Language Notes* 56, no. 2 (2018): 71–89.

Danky, James P. "Reading, Writing, and Resisting: African American Print Culture." In *A History of the Book in America. Vol. 4: Print in Motion: The Expansion of Publishing and Reading in the United States, 1880–1940*, edited by Carl F. Kaestle and Janice A. Radway, 339–58. Chapel Hill: University of North Carolina Press, 2009.

Dávila, Arlene. *Latinx Art: Artists, Markets, and Politics*. Durham: Duke University Press, 2020.

Davis, David A. Introduction to *Not Only War: A Story of Two Great Conflicts* by Victor Daly, edited by David A. Davis, vii-xxxii. Charlottesville: University of Virginia Press, 2010.

Davis, David A. "Not Only War Is Hell: World War I and African American Lynching Narratives." *African American Review* 42, no. 3–4 (2008): 477–91.

Dawes, Henry L. "Solving the Indian Problem." In *Americanizing the American Indians: Writings by the "Friends of the Indian" 1880–1900*, edited by Francis P. Prucha, 27–30. Cambridge, MA: Harvard University Press, 1973.

Day, Iyko. *Alien Capital: Asian Racialization and the Logic of Settler Colonial Capitalism*. Durham: Duke University Press, 2016.

Dayton, Tim, and Mark Van Wienen, eds. *A History of American Literature and Culture of the First World War*. New York: Cambridge University Press, 2021.

De Santis, Christopher, ed. *Langston Hughes and the Chicago Defender. Essays on Race, Politics, and Culture, 1942–62*. Champaign: University of Illinois Press, 1995.

Delgado, Linda. "Jesús Colón and the Making of a New York City Community, 1917 to 1974." In *The Puerto Rican Diaspora: Historical Perspectives*, edited by Carmen Teresa Whalen and Víctor Vázquez-Hernández, 68–87. Philadelphia: Temple University Press, 2005.

Delmont, Matthew F. *Half American: The Epic Story of African Americans Fighting World War II at Home and Abroad*. New York: Viking, 2022.

Denis, Nelson A. *War against All Puerto Ricans: Revolution and Terror in America's Colony*. New York: Bold Type, 2015.

Du Bois, W. E. B. *The Autobiography of W. E. B. Du Bois*. New York: International Publishers, 1968.

Du Bois, W. E. B. "Awake America." *Crisis*, September 1917. In *The Oxford W. E. B. Du Bois Reader*, edited by Eric J. Sundquist, 379. New York: Oxford University Press, 1996.

Du Bois, W. E. B. "Criteria of Negro Art." *Crisis*, October 1926. In *The New Negro: Readings on Race, Representation, and African American Culture, 1892–1938*, edited by Henry L. Gates and Gene Andrew Jarrett, 257–60. Princeton: Princeton University Press, 2007.

Du Bois, W. E. B. *Dusk of Dawn*. New York: Oxford University Press, 2007.

Du Bois, W. E. B. Letter to Arturo Schomburg, May 6, 1927. Arturo Alfonso Schomburg Papers. Schomburg Center for Research in Black Culture, Manuscripts, Archives, and Rare Books Division, New York Public Library. Box 2, folder 14.

Du Bois, W. E. B. Letter to [Charles] F. Heartman, July 30, 1915. Arturo Alfonso Schomburg Papers. Schomburg Center for Research in Black Culture, Manuscripts, Archives, and Rare Books Division, New York Public Library. Box 2, folder 14.

Du Bois, W. E. B. "On Stalin." In *W. E. B. Du Bois: A Reader*, edited by David Levering Lewis, 796–97. New York: Henry Holt, 1995.

Du Bois, W. E. B. "Phillis Wheatley and African American Culture." *Fisk News*, May 1941. In *The Oxford W. E. B. Du Bois Reader*, edited by Eric J. Sundquist, 328–42. New York: Oxford University Press, 1996.

Du Bois, W. E. B. "The Real Reason behind Robeson's Persecution." In *W. E. B. Du Bois: A Reader*, edited by David Levering Lewis, 798–800. New York: Henry Holt, 1995.

Du Bois, W. E. B. "Returning Soldiers." *Crisis*, May 1919. In *The Oxford W. E. B. Du Bois Reader*, edited by Eric J. Sundquist, 380–81. New York: Oxford University Press, 1996.

Dunbar-Ortiz, Roxanne. *An Indigenous Peoples' History of the United States*. Boston: Beacon Press, 2014.

Edwards, Brent Hayes. *Practice of Diaspora: Literature, Translation, and the Rise of Black Internationalism*. Cambridge, MA: Harvard University Press, 2003.

Eggleston, Edward. "The Aborigines and the Colonists." *Century* 26 (1883): 96–114.

English, James F. *The Economy of Prestige: Prizes, Awards, and the Circulation of Cultural Value*. Cambridge, MA: Harvard University Press, 2005.

Ernest, John. *Chaotic Justice: Rethinking African American Literary History*. Chapel Hill: University of North Carolina Press, 2009.

Ernest, John. *Liberation Historiography. African American Writers and the Challenge of History, 1794–1861*. Chapel Hill: University of North Carolina Press, 2004.

Ferguson, Niall. *The War of the World: Twentieth-Century Conflict and the Descent of the West*. New York: Penguin Press, 2006.

Ferrer, Ada. *Insurgent Cuba: Race, Nation, and Revolution, 1868–1898*. Chapel Hill: University of North Carolina Press, 1999.

Feu, Montse, and Yolanda Padilla, eds. *Latina Histories and Cultures. Feminist Readings and Recoveries of Archival Knowledge*. Houston: Arte Público Press, 2023.

Figueroa, Sotero. *Ensayo biográfico de los que más han contribuido al progreso de Puerto Rico*. Ponce, Puerto Rico: El Vapor, 1888.

Figueroa, Sotero. *La verdad de la historia*. San Juan, Puerto Rico: Instituto de cultura Puertorriqueña, 1977.

Fitzpatrick, Kathleen. *Planned Obsolescence: Publishing, Technology, and the Future of the Academy*. New York: New York University Press, 2011.

Flores, Juan. Foreword to *A Puerto Rican in New York and Other Sketches* by Jesús Colón, ix–xvii. New York: International Publishers, 1982.

Flores, Juan. *The Diaspora Strikes Back: Caribeño Tales of Learning and Turning*. New York: Routledge, 2009.

Flores, Juan. *Divided Borders: Essays on Puerto Rican Identity*. Houston: Arte Público Press, 1993.

Flores, Lori A. *Grounds for Dreaming: Mexican Americans, Mexican Immigrants, and the California Farmworker Movement*. New Haven: Yale University Press, 2016.

Fonseca-Chávez, Vanessa. *Colonial Legacies in Chicana/o Literature and Culture: Looking through the Kaleidoscope*. Tucson: University of Arizona Press, 2020.

Fountain, Anne. *José Martí, the United States, and Race*. Gainesville: University of Florida Press, 2014.

Frymer, Paul. *Building an American Empire: The Era of Territorial and Political Expansion*. Princeton: Princeton University Press, 2017.

Gandal, Keith. *The Gun and the Pen: Hemingway, Fitzgerald, Faulkner, and the Fiction of Mobilization*. New York: Oxford University Press, 2008.

Gandal, Keith. *War Isn't the Only Hell. A New Reading of World War I American Literature*. Baltimore: Johns Hopkins University Press, 2018.

García, Mario T. "Alonso S. Perales and the Catholic Imaginary: Religion and the Mexican-American Mind." In *In Defense of My People: Alonso S. Perales and the Development of Mexican-American Public Intellectuals*, edited by Michael A. Olivas, 151–69. Houston: Arte Público Press, 2012.

García, Mario T. *Católicos: Resistance and Affirmation in Chicano Catholic History*. Austin: University of Texas Press, 2008.

García, Mario T. *Mexican Americans: Leadership, Ideology, and Identity, 1930–1960*. New Haven: Yale University Press, 1989.

Garcia, Richard A. "Alonso S. Perales: The Voice and Visions of a Citizen Intellectual." In *Leaders of the Mexican American Generation: Biographical Essays*, edited by Anthony Quiroz, 85–117. Denver: University Press of Colorado, 2015.

García Peña, Lorgia. *Translating Blackness. Latinx Colonialities in Global Perspective*. Durham: Duke University Press, 2022.

Gardner, Eric. "African American Literary Reconstructions and the 'Propaganda of History.'" *American Literary History* 30, no. 3 (2018): 429–49.

Gardner, Eric. *Black Print Unbound: The Christian Recorder, African American Literature, and Periodical Culture*. New York: Oxford University Press, 2015.

Garza, Gregorio. Letter to Américo Paredes, August 25, 1937. Américo Paredes Papers. Nettie Lee Benson Latin American Collection. University of Texas at Austin. Box 18, folder 8.

Gates, Henry L. *Trials of Phillis Wheatley: America's First Black Poet and Her Encounters with the Founding Fathers*. New York: Basic Books, 2003.

Gates, Henry L. and Gene Andrew Jarrett, eds. *The New Negro: Readings on Race, Representation, and African American Culture, 1892–1938*. Princeton: Princeton University Press, 2007.

Genette, Gérard. *Paratexts: Thresholds of Interpretation*. Translated by Jane E. Lewin. New York: Cambridge University Press, 1997.

Gillman, Susan. "*Ramona* in 'Our America.'" In *José Martí's "Our America": From National to Hemispheric Cultural Studies*, edited by Jeffrey Belnap and Raúl Fernández, 91–111. Durham: Duke University Press, 1998.

Gilpin, Patrick J., and Marybeth Gasman. *Charles S. Johnson: Leadership Beyond the Veil in the Age of Jim Crow*. Albany: State University of New York Press, 2003.

Ginna, Peter. Introduction to *What Editors Do: The Art, Craft, and Business of Book Editing*, edited by Peter Ginna, 1–13. Chicago: University of Chicago Press, 2017.

Gómez, Laura E. *Manifest Destinies: The Making of the Mexican American Race*. New York: New York University Press, 2018.

Gómez-Quiñones, Juan. *Roots of Chicano Politics, 1600–1940*. Albuquerque: University of New Mexico Press, 1994.

Gonzales-Berry, Erlinda, ed. *Pasó por Aquí: Critical Essays on the New Mexican Literary Tradition, 1542–1988*. Albuquerque: University of New Mexico Press, 1989.

González, Gabriela. *Redeeming La Raza: Transborder Modernity, Race, Respectability, and Rights*. New York: Oxford University Press, 2018.

González, John M. *Border Renaissance: The Texas Centennial and the Emergence of Mexican American Literature*. Austin: University of Texas Press, 2009.

González, John M., ed. *The Cambridge Companion to Latina/o American Literature*. New York: Cambridge University Press, 2016.

González, John M. "The Warp of Whiteness: Domesticity and Empire in Helen Hunt Jackson's Ramona." *American Literary History* 16, no. 3 (2004): 437–65.

González, Jovita. *Life Along the Border: A Landmark Tejana Thesis*, edited by María E. Cotera. College Station: Texas A&M University Press, 2006.

González, Juan, and Joseph Torres. *News for All the People: The Epic Story of Race and the American Media*. New York: Verso, 2011.

Greenidge, Kerri K. *Black Radical: The Life and Times of William Monroe Trotter*. New York: Liveright, 2020.

Greenwald, Emily. *Reconfiguring the Reservation: The Nez Perces, Jicarilla Apaches, and the Dawes Act*. Albuquerque: University of New Mexico Press, 2002.

Gruesz, Kirsten Silva. *Ambassadors of Culture: The Transamerican Origins of Latino Writing*. Princeton: Princeton University Press, 2002.

Gruesz, Kirsten Silva. *Cotton Mather's Spanish Lessons: A Story of Language, Race, and Belonging in the Early Americas*. Cambridge, MA: Harvard University Press, 2022.

Gruesz, Kirsten Silva. "What Was Latino Literature?" *PMLA* 127, no. 2 (2012): 335–41.

Guerra, Lillian. *The Myth of José Martí: Conflicting Nationalisms in Early Twentieth-Century Cuba*. Chapel Hill: University of North Carolina Press, 2005.

Guillory, John. *Cultural Capital: The Problem of Literary Canon Formation*. Chicago: University of Chicago Press, 1993.

Gutiérrez, José Angel. *The Making of a Chicano Militant: Lessons from Cristal*. Madison: University of Wisconsin Press, 1998.

Haney López, Ian. *White by Law: The Legal Construction of Race*. New York: New York University Press, 2006.

Harper's Magazine. Rejection Slip to Américo Paredes, February 1953. Américo Paredes Papers. Nettie Lee Benson Latin American Collection. University of Texas at Austin. Box 18, folder 11.

Hartman, Saidiya. *Scenes of Subjection: Terror, Slavery, and Self-Making in Nineteenth-Century America*. New York: Norton, 2022.

Hawes, Gene R. *To Advance Knowledge: A Handbook on American University Press Publishing*. New York: American University Press Publishing, 1967.

Heartman, Charles F. *Phillis Wheatley (Phillis Peters): A Critical Attempt and a Bibliography of Her Writings*. New York: Charles F. Heartman, 1915.

Helton, Laura E. "Making Lists, Keeping Time: Infrastructures of Black Inquiry, 1900–1950." In *Against a Sharp White Background: Infrastructures of African American Print*, edited by Brigitte Fielder and Jonathan Senchyne, 82–108. Madison: University of Wisconsin Press, 2019.

Helton, Laura E. and Rafia Zafar. "Arturo Alfonso Schomburg in the Twenty-First Century: An Introduction." *African American Review* 54, no. 1–2 (2021): 1–18.

Hemingway, Andrew. *Artists on the Left: American Artists and the Communist Movement 1926–1956*. New Haven: Yale University Press, 2002.

Hernández, Kelly Lytle. *Bad Mexicans: Race, Empire, and Revolution in the Borderlands*. New York: Norton, 2022.

Hernández, Sonia, and John M. González, eds. *Reverberations of Racial Violence: Critical Reflections on the History of the Border*. Austin: University of Texas Press, 2021.

Hernández, Tanya Katerí. *Racial Innocence: Unmasking Latino Anti-Black Bias and the Struggle for Equality*. Boston: Beacon Press, 2022.

Hinojosa, Rolando. Introduction to *George Washington Gómez* by Américo Paredes, 5–6. Houston: Arte Público Press, 1990.

Hochschild, Adam. *American Midnight: The Great War, A Violent Peace, and Democracy's Forgotten Crisis*. Boston: Mariner, 2022.

Hoffnung-Garskof, Jesse E. "The Migrations of Arturo Schomburg: On Being *Antillano, Negro*, and Puerto Rican in New York 1891–1938." *Journal of American Ethnic History* 21, no. 1, (2001): 3–49.

Hoffnung-Garskof, Jesse E. *Racial Migrations: New York City and the Revolutionary Politics of the Spanish Caribbean, 1850–1902*. Princeton: Princeton University Press, 2019.

Holbo, Christine. "'Industrial & Picturesque Narrative': Helen Hunt Jackson's California Travel Writing for the *Century*." *American Literary Realism* 42, no. 3 (2010): 243–66.

Holton, Adalaine. "Arturo Alfonso Schomburg's Archival Encounters in Spain." *African American Review* 54, no. 1–2 (2021): 31–47.

Holton, Adalaine. "Decolonizing History. Arthur Schomburg's Afrodiasporic Archive." *Journal of African American History* 92, no. 2 (2007): 218–38.

Holton, Adalaine. "Little Things Are Big: Race and the Politics of Print Community in the Writings of Jesús Colón." *MELUS* 38, no. 2 (2013): 5–23.

"Hombro a hombro." Editorial. *Pueblos Hispanos*, February 20, 1943.

Hong, Christine. *A Violent Peace: Race, U.S. Militarism, and Cultures of Democratization in Cold War Asia and the Pacific*. Stanford: Stanford University Press, 2020.

Hughes, Langston. *The Big Sea: An Autobiography*. New York: Knopf, 1940.

Hutchinson, George. *The Harlem Renaissance in Black and White*. Cambridge, MA: Harvard University Press, 1995.

Hutchinson, George, and John K. Young. Introduction to *Publishing Blackness: Textual Constructions of Race since 1850*, edited by George Hutchinson and John K. Young, 1–17. Ann Arbor: University of Michigan Press, 2013.

"Importante reunión en Mission, Texas." *La Prensa*, March 14, 1952.

"Importantes trabajos en Mission, Texas: Los realiza el comité formado para combatir la segregación de los niños escolares mexicanos." *La Prensa*, December 14, 1930.

Isherwood, Ian A. "Memoirs: Negotiating the Great War's Social Memory." In *A History of American Literature and Culture of the First World War*, edited by Tim Dayton and Mark Van Wienen, 108–20. New York: Cambridge University Press, 2021.

Jackson, Helen Hunt. *A Century of Dishonor: A Sketch of the United States Government's Dealings with Some of the Indian Tribes.* Norman: University of Oklahoma Press, 1995.

Jackson, Helen Hunt. "Father Junipero and His Work: A Sketch of the Foundation, Prosperity, and Ruin of the Franciscan Missions in California." *Century* 26 (1883): 1–18.

Jackson, Helen Hunt. *Ramona.* New York: Signet, 2002.

Jackson, Helen Hunt and Abbot Kinney. "Report on the Condition and Needs of the Mission Indians of California." In *A Century of Dishonor* by Helen Hunt Jackson, 458–514. Norman: University of Oklahoma Press, 1995.

Jackson, Lawrence P. *The Indignant Generation: A Narrative History of African American Writers and Critics, 1934–1960.* Princeton: Princeton University Press, 2011.

Jackson, Leon. "The Talking Book and the Talking Book Historian: African American Cultures of Print—The State of the Discipline." *Book History* 13, no. 1 (2010): 251–308.

James, Jennifer C. *A Freedom Bought with Blood: African American War Literature from the Civil War to World War II.* Chapel Hill: University of North Carolina Press, 2007.

James, Pearl. "Propaganda: Martialing Media." In *A History of American Literature and Culture of the First World War,* edited by Tim Dayton and Mark Van Wienen, 204–19. New York: Cambridge University Press, 2021.

James, Winston. *Holding Aloft the Banner of Ethiopia: Caribbean Radicalism in Early Twentieth-Century America.* New York: Verso, 1998.

James, Winston. *The Struggles of John Brown Russwurm: The Life and Writings of a Pan-Africanist Pioneer, 1799–1851.* New York: New York University Press, 2010.

Jaramillo, Cleofas M. *Romance of a Little Village Girl.* Albuquerque: University of New Mexico Press, 2000.

Jiménez Román, Miriam, and Juan Flores, eds. *The Afro-Latin@ Reader: History and Culture in the United States.* Durham: Duke University Press, 2010.

Johnson, Benjamin H. "The Cosmic Race in Texas: Racial Fusion, White Supremacy, and Civil Rights Politics." *Journal of American History* 98, no. 2 (2011): 404–19.

Johnson, Benjamin H. *Revolution in Texas: How a Forgotten Rebellion and Its Bloody Suppression Turned Mexicans into Americans.* New Haven: Yale University Press, 2003.

Johnson, Charles S. Letter to Arturo Schomburg, Thanksgiving [November 28,] 1935. Arturo Alfonso Schomburg Papers. Schomburg Center for Research in Black Culture, Manuscripts, Archives, and Rare Books Division, The New York Public Library. Box 4, folder 25.

Johnson, Charles S. Letter to Arturo Schomburg, October 12, 1936. Arturo Alfonso Schomburg Papers. Schomburg Center for Research in Black Culture, Manuscripts, Archives, and Rare Books Division, The New York Public Library. Box 4, folder 26.

Johnson, James Weldon, ed. Preface to *The Book of American Negro Poetry,* edited by James Weldon Johnson, vii-xlviii. New York: Harcourt, Brace and Co., 1922.

Jordan, William G. *Black Newspapers and America's War for Democracy, 1914–1920.* Chapel Hill: University of North Carolina Press, 2001.

Kabalen de Bichara, Donna M. "Expressions of Dissent in the Writing of Adela Sloss Vento." In *Recovering the U.S. Hispanic Literary Heritage, Vol. 9,* edited by Donna M. Kabalen de Bichara and Blanca López de Mariscal, 191–207. Houston: Arte Público Press, 2014.

Kabalen de Bichara, Donna M. "Self-Writing and Collective Representation: The Literary Enunciation of Historical Reality and Cultural Values." In *In Defense of My People: Alonso*

S. *Perales and the Development of Mexican-American Public Intellectuals*, edited by Michael A. Olivas, 241–63. Houston: Arte Público Press, 2012.

Kabalen Vanek, Donna M., and María Teresa Mijares Cervantes, eds. *Women and Print Culture: A Critical Exploration of the Archives of the Border Region of Mexico and the United States*. Houston: Arte Público Press, 2021.

Kaestle, Carl, and Janice Radway. "A Framework for the History of Publishing and Reading in the United States, 1880–1940." In *A History of the Book in America. Vol. 4: Print in Motion: The Expansion of Publishing and Reading in the United States, 1880–1940*, edited by Carl F. Kaestle and Janice A. Radway, 7–21. Chapel Hill: University of North Carolina Press, 2009.

Kanellos, Nicolás. "*Cronistas* and Satire in Early Twentieth Century Hispanic Newspapers." *MELUS* 23, no. 1 (1998): 3–25.

Kanellos, Nicolás. *Hispanic Immigrant Literature: El Sueño del Retorno*. Austin: University of Texas Press, 2011.

Kanellos, Nicolás. *Latinos and Nationhood: Two Centuries of Intellectual Thought*. Tucson: University of Arizona Press, 2023.

Kanellos, Nicolás. "Recovering and Re-constructing Early Twentieth-Century Hispanic Immigrant Print Culture in the US." *American Literary History* 19, no. 2 (2007): 438–55.

Kanellos, Nicolás. "Sotero Figueroa: Writing Afro-Caribbeans into History in the Late Nineteenth Century." In *The Latino Nineteenth Century*, edited by Rodrigo Lazo and Jesse Alemán, 323–340. New York: New York University Press, 2016.

Kanellos, Nicolás, and Helvetia Martell. *Hispanic Periodicals in the United States: Origins to 1960: A Brief History and Comprehensive Bibliography*. Houston: Arte Público Press, 2000.

Koshiro, Yukiko. *Trans-Pacific Racisms and the U.S. Occupation of Japan*. New York: Columbia University Press, 1999.

Kreitz, Kelley. "American Alternatives: Participatory Futures of Print from New York City's Nineteenth-Century Spanish-Language Press." *American Literary History* 30, no. 4 (2018): 677–702.

Kreitz, Kelley. "Sotero Figueroa: Creating a Communal Voice in *La Revista Ilustrada de Nueva York, Patria*, and *La Doctrina de Martí*." *American Periodicals* 30, no. 2 (2020): 105–9.

Lamas, Carmen E. *The Latino Continuum and the Nineteenth-Century Americas: Literature, Translation, and Historiography*. New York: Oxford University Press, 2021.

Lazo, Rodrigo. *Letters from Filadelfia: Early Latino Literature and the Trans-American Elite*. Charlottesville: University of Virginia Press, 2020.

Lazo, Rodrigo. *Writing to Cuba: Filibustering and Cuban Exiles in the United States*. Chapel Hill: University of North Carolina Press, 2005.

Lazo, Rodrigo, and Jesse Alemán, eds. *The Latino Nineteenth Century*. New York: New York University Press, 2016.

Lee, Erika. *America for Americans: A History of Xenophobia in the United States*. New York: Basic Books, 2019.

Lee, Erika. *The Making of Asian America: A History*. New York: Simon & Schuster, 2015.

Lee, Julia H. *Interracial Encounters: Reciprocal Representations in African and Asian American Literatures, 1896–1937*. New York: New York University Press, 2011.

Lee Tapia, Consuelo. "Día internacional de la mujer Brooklyn." *Pueblos Hispanos*, April 3, 1943.

Lentz-Smith, Adriane. *Freedom Struggles: African Americans and World War I*. Cambridge, MA: Harvard University Press, 2009.

Lew-Williams, Beth. *The Chinese Must Go: Violence, Exclusion, and the Making of the Alien in America*. Cambridge, MA: Harvard University Press, 2018.

Lewis, David Levering. *W. E. B. Du Bois: The Fight for Equality and the American Century 1919–1963*. New York: Henry Holt, 2000.

Limerick, Patricia Nelson. *The Legacy of Conquest. The Unbroken Past of the American West*. New York: Norton, 1987.

Limón, José E. *Américo Paredes: Culture and Critique*. Austin: University of Texas Press, 2012.

Limón, José E. *Dancing with the Devil: Society and Cultural Poetics in Mexican-American South Texas*. Madison: University of Wisconsin Press, 1994.

Limón, José E. "Imagining the Imaginary: A Reply to Ramón Saldívar." *American Literary History* 21, no. 3 (2009): 595–603.

Locke, Alain. "The Negro in Literature." In *The New Negro*, edited by Alain Locke, 427–31. New York: Simon & Schuster, 1997.

Locke, Alain, ed. *The New Negro*. New York: Simon & Schuster, 1997.

Lomas, Clara. Introduction to *The Rebel* by Leonor Villegas de Magnón, edited by Clara Lomas, xi–lvi. Houston: Arte Público Press, 1994.

Lomas, Laura. *Translating Empire: José Martí, Migrant Latino Subjects, and American Modernities*. Durham: Duke University Press, 2008.

López, Antonio. *Unbecoming Blackness: The Diaspora Cultures of Afro-Cuban America*. New York: New York University Press, 2012.

López Morín, José R. "The Life and Early Works of Américo Paredes." *Western Folklore* 64, no. 1–2 (2005): 7–28.

Lossing, Benson J. *Eminent Americans: Comprising Brief Bibliographies of Leading Statesmen, Patriots, Orators and Others, Men and Women, Who Have Made American History*. New York: Hurst & Company, 1890.

Lovett, Bobby L. *America's Historically Black Colleges & Universities: A Narrative History from the Nineteenth Century into the Twenty-first Century*. Macon: Mercer University Press, 2011.

Luis, William. *Dance between Two Cultures: Latino Caribbean Literature Written in the United States*. Nashville: Vanderbilt University Press, 1997.

Luis-Brown, David. *Waves of Decolonization: Discourses of Race and Hemispheric Citizenship in Cuba, Mexico, and the United States*. Durham: Duke University Press, 2008.

Luis-Brown, David. "'White Slaves' and the 'Arrogant Mestiza': Reconfiguring Whiteness in *The Squatter and the Don* and *Ramona*." *American Literature* 69, no. 4 (1997): 813–39.

Madley, Benjamin. *An American Genocide: the Unites States and the California Indian Catastrophe*. New Haven: Yale University Press, 2017.

Mark, Joan. *A Stranger in Her Native Land: Alice Fletcher and the American Indians*. Lincoln: University of Nebraska Press, 1988.

Martí, José. *En los Estados Unidos, Escenas Norteamericanas I. Obras Completas, Vol. 9*. Habana: Editorial Nacional de Cuba, 1963.

Martí, José. *En los Estados Unidos, Escenas Norteamericanas II. Obras Completas, Vol. 10*. Habana: Editorial Nacional de Cuba, 1963.

Martí, José. *En los Estados Unidos, Escenas Norteamericanas III. Obras Completas, Vol. 11.* Habana: Editorial Nacional de Cuba, 1963.

Martí, José. *En los Estados Unidos, Escenas Norteamericanas IV. Obras Completas, Vol. 12.* Habana: Editorial Nacional de Cuba, 1964.

Martí, José. *En los Estados Unidos, Norteamericanos; Letras, Pintura y Artículos Varios. Obras Completas, Vol. 13.* Habana: Editorial Nacional de Cuba, 1964.

Martí, José. *Nuestra America VI. Obras Completas, Vol. 6.* Habana: Editorial Nacional de Cuba, 1963.

Martí, José. *Nuestra América VIII. Obras Completas, Vol. 8.* Habana: Editorial Nacional de Cuba, 1963.

Martí, José. *Traducciones, Obras Completas, Vol. 24.* Habana: Editorial Nacional de Cuba, 1965.

Martí, José. *José Martí Selected Writings.* Edited and translated by Esther Allen. New York: Penguin, 2002.

Martín-Rodríguez, Manuel M. *Life in Search of Readers: Reading (in) Chicano/a Literature.* Albuquerque: University of New Mexico Press, 2003.

Martinez, Monica Muñoz. *The Injustice Never Leaves You: Anti-Mexican Violence in Texas.* Cambridge, MA: Harvard University Press, 2018.

Masarik, Elizabeth Garner. "Por la Raza, Para la Raza: Jovita Idar and the Progressive-Era Mexicana Maternalism along the Texas-Mexico Border." *Southwestern Historical Quarterly* 122, no. 3 (2019): 278–99.

Mathes, Valerie Sherer. Afterword to *Ramona* by Helen Hunt Jackson, 391–402. New York: Signet, 2002.

Mathes, Valerie Sherer. Foreword to *A Century of Dishonor* by Helen Hunt Jackson, vii-xviii. Norman: University of Oklahoma Press, 1995.

Mathes, Valerie Sherer. *Helen Hunt Jackson and Her Indian Reform Legacy.* Norman: University of Oklahoma Press, 1990.

Maxwell, William J. "Editorial Federalism: The Hoover Raids, the New Negro Renaissance, and the Origins of FBI Literary Surveillance." In *Publishing Blackness: Textual Constructions of Race since 1850*, edited by George Hutchinson and John K. Young, 136–59. Ann Arbor: University of Michigan Press, 2013.

Maxwell, William J. *New Negro, Old Left: African-American Writing and Communism between the Wars.* New York: Columbia University Press, 1999.

May, Cedrick. Preface to *The Collected Works of Jupiter Hammon: Poems and Essays*, edited by Cedrick May, xi-xvii. Knoxville: University of Tennessee Press, 2017.

McGurl, Mark. *Everything and Less: The Novel in the Age of Amazon.* New York: Verso, 2021.

McHenry, Elizabeth. *Forgotten Readers: Recovering the Lost History of African American Literary Societies.* Durham: Duke University Press, 2002.

McHenry, Elizabeth. *To Make Negro Literature: Writing, Literary Practice, and African American Authorship.* Durham: Duke University Press, 2021.

Medrano, Manuel F. *Américo Paredes: In His Own Words, an Authorized Biography.* Denton: University of North Texas Press, 2010.

Meléndez, A. Gabriel. *So All Is Not Lost: The Poetics of Print in Nuevomexicano Communities, 1834–1958.* Albuquerque: University of New Mexico Press, 1997.

Meléndez, A. Gabriel, and Francisco A. Lomelí, eds. *The Writings of Eusebio Chacón*. Albuquerque: University of New Mexico Press, 2012.

Meléndez, Edgardo. *Patria: Puerto Rican Revolutionary Exiles in Late Nineteenth Century New York*. New York: Centro Press, 2020.

Menchaca, Martha. *The Mexican American Experience in Texas: Citizenship, Segregation, and the Struggle for Equality*. Austin: University of Texas Press, 2022.

Menchaca, Martha. *Recovering History, Constructing Race: The Indian, Black, and White Roots of Mexican Americans*. Austin: University of Texas Press, 2001.

Mills, Charles W. *The Racial Contract*. Ithaca: Cornell University Press, 1997.

Mirabal, Nancy Raquel. *Suspect Freedoms: The Racial and Sexual Politics of Cubanidad in New York, 1823–1957*. New York: New York University Press, 2017.

Molasky, Michael S. *The American Occupation of Japan and Okinawa: Literature and Memory*. New York: Routledge, 1999.

Molina, Natalia. *How Race Is Made in America: Immigration, Citizenship, and the Historical Power of Racial Scripts*. Berkeley: University of California Press, 2014.

Morales, Ed. *Fantasy Island: Colonialism, Exploitation, and the Betrayal of Puerto Rico*. New York: Bold Type, 2019.

Morales, Ed. *Latinx: The New Force in America Politics and Culture*. New York: Verso, 2019.

Morgan, Ted: *Reds: McCarthyism in the Twentieth-Century America*. New York: Random House, 2003.

Morris, Burnis R. *Carter G. Woodson: History, the Black Press, and Public Relations*. Jackson: University Press of Mississippi, 2017.

Mudditt, Alison. "The Past, Present, and Future of American University Presses: A View from the Left Coast." *Learned Publishing* 29, no. 1 (2016): 330–34.

Nerone, John. "Newspapers and the Public Sphere." In *A History of the Book in America, Vol. 3. The Industrial Book 1840–1880*, edited by Scott E. Casper, Jeffrey D. Groves, Stephen W. Nissenbaum, and Michael Winship, 230–48. Chapel Hill: University of North Carolina Press, 2007.

New Yorker. Rejection Slip to Américo Paredes, February 1953. Américo Paredes Papers. Nettie Lee Benson Latin American Collection. University of Texas at Austin. Box 18, folder 11.

Nwankwo, Ifeoma Kiddoe. "More than McKay and Guillén: The Caribbean in Hughes and Bontemps's *The Poetry of the Negro* (1949)." In *Publishing Blackness: Textual Constructions of Race since 1850*, edited by George Hutchinson and John K. Young, 108–35. Ann Arbor: University of Michigan Press, 2013.

O'Shea, Elena Zamora. "Life of General Juan Nepomuceno Cortina." Translated by José de la Luz Sáenz. October 1947. José de la Luz Sáenz Papers. Nettie Lee Benson Latin American Collection. University of Texas at Austin. Box 3, folder 3.

O'Shea, Elena Zamora. *El Mesquite*. College Station: Texas A&M University Press, 2000.

Olguín, B. V. *Violentologies: Violence, Identity, and Ideology in Latina/o Literature*. New York: Oxford University Press, 2021.

Olguín, B. V., and Omar Vásquez Barbosa. Introduction to *Cantos de adolescencia/Songs of Youth (1932–1937)* by Américo Paredes, xxiii–lxiii. Houston: Arte Público Press, 2007.

Orozco, Cynthia E. *Agent of Change: Adela Sloss-Vento, Mexican American Civil Rights Activist and Texas Feminist*. Austin: University of Texas Press, 2020.

Orozco, Cynthia E. "Alice Dickerson Montemayor: Feminism and Mexican American Politics in the 1930s." In *Leaders of the Mexican American Generation: Biographical Essays*, edited by Anthony Quiroz, 57–83. Denver: University Press of Colorado, 2015.

Orozco, Cynthia E. "Del Rio ISD v. Salvatierra." *Handbook of Texas*. Texas State Historical Association. October 21, 2022. https://www.tshaonline.org/handbook/entries/del-rio-isd-v-salvatierra.

Orozco, Cynthia E. "J. T. Canales's Contributions in Law, Civil Rights, and Education, 1920–1976." In *Reverberations of Racial Violence: Critical Reflections on the History of the Border*, edited by Sonia Hernández and John M. González, 178–208. Austin: University of Texas Press, 2021.

Orozco, Cynthia E. *No Mexicans, Women, or Dogs Allowed: The Rise of the Mexican American Civil Rights Movement*. Austin: University of Texas Press, 2009.

Orozco, Cynthia E. *Pioneer of Mexican-American Civil Rights: Alonso S. Perales*. Houston: Arte Público Press, 2020.

Ortega, Enrique. "El Diario de un Adolescente." *La Prensa*, October 18, 1937.

Owen, Chandler. "The Failure of Negro Leadership." *The Messenger*, January 1918. In *These Truly Are the Brave: An Anthology of African American Writings on War and Citizenship*, edited by Yẹmisi Jimoh and Françoise N. Hamlin, 299–301. Gainesville: University of Florida Press, 2015.

Padilla, Edwin K. Introduction to *"Lo que el pueblo me dice . . .": Crónicas de la colonia Puertorriqueña en Nueva York* by Jesús Colón, xiii–xxxix. Houston: Arte Público Press, 2001.

Padilla, Edwin K. "Jesús Colón: Relación entre crónica periodística, lenguaje y público." In *Recovering the U.S. Hispanic Literary Heritage, Vol. III*, edited by María Herrera-Sobek and Virginia Sánchez Korrol, 371–82. Houston: Arte Público Press, 2000.

Padilla, Genaro M. *My History, Not Yours: The Formation of Mexican American Autobiography*. Madison: University of Wisconsin Press, 1993.

Paralitici, Ché. *Historia de la lucha por la independencia de Puerto Rico*. Río Piedras, Puerto Rico: Gaviota, 2017.

Paredes, Américo. *Between Two Worlds*. Houston: Arte Público Press, 1991.

Paredes, Américo. *Cantos de adolescencia/Songs of Youth (1932–1937)*. Translated by B. V. Olguín and Omar Vásquez Barbosa. Houston: Arte Público Press, 2007.

Paredes, Américo. "Co-Defendant Slaps Tojo on Head during Session: 47 Indictments Counts Read." *Pacific Stars and Stripes*, May 4, 1946.

Paredes, Américo. "Al cumplir veintiún años." *La Prensa*, November 16, 1936.

Paredes, Américo. *George Washington Gómez: A Mexicotexan Novel*. Houston: Arte Público Press, 1990.

Paredes, Américo. *The Hammon and the Beans and Other Stories*. Houston: Arte Público Press, 1994.

Paredes, Américo. "L'Amour." *La Prensa*, April 13, 1936.

Paredes, Américo. Letter to Frank H. Wardlaw, February 21, 1957. Américo Paredes Papers. Nettie Lee Benson Latin American Collection. University of Texas at Austin. Box 15, folder 1.

Paredes, Américo. Letter to Frank H. Wardlaw, March 4, 1957. Américo Paredes Papers. Nettie Lee Benson Latin American Collection. University of Texas at Austin. Box 15, folder 1.
Paredes, Américo. Letter to José David Saldívar, February 7, 1992. Américo Paredes Papers. Nettie Lee Benson Latin American Collection. University of Texas at Austin. Box 71, folder 2.
Paredes, Américo. Letter to Louis Cortez, May 23, 1955. Américo Paredes Papers. Nettie Lee Benson Latin American Collection. University of Texas at Austin. Box 15, folder 1.
Paredes, Américo. Letter to Nicolás Kanellos, June 23, 1989. Américo Paredes Papers. Nettie Lee Benson Latin American Collection. University of Texas at Austin. Box 18, folder 3.
Paredes, Américo. Letter to Ramón Saldívar, October 2, 1991. Américo Paredes Papers. Nettie Lee Benson Latin American Collection. University of Texas at Austin. Box 71, folder 2.
Paredes, Américo. Letter to Ramón Saldvíar, December 13, 1993. Américo Paredes Papers. Nettie Lee Benson Latin American Collection, University of Texas at Austin. Box 71, folder 2.
Paredes, Américo. Letter to Sharon Reynolds, August 7, 1992. Américo Paredes Papers. Nettie Lee Benson Latin American Collection. University of Texas at Austin. Box 71, folder 2.
Paredes, Américo. "A México." *La Prensa*, October 18, 1937.
Paredes, Américo. "México, la ilusión del continente." *La Prensa*, October 18, 1937.
Paredes, Américo. "The Mexico-Texan." *Brownsville Herald*, October 17, 1937.
Paredes, Américo. "Mis tres novias." *La Prensa*, July 8, 1940.
Paredes, Américo. "Tojo Heads List of Defendants; Legal Papers Now Being Served." *Pacific Stars and Stripes*, April 30, 1946.
Paredes, Américo. "Tojo's Defense Asks Charges Be Dismissed." *Pacific Stars and Stripes*, May 15, 1946.
Paredes, Américo. "Tojo['s] Defense Head Prepares for Trial as Jap-U.S. Press Accept Indictments." *Pacific Stars and Stripes*, May 1, 1946.
Paredes, Américo. *"With His Pistol in His Hand": A Border Ballad and Its Hero*. Austin: University of Texas Press, 1958.
Partisan Review. Rejection Slip to Américo Paredes, March 3, 1953. Américo Paredes Papers. Nettie Lee Benson Latin American Collection, University of Texas at Austin. Box 18, folder 11.
Perales, Alonso S. *Are We Good Neighbors?* New York: Arno Press, 1974.
Perales, Alonso S. "Arquitectos de nuestros propios destinos: Continua el entusiasmo con motivo de la reaparición de *La Prensa*." *La Prensa*, July 18, 1957.
Perales, Alonso S. "Arquitectos de nuestros propios destinos: Ha muerto otro gran líder de nuestro pueblo en el estado de Texas." *La Prensa*, November 6, 1958.
Perales, Alonso S. "Arquitectos de nuestros propios destinos: ¿Quiénes son los mexicanos que residen en Texas?" *La Prensa*, December 7, 1952.
Perales, Alonso S. "Arquitectos de nuestros propios destinos: ¿Quiénes son los mexicanos que residen en Texas?" *La Prensa*, December 21, 1952.
Perales, Alonso S. *In Defense of My People*. Edited and translated by Emilio Zamora. Houston: Arte Público Press, 2021.
Perales, Alonso S. Letter to Adela Sloss-Vento, December 14, 1951. Alonso S. Perales Papers. University of Houston Libraries Special Collections. Box 5, folder 8.

Perales, Alonso S. Letter to Adela Sloss-Vento, November 7, 1927. Alonso S. Perales Papers. University of Houston Libraries Special Collections. Box 5, folder 8.

Pérez, Emma. *The Decolonial Imaginary: Writing Chicanas into History*. Bloomington: Indiana University Press, 1999.

Pérez, Lisandro. *Sugar, Cigars, and Revolution: The Making of Cuban New York*. New York: New York University Press, 2018.

Pérez Rosario, Vanessa. *Becoming Julia de Burgos: The Making of a Puerto Rican Icon*. Champaign: University of Illinois Press, 2014.

Phillips, Frances. Letter to J. Luz Sáenz, August 20, 1945. José de la Luz Sáenz Papers. Nettie Lee Benson Latin American Collection. University of Texas at Austin. Box 2, folder 14.

Phillips, Kate. *Helen Hunt Jackson: A Literary Life*. Berkeley: University of California Press, 2003.

Piñeiro de Rivera, Flor, ed. *Arthur A. Schomburg: A Puerto Rican's Quest for His Black Heritage*. San Juan, Puerto Rico: Centro de Estudios Avanzados de Puerto Rico y el Caribe, 1989.

Porter, Dorothy. "Black Antiquarians and Bibliophiles Revisited, with a Glance at Today's Lovers of Books and Memorabilia." In *Black Bibliophiles and Collectors. Preservers of Black History*, edited by Elinor Des Verney Sinnette, W. Paul Coates, and Thomas C. Battle, 3–20. Washington, DC: Howard University Press, 1990.

Porter, Dorothy, ed. *Early Negro Writing 1760–1837*. Boston: Beacon Press, 1971.

Porter, Dorothy. *North American Negro Poets: A Bibliographical Checklist of Their Writings 1760–1944*. Hattiesburg: Book Farm, 1945.

Porter, Lavelle. *The Blackademic Life: Academic Fiction, Higher Education, and the Black Intellectual*. Evanston: Northwestern University Press, 2020.

Proceedings of the Third Annual Meeting of the Lake Mohonk Conference of Friends of the Indian. Philadelphia: Sherman & Co., 1886.

Radway, Janice A. *A Feeling for Books: The Book-of-the-Month Club, Literary Taste, and Middle-Class Desire*. Chapel Hill: University of North Carolina Press, 1997.

Ramírez, José A. *To the Line of Fire!: Mexican Texans and World War I*. College Station: Texas A&M University Press, 2009.

Ramirez, Pablo A. "Inherited Obligations: Conquest, Californio Promises, and Native American Land in Helen Hunt Jackson's *Ramona*." *J19* 8, no. 1 (2020): 147–69.

Ramos, Julio. *Divergent Modernities: Culture and Politics in Nineteenth-Century Latin America*. Translated by John D. Blanco. Durham: Duke University Press, 2001.

Rampersad, Arnold. Introduction to *The New Negro*, edited by Alain Locke, ix–xxiii. New York: Simon and Schuster, 1997.

Rampersad, Arnold. *The Life of Langston Hughes. Vol. I: 1902–1941. I, Too, Sing America*. New York: Oxford University Press, 1986.

Rampersad, Arnold. *The Life of Langston Hughes. Vol. II: 1941–1967. I Dream a World*. New York: Oxford University Press, 1988.

Rebolledo, Tey Diana. *Women Singing in the Snow: A Cultural Analysis of Chicana Literature*. Tucson: University of Arizona Press, 1995.

Rennie, David. A. *American Writers and World War I*. New York: Oxford University Press, 2020.

Reséndez, Andrés. *The Other Slavery: The Uncovered Story of Indian Enslavement in America.* Boston: Mariner, 2017.

"Revista de comercio e industria." *La Prensa*, December 18, 1930.

Rezek, Joseph. "The Racialization of Print." *American Literary History* 32, no. 3 (2020): 417–45.

Rifkin, Mark. *Beyond Settler Time: Temporal Sovereignty and Indigenous Self-Determination.* Durham: Duke University Press, 2017.

Rodríguez, Angélica Aguilar, Julian Vasquez Heilig, and Allison Prochnow. "Higher Education, the GI Bill, and the Postwar Lives of Latino Veterans and their Families." In *Latina/os and World War II: Mobility, Agency and Ideology*, edited by Maggie Rivas-Rodríguez and B. V. Olguín, 59–74. Austin: University of Texas Press, 2014.

Rosales, Steven. *Soldados Razos at War: Chicano Politics, Identity, and Masculinity in the U.S. Military from World War II to Vietnam.* Tucson: University of Arizona Press, 2017.

Rosas, Ana Elizabeth. *Abrazando el Espíritu: Bracero Families Confront the US-Mexico Border.* Berkeley: University of California Press, 2014.

Rotker, Susana. *The American Chronicles of José Martí: Journalism and Modernity in Spanish America.* Hanover: University Press of New England, 2000.

Rotker, Susana. "The (Political) Exile Gaze in Martí's Writing on the United States." In *José Martí's "Our America": From National to Hemispheric Cultural Studies*, edited by Jeffrey Belnap and Raúl Fernández, 58–76. Durham: Duke University Press, 1998.

Ruiz, Vicki L., and Virginia Sánchez Korrol, eds. *Latina Legacies: Identity, Biography, and Community.* New York: Oxford University Press, 2005.

Rusert, Britt. *Fugitive Science. Empiricism and Freedom in Early African American Culture.* New York: New York University Press, 2017.

Sae-Saue, Jayson Gonzales. *Southwest Asia: The Transpacific Geographies of Chicana/o Literature.* New Brunswick: Rutgers University Press, 2016.

Sáenz, José de la Luz. "Demostraremos que somos dignos de ocupar un sitio en estos campos donde se lucha por un noble ideal." *La Prensa*, August 12, 1918.

Sáenz, José de la Luz. "El diario de un soldado méxico-texano." *La Prensa*, October 27, 1918.

Sáenz, José de la Luz. "La discriminación racial." José de la Luz Sáenz Papers. Nettie Lee Benson Latin American Collection. University of Texas at Austin. Box 3, folder 2.

Sáenz, José de la Luz. "I by Myself." José de la Luz Sáenz Papers. Nettie Lee Benson Latin American Collection. University of Texas at Austin. Box 3, folder 8.

Sáenz, José de la Luz. Letter to Alonso S. Perales, May 26, 1927. Alonso S. Perales Papers. University of Houston Libraries Special Collections. Box 4, folder 27.

Sáenz, José de la Luz. "Mi linaje Azteca." José de la Luz Sáenz Papers. Nettie Lee Benson Latin American Collection. University of Texas at Austin. Box 3, folder 5.

Sáenz, José de la Luz. *Los méxico-americanos en la gran guerra y su contingente en pró de la democracia, la humanidad y la justicia.* San Antonio: Artes Gráficas, 1933.

Sáenz, José de la Luz. "Del público: la nueva ley escolar obligatoria." *La Prensa*. August 15, 1916.

Sáenz, José de la Luz. "Racial Discrimination." In *Are We Good Neighbors?* by Alonso S. Perales, 29–33. New York: Arno Press, 1974.

Sáenz, José de la Luz. "Los últimos días en las trincheras." *La Prensa*, February 2, 1919.

Sáenz, José de la Luz. "Una carta del Profesor J. Luz Sáenz, Director de la Escuela de las 'Caleras de Dittlinger." *La Prensa*, January 26, 1917.

Sáenz, José de la Luz. "Una fiesta de los soldados méxico-texanos que se encuentran en Alemania." *La Prensa*, March 31, 1919.

Sáenz, José de la Luz. *The World War I Diary of José de la Luz Sáenz*. Edited and translated by Emilio Zamora and Ben Maya. College Station: Texas A&M University Press, 2014.

Saldaña-Portillo, María Josefina. *Indian Given: Racial Geographies across Mexico and the United States*. Durham: Duke University Press, 2016.

Saldívar, José David. *Border Matters: Remapping American Cultural Studies*. Berkeley: University of California Press, 1997.

Saldívar, José David. *Trans-Americanity: Subaltern Modernities, Global Coloniality, and the Cultures of Greater Mexico*. Durham: Duke University Press, 2012.

Saldívar, Ramón. "Asian Américo: Paredes in Asia and the Borderlands: A Response to José E. Limón." *American Literary History* 21, no. 3 (2009): 584–94.

Saldívar, Ramón. *The Borderlands of Culture: Américo Paredes and the Transnational Imaginary*. Durham: Duke University Press, 2006.

Saldívar, Ramón. *Chicano Narrative: The Dialectics of Difference*. Madison: University of Wisconsin Press, 1990.

Saldívar, Ramón. Introduction to *The Hammon and the Beans and Other Stories* by Américo Paredes, vii–li. Houston: Arte Público Press, 1994.

Salinas, Lupe S. "Legally White, Socially Brown: Alonso S. Perales and His Crusade for Justice for La Raza." In *In Defense of My People: Alonso S. Perales and the Development of Mexican-American Public Intellectuals*, edited by Michael A. Olivas, 75–95. Houston: Arte Público Press, 2012.

Sánchez, Aaron E. *Homeland: Ethnic Mexican Belonging since 1900*. Norman: University of Oklahoma Press, 2021.

Sánchez, Aaron E. "*Mendigos de nacionalidad*: Mexican-Americanism and Ideologies of Belonging in a New Era of Citizenship, Texas 1910–1967." In *In Defense of My People: Alonso S. Perales and the Development of Mexican-American Public Intellectuals*, edited by Michael A. Olivas, 97–118. Houston: Arte Público Press, 2012.

Sánchez, George I. Foreword to *The Wetback in the Lower Rio Grande Valley of Texas* by Lyle Saunders and Olen E. Leonard, 3–4. Austin: University of Texas, 1951.

Sánchez González, Lisa. *Boricua Literature: A Literary History of the Puerto Rican Diaspora*. New York: New York University Press, 2001.

Sánchez González, Lisa. "Decolonizing Schomburg." *African American Review* 54, no. 1–2 (2021): 129–42.

Sánchez González, Lisa, ed. *The Stories I Read to the Children: The Life and Writings of Pura Belpré, the Legendary Storyteller, Children's Author, and New York Public Librarian*. New York: Center for Puerto Rican Studies, 2013.

Sánchez Korrol, Virginia. "Antonia Pantoja and the Power of Community Action." In *Latina Legacies: Identity, Biography, and Community*, edited by Vicki L. Ruiz and Virginia Sánchez Korrol, 209–24. New York: Oxford University Press, 2005.

Sánchez Korrol, Virginia. *From Colonia to Community: The History of Puerto Ricans in New York City*. Berkeley: University of California Press, 1983.
Sánchez, Rosaura, and Beatrice Pita. "María Amparo Ruiz de Burton and the Power of Her Pen." In *Latina Legacies: Identity, Biography, and Community*, edited by Vicki L. Ruiz and Virginia Sánchez Korrol, 72–83. New York: Oxford University Press, 2005.
Sandburg, Carl. *The Chicago Race Riots: July 1919*. New York: Dover, 2013.
Schappes, Morris U. *The Daily Worker: Heir to the Great Tradition*. New York: Daily Worker, 1944.
Schlau, Stacey. "A Cultural Leader in Pre-1950 Puerto Rican New York: Josefina Silva de Cintrón." *Letras Femeninas* 38, no. 1, (2012): 71–91.
Schmidt Camacho, Alicia. *Migrant Imaginaries: Latino Cultural Politics in the U.S.-Mexico Borderlands*. New York: New York University Press, 2008.
Schomburg, Arturo A. "Antonio Carlos Gomes: Negro Opera Composer." *New York Amsterdam News*, August 30, 1933.
Schomburg, Arturo A. "An Appreciation." In *Phillis Wheatley Poems and Letters*, edited by Charles F. Heartman, 7–19. New York: Charles F. Heartman, 1915.
Schomburg, Arturo A. *A Bibliographical Checklist of American Negro Poetry*. New York: Charles F. Heartman, 1916.
Schomburg, Arturo A. "Crispus Attucks—Free Patriot." *New York Amsterdam News*, August 24, 1935.
Schomburg, Arturo A. "General Evaristo Estenoz." *Crisis* 4, no. 3, (1912): 143–44.
Schomburg, Arturo A. "Jupiter Hammon Before the New York African Society." *New York Amsterdam News*, January 22, 1930.
Schomburg, Arturo A. Letter to W. E. B. Du Bois, May 21, 1927. W. E. B. Du Bois Papers. Special Collections and University Archives, University of Massachusetts Amherst Libraries.
Schomburg, Arturo A. "The Negro Brotherhood of Sevilla." *Opportunity*, June 1927, 162–64.
Schomburg, Arturo A. "The Negro Digs Up His Past." In *The New Negro*, edited by Alain Locke, 231–37. New York: Simon & Schuster, 1997.
Schomburg, Arturo A. "Negroes in Sevilla." *Opportunity*, March 1928, 70–71.
Schomburg, Arturo A. "Our Pioneers: Saga of Peter Williams; Creating a Church; Distinguished Issue; Anchor in America." *New York Amsterdam News*, July 25, 1936.
Schomburg, Arturo A. "Our Pioneers: 'Freedom's Journal'; Pioneer Negro Editors; Turns to Religion; 'Back to Africa.'" *New York Amsterdam News*, September 19, 1936.
Schomburg, Arturo A. "Our Pioneers: Statesmen from Jamaica; S.C. Attorney General; Twice in Congress; Rebuking a Confederate." *New York Amsterdam News*, August 29, 1936.
Schomburg, Arturo A. "Racial Integrity: A Plea for the Establishment of a Chair of Negro History in Our Schools and Colleges." Negro Society for Historical Research. August Valentine Bernier, 1913. Arturo Alfonso Schomburg Papers. Schomburg Center for Research in Black Culture, Manuscripts, Archives, and Rare Books Division, The New York Public Library. Box 13, folder 12.
Schomburg, Arturo A. "A Select List of Negro-Americana and Africana." In *The New Negro*, edited by Alain Locke, 421–26. New York: Simon & Schuster, 1997.

Schultz de Mantovani, Fryda. Prologue to *La Edad de Oro* by José Martí, 9–33. San Salvador: Ministro de Cultura, 1955.
"Se levantará en San Antonio un monumento a los méxico-texanos que murieron en Francia." *La Prensa*, May 27, 1928.
"Segundo tomo de la obra *En defensa de mi raza.*" *La Prensa*, July 11, 1937.
Senier, Siobhan. *Voices of American Indian Assimilation and Resistance: Helen Hunt Jackson, Sarah Winnemucca, and Victoria Howard*. Norman: University of Oklahoma Press, 2001.
Sherman, Joan R. Introduction to *The Black Bard of North Carolina: George Moses Horton and His Poetry*, edited by Joan R. Sherman, 1–46. Chapel Hill: University of North Carolina Press, 1997.
Silverman, Al. *The Time of Their Lives: The Golden Age of Great American Book Publishers, Their Editors and Authors*. New York: Truman Talley, 2008.
Simpson, Audra. "On Ethnographic Refusal: Indigeneity, 'Voice' and Colonial Citizenship." *Junctures*, no. 9 (2007): 67–80.
Simpson, Audra. *Mohawk Interruptus: Political Life across the Borders of Settler States*. Durham: Duke University Press, 2014.
Sinnette, Elinor Des Verney. *Arthur Alfonso Schomburg: Black Bibliophile and Collector*. Detroit: Wayne State University Press, 1989.
Sinykin, Dan. *Big Fiction: How Conglomeration Changed the Publishing Industry and American Literature*. New York: Columbia University Press, 2023.
Slater, Robert Bruce. "The First Black Faculty Members at the Nation's Highest-Ranked Universities." *The Journal of Blacks in Higher Education* 22, no. 1 (1998–1999): 97–106.
Sloss-Vento, Adela. *Alonso S. Perales: His Struggle for the Rights of Mexican-Americans*. San Antonio: Artes Gráficas, 1977.
Sloss-Vento, Adela. "Alonso S. Perales: Precursor and Founder of LULAC." October 1978. Alonso S. Perales Papers. University of Houston Libraries Special Collections. Box 10, folder 10.
Sloss-Vento, Adela. "Es Encomiada La Labor del Lic. Perales" *La Prensa*, May 20, 1931.
Sloss-Vento, Adela. Letter to Alonso S. Perales, December 6, 1947. Alonso S. Perales Papers. University of Houston Libraries Special Collections. Box 5, folder 8.
Sloss-Vento, Adela. Letter to Alonso S. Perales, December 17, 1951. Alonso S. Perales Papers. University of Houston Libraries Special Collections. Box 5, folder 8.
Sloss-Vento, Adela. Letter to Alonso S. Perales, November 12, 1947. Alonso S. Perales Papers. University of Houston Libraries Special Collections. Box 5, folder 8.
Sloss-Vento, Adela. Letter to Alonso S. Perales, Sepember. 8, 1947. Alonso S. Perales Papers. University of Houston Libraries Special Collections. Box 5, folder 8.
Sloss-Vento, Adela. Letter to J. T. Canales, March 29, 1961. Alonso S. Perales Papers. University of Houston Libraries Special Collections. Box 5, folder 9.
Sloss-Vento, Adela. Letter to Joe Benitez, June 20, 1974. Alonso S. Perales Papers. University of Houston Libraries Special Collections. Box 4, folder 9.
Sloss-Vento, Adela. Letter to José de la Luz Sáenz, January 3, 1952. Alonso S. Perales Papers. University of Houston Libraries Special Collections. Box 5, folder 8.

Sloss-Vento, Adela. Letter to Marta Perez de Perales, June 2, 1980. Alonso S. Perales Papers. University of Houston Libraries Special Collections. Box 5, folder 10.

Sloss-Vento, Adela. "La Política del Mexico-Americano: La Srita. Adela Sloss dice cuál debe ser la política ideal del elemento de nuestra raza." *La Prensa*, May 7, 1932.

Sloss-Vento, Adela. "Por qué en muchos hogares Latinos no existe verdadera felicidad." *LULAC News*, March 1, 1934, 31–32.

Sloss-Vento, Adela. "Tribuna del Publico: Importancia de la Liga de Ciudadanos Unidos Latino-Americanos." *La Prensa*, October 19, 1932.

Sloss-Vento, Adela. "Tribuna del Publico: Sobre el votante latino-americano." *La Prensa*, September 13, 1934.

So, Richard Jean. *Redlining Culture: A Data History of Racial Inequality and Postwar Fiction*. New York: Columbia University Press, 2021.

Spires, Derrick R. "'Faithful Reflection' and the Work of African American Literary History." In *Race in American Literature and Culture*, edited by John Ernest, 59–75. New York: Cambridge University Press, 2022.

Spires, Derrick R. "On Liberation Bibliography: The 2021 BSA Annual Meeting Keynote." *The Papers of the Bibliographical Society of America* 116, no. 1 (2022): 1–20.

Spires, Derrick R. "Order and Access: Dorothy Porter and the Mission of Black Bibliography." *The Papers of the Bibliographical Society of America* 116, no. 2 (2022): 255–75.

Spires, Derrick R. *The Practice of Citizenship: Black Politics and Print Culture in the Early United States*. Philadelphia: University of Pennsylvania Press, 2019.

Stewart, Jeffrey C. *The New Negro: The Life of Alain Locke*. New York: Oxford University Press, 2018.

Sugita, Yoneyuki. *Pitfall or Panacea: The Irony of US Power in Occupied Japan, 1945–1952*. New York: Routledge, 2003.

Sundquist, Eric J. *Empire and Slavery in American Literature 1820–1865*. Jackson: University Press of Mississippi, 2006.

Tebbel, John. *Between Covers: The Rise and Transformation of Book Publishing in America*. New York: Oxford University Press, 1987.

Tebbel, John. *A History of Book Publishing in the United States. Vol. II: The Expansion of an Industry 1865–1919*. New York: R. R. Bowker, 1975.

"Termino una jira de conferencias: La llevaron a cabo Alonso S. Perales y José de la Luz Sáenz." *La Prensa*, August 31, 1924.

"They Must Go. The Crow Indians Have Rich Lands and They Must Move Off." *Kansas City Star*, February 8, 1882.

Thomas, Evan. Letter to Américo Paredes, July 3, 1957. Américo Paredes Papers. Nettie Lee Benson Latin American Collection. University of Texas at Austin. Box 18, folder 11.

Thompson, John B. *Merchants of Culture: The Publishing Business in the Twenty-First Century*. Cambridge: Polity, 2010.

Tillman, Katherine. "Afro-American Women and Their Work." *A.M.E. Church Review*, April 1895. In *The New Negro: Readings on Race, Representation, and African American Culture, 1892–1938*, edited by Henry L. Gates and Gene Andrew Jarrett, 277–86. Princeton: Princeton University Press, 2007.

Torres, Luis A., ed. *The World of Early Chicano Poetry, 1846–1910*. Encino: Floricanto Press, 1994.
Torres-Saillant, Silvio. *An Intellectual History of the Caribbean*. New York: Palgrave, 2006.
Trujillo, Simón Ventura. *Land Uprising: Native Story Power and the Insurgent Horizons of Latinx Indigeneity*. Tucson: University of Arizona Press, 2020.
Uranga, Rodolfo. "Glosario del día." *La Prensa*, January 8, 1928.
Valdés, Vanessa K. *Diasporic Blackness: The Life and Times of Arturo Alfonso Schomburg*. Albany: State University of New York Press, 2017.
Vallejo, Catherine. "José Martí y su transpensamiento de Ramona por Helen Hunt Jackson: Un diálogo de sustancia y estilo." *Revista Iberoamericana* 79, no. 244–245 (2013): 777–95.
Van Wienen, Mark. *American Socialist Triptych: The Literary-Political Work of Charlotte Perkins Gilman, Upton Sinclair, and W. E. B. Du Bois*. Ann Arbor: University of Michigan Press, 2012.
Varel, David A. *The Lost Black Scholar: Resurrecting Allison Davis in American Social Thought*. Chicago: University of Chicago Press, 2018.
Varon, Alberto. "Archival Excess in Latinx Print Culture: US National Latinx Literature." *English Language Notes* 56, no. 2 (2018): 67–70.
Varon, Alberto. *Before Chicano: Citizenship and the Making of Mexican American Manhood, 1848–1959*. New York: New York University Press, 2018.
Vázquez, David J. *Triangulations: Narrative Strategies for Navigating Latino Identity*. Minneapolis: University of Minnesota Press, 2011.
Vega, Bernardo. *The Memoirs of Bernardo Vega: A Contribution to the History of the Puerto Rican Community in New York*. Edited by César Andreu Iglesias. Translated by Juan Flores. New York: Monthly Review, 1984.
Vento, Arnoldo C. *Adela Sloss-Vento: Writer, Political Activist, and Civil Rights Pioneer*. Boulder: Hamilton, 2017.
Vento, Arnoldo C. Introduction to *Alonso S. Perales: His Struggle for the Rights of Mexican-Americans* by Adela Sloss-Vento, ix-xii. San Antonio: Artes Gráficas, 1977.
Walker, Lara. Introduction to *Absolute Equality: An Early Feminist Perspective* by Luisa Capetillo, v-xxxix. Houston: Arte Público Press, 2009.
Wardlaw, Frank H. Letter to Américo Paredes, January 14, 1956 [1957]. Américo Paredes Papers. Nettie Lee Benson Latin American Collection. University of Texas at Austin. Box 15, folder 1.
Wardlaw, Frank H. Letter to Américo Paredes, February 25, 1957. Américo Paredes Papers. Nettie Lee Benson Latin American Collection. University of Texas at Austin. Box 15, folder 1.
Wardlaw, Frank H. Letter to Américo Paredes, July 18, 1957. Américo Paredes Papers. Nettie Lee Benson Latin American Collection. University of Texas at Austin. Box 15, folder 1.
Wardlaw, Frank H. Letter to George I. Sánchez, May 12, 1959. Américo Paredes Papers. Nettie Lee Benson Latin American Collection. University of Texas at Austin. Box 15, folder 1.
Waldstreicher, David. *The Odyssey of Phillis Wheatley: A Poet's Journeys through American Slavery and Independence*. New York: Farrar, Straus and Giroux, 2023.
West, Cornel. *Black Prophetic Fire*. In dialogue and edited by Christa Buschendorf. Boston: Beacon Press, 2014.

Whalen, Carmen Teresa. "Colonialism, Citizenship, and the Making of the Puerto Rican Diaspora: An Introduction." In *The Puerto Rican Diaspora: Historical Perspectives*, edited by Carmen Teresa Whalen and Víctor Vázquez-Hernández, 1–42. Philadelphia: Temple University Press, 2005.

White, Edward. *The Tastemaker: Carl Van Vechten and the Birth of Modern America*. New York: Farrar, Straus, and Giroux, 2014.

Wilder, Craig Steven. *Ebony and Ivy: Race, Slavery, and the Troubled History of America's Universities*. London: Bloomsbury, 2013.

Williams, Chad L. *The Wounded World: W.E.B. Du Bois and the First World War*. New York: Farrar, Straus and Giroux, 2023.

Wilson, Ivy G. "The Brief Wondrous Life of the *Anglo-African Magazine*; or, Antebellum African American Editorial Practice and Its Afterlives." In *Publishing Blackness: Textual Constructions of Race since 1850*, edited by George Hutchinson and John K. Young, 18–38. Ann Arbor: University of Michigan Press, 2013.

Wood, C. E. S. "Chief Joseph, The Nez-Percé." *Century Magazine*. May 1884, 135–42.

Wright, Richard. *Black Boy*. New York: Perennial Classics, 1998.

Young, John K. *Black Writers, White Publishers: Marketplace Politics in Twentieth-Century African American Literature*. Jackson: University Press of Mississippi, 2006.

Zamora, Emilio. *Claiming Rights and Righting Wrongs in Texas: Mexican Workers and Job Politics during World War II*. College Station: Texas A&M University Press, 2009.

Zamora, Emilio. Introduction to *In Defense of My People* by Alonso S. Perales, xi–xxviii. Houston: Arte Público Press, 2021.

Zamora, Emilio. Introduction to *The World War I Diary of José de la Luz Sáenz*, 1–19. College Station: Texas A&M University Press, 2014.

Zamora, Emilio. "Fighting on Two Fronts: José de la Luz Sáenz and the Language of the Mexican American Civil Rights Movement." In *Recovering the U.S. Hispanic Literary Heritage. Vol. 4*, edited by José Aranda and Silvio Torres-Saillant, 214–39. Houston: Arte Público Press, 2002.

Zamora, Emilio. "José de la Luz Sáenz: Experiences and Autobiographical Consciousness." In *Leaders of the Mexican American Generation: Biographical Essays*, edited by Anthony Quiroz, 25–55. Denver: University Press of Colorado, 2015.

INDEX

Acosta-Belén, Edna, 75, 79, 98, 206n4, 210n87, 212n118
afrolatinidad, 51
Afro-Latinxs, 51–52, 72, 75, 91–92, 129, 186, 191n2, 206n4, 219n150
Alarcón, Norma, 187
Alemán, Jesse, 9, 192n19, 193n1, 233n6
Alonso S. Perales: His Struggle for the Rights of Mexican-Americans (Sloss-Vento): archival practices in, 18, 128; authorial voice in, 139; as biography, 128–29, 131, 138; as book-archive, 18, 128–29, 132–33, 137; and Bracero Program, 142, 145; Catholicism in, 147; and early Mexican American civil rights, 137, 149, 150–51; and Mexican American history, 134–36; as nontraditional book, 133
América, La (magazine), 28, 31, 195n30
Anglo-African Magazine, 49, 65, 71, 200n4
Arte Público Press, 3, 20, 98–99, 168, 187, 191n1, 226n13, 227n23, 231n132
Artes Gráficas, 18, 103, 117, 131, 134, 211n92, 217n98, 220n23

Aztlán (periodical), 187

Betances, Ramón Emeterio, 81
Bibliographical Checklist of American Negro Poetry, A (Schomburg), 16, 50, 59–63, 66, 204n73
Big Sea, The (Hughes), 76, 92, 212n109
Black Boy (Wright), 76, 92–93
Blackwell, Maylei, 131
Blanton, Carlos, 145, 213n13, 224n109
Bolivar, William Carl, 52
Borderlands, 19, 104, 135, 143, 148, 156–57, 158–60, 162–64, 177, 179–81, 226n12, 228n43. *See also* U.S.-Mexico border
Bourdieu, Pierre, 7, 192n9
Bracero Program, 128–29, 142–45, 223n86
braceros, 143–45
Braithwaite, William Stanley, 49, 50, 200n7
Brown, William Wells, 49, 57, 64, 200n2
Brownsville Herald (periodical), 157, 158
Bruce, John Edward, 52, 106, 201nn24–25, 201n27
Burgos, Julia de, 13, 77, 90, 126–27, 130

Burnett, Peter, 43
Byrd, Jodi, 30, 42, 45, 194n10

Californios, 13
Camacho, Jorge, 25, 38, 196n52, 200n139
Campa, Arthur L., 155, 176, 226n10
Campos, Pedro Albizu, 77, 81, 207n18
Camprubí, José, 74
Canales, José Tomás: as early Latinx writer, 186, 221nn39–40, 221n44; and early Mexican American civil rights, 136–37, 138, 146–47, 149, 151, 226n150; and LULAC, 115, 128, 138, 225n146; and Texas Rangers investigation, 221n48. See also *Juan N. Cortina: Bandit or Patriot?*
Cantos de adolescencia (Songs of Youth) (Paredes), 9, 12, 157, 159–63, 181, 227n29, 227n42
Capetillo, Luisa, 130, 186
Caracol (periodical), 187
Casanova, Emilia, 22
Castañeda, Carlos E.: and Catholicism in Texas, 147–49, 224n119; as early Latinx writer and intellectual, 101, 162, 176, 226n150; and higher education, 155; on Indigenous people, 225n130. See also *Our Catholic Heritage in Texas: 1519–1936*
Century (magazine), 26–28, 31, 37, 195n21, 195n28, 196n50, 196n52, 211n91
Century of Dishonor, A (Jackson), 15, 24, 26, 30, 32, 34–35, 37–38, 195n21, 199n120
Chacón, Eusebio, 13
Cheyenne, 24, 28–30, 196n52
Chicago Defender (periodical), 49, 67, 83, 91, 106, 211n97
Chicanx Movement. *See* Mexican American civil rights movement
Child, Lydia Maria, 58
Chinese Exclusion Act, 164
Clarkson, Thomas, 58, 203n62
Cold War, 5, 14
Colins, Carlos de, 73
Colón, Jesús: and CPUSA, 78, 88–89; and *crónica* as genre, 78, 208nn29–30; and ethnic and working class solidarity, 5,

80–82, 86, 92–93; on *Hispano* identity, 75–77, 80, 82, 96–97; "*Lo que el pueblo me dice...*," 99; and McCarthyism, 88; on Puerto Rican identity, 79–80, 87, 96; and Puerto Rican independence, 5, 78, 80, 86, 96–97; and Puerto Rican migration to New York City, 75, 77–79, 85, 91, 96–98; and racial discrimination, 75, 79, 91–92; and sketches for *Daily Worker*, 11, 14, 17, 75–76, 82, 84–90, 96–97, 210n72, 210n83; and sketches for *Pueblos Hispanos*, 11, 14, 17, 75–78, 80–82, 207n11; as writer and intellectual, 4, 12, 16, 75, 83, 98–99, 133, 183–84. See also *A Puerto Rican in New York and Other Sketches*; *The Way It Was and Other Writings*
Colored American, The (periodical), 48
Committee on Un-American Activities, 89
Communist Party of the USA (CPUSA), 78, 83–85, 88–89, 127, 210n84
Cornish, Samuel E., 49, 54, 64, 65, 69–71, 206n115
Coronado, Raúl, 12, 13
Corretjer, Juan Antonio, 13, 76–78, 186, 207n19
Cortez, Gregorio, 19, 100, 135, 157, 163, 177, 179–80, 232n141
Cortina, Juan N., 129, 134–37, 147, 221nn39–40, 221n46
Cotera, María E., 132
Cotto-Thorner, Guillermo, 85, 90
criollos, 25, 27
Crisis (periodical), 49, 53–54, 67, 83, 106–07, 109, 113, 200n7, 202nn28–29
Crónica, La (periodical), 100, 126, 213nn4–5
Crow, 24, 28–30
Cutler, John Alba, 21, 74, 101, 192n19, 194n3, 226n12

Daily Worker (periodical): 83–84, 209n61; Colón's writings for, 11, 16–17, 75–76, 82, 84–90, 96–98, 210n72, 210n83; Wright's writings for, 84–85, 209n65
Daly, Victor, 117, 217n96

Dana, Charles Anderson, 27
Davis, W. Allison, 154
Dawes, Henry L., 44
Dawes Act, 5, 15, 24, 43–46
Day, Iyko, 164
Debs, Eugene V., 82
Defense of My People, In (Perales), 133, 139, 162, 183, 215n76, 218n115, 220n25, 222n66, 224n128
Delany, Martin, 57, 64, 65, 200n4
Delgado, Martín Morúa, 22, 36, 52, 74
Del Rio ISD v. Salvatierra, 116, 216n91
Díaz Guerra, Alirio, 9, 182
Diosa y Hembra (M. Cotera), 152
Dobie, J. Frank, 177, 231n136
Doctrina de Martí (periodical), 52, 73
Dos Antillas, Las (The Two Antilles), 51, 201n17
Douglass, Frederick, 49, 57, 64, 65, 67, 202nn35–36
Du Bois, W. E. B.: and bibliography, 204n68, 205n91; and Black print culture, 49, 67, 83; and Black soldiers, 102, 106–7, 108–9; and communism, 78, 88–89, 210n84, 210n86; and *Crisis*, 49, 106–7, 202n29; and Harlem Renaissance, 61, 154; on racial violence, 113–14; on World War I, 102, 106–7, 113–14, 214n31; as writer and intellectual, 50, 52, 54, 76, 113, 125, 201nn27–28
Dunbar, Paul Laurence, 60, 62–63, 64, 65
Dunbar Nelson, Alice, 186
Dunbar-Ortiz, Roxanne, 30

early Mexican American civil rights movement, 14, 18, 112–13, 128–29, 130–31, 149, 181. *See also* Mexican American civil rights movement
Ernest, John, 48, 200n10
escuelitas, 104
Espinoza, Conrado, 9, 182
Espionage Act, 106
Estenoz, Evaristo, 53, 202n32

Fauset, Jessie, 66, 186
F.B.I., 88–89, 210n84, 210n86
Ferguson, Niall, 171, 230n104

Figueroa, Sotero, 13, 51–52, 73, 186, 201n19, 201n22
Fitzpatrick, Kathleen, 153
Fletcher, Alice, 33–34, 197n61, 197n63, 197n67
Flores, Juan, 17, 51, 85, 91, 98, 186, 207n7, 211n93
Ford, Nick Aaron, 154–55, 226n8
Forgotten People: A Study of New Mexicans (Sánchez), 155
Freedom's Journal (periodical), 48, 54, 65, 69–71, 206n109
Frymer, Paul, 45, 193n37

García, Héctor P., 146, 224n108
García, Mario T., 149, 215n79, 219n11, 224n119, 225n131
García Peña, Lorgia, 53, 201n12, 205n14
Garza, Bernardo "Ben," 138
Gates, Henry L., 54, 56, 202n38
George Washington Gómez (Paredes), 19, 156, 157, 162–63, 176, 179–81, 226nn12–13, 228n45
GI Bill, 176, 231n131
GI Forum, 142, 146, 224n108
GIs, 169–71, 173, 231n121
Gómez, Laura E., 104, 116, 192n4, 218n134
Gómez-Quiñones, Juan, 115, 181, 215n79
González, Gabriela, 120, 150, 213nn4–5, 218n115, 219n5
González, John M., 43, 112, 127, 135, 192n19, 221n46, 221n48, 226n12, 227n23, 231n136
González, Jovita, 9, 90, 130, 155
Gráfico (periodical), 16, 74–75, 76, 78, 99, 127, 207n6, 208n29
Great Depression, 75, 83, 209n53
Great War. *See* World War I
Grito, El (periodical), 187
Gruesz, Kirsten Silva, 10, 186, 191n2, 192n19, 193n1
Guerra, Lillian, 23
Guillory, John, 7, 192n9
Gutiérrez, José Angel, 151–52, 225n148

Hamilton, Thomas, 49, 65, 67, 71, 200n4
Hammon, Jupiter, 49, 54, 64, 67–69, 202n38, 204n73, 206n106

Harlem Renaissance, 8, 49, 50–51, 52, 61, 63, 66, 71–72, 83, 154, 209n54
Harper's (magazine), 27–28, 157, 169, 195n28, 229n85
Hartman, Saidiya, 57
Heartman, Charles F., 50, 54–55, 59, 202n37
Hernández, Kelly Lytle, 101
Hispanos, 76–77, 80–82, 86–87, 97–98, 207n11, 207n15, 207n22
Historically Black Colleges and Universities (HBCUs), 154
Hochschild, Adam, 112
Holton, Adalaine, 92, 132, 208n30
Homestead Act, 26
Hong, Christine, 173
Hopkins, Pauline, 65, 186
Howard, Oliver, 31, 196n52
Howells, William Dean, 60, 65
Hughes, Langston: and autobiography, 17, 93, 212n109; and Black print culture, 67, 83, 85, 91, 205n96, 209n58, 209n66, 211n97; and communism, 76, 78, 83, 88–89, 210nn85–86; and Harlem Renaissance, 63; *Simple Speaks His Mind*, 91; *The Weary Blues*, 83, 205n96. See also *The Big Sea*
Hutchinson, George, 8, 192n12, 200n5, 202n29, 209n54

Idar, Jovita, 13, 100, 126–27, 186, 213n4, 219n5. See also *La Crónica*
Idar, Nicasio, 100, 213nn4–5. See also *La Crónica*
Iglesias, César Andreu, 85

Jackson, Helen Hunt: and Indigenous peoples' rights, 15, 23–24, 26, 34–35, 37–43, 198n86, 199n120; as reformer, 26, 34–35, 43–46, 197n67; and report on Mission Indians of California, 37, 41, 42, 198n103, 199n106; and U.S. print culture, 26, 37, 195n21, 195n28. See also *A Century of Dishonor*; *Ramona*
Jackson, Lawrence, 83, 155, 192n12, 200n5, 209n53, 226n8

Jaeger, Clotilde Betances, 13
James, Winston, 70, 92, 206n115, 211n101
Jaramillo, Cleofas M., 130, 219n1
Jicoténcal (anonymous), 9
Jim Crow segregation, 5, 56–57, 93, 104, 106–7, 125, 174
Jiménez Román, Miriam, 51
Johnson, Charles S., 16, 49, 52, 63, 71–72, 83, 154, 202n28, 206n120
Johnson, James Weldon, 52, 61, 63, 66, 106, 114, 203n57
Johnson-Reed Act, 112, 164, 228n55
Jones Act, 74
Juan Crow segregation, 104, 112–13, 114, 118, 144
Juan N. Cortina: Bandit or Patriot? (Canales), 129, 134–36, 220n25, 221nn39–40
Juárez, Benito, 121, 218n129

Kabalen de Bichara, Donna, 137, 143–44, 219n2, 220n13
Kanellos, Nicolás, 3, 9–10, 52, 82, 162, 187, 192n19, 192n21, 193n1, 207n4, 211n93, 213n1
Knopf, Alfred A., 8, 83, 219n58
Knopf, Blanche, 8
Korematsu v. United States, 164
Koshiro, Yukiko, 165, 169, 228n55

Lamas, Carmen, 22, 35–36, 47, 191n2, 192n19, 193n1, 197n81, 198n95, 206n1, 207n4
Latinidad: in Colón's sketches, 11, 75–78, 82, 85, 96; and pan-ethnic identity, 3, 5, 13, 74–78, 98, 127, 183–85, 191n1; and Spanish-language print culture, 13–14, 74
Lazo, Rodrigo, 9, 10, 192n19, 193n1, 206n1, 233n6
League of United Latin American Citizens (LULAC): and claims to whiteness, 116, 120; formation of, 102, 114, 132, 136–37, 151, 215n76, 215n79, 222n66, 225n146; ideology of, 102–3, 115–16, 145–46, 216n81, 216n86, 218n130; and Ladies LULAC, 127–28, 141; and *LULAC News*, 141, 219n6, 223n81; and Mexican American civil rights, 17, 103, 129,

138–39, 142, 222n77, 223n78; and school desegregation, 18, 116, 216n91; and Spanish-language print culture, 114–15, 134
lectores, 77, 92–93, 208n23
Lee, Erika, 164, 228n55
Lee Tapia, Consuelo, 77, 126–27, 186, 219n9
Limón, José, 167, 181, 226n12, 228n52, 230n120, 231n136, 232n152
Locke, Alain, 16, 50, 52, 61, 63, 65–66, 154, 205n93. See also *The New Negro*
Lomas, Laura, 23, 27, 36, 38, 192n19, 193n1, 194n9, 195n22
López Morín, José, 158, 228n62
Lozano, Ignacio E., 101, 134, 159, 186, 213n18. See also *La Prensa*

Madley, Benjamin, 41, 43, 195n19, 196n35, 199n122
Magón, Ricardo Flores, 100–101, 213n21. See also *Regeneración*
magonistas, 101, 213n5, 228n45
Mainstream (magazine). See *Masses and Mainstream*
Manifest Destiny, 24, 26, 149, 176–77
Marcantonio, Vito, 80–81
Marín, Francisco Gonzalo "Pachín," 74
Martell, Helvetia, 9, 208n24, 213n1
Martí, José: *crónicas* of, 14, 15, 22–25, 27–35, 38, 47, 195nn26–27; and Cuban independence, 47, 51–52, 73, 87, 194n7; and Indigenous people in Latin America, 25, 46; and Latin American newspapers, 25, 27–35, 43–46, 78, 183; as Latinx writer and intellectual, 4, 23, 51, 184–85, 194n11; and Spanish-language print culture, 28, 51, 73–74, 195n30, 198n95, 200n140; and translation of *Ramona*, 12, 24, 35–43, 184, 198n92; and U.S. Indigenous peoples, 24, 28–32, 194n10, 196n52; and U.S. Indigenous peoples' rights, 5, 11, 15, 32–35, 36–43, 44–46, 185–86; and U.S. print culture, 23, 26–28, 31, 47, 195nn22–23, 198n83; *Versos sencillos* (Simple Verses), 12

Martinez, Monica Muñoz, 104, 228n43, 231n134
Masses and Mainstream (magazine), 90–91, 211n96
Maya, Ben, 103, 117
McCarthyism, 88–89, 210n79, 210n84
McHenry, Elizabeth, 12, 48–50, 54, 58–59, 63, 70, 168, 200n4, 200n10, 204n68, 205n91, 206n109
McKay, Claude, 8, 63, 209n66
Medrano, Manuel, 176, 231nn133–34
Mesquite, El (Zamora O'Shea), 9, 127, 211n92, 221n46, 233n8
mestizaje, 25, 149
Mexican American civil rights movement, 14, 19, 98, 115–16, 128–29, 131, 151–52, 155, 181. See also early Mexican American civil rights movement
Mexican Americans: and early fights for civil rights, 19, 113–16, 128, 133, 151, 185, 222n77; and racialization, 116, 118–19, 128, 155–56, 199n129, 216nn85–86, 219n11; and segregation in Texas, 19, 104–7, 114, 116, 124, 129–31, 137, 144, 228n43; and Spanish-language print culture, 100–101, 108–9, 134, 140–41; and U.S. historical narratives, 5, 17, 122–23, 127, 132, 134–36, 147, 221n40; in World War I, 17–18, 102–3, 107–12, 117–25; in World War II, 164–75, 179–81
méxico-americanos en la gran guerra, Los (The Mexican Americans during the Great War) (Sáenz), 12, 14, 18, 103, 108, 110, 117–25, 214n48, 214n52, 217n99, 217n103, 218n115, 218n121
México de afuera (a Mexican nation abroad), 101, 150
méxico-texanos (Texas Mexicans), 108–9, 158–59, 161–63, 177, 214n40
Miles, Nelson, 30–31, 196n52
Molasky, Michael, 175
Montemayor, Alice Dickerson, 13, 126–27, 219n6
Moorland, Jesse Edward, 52

Mossell, Gertrude Bustill, 63
Morúa Delgado, Martín, 22, 36, 52, 74

Nación, La (periodical), 27, 32, 44–45, 195n24
National Association for the Advancement of Colored People (NAACP), 107, 114
New Masses (periodical), 83, 84, 91, 209n66
New Negro, The (Locke), 16, 49–50, 62–63, 65–66, 204n87
New York Amsterdam News (periodical), 16, 49–50, 67–72, 205nn94–98
New York Daily Tribune (periodical), 26
New York Sun (periodical), 27
New York Times (periodical), 33, 188
Nez Perce, 24, 31–32, 196n50, 197n61
Niggli, Josefina, 9, 182, 211n91, 226n10
North American Negro Poets: A Bibliographical Checklist of Their Writings 1760–1944 (Porter), 61–62, 204n84
Nuevomexicanos, 13, 187, 193n29
Nuyorican poets, 98–99, 212n137

O'Farrill, Alberto, 74, 186
Olguín B. V., 108, 227n29, 228n51
Opinión Nacional, La (periodical), 27, 28, 30
Opportunity (periodical), 16, 49, 53, 67, 83, 202n28, 202n33
Orozco, Cynthia, 129, 132, 137, 140, 141, 151, 215n73, 215n76, 219n11, 220n21, 221n44, 223n89, 225n131, 227n15
Ortega, Enrique, 160, 161–62
O'Shea, Elena Zamora, 90, 126–27, 130, 135, 186, 221n46. See also El Mesquite
Our Catholic Heritage in Texas: 1519–1936 (Castañeda), 147, 149, 220n25, 224n120, 225n130

Pacific Stars and Stripes (periodical), 11, 19, 156–57, 165–66, 181
Padilla, Edwin K., 75, 78, 98, 208nn29–30
Paredes, Américo: "Alma Pocha" (Pocho Soul), 156, 158–60, 227n23; "A México," 156, 160; as early Latinx writer and intellectual, 4, 156; "The Gift," 169–71, 174–75; and Gregorio Cortez, 100, 135, 157, 179–80; The Hammon and the Beans and Other Stories, 168, 176; "Ichiro Kikuchi," 170–72, 230n98; and Mexican American identity, 155, 157, 160–63, 181; "México, la ilusión del continente" (Mexico, the Illusion of the Continent), 156, 160; "The Mexico-Texan," 156, 158–59, 161, 227n18; "Over the Waves Is Out," 157, 176, 229n85; and racialization, 155–56, 158–59, 164; The Shadow, 176, 231n132; and Spanish-language print culture, 14, 101, 156–57; "Sugamo," 174–75, 229n85, 230nn120–21; "The Terrible High Cost," 172–74; and Tokyo war crimes trial, 11, 19, 156, 165–68, 170–72, 174–75, 229n71, 230n121; and University of Texas–Austin, 19, 175–77, 231n133, 231n138; and U.S. occupation of Japan, 5, 172–74, 228n62, 230n116; and U.S. publishing industry, 9, 12, 19–20, 90, 175–79, 183, 184, 229n85, 231n132. See also Cantos de adolescencia (Songs of Youth); George Washington Gómez; University of Texas Press; "With His Pistol in His Hand"
Partido Liberal, El (periodical), 27
Partido Revolucionario Cubano (Cuban Revolutionary Party), 51, 73
Partisan Review (magazine), 84, 157, 169, 209n66, 229n85
Patria (periodical), 47, 51–52, 73, 200n140, 201n22
peninsulares, 25
Perales, Alonso A.: "Arquitectos de nuestros propios destinos" (Architects of Our Own Destinies), 148, 152; and Bracero Program, 142–43, 145–46; as early Latinx writer and intellectual, 182; as founder of LULAC, 114–16, 128, 132, 138–39, 150–51, 215n76, 222n66, 225n146; and Mexican American civil rights, 101–2, 128, 136–39, 150–51, 162, 215n73; and racial segregation of Mexican Americans, 102–3, 139; racial views of,

124, 148–49, 219n150, 224n128; on racial violence, 113; and Spanish-language print culture, 13, 90, 114–15, 131, 134, 148, 152, 211n92, 224n121, 226n150. See also *In Defense of My People*

Pérez, Emma, 155

Phillis Wheatley: A Critical Attempt and a Bibliography of Her Writings (Heartman), 54

Phillis Wheatley Poems and Letters (Heartman), 50, 55

Plan de San Diego, 104, 106, 136, 162, 228n45

Poems on Various Subjects, Religious and Moral (Wheatley), 54, 56, 62, 64

Poncas, 26

Porter, Dorothy, 50, 60, 61–62, 204n75, 204n84. See also *North American Negro Poets: A Bibliographical Checklist of Their Writings 1760–1944*

Predominately White Institutions (PWIs), 154–55

Prensa, La (periodical): Lozano as editor of, 101, 109; and LULAC, 114–15; and Mexican American civil rights, 11, 101; Paredes's poetry in, 19, 157, 158–62; Perales's writings in, 148, 152, 211n92, 222n70, 224n121; Sáenz's writings in, 11, 17–18, 102, 105, 107–12, 113, 118, 121, 125, 211n92, 214n52, 217n115; Sloss-Vento's writings in, 18–19, 128, 134, 139–41, 148, 211n92, 223n78; and Spanish-language print culture, 101–2, 105

Prisoners of War (POWs), 164, 169–71, 174

Pueblos Hispanos (periodical): and Burgos, 77, 90, 127; Colón's writings in, 11, 16–17, 75–76, 78–82, 89, 94, 97; Corretjer as editor of, 76; and *Hispano* identity, 77, 78, 82, 207n11; and Lee Tapia, 77, 127; and Puerto Ricans in New York City, 77; and Spanish-language print culture, 75, 82

Puerto Rican in New York and Other Sketches, A (Colón): 75–76, 90–99; as literary and intellectual journey, 17, 91–96, 98; as nontraditional book, 86, 91, 210n72; publication history of, 91, 98–99, 211n94, 211n101; on Puerto Rican history, 94–95

puertorriqueñidad (Puertoricanness), 78–79

"Race War of 1912," 53

racialization: and Black people in the U.S., 14, 45; and Indigenous people, 15, 22, 24, 43–47, 125, 186, 199n129; and Mexican Americans, 17, 102–4, 107, 119, 121–22, 128, 216nn85–86, 219n11, 227n15; and non-white groups, 4, 14, 76, 123, 185, 199n129; in the Pacific, 5, 14, 19, 155–57, 169, 174, 179; and Puerto Ricans, 79, 96; in the Southwest, 116, 121, 134–35, 136, 158–59, 161–64, 192n4, 216n86; during World War II, 164–65, 181

Ramírez, José, 105, 113, 213n21, 215n76

Ramona (Jackson), 15, 22–24, 34–35, 36–43, 45, 47, 194n9, 198n92, 198n95

Ramos, Julio, 36, 195n22, 195n26, 198n83

raza, la (our people), 103, 115, 119–22, 124, 217n115

Redding, J. Saunders, 154, 204n73, 204n84

Red Summer of 1919, 113

Regeneración (periodical), 100–101, 213n5, 213n21

Revista Chicano-Riqueña (periodical), 187

Revista de Artes y Letras (Magazine of Arts and Letters), 76, 127, 207n15

Revista Ilustrada de Nueva York, La (magazine), 73, 200n140, 201n19

Revista Universal, La (magazine), 25, 36

Rezek, Joseph, 7

Rifkin, Mark, 30, 33, 46, 194n10

Romano, Octavio I., 187

Rotker, Susana, 27, 195n22, 195n24, 295n27

Ruiz de Burton, María Amparo, 9, 182

Russwurm, John B., 49, 54, 69–71, 206n115

Sáenz, José de la Luz: and Bracero Program, 142–43, 146–47, 224n109, 225n138; as early Latinx writer and intellectual, 4, 184; "I by Myself," 213n14, 218n124; and Indigenous identity, 18, 103, 120–25; and LULAC, 114–15, 128; and Mexican American civil rights, 5, 17–18, 101, 131, 136–39, 149, 151, 185, 226n150; and Mexican American identity, 117–19, 150, 185; and Mexican American soldiers, 17, 102, 107–12, 117–25; "Mi linaje Azteca" (My Aztec Lineage), 120; *La Prensa* writings of, 11, 17–18, 102, 105, 107–12, 113, 118, 121, 125, 211n92, 214n52, 217n115; "Racial Discrimination," 112–13, 122–23; on racial violence, 113; and segregation of Mexican Americans, 14, 17, 102, 104–5, 112, 117–20, 213n18; and U.S. publishing industry, 9, 90, 117, 217n99. See also *Los méxico-americanos en la gran guerra, Los* (The Mexican Americans during the Great War)

Saldaña-Portillo, María Josefina, 44–45, 116, 123, 194n10, 216n89, 228n51

Saldívar, Ramón, 156–57, 165, 166, 171, 175, 179, 229n83, 229n86, 230n121, 231n134, 232n152

Sánchez, Aaron, 135, 150, 216n81

Sánchez, George I., 145–46, 155, 176, 178. See also *Forgotten People: A Study of New Mexicans*

Sánchez Korrol, Virginia, 75, 98, 207nn6–7, 207n15, 210n87, 212n118, 220n13, 220n15

Santiago, Carlos, 79, 206n4

Schmidt Camacho, Alicia, 158, 227n18

Schomburg, Arturo A.: "An Appreciation [of Phillis Wheatley]," 55–58, 203n57; and bibliography, 12, 14, 50, 58–66, 184, 205n93; and Black diasporic thinking, 5, 51, 52–53, 60–62, 132, 185; and Black literary past, 11, 16, 49, 51, 63–66, 67–70, 186, 202n35, 202n37, 204n73; and Black print culture, 16, 49, 53–54, 67, 69–72, 202n30, 205nn94–95; as book collector, 52, 95, 132, 212n118; as early Latinx writer and intellectual, 4, 15, 53, 72, 201n16; and Harlem Renaissance, 50, 52, 201nn27–28; *New York Amsterdam News* writings of, 16, 50, 67–71, 205nn94–95, 205n97; "A Select List of Negro-Americana and Africana," 16, 50, 62–63, 65. See also *A Bibliographical Checklist of American Negro Poetry*

Seminoles, 46

Serra, Rafael, 22, 51–52, 73

Silva de Cintrón, Josefina, 126–27, 186, 207n15. See also *Revista de Artes y Letras* (Magazine of Arts and Letters)

Simpson, Audra, 35, 194n10

Sinnette, Elinor Des Verney, 50, 59, 201nn27–28, 202n37, 205n94

Sioux, 28, 30, 197n61

Slaughter, Henry Proctor, 52

Sloss-Vento, Adela: and archival practices, 12, 128–29, 131–34, 220n25, 224n121; and Bracero Program, 142–47; and Catholicism, 147–50, 225n131; and Chicanx Movement, 19, 151–52, 181; and discrimination of Mexican Americans, 134–35, 139–40, 150–51; as early Latina writer and intellectual, 4, 128, 133, 183–84, 220n32; and education of Latinas before 1960s, 131; and Ladies LULAC, 141; and LULAC, 136–39, 151, 222n66, 222n77, 223n78, 225n146; and *LULAC News*, 141–42, 223n81; and Mexican American civil rights, 11, 18, 128, 130–32, 136–42, 152, 226n150; and Mexican Americans in Southwest, 129, 134–37, 147–49; *La Prensa* writings of, 18–19, 128, 134, 139–41, 148, 211n92, 223n78; racial views of, 148–49, 224n128; on Spanish-language print culture, 90, 101, 133–34, 183, 221n35; "The Wetback Problem," 144–45. See also *Alonso S. Perales: His Struggle for the Rights of Mexican-Americans*

Solis, John C., 114, 215n76

Spanish-Language print culture: and civil rights, 17, 100–101, 105, 126, 213n18; emergence of, 9–10, 14–17, 21–22, 36, 126, 192n19, 192n21; and early notions of Latinidad, 74, 76–78; in New York City, 9, 16–17, 75, 76, 85, 206n3, 207n11; as platform for early Latinx writers, 9–10, 16–17, 101,

133, 194n3, 219n2; in Texas, 9, 17, 100–101, 105, 126–27, 133
Spires, Derrick, 10, 200n10, 202n38, 204n75
Stowe, Harriet Beecher. See *Uncle Tom's Cabin*
Sugita, Yoneyuki, 169

tabaqueros, 77, 92, 97
Tebbel, John, 11
Tejanos, 13, 101–8, 113, 115, 158, 227n15
Texas Rangers, 19, 104, 136, 162, 176–79, 221n48, 228n45
Third Lake Mohonk Conference of 1885, 32–35, 197n63, 197n67
Tibbles, Thomas Henry, 26, 195n19
Tojo, Hideki, 165–67, 231n121
Tokyo war crimes trial, 11, 19, 156, 165–68, 170–72, 174, 181, 228n60, 230n121
Tolón, Miguel T., 22, 35, 197n81
Treaty of Guadalupe Hidalgo, 104, 116, 134–35, 216n86
Trotter, William Monroe, 106

Uncle Tom's Cabin (Stowe), 37, 38–39, 66, 198n86, 198n92
University of Texas Press, 19, 155, 157, 175–79, 181, 231n137
university presses, 19, 68, 153–55, 177, 179, 181, 187, 226n6, 226n8, 231n137, 233n8
U.S. Army: and Black soldiers, 125, 174–75; and Indigenous peoples, 24, 29, 30–32, 123; and occupation of Japan, 166–68, 180; and racialization of soldiers of color, 117, 118–19, 123, 125, 156, 164–65, 170, 174–75, 180; and World War I, 117; and World War II, 156, 163, 163–70
U.S. citizenship: and Asian Americans, 164; and Indigenous people, 15, 24, 34–35, 38, 43–44, 124, 199n120; and Mexican Americans, 103, 112, 115–16; and whiteness, 103, 116, 122, 216n89
U.S.-Mexican War, 5, 113, 116, 121, 134, 198n97, 218n134

U.S.-Mexico border, 100–101, 106, 123, 158, 160, 226n12. *See also* Borderlands
Utes, 28

Valdés, Vanessa, 51, 59, 202n30, 205n94
Varela, Félix, 22, 35
Vasconcelos, José, 121–22, 218n130
Vázquez, David, 92, 94
Vega, Bernardo, 72, 74, 78, 85, 90, 127, 186, 207n8, 208nn23–24
Velázquez, Eulalio, 104–5, 121
Venegas, Daniel, 9
Vento, Arnoldo, 137, 221n34, 223n81
Villarreal, José Antonio, 9, 182, 211n91
Villaverde, Cirilo, 22
Villegas de Magnón, Leonor, 130, 186

Wardlaw, Frank H., 19, 176–78, 231n137, 232n142
Way It Was and Other Writings, The (Colón), 98
Webb, Walter Prescott, 135, 176–78, 221n40, 231n136. *See also* Texas Rangers
Wells, Ida B., 106, 114, 186
West, Dorothy, 186
Wetback in the Lower Rio Grande Valley of Texas, The (Saunders and Leonard), 145
Wheatley, Phillis: background of, 56; and Black literary past, 16, 49, 51, 54–58, 68, 202n36, 202n38, 204n73; poetry of, 50, 54–55, 56–58, 62, 64, 203n62. *See also Poems on Various Subjects, Religious and Moral*
White, Walter, 66, 106
Wilson, Ivy, 71, 200n4
Wilson, Woodrow, 105
"With His Pistol in His Hand" (Paredes), 19, 135, 155–57, 175–81, 221n40, 226n12, 231n134
Woodson, Carter G., 52, 67, 154, 205n96
World War I: and Black soldiers, 113–14, 117, 124–25, 214n31; and Great Migration, 67; and Indigenous soldiers, 14, 124; and

Mexican American civil rights, 114–16, 130, 136, 137, 215n76; and Mexican American soldiers, 5, 14, 17–18, 102–3, 107–12, 117–25; and Russian Revolution, 84

World War II: and Asian Americans, 164–65; and Black soldiers, 174–75; and Bracero Program, 142; and Mexican American soldiers, 19, 156, 169–75, 179–81, 232n152, 232n157; and occupation of Japan, 5, 164, 165–68, 172–74; and Pacific war, 169, 174–75, 179–81

Wright, Richard, 8, 17, 76, 83–86, 88–89, 92–93, 209nn65–66, 210n86, 220n12. See also *Black Boy*

Young, John K., 8, 192n12

Young Lords, 98, 212n137

Zamora, Emilio, 103, 108, 117, 120, 121, 123, 213n14, 214n48, 218n121, 219n150, 232n154

ABOUT THE AUTHOR

Jose O. Fernandez is an assistant professor in the Latina/o/x Studies Program at the University of Iowa. He is the author of *Against Marginalization: Convergences in Black and Latinx Literatures*, published by the Ohio State University Press.